# WORKSHOPS IN COMPUTING
Series edited by C. J. van Rijsbergen

## *Also in this series*

**Interfaces to Database Systems (IDS92)**
Proceedings of the First International Workshop
on Interfaces to Database Systems,
Glasgow, 1–3 July 1992
Richard Cooper (Ed.)

**AI and Cognitive Science '92**
University of Limerick, 10–11 September 1992
Kevin Ryan and Richard F.E. Sutcliffe (Eds.)

**Theory and Formal Methods 1993**
Proceedings of the First Imperial College
Department of Computing Workshop on Theory
and Formal Methods, Isle of Thorns Conference
Centre, Chelwood Gate, Sussex, UK,
29–31 March 1993
Geoffrey Burn, Simon Gay and Mark Ryan (Eds.)

**Algebraic Methodology and Software
Technology (AMAST'93)**
Proceedings of the Third International Conference
on Algebraic Methodology and Software
Technology, University of Twente, Enschede,
The Netherlands, 21–25 June 1993
M. Nivat, C. Rattray, T. Rus and G. Scollo (Eds.)

**Logic Program Synthesis and Transformation**
Proceedings of LOPSTR 93, International
Workshop on Logic Program Synthesis and
Transformation, Louvain-la-Neuve, Belgium,
7–9 July 1993
Yves Deville (Ed.)

**Database Programming Languages (DBPL-4)**
Proceedings of the Fourth International
Workshop on Database Programming Languages
– Object Models and Languages, Manhattan, New
York City, USA, 30 August–1 September 1993
Catriel Beeri, Atsushi Ohori and
Dennis E. Shasha (Eds.)

**Music Education: An Artificial Intelligence
Approach**, Proceedings of a Workshop held as
part of AI-ED 93, World Conference on Artificial
Intelligence in Education, Edinburgh, Scotland,
25 August 1993
Matt Smith, Alan Smaill and
Geraint A. Wiggins (Eds.)

**Rules in Database Systems**
Proceedings of the 1st International Workshop on
Rules in Database Systems, Edinburgh, Scotland,
30 August–1 September 1993
Norman W. Paton and
M. Howard Williams (Eds.)

**Semantics of Specification Languages (SoSL)**
Proceedings of the International Workshop on
Semantics of Specification Languages, Utrecht,
The Netherlands, 25–27 October 1993
D.J. Andrews, J.F. Groote and
C.A. Middelburg (Eds.)

**Security for Object-Oriented Systems**
Proceedings of the OOPSLA-93 Conference
Workshop on Security for Object-Oriented
Systems, Washington DC, USA,
26 September 1993
B. Thuraisingham, R. Sandhu and
T.C. Ting (Eds.)

**Functional Programming, Glasgow 1993**
Proceedings of the 1993 Glasgow Workshop on
Functional Programming, Ayr, Scotland,
5–7 July 1993
John T. O'Donnell and Kevin Hammond (Eds.)

**Z User Workshop, Cambridge 1994**
Proceedings of the Eighth Z User Meeting,
Cambridge, 29–30 June 1994
J.P. Bowen and J.A. Hall (Eds.)

**6th Refinement Workshop**
Proceedings of the 6th Refinement Workshop,
organised by BCS-FACS, London,
5–7 January 1994
David Till (Ed.)

**Incompleteness and Uncertainty in
Information Systems**
Proceedings of the SOFTEKS Workshop on
Incompleteness and Uncertainty in Information
Systems, Concordia University, Montreal,
Canada, 8–9 October 1993
V.S. Alagar, S. Bergler and F.Q. Dong (Eds.)

**Rough Sets, Fuzzy Sets and
Knowledge Discovery**
Proceedings of the International Workshop on
Rough Sets and Knowledge Discovery
(RSKD'93), Banff, Alberta, Canada,
12–15 October 1993
Wojciech P. Ziarko (Ed.)

**Algebra of Communicating Processes**
Proceeedings of ACP94, the First Workshop on
the Algebra of Communicating Processes,
Utrecht, The Netherlands,
16–17 May 1994
A. Ponse, C. Verhoef and
S.F.M. van Vlijmen (Eds.)

*continued on back page...*

Pete Sawyer (Ed.)

# Interfaces to Database Systems (IDS94)

Proceedings of the Second International Workshop on Interfaces to Database Systems, Lancaster University, 13–15 July 1994

Published in collaboration with the
British Computer Society

Springer-Verlag
London  Berlin  Heidelberg  New York
Paris  Tokyo  Hong Kong
Barcelona  Budapest

Pete Sawyer, BSc, PhD
Computing Department, Lancaster University,
Bailrigg, Lancaster, LA1 4YR, UK

ISBN 3-540-19910-1 Springer-Verlag Berlin Heidelberg New York

British Library Cataloguing in Publication Data
Interfaces to Database Systems (IDS94):
Proceedings of the Second International Workshop on Interfaces to Database Systems, Lancaster University, 13-15 July 1994. - (Workshops in Computing Series)
 I. Sawyer, P.H. II. Series
 005.74
 ISBN 3-540-19910-1

Library of Congress Cataloging-in-Publication Data
International Workshop on Interfaces to Database Systems (2nd : 1994 : Lancaster University)
Interfaces to database systems (IDS94) : proceedings of the Second International Workshop on Interfaces to Database Systems, Lancaster University, 13-15 July, 1994 / Pete Sawyer (ed.).
    p. cm. - (Workshops in computing)
 "Published in collaboration with the British Computer Society."
 Includes bibliographical references and index.
 ISBN 3-540-19910-1 (U.S. : acid-free paper)
  1. Database management–Congresses.  2. User interfaces (Computer systems)–Congresses.  I. Sawyer, Pete (Pete H.), 1958- .
II. British Computer Society. III. Title. IV. Series.
QA76.9.D3I58545 1994                                                94-38463
005.74–dc20                                                          CIP

Apart from any fair dealing for the purposes of research or private study, or criticism or review, as permitted under the Copyright, Designs and Patents Act 1988, this publication may only be reproduced, stored or transmitted, in any form, or by any means, with the prior permission in writing of the publishers, or in the case of reprographic reproduction in accordance with the terms of licences issued by the Copyright Licensing Agency. Enquiries concerning reproduction outside those terms should be sent to the publishers.

©British Computer Society 1995
Printed in Great Britain

The use of registered names, trademarks etc. in this publication does not imply, even in the absence of a specific statement, that such names are exempt from the relevant laws and regulations and therefore free for general use.

The publisher makes no representation, express or implied, with regard to the accuracy of the information contained in this book and cannot accept any legal responsibility or liability for any errors or omissions that may be made.

Typesetting: Camera ready by contributors
Printed by Athenæum Press Ltd., Gateshead
34/3830-543210 Printed on acid-free paper

# Preface

A brief survey of the major DBMS and HCI conference proceedings over the past 10 years will reveal isolated pockets of research in database user interfaces but little sense of being swept along with the general advances in DBMS technology and HCI. New data models have evolved to meet the needs of different application domains; persistent programming languages are blurring the traditional distinction between data definition and application programming languages; distribution and inter-operability have become issues as have the storage of heterogeneous media types; yet it is still rare to read of the HCI issues raised by these technological innovations being expressly addressed and rarer still to find recognition of the usability problems with longer-established database technologies.

There are at least two reasons why this should be surprising:

- Database systems are not like other computer systems; existing both as back-ends to other applications and as stand-alone data stores, they are typically slow, deal with very large volumes of data and can involve all sorts of security, confidentiality and even cooperability issues.

- Databases are everywhere. Perhaps only word processors and spreadsheets are more widespread. In addition, as business cultures change and personal computing continues to mould expectations, end-users find themselves interacting increasingly closely with database systems.

Hence, databases present particular problems and challenges to the user interface designer. While there has been some very valuable work (Zloof's work on by-example querying in the 1970's [1] for example) the huge body of database users has been greatly under-represented in HCI research. However, there are signs that attitudes are changing; soundings taken at recent VLDB conferences indicate that the DBMS community is becoming sensitised to the importance of database usability [2], identifying user interface issues as one of the crucial areas for future database research. The series of workshops on user interfaces to database systems, of which this collection of papers represents the proceedings of the second, was initiated to exploit and stimulate this awakening interest.

The papers cover a range of topics within the area of database user interfaces, and are by authors whose research backgrounds span both the DBMS and the HCI camps. The papers accepted for the workshop were selected for their quality and relevance to the area. We hoped to encourage submissions on a range of topics and the papers we received admirably met this criterion. All the topics covered by the papers in this volume have an important relevance to database user interface research, but it is perhaps interesting to note two of the topics; 3-dimensional visualisation and evaluation methods. The visualisation papers demonstrate that one of HCI's hottest topics has found a real, and really useful, application in databases. The evaluation papers show that database user interface researchers are aware of the pitfalls of concentrating on technology in the search for solutions while ignoring the need to evaluate users' needs and experiences. The presence of papers on these topics demonstrates that within database user interface research there is both a willingness to innovate technologically, and a mature determination to learn from the mistakes of other areas of HCI.

The short paper by Haber will make interesting reading for researchers as it reports a first attempt to add flesh to the general observation that database user interfaces need more research. The workshop delegates were asked to identify what we saw as the crucial areas within the general area. The survey represents a relatively small sample of opinions but it will be interesting to see how closely our current perceptions match future developments.

Finally, I would like to express my thanks to the many people who have helped with the workshop and the proceedings: the programme committee and their reviewing teams for performing an admirable and extremely efficient job; the authors who provided such high-quality submissions, mostly to time and in format; Jacqui Forsyth for performing nearly all of the actual organisation and management of the workshop; Simon Monk for doing my job while I was away over a critical period; Kath Teasdale and the staff at Charlotte Mason College for their help and for providing such an excellent venue. I am particularly grateful to Richard Cooper, who as inaugurator of the series provided advice and ideas on many aspects of the workshop's content and organisation.

Pete Sawyer                                                                August 1994

## References

[1] Zloof, M.M. Query-by-Example: A database language. IBM Syst. J., vol 16, no 4, 1982, pp 324–343
[2] Stonebraker, M. et. al. DBMS Research at a Crossroads: The Vienna Update, Proc. 19th VLDB Conference, Dublin, 1993, pp 688–692

# IDS94 Programme Committee

| | |
|---|---|
| Pete Sawyer (Chair) | Lancaster University, UK |
| Hans Dieter Böecker | GMD, Darmstadt, Germany |
| Richard Cooper | Glasgow University, UK |
| Maria Costabile | University of Bari, Italy |
| Alan Dix | University of York, UK |
| David England | Glasgow Unviersity, UK |
| Alistair Kilgour | Heriot-Watt University, UK |
| Roger King | University of Colorado, USA |
| Norman Paton | Heriot-Watt University, UK |

# Reviewers

Hans-Dieter Böecker
Jack Campin
Berardina de Carolis
Richard Cooper
Maria Costabile
Alan Dix
Geoff Ellis
David England
Alvaro Fernandes
Alistair Kilgour
Roger King
John Mariani
Simon Monk
Norman Paton
Sebastiano Pizzutilo
Pete Sawyer

# Contents

**Invited Paper**

Configuring Database Query Languages
*R. Cooper* .................................................................................... 3

**Naive and Application-Specific User Interfaces**

GUIDANCE: Making it Easy for the User to be an Expert
*D. Haw, C. Goble and A. Rector* ....................................... 25

HIBROWSE for Hotels: Bridging the Gap Between User and System Views of a Database
*G.P. Ellis, J.E. Finlay and A.S. Pollitt* ............................... 49

**Formal Approaches**

A Visual Approach to Multilinear Recursion
*T. Catarci and G. Santucci* ................................................ 65

Database Querying by Hypergraph Manipulation
*T. Catarci and L. Tarantino* ............................................... 84

SFQI: Semi-Formal Query Language Interface to Relational Databases
*M.N. MdSap and D.R. McGregor* ...................................... 104

**3-Dimensional Visualization and Virtual Reality**

Design of a 3D User Interface to a Database
*J. Boyle, J.E. Fothergill and P.M.D. Gray* ........................ 127

Three Dimensional Interface for an Object Oriented Database
*M.H. Rapley and J.B. Kennedy* ......................................... 143

Virtual Environments for Data Sharing and Visualisation – Populated Information Terrains
*S. Benford and J. Mariani* .................................................. 168

**Data Model Issues I**

A Graphical User Interface for Schema Evolution in an Object-Oriented Database
*S. Monk* ................................................................................ 185

Unifying Interaction with Persistent Data and Program
R.C.H. Connor, Q.I. Cutts, G.N.C. Kirby, V.S. Moore and
R. Morrison .................................................................................. 197

## Metaphors

Bags and Viewers: A Metaphor for Intelligent Database Access
R. Inder and J. Stader ................................................................... 215

Query by Browsing
A. Dix and A. Patrick .................................................................... 236

A Dynamic Form-Based Data Visualiser for Semantic
Query Languages
G. Santucci and F. Palmisano ...................................................... 249

Domain Restrictive User Interfaces Using Databases
P. Messer and N. Patel ................................................................. 266

## Data Model Issues II

A Graphical User Interface for a Cooperative Design
Database
M. Machura ................................................................................... 289

Interfaces to Data Models: Taking a Step Backwards
P. Barclay, A. Crerar and K. Davidson ......................................... 306

## Evaluation and Experimentation

Intuitive Human Interfaces for an Audio-Database
B. Eaglestone and R. Vertegaal ................................................... 329

Techniques for the Effective Evaluation of
Database Interfaces
N.W. Paton, G. al-Qaimari, K. Doan and A.C. Kilgour ................. 343

## Future Directions

The Ambleside Survey: Important Topics in DB//HCI
Research
E.M. Haber ................................................................................... 361

**Author Index** ............................................................................ 365

Invited Paper

# Configuring Database Query Languages

## Richard Cooper

Dept. of Computing Science, University of Glasgow, Glasgow G12 8QQ, Scotland

### Abstract

The three level architecture of the ANSI/SPARC model promises multiple interfaces to DBMS. The reality is a few impoverished interfaces - usually a form interface, sometimes a graphical schema design tool as well as a query language, perhaps also embedded in a programming language. Argument reigns over the relative merits of various query languages and yet the option of providing multiple query languages is rarely addressed. This paper demonstrates an architecture in which the addition of new query languages to a DBMS is greatly simplified. In order to build such an architecture, it is necessary to create a model of query languages and of the functionality of a DBMS. The paper shows how such a model is used to allow query languages to be configured.

## 1 Introduction

The three level architecture of the ANSI/SPARC model supports the notion of multiple interfaces to the DBMS, by separating the external user level from the internal data model. For instance, a database which is constructed out of relations can be realised to users as a set of forms, ER diagrams, tables and so on. In theory, this promises a rich variety of interfaces varying according to user need and experience. The reality, of course, is that most DBMS provide a very small number of extremely impoverished interfaces. Sometimes there will be a graphical schema design tool, often a forms interface and usually a textual language for expressing *ad hoc* queries, which may perhaps also be embedded in a programming language. The paucity of database interfaces has been identified as one of the most pressing problems facing database researchers [Bernstein *et al.*, 1989, Stonebraker *et al.*, 1993].

The reason for this surprising state of affairs is that the design and the implementation of user interfaces to DBMS is a costly business. Extending the DBMS to provide additional interfaces is achieved by a great deal of intricate low-level programming. For a graphical interface, there will need to be careful placement of screen objects. For a textual language interface, at least some aspects of compiler technology need to be tackled. Consequently, few interface tools will be provided and this is justified in the name of supplying a single uniform interface to all users.

In fact, DBMS are intended to be used by a wide variety of kinds of user - a variety which is being greatly extended with the intention of using DBMS for an increasing range of different kinds of applications, which bring with them added complexity, both of data structure and of iuser interaction. In order to support the access of many kinds of user to complex data, many interfaces will be needed, which, for instance, provide differing levels of detail. Therefore, the creation of interfaces needs to be greatly simplified. In the context of query languages, the adoption of SQL as a standard has been accompanied with considerable controversy [Date, 1984]. Many database specialists are extremely critical of SQL, preferring languages such as QUEL which have a cleaner structure [Stonebraker, 1986]. There seems no reason why a system should not provide QUEL for some uses and SQL for others (principally standardisation) - other than the cost of implementing two equivalent interfaces. If the cost of providing interfaces is reduced, each user can have their interface of choice.

It is important, however, that if multiple interfaces are provided that this is done in a coherent and integrated manner for at least two reasons [Cooper, 1993]. Firstly, it is important that they are tightly coupled in the sense they provide access to (possibly a subset of) the same database functionality, otherwise the multiple inetrfaces may interact in a chaotic manner. Secondly, the integration should greatly reduce the cost of building each interface.

The Configurable Data Modelling System (CDMS) is being constructed to tackle this problem [Cooper, 1990]. CDMS allows the creation of conceptual data models and multiple concrete user interfaces to those models to be built quickly using menus and direct manipulation. CDMS contains a highly abstract generic data model, of which models such as the relational model, object oriented models, the ER model or IFO are instances. CDMS also contains a set of user interface primitives which may then be attach to each component. CDMS deals not only with the static data structuring part of a model, but also with constraints and active values. The CDMS has similarities with other work, in which the conceptual model is configurable [Durand *et al.*, 1993; Radermacher, 1993].

Initially, CDMS concentrated on graphical interfaces, but it has always been the intention to support the creation of all kinds of interface, since all are essentially formal languages, which may be subject to equivalent kinds of manipulation. This paper presents the first prototype of the component which will deal with textual interfaces. Query languages are considered first - with a description of the important components of query languages followed by a tool to build them. A prototype component for configuring query languages is then described.

## 2   Query Language Interfaces

We propose here a DBMS component which allows query languages to be configured and added to the range of interfaces of the DBMS without recourse to low-level programming. This achieved by allowing the user to specify:

(a) the data model that is supported by the query language;

(b) the operations supported by the DBMS;

(c) the syntax of the language;

and

(d) associations between operations and command syntaxes.

The configuration of the data model is described in detail elsewhere [Cooper and Qin, 1994a] but will be discussed cursorily in the next section. The paper concentrates on the other three steps - the design of a component, which given a data model, assists the DBMS engineer to configure a query language for it. Just like any other computerised application, this component must have an adequate model of the data it is dealing with - in this case it must have a model of a query language, a meta-model of the DBMS functionality and a model of how the two are connected. To this end, a general description of query languages will be given and an example will introduce the components.

## 2.1 An Introductory Example

A **database query language** (QL) provides a concrete basis for user interaction, in order that users can not only pose queries to a database, but can also define the database and perform updates. In essence the QL supports the creation, deletion, modification and retrieval of data and meta-data.

In order to do this, the QL consists of a set of **sentence syntaxes**, each of which provides user access to a particular facility of the DBMS. Thus in SQL, one of the sentence syntaxes is:

**create table** <rname> ( <aname> : <atype> { , <aname> : <atype>}* )

in which literals are emboldened, slots for user specified values are in angle brackets and the syntax {...}* means an optional numbers of repetitions (including zero).

The sentence syntax gives the user access to the operation to create a relation, which might be written as[1]:

createRelation = **proc**( Rname:**string**; Anames:*****string**; Atypes:*****string** )

which means that the *createRelation* operation takes a single string for the relation name and arrays of strings for the names and types of the attributes.

This in turn is probably composed of the following:

    R := createNullRelation( Rname )
    **for** i := 1 **to upb**(Anames) **do**
      **begin**
        A := createAttribute( Anames[i], Atypes[i] )
        addAttribute( R, A )
      **end**

which is built out of primitive operations which create the fundamental categories of the data model - in this case a relation and an attribute and the relationship between

---

[1] The syntax used here for code examples is similar to that of the persistent language Napier88.

them. Each tuple is composed of a set of attributes. In general, the primitive operations out of which the functionality of the QL is built consists of creation, deletion, update and display facilities for each fundamental construct in the data model.

The QL is made complete by associating each of the sentences with an operation, which includes associating the parameters of the operation with slots in the sentence syntax. An interpreter for the sentences which have been defined can then be created, which embeds the operations and calls them on demand.

Thus, in order to create a component for configuring query languages, we need the following:

i) a set of primitive operations for manipulating each kind of data and meta-data in the data model;

ii) a mechanism for creating compound operations out of these;

iii) a meta-syntax in which sentences can be described;

iv) a mechanism for inputing sentences;

v) a facility for associating operations with sentence structures;

vi) a template for a query language interpreter;

vii) the ability to fill out the template with operations and syntaxes, to compile it and then to add it to the DBMS.

## 2.2 An Abstract Description of Database Functionality

The CDMS [Cooper and Qin, 1994a] architecture consists of four levels in which there is a global model, which can be instantiated as a number of data models, which in turn can be instantiated to create schemata and these, in turn, can be instantiated to create databases as usual. The global model contains a number of highly abstract constructs for describing sorts of values, the connections between sorts, constraints [Cooper and Qin, 1994b] and active values. Here we concentrate on the first two of these.

### The Global Constructs

The global constructs for describing sorts are:

**entity** - which is the sort used for any data model construct which includes the notions of object identity or reference semantics;

**base** - which is the sort for any data model construct for atomic values, such as integers and strings;

**composite** - which is the sort of any data model construct for describing values with multiple components and value semantics - sets and records are covered by these.

The global constructs for describing connections are:

**property** - which is the construct that links two sorts implying that instances of one are attributes of instances of the other;

**component** - which is the construct which connects a composite sort with its components;

**inheritance** - which is the relationship between two sorts indicating that instances of one form a subset of instances of the other.

The task of configuring data models out of this global architecture then consists of instantiating these global constructs - i.e. creating named instances and constraining them. For instance, we might create a simple ER model as follows:

out of entity, create an instance named **strong entity**;

out of base, create an instance named **attribute**;

out of composite, create an instance called **relationship**;

out of property, create an instance called **attributeOfEntity** linking strong entity and attribute;

out of property, create an instance called **attributeOfRelationship** linking relationship and attribute;

and

out of component, create an instance called **connection** linking relationship and entity.

The result of this instantiation is a program which manages data described using these constructs. Such a program has slots left which connect it to a concrete user interface, and this interface may be graphical, form-based or textual. This paper describes how a textual interface is added, but first a little more detail on the data modelling program must be given.

## The Underlying Data Model Structures

Each of the global constructs has associated with it two template data structures, which can hold the appropriate kinds of data and meta-data. In designing a data model using CDMS, each of the data model construction decisions (illustrated above) leads to the installation of instantiations of these templates into the program which supports the data model. In the case of the constructs for sorts, these take the form of (nested) record structures. Thus for instance, **entity** has the structures[1]:

---

[1] The syntax for record structures consists of a name for the structure and a set of fields separated by semi-colons. The fields are named and typed. The type may be either a base type, such as string, or another record type and may be indicated as being a set of values by preceding the type with a "*".

> *construct*Type( *construct*Name: string; *construct*Instances: **construct*Instance)

and

> *construct*Instance( *construct*Owner: *construct*Type )

in which the text in the italicised font indicates a placeholder, which in this case will be filled in by the given name of the construct - for instance the first instantiations generated in our example will be:

> strongEntityType( strongEntityName: string;
> strongEntityInstances: *strongEntityInstance )

and

> strongEntityInstance( strongEntityOwner: strongEntityType )

The two structures associated with **base** have a little more structure:

> *construct*Type( *construct*Name: string; *construct*Domain: string;
> *construct*Instances: **construct*Instance )

and

> *construct*Instance( c*construct*Value: value; *onstruct*Owner: *construct*Type )

where the domain *value* is a variant type of all the base domains.

The global relationship constructs are not held directly as a record structures, but as fields which can be embedded in the above structures. In general, the connections will be embedded in both directions. For instance, adding *attributeOfStrongEntity* changes the above record structures by adding an extra field in the record structures for attribute and strong entity, each holding the pointer to the other. In general, the fields refer to sets of related objects - thus there is a field referring to the set of attributes of a strong enetity. Once again the base types form an exception, since they are only allowed to be associated with one object at a time - thus each attribute is attached to only one strong entity. After adding the pointers for the three relationship constructs, the record structures for the three sorts in our example will finally be:

> strongEntityType - name, set of attribute types, set of relationship types, set of instances;

> attributeType - name, domain, related entity type, related relationship type, set of instances;

> relationshipType - name, set of attribute types, set of entity types, set of instances;

> strongEntityInstance - set of attributes, set of relationships, entity type;

> attributeInstance - value, related entity, related relationship, attribute type

> relationshipInstance - set of attributes, set of entities, relationship type.

To finish the description, here are the instances that would be created for data and meta-data to hold a person aged 33 (where the curly braces indicate a set of objects ):

> a strong entity type, *PERSON*:
> 
> PERSON := strongEntityType( "PERSON", { AGE }, { }, { P33 } )

an attribute type, *AGE*:
> AGE := attributeType( "age", "integer", PERSON, nil, { A33 } )

a strong entity, *P33*, which is an instance of *PERSON*:
> P33 := strongEntityInstance( {A33}, {}, PERSON )

an attribute of *P33*, called *A33*:
> A33 := attributeInstance( value( 33 ), P33, nil, AGE )

The result of this organisation is that the operations which implement the functionality of the database system manage an explicitly constructed graph containing both the intension and the extension of the database. These operations are built out of a set of primitive operations, which will be described next.

## The Primitive Operations

In constructing a query language to support this data model, we need next to describe the operations which will be provided. The approach here is to provide a uniform set of primitive operations, together with ways of combining them to create compound operations. The primitive operations comprise two parallel sets, one for manipulating schema elements as instances of the data model constructs and one for manipulating data values as instances of the schema elements. In each case there will be operations to create, delete, edit and display values. These operations are provided for each of the constructs in the global model.

The primitive operations in the global data model are instantiated to create primitive operations in the data model. Thus in the example data model, there will be the following operations:

| **Operation** | **Example** |
|---|---|
| createStrongEntityType( Ename:string -> strongEntityType ) | Person := createStrongEntityType( "Person" ); |
| createAttributeType( Aname: string; domain: string -> attributeType ) | age := createAttributeType( "age", "integer" ); |
| createRelationshipType( Rname: string -> relationshipType ) | worksFor:=createRelationshipType("worksFor") |
| createAttributeOfEntityType( E: entityType; A: attributeType ) | createAttributeOfEntityType( Person, age ) |
| createStrongEntityInstance( E: entityType -> entity ) | aPerson := createStrongEntityInstance( Person ) |
| createAttributeInstance(A:attributeType; V:value -> attribute) | anAge := createAttributeInstance( age,value(32) ) |
| createAttributeOfEntityInstance( anE: entity; anA: attribute ) | createAttributeOfEntityInstance(aPerson,anAge) |

etc.

Notice that these operations can all be generated automatically from information residing either in the global model or in the choices made in configuring the data model, since all of the individual parts of the names and types of the operations are completely determined. To take two examples:

*createAttributeType* is instantiated from the global primitive *createBaseType*, which looks as follows:

```
createBaseType( Bname: string; domain:string -> baseType )
    begin
        .... code to add the base value type to the set of base value types
    end
```

The instantiation here is quite simple - the word "base" is replaced by the name "attribute" throughout, and "Bname" is replaced by "Aname". "attribute" has been derived directly from the interface designer in the configuring process and "Aname" is the first letter of "attribute" concatenated with "name".

*createAttributeInstance* is instantiated from the global *createBaseInstance* which looks like:

```
createIntegerInstance( B:baseType; V:value -> base )
    begin
        .... code to add the instance to the set of instances of this base type
    end
```

The instantiation is again by simple renaming. As will be seen later, the interpreter is provided with a facility for deriving values from the input command.

## Constructing Compound Operations

Clearly we cannot limit the query language to providing commands which use these primitive operations on an individual basis. Instead, we must allow more complex operations to exist, such as create an entity types and its attributes. An operation to achieve this might look like this:

```
createEntityAndAttributeTypes( Ename: string; Anames:*string;
                                              Adomains: *string )
    begin
        let theE := createStrongEntityType( Ename )
        for i := 1 to upb( Anames ) do
            begin
                let theA := createAttributeType( Anames[i], Adomains[i] )
                createAttributeOfEntity( theE, theA )
            end
    end
```

We therefore provide a menu-driven interface for building compound operations out of the primitive operations. The compound operation is a sequence of sub-operations, where the sub-operations may include conditional or iterating expressions. The implementation of this is described in Section 3.1.

## 2.2 The Query Language

A query language is a set of sentence type definitions, each of which specifies the syntax for instigating the execution of one of the operations permitted by the DBMS and instantiating any parameters required by the operations.

A sentence definition is a description of a set of allowable sentences in the query language. These are described in a meta-language. The definition contains a mixture of literals and slots. The former consist of textual symbols which must appear exactly as they are in the sentence. The latter are placeholders which will be filled with actual text identifying a database element. Thus the example in section 2.1 above must start with the words "create" and "relation" and these will be followed by some string which names a new relation.

To complete the definition of the query language, it is necessary to associate each description with a concrete operation and this involves identifying the category of database object associated with each of the slots in the definition.

Thus we can define a query language, QL, to be an interface of the functionality of a data model, DMF, as follows:

DMF ::= { $O_1, ... O_n$ }

where each operation $O_i$ ::= { $Oname_i$; {$Oparam_{i,1}, ... Oparam_{i,np_i}$} }

and QL ::= { $S_1, ... S_m$ }

where each sentence $S_j$ ::= { $O_j$; $Synt_j$ }

where each $O_j$ is one the $O_i$ above

and

$Synt_j$ ::= sequence of atoms

and each atom is either a literal or a slot

and a slot indicates one of the $Oparam_{i,k}$

Thus an appropriate syntax to associate with *createEntityAndAttributeTypes* above might be:

create entity <E> with attributes { <A[i]> : <T[i]> }*

after which, there remains the task of associating <E> with *Ename* and the <A[i]> and <T[i]> with *Anames(i)* and *Adomains(i)* respectively.

# 3   Configuring Query Languages

This section concentrates on an implementation of a system for configuring query languages. The process consists of three parts - identifying an operation, perhaps building it out of some primitive operations; entering a syntax in the meta-language; and associating a sentence description with an operation. This is controlled by a central screen (shown as Figure 1) most of which is divided into four quarters: the left side of the screen contains interfaces to the operations, while the right hand side contains the sentence descriptions. The lower half of the screen contains operations and sentence descriptions that are as yet unpaired, while the upper half of the screen contains pairs of operations and sentence descriptions which have been associated. At the bottom of the screen is a window for messages from the program and a set of buttons which guide the process. The three principal activities will now be dealt with.

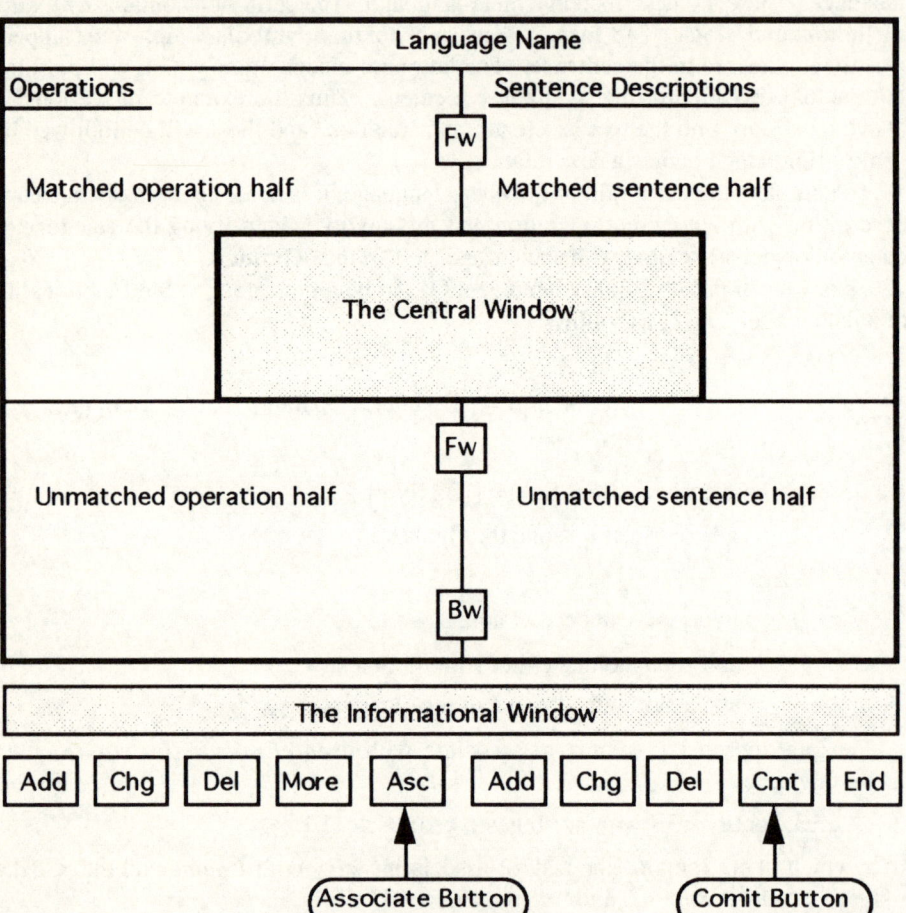

**Figure 1** The Definition Screen

## 3.1 Defining an Operation

The left hand button in Figure 1 summons the activity of adding a new operation to the functionality of the query language. An operation is a small piece of code built out of the primitive operations in the data model. First of all, an interface to the operation must be provided. This will include giving a name for the operation and then specifying parameters for the operation, i.e. a name for the parameter and a type. Types are chosen from a menu of any of the model constructs or the base domain types or the bulk type constructors.

Then code is constructed for the operation using the menu shown in Figure 2 below, which allows the code to be built up in stages. The operations have the following effects:

*Add a Primitive Operation* - summons a window to choose one of the primitive operations - create, delete, modify and display of each category in the data model - the window has a set of four radio buttons for the kinds of operation and a menu of the data model categories. The operations will be parameterised and the parameter values for the operation must now be specified. There are two possibilities for each parameter here. Either its value can be fixed now (either as a constant, one of the input parameters of the operation or any local variables which have been created) or the choice can be passed on to the user - in the latter case, it will become a parameter of the operation and need to be associated with a slot in a syntax structure;

*Mark Beginning Of An Optional Block* - this starts a block of code which may or may not be executed depending upon whether or not an optional part of the syntax is supplied by the user or not;

*Mark End Of An Optional Block* - this ends such a block;

*Mark Start Of An Iterative Block* - this starts a block of code which is associated with an iterative part of the sentence syntax. An iterative block is usually associated with some set of values to be iterated over. This may be one of the multi-valued components of data already associated with the operations or it may be a new set introduced as a a parameter;

*Mark End Of An Iterative Block* - this ends such a block;

*Show The Current Operation* - bring up a textual display of the operation;

*Quit* - terminate the operation, checking that all the blocks are terminated effectively, and enter this into the query language.

| DEFINE OPERATION |
|---|
| Add A Primitive Operation |
| Mark Beginning Of An Optional Block |
| Mark End Of An Optional Block |
| Mark Beginning Of An Iterative Block |
| Mark End Of An Iterative Block |
| Show The Current Operation |
| Quit |

**Figure 2.** Defining an Operation

The process is now illustrated with regard to the compound operation shown in section 2.2, *createEntityAndAttributeTypes*, which is built in the following steps:

i) Give the name - *createEntityAndAttributeTypes*

ii) The names and types of the parameters - in this case *Ename*, string, *Anames*, set of string, *Adomains*, and set of string.

iii) Now the operation is started and the first thing to do is to insert the primitive operation *createStrongEntityType* and to determine its actual parameters - in this case, we select the parameter *Ename* and we create a variable to hold the output, *theE*.

iv) Then we start an iterative block, indicating that the number of *Anames* determines the number of iterations.

v) Now we add another primitive type - *createStrongEntityType*, selecting *Anames* and *Adomains* for the parameters - the index is added automatically - a variable to hold the output is added as well.

vi) Next the primitive *createAttributeOfEntity* is added and its parameters are fixed to be the two variables created.

vii) The iterative loop is ended.

viii) The operations is finished by selecting the quit option.

## 3.2 Specifying a Sentence Description

This is much simpler than defining an operation. It consists merely of specifying the structure by typing in the description using a meta-language. The important issue is to ensure that there are the correct number of slots to be associated with parameters in the operation. Slots may be either simple slots, which will hold single values, or indexed slots, where the slot is to be associated with a multi-valued parameter. Thus we would write the following as a syntax for *createEntityAndAttributeTypes*:

create entity <E> with attributes <A[i]>:<T[i]> {, <A[i]>:<T[i]> }

## 3.3 Associating a Syntax Structure with an Operation

This is summoned by selecting the *Associate* button in the main definition screen. The user selects firstly the operation, from the set of unpaired operations, and then an unpaired sentence description. Finally, for each operation parameter, a menu of the sentence description slots is given. To illustrate the process, consider two ways in which the same operation might be added to the language.

The operation creates an entity with a single attribute and is:

CreateEntityAttribute( Aname: string; Atype: baseType, Ename: string )

which adds an attribute to the entity type named *Ename*, where the attribute is named *Aname* with type *Atype*.

The two alternate syntaxes we wish to add for this are:

**create attribute <A> : <T> of entity <E>**

which is a general sentence for this operation and

**create integer attribute <A> of entity <E>**

which fixes the type of the attribute.

To associate the operation with the first of these, both are selected from the sets of unpaired components and the window shown in Figure 3 pop up:

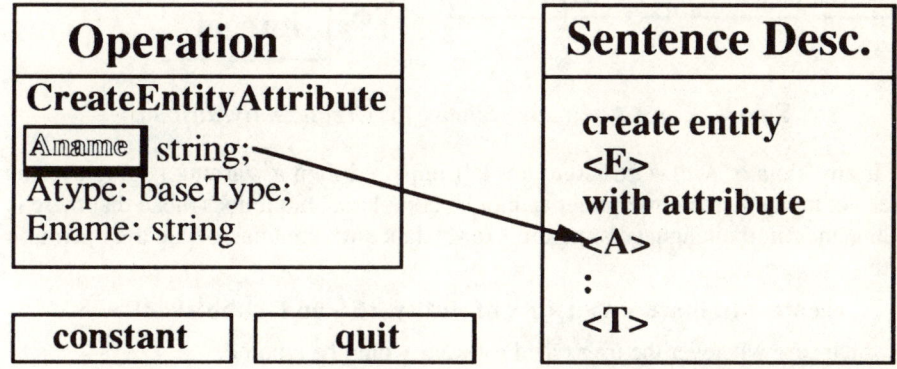

**Figure 3.** Associating an Operation with a Sentence Description

In the figure, we see the operation signature on the left and the associated sentence syntax on the right. The goal of using the window is to provide ways of deriving actual values for all of the formal parameters of the operation. To do this each is selected in turn and this may be associated with either one of the slots in the description or with a constant, in which case the operation would have its generality limited. We see here that the first parameter *Aname* has been associated with the slot *<A>*. As each parameter is selected, the slots of syntax structure and the **constant** button become available for selection. When a selection has been made the parameter name is inverted to show this. To create the association with "**create attribute <A> : <T> of entity <E>**", the pairings *Aname* with *<A>*, *Atype* with *<T>* and *Ename* with *<E>* would be made, at which point the quit button becomes active.

To achieve the association with "**create entity <E> with integer attribute <A>**", the pairings of *Ename* with *<E>* and *Aname* with *<A>* are the same. However, *Atype* is fixed by selecting constant, at which point a menu of all the base types comes up and "integer" is selected. Had either of the other attributes been fixed, then as they are strings, a string editor would be brought up to take in the value.

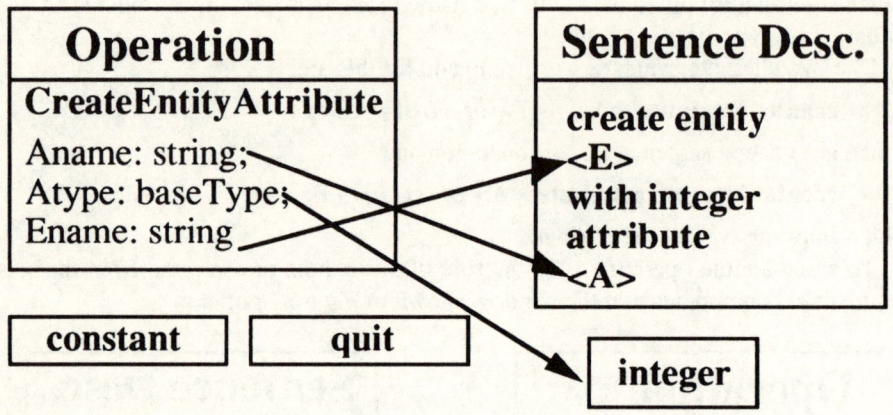

**Figure 4.** An Alternative Syntax for *CreateEntityAttribute*

If any slots of syntax structure are left unpaired then a warning is given. This does not mean that the interpreter cannot be completed, but it does mean that there is redundancy in the language structure - for instance we could associate the operation with:

**create attribute <A> : <T> of entity <E> and rubbish <R>**

in which case whatever the user typed for *<R>* would be ignored.

In the case where there are multiple copies of the same slot in the same syntax as in:

**create entity <E> with attributes <A[i]>:<T[i]> {, <A[i]>:<T[i]> }**

selecting any copy selects them all. Thus either copy of "A[i]" can be chosen for association with *Anames*.

### 3.4 Update and Query Operations

The examples above have consisted of data definition operations, since these are easier to describe (and implement). A query language will, of course, have data manipulation and querying operations. These are subject to the same kind of structural decomposition as are data definition operations, both in terms of the code and the syntax. For instance, we might wish to have the SQL-like operation

**select <A>\* from <E> where <C>**

in our model. This would be bound to the following compound operation:

selectFromWhere( Anames: \*string; Ename: string; C: condition )

which introduces a new type which is built into the interpreter - the type of boolean conditions. This is just one example of general expression handling which a query language interpreter must manage and in the design of the system, the possibility existed of allowing the expression sub-language to be user-configurable. It was not a possibility that was explored however, since it was felt that there would be very little value in allowing this. Configuring expression syntax is intricate and any standard syntax will probably suffice. Configuring expression management is a possibility for future development however.

Update operation are similarly handled. An operation such as:

    **update** <name> := <expression> **in** <E> **where** <C>

would be bound to a compound operation:

    updateSelected( Aname:string; Ename:string; Exp: expression; C:condition )

which again can be configured out of an iteration over the instances of the entity type, but this time calling the primitive update operation on attributes.

The discussion has centred on declarative languages. The querying and update operations depend on selection based on values in the data. We are exploring the possibility of extending the system to handle procedural languages in which the operations can use local variables.

## 3.5 Miscellaneous Operations

The other buttons.in Figure 1 have the following effects:
- the *Chg* buttons allow operations and sentence syntaxes to be replaced;
- the *Del* buttons allow operations and sentence syntaxes to be removed;
- the *More* button allows the details of an operation to be displayed;
- the *Cmt* buttons saves the work;
- the *End* button completes the process and builds, compiles and installs an interpreter in the DBMS.

## 3.6 Finishing Off

The process of configuring a language is completed when the *End* button is selected. This checks if the definition is consistent and complete. It then pulls together all of the pieces of code which exist as templates into a complete program. The completed program once compiled is added to the set of interfaces to the database system.

## 3.7 The Implementation Environment

The system described above has been implemented in Napier88, a procedural persistent programming language. The language is well suited to the implementation of configurable systems, such as this, since it has a rich type system, first-class procedures, orthogonal persistence and type safe linguistic reflection. The value of each of these will now be described in turn.

Napier88 [Morrison et al. 1989] belongs syntactically to the same family of languages as Pascal and Ada, but has a much **richer type system** than the former and has a much simpler computational model than the latter. The base types provided by Napier88 include integers, reals, strings, booleans and also graphical types for line drawings and bitmaps. The type system is characterised by the orthogonal applicability of the type constructors, which include constructors for arrays, records, variants and abstract data types. Each of these types can be made generic by providing type parameters. There are, moreover, the dynamic types **any** (the union of all types) and **env** (which is the type of extensible records). Each of these has proved valuable in creating a direct representation of complex information.

The provision of **procedures as first-class values** is one of the great strengths of Napier88. CDMS is principally a program for managing **code** and the ability to write the managing programs to make direct references to the code as data simplifies a daunting task. Much of the work is achieved by string manipulation over source fragments, but some parts of the programming are effected by passing compiled code about. The interpreter which is finally created is compiled and this is placed into the persistent store for later re-use.

The term **orthogonal persistence** means that values of **every** type are allowed to be stored in the database **without transformation**. By "every type" is meant any type, no matter how richly structured and includes procedures, freely mixed with values of other types. The construction of CDMS has been greatly simplified by the removal of any requirement to find permanent representations of any of the values (including code) being managed. The way in which the persistent store is used to house CDMS information is shown in Figure 5. The persistent store houses not only the databases, but also all of the support software.

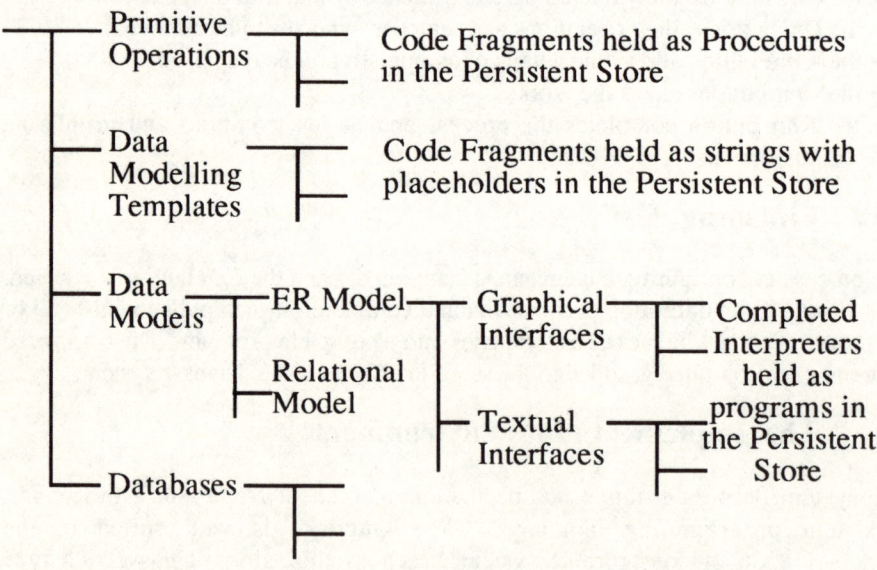

**Figure 5** The CDMS Implementation Architecture

Critical to the success of the implementation has been **strongly typed linguistic reflection** [Kirby, 1992; Cooper and Kirby, 1994]. This is provided in the form of a system procedure which contains the compiler and which can be called at run-time. Extensible efficient systems are much simpler to write if the compiler is available at run-time. CDMS uses this feature to compile the interpreter when the building of the source is complete. This means that by providing appropriate templates and string-handling techniques, it is possible to write a programs which itself writes the query language interpreter that a programmer would have written had all the confuguration information been available.

# 4 Conclusions

A database system has been presented in which novel end user query languages can be configured and added to the system. Such a query language is specified against a data model which is instantiated from a general model using other facilities of the Configurable Data Modelling System. The process of configuring the query language consists of three parts:

> the specification of operations out of primitives which have been programmed against the general data model and which are automatically tailored to the specific data model;
> 
> the specification of a concrete syntax which will summon each operation;
> 
> the association of the syntax for individual sentences with their operations.

The work described here is only one strand of a general effort to encompass every sort of database interface in the same system. The management of graphical interfaces was described previously [Cooper, 1990]. This was carried out first since there is a sense in which configurability and graphic interfaces seem to fit together. The present work demonstrate that textual interfaces are subject to precisely the same kinds of manipulation.

One concern which is commonly raised when discussing work such as this is the problem of efficiency. It is commonly felt that the only way of providing generic tools is to use some form of indirection, but as long as the system provides linguistic reflection this is not necessarily the case. In the current work, the ways in which values have been managed has been indirectly through the use of a variant type. We have done this to speed up the production of a prototype. This was not, however, strictly necessary, since by use of a second layer of reflection, it is possible to build code to manage the precise structure which is described by the schema. Thus instead of using the *strongEntitInstance* structure which is generic and indirect, it is possible to build specific structures and the code to manipulate them. For instance, we could configure the structure:

> PERSONinstance( age: integer )

in the example above. The reader is referred to a description how this was achieved for the relational model [Cooper *et al.*, 1987].

Query optimisation.is a concern we have not as yet tackled. Since all of the operations are provided as structures built out of primitives, it should prove possible to construct an algebra or meta-algebra at the generic level and make use of this. We look to explore this in the near future.

## Acknowledgements

The author would like to thank Darrell Robertson and Dave Tan for working on early versions of this part of the Configurable Data Modelling System. Zhenzhou Qin and David England have provided continued input on the main ideas here. I would also like to thank the Napier group at the University of St. Andrews, led by Professor Ron Morrison. They provide a software environment with which it is possible to try out complex ideas quickly, both because Napier88 provides very powerful constructs and because the Napier88 system works and works well. The research described in this paper was supported by SERC grant H17671 Configurable Data Modelling.

## Bibliography

Bernstein *et al.*, 1989
> The Laguna Beach Participants, "Future Directions in DBMS Research", *ACM SIGMOD Record*, <u>18</u>, 1, 17-26, March 1989.

Cooper *et al.*, 1987
> R.L. Cooper, M.P. Atkinson, D. Abderrahmane and A. Dearle, "Constructing Database Systems in a Persistent Environment", in *Proceedings of the 13th International Conference on Very Large Databases*, Brighton, England, 117-126, September 1987.

Cooper, 1990
> R.L. Cooper, "Configurable Data Modelling Systems", *Proc. of 9th Conference on the Entity Relationship Approach*, 35-52, Lausanne, October 1990 - also in Cooper 1991.

Cooper, 1993
> R.L. Cooper, "The Interaction between DBMS and User Interface Research", editorial of "Interfaces to Database Systems 1992", 1-5, Workshops in Computer Science, Springer Verlag, 1993.

Cooper and Qin, 1994a
> R.L. Cooper and Z. Qin, "A Generic Data Model for the Support of Multiple User Access Mechanisms", *to be presented at the Enity Relationship 94 Conference, December, 1994.*

Cooper and Qin, 1994b
> R.L. Cooper and Z. Qin, "Generalised Configurable Constraint Management", *n preparation.*

Cooper and Kirby, 1994
> R.L. Cooper and G. Kirby, "Type-Safe Linguistic Run-time Reflection - A Practical Perspective", to be presented at the the 6th International Workshop on Persistent Object Systems, Tarascon, France, September, 1994.

Date, 1984
: C. Date, "A Critique of the SQL Database Language", ACM SIGMOD Record, 14:3, November, 1984.

Durand et al., 1993
: J Durand, H. Brunner, R. Cuthbertson, S. Fogel, Tim McCandless, R. Sparks and L. Sylvan, "Data Model and Query Algebra for a Model Based Multi-Modal User Interface" in "Interfaces to Database Systems 1992", R.L. Cooper, (ed), Workshops in Computer Science, Springer Verlag, 1993.

Kirby, 1992
: G. Kirby, "Persistent Programming with Type Safe Linguistic Reflection", *Proc. Hawaii ICSS*, January 1992.

Morrison et al, 1989
: R. Morrison, A. Brown, R. Carrick, R. Connor and A. Dearle, "The Napier Reference Manual", Computational Science, University of St. Andrews.

Radermacher, 1993
: K. Radermacher, "An Extensible Graphical Programming Environment for Semantic Modelling", in "Interfaces to Database Systems 1992", R.L. Cooper, (ed), Workshops in Computer Science, Springer Verlag, 1993.

Stonebraker, 1986
: M. Stonebraker (ed), "The INGRES Papers", Addison-Wesley, 1986.

Stonebraker et al., 1993
: M. Stonebraker, R. Agrawal, U. Dayal, E.J. Neuhold and A. Reuter, "DBMS Research at a Crossroads: The Vienna Update", *Proc VLDB19.*, 688-692, Dublin, August 1993.

# Naive and Application-Specific User Interfaces

# GUIDANCE:
# Making it Easy for the User to be an Expert

David Haw[1], Carole Goble[2], Alan Rector[2]

[1]Harlequin Ltd, 2nd Floor, Queens Court, Wilmslow Road,
Alderley Edge, Cheshire, SK9 7QD. tel: +44 625 588019;
internet: dh@harlequin.co.uk

[2]Department of Computer Science, University of Manchester,
Oxford Road, Manchester M13 9PL; tel: +44 61 275 6195/6188;
internet: <cag, alr>@cs.man.ac.uk

## Abstract

This paper describes an information retrieval system—GUIDANCE[1]—that is accessible and usable by people who are not experts in computing but are experts in their own domain. This particular user group needs to be supported by a system that is easy to use and reflects their own knowledge of the world. The system presented is based on descriptions - the logical structure of the database is *concealed* in favour of an interface which supports the question 'What can I say about People?' regardless of how many objects, roles, or attributes represent 'People'. A full and relevant description is implemented by two models, one containing conceptual knowledge, and the other database specific information. These models are represented in, and related by, a descriptive subsumption-based classification formalism GRAIL[2], which has a system of semantic sanctions to control the creation of implied concepts and a mechanism for ensuring their uniqueness.

---

[1]Grail User IndepenDent Advice oN Concept Enquiry
[2]GALEN Representation and Integration Language

# 1 Introduction

> "The information provided by an information system is normally used by people who are not experts in computing." [1, p7].

It is most often the case that the development of a information retrieval system starts from the misguided notion that it is being produced for 'people like us'- the developers[3]. Generally, the people with the expertise to utilise an information resource (managers, economists or bankers) will not, and should not, also be experts in software development. Badly designed and unintelligent application software frequently forces these users to refer their query to computer professionals who have no expertise in the domain of enquiry. This state of affairs is neither timely nor appropriate, and represents an 'impedance mismatch' of expertise between the professional and casual user groups. Direct retrieval by the user group concerned would facilitate full use of the database resource—information—upon which important decisions can be made, and would also serve to 'de-mystify' computer systems.

Contemporary application software that is based on views of data in the relational database often makes an implicit assumption that the coding of the data into the entity-relationship model and subsequently into the database is a true reflection of the knowledge of the user. This may or may not be the case, but it is a simplistic assumption. The 'bedrock' knowledge representation of these particular applications - the relational model - can be carried over into views where a reconsideration of the precise semantics of the data may be appropriate. There are two broad views: (a) to elaborate a base relational model with a conceptual model or (b) to re-express the data model in a higher level semantic data model [2]. Both put a layer of abstraction on top of the relational model. In this paper we subscribe to the first view. Whether or not a relational database is intended to be used by 'non-experts', its semantic baggage is carried over into the views that are intended for the casual user.

To discover and articulate the problems casual users may have in interacting with a relational database or possible views based upon it, a human factors analysis is presented from the theoretical perspective provided by Norman [3] and Hutchins et al. [4]. Factoring out the issues from first principles means that it is possible to suggest a system-wide resolution with reference to a set of partial solutions suggested by other work in the field.

GUIDANCE is a carefully scoped co-operative assistant system. It is:

- not an instructional system, nor a teaching aid.
- directed at a group who are experts in the domain, but not in computing.
- primarily intended for a single domain of enquiry.
- intended to primarily serve the poorly formed or 'discovery-based' query .
- designed to allow users to query it without specific knowledge of the data's structure (or distribution).

---

[3]Thanks to Jerri Pries for this neat articulation of the problem.

The case study used throughout is a real database for handling the computer system management requirements for the Department of Computer Science at Manchester. The database is implemented in the RDBMS Sybase, and has over 20 tables.

The rest of the paper is organised as follows. Section 2 presents the theoretical perspective of semantic and articulatory directness with reference to problems of retrieval from a relational database. Section 3 presents the GUIDANCE strategic approach, and describes the architecture in broad terms. Section 4 presents the interface, and section 5 describes the notion of Natural Categories which remove the need for a definitive identifier for an object. Section 6 goes into more depth about the embedded models and their construction, and the operation of the system. Section 7 describes a qualitative evaluation of the system by members of the target user group. Section 8 looks at related work, and section 9 closes the paper with a discussion.

## 2   Gulfs of Execution and Evaluation

Norman [3] suggests that many problems that are encountered by users of computer systems are to do with mismatches between a users intention and the task variables, and that effective human computer interaction occurs when it is possible for a user to easily map their intentions onto actions on the screen, and that the actions produce the desired results. The problems encountered are therefore due to a *Gulf of Execution*—mapping a goal to an action specification—and a *Gulf of Evaluation*—mapping a new system state to an expectation of results. Hutchins, Hollan and Norman [4] extended this idea by suggesting that within each gulf lay two 'distances'—semantic and articulatory. The idea being that the more direct the relationship, the less the distance (see figure 1). *Semantic directness* is concerned with the relationship between the user's intentions and the meanings of expressions. *Articulatory directness* is the relationship between the meanings of expressions and their physical form.

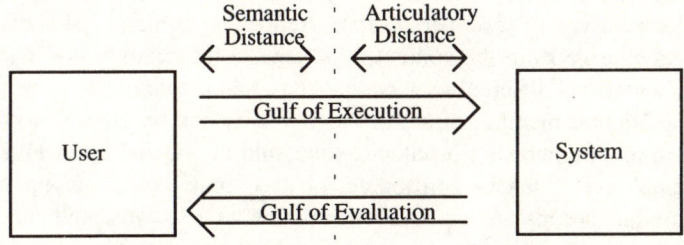

**Figure 1**. The relationship between semantic and articulatory distances and the gulfs of execution and evaluation [3,4].

When considering information retrieval from a relational database, using a traditional interface language such as SQL, it is possible to categorise a series of problems using this theoretical framework.

## 2.1 Problems in the Gulf of Execution

Let us suppose that a particular user would like to find out the room number of a particular member of staff in a database. Assuming that there is no interface language problem, there are potentially three problems in specifying the action, which neatly fit the analysis provided by the framework in figure 1. Firstly the user must know the *naming* conventions in the database, and knowledge of what symbol is used to denote information in the system, can be considered a problem of 'articulatory' distance[4]:

- Knowledge of the name of the relation(s) holding the required information.
- Knowledge of whether the column name holding the data values for room number are held in a column called 'Room', 'Room_No', 'Room_Number'....
- Knowledge of whether the data value denoting a particular room is in the form 'CB-2.100' or perhaps '2.100'

A second problem of semantic distance may occur when an assumption is made by the user on the basis of their particular intention—the user query is based on the assumption that there is a relation that corresponds to the description 'Rooms_of_Staff_Members'. Although it may be reasonable to believe that the 'Room_Number' column is contained in the same relation as 'Surname' because staff do have rooms, this need not be the case. It is not necessarily so that the organisation of data in the relational model is the same as the organisation of concepts in the world as the user conceives of them. It may not be possible to *phrase* the query as the user would do. Hutchins et al. [4] pose two important questions about semantic directness that are of central importance here: a) does the language support the user's conception of the task domain? and b) can the user say what is wanted in a straightforward fashion?

The last question concerning conceptual simplicity reveals an issue that also increases the semantic distance and is very closely related to the previous phrasing problem. Information tends to be viewed by different users with different goals from different perspectives. These perspectives represent a major part of the user's intention and emerge from the context in which the information is sought, and can be used. As such, it is different user *perspective*s that create phrasing problems. For instance, a particular member of staff at a university can be viewed in many ways, all leading to unique phrasing problems; she could be viewed as an inhabitant of a room, an employee, a teaching resource, or a computer user, among others. The relational model, because it encodes information as *relations*, and not as *objects* cannot in all cases support *concise queries* which the user would consider to be "conceptually simple."

---

[4]Also called the vocabulary problem [5].

## 2.2 Problems in the Gulf of Evaluation

One positive point about evaluation is that there is no naming problem. Whether a single value returned to a simple query concerning a room number is either 'CB-2.92' or '2.92', the user will make a simple inference, based on context, to recognise that data value as a room number[5]. Giving computer systems the capacity to produce this kind of inference, however, is not a trivial matter. But a tabular representation of information may not always be the most appropriate for its *interpretation*. An inadequate representation can thus increase articulatory distance.

A rich representation would provide an opportunity to interpret the information received with regard to the bigger picture of the user's intentions, and allow *refinement* and encourage exploration and discovery. The relational model volunteers no extra, potentially relevant, information such as that a human respondent may give, it is only concerned with answering correctly and efficiently [7].

The series of problems that have been identified are summarised diagramatically in figure 2.

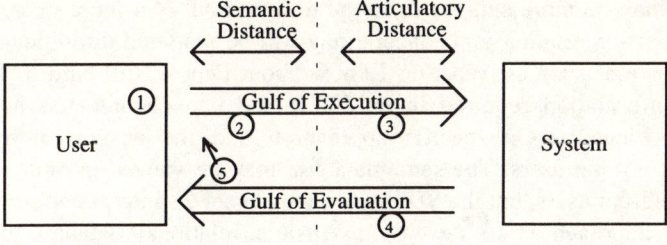

1. The perspective problem.
2. The phrasing problem.
3. The naming problem.
4. The interpretation problem.
5. The refinement problem.

**Figure 2.** Database communication problems in relation to the theoretical framework.

## 2.3 Problems with the Relational Model

The relational model is a particular representation of knowledge, favouring the coding of relations rather than the complete and coherent entities that hold those relations [8]. The structural simplicity of the conventional data models, such as the relational, forces database designers into 'flattening' the structural complexities of the universe of discourse, which leads to the loss of semantic information. Generic-

---

[5]This phenomenon was first remarked upon by Bartlett [6] as 'effort after meaning'.

specific relationships are not well supported, and although the logical or conceptual data model from which the relational model was derived may have been quite explicit about a categorical structure, it does not map well onto the relational model. The reduction to a normalised form does not necessarily provide a representation for the user that is unambiguous, or naturally applicable to different perspectives. Users are reduced to reconstructing the semantic information by virtue of their understanding of domain and context; hence the relational model in itself is not a sufficiently rich representation to support communication with the casual user.

The Semantic Data Models (SDM) place a conceptual layer upon the relational model in the same way that the relational model is a semantically richer abstraction of file system. The most well known of the SDMs is the Entity-Relationship model (ER) [2, ,8, 9]. The relational model is used by SDMs as one of many possible implementational representations. Consequentially there has been a great deal of research into using SDMs as the design interface and user's interface, with a behind-the-scenes mapping to the relational model [10]. We are still using the relational model behind a veneer of graphical user interface.

However, this approach merely presents the user with a new design-oriented structural model which the user is still expected to conform to and to navigate. An ER model may be more expressive to the designer but is it more expressive to the user? Information relating to a concept may still be scattered throughout the model, making questions such as 'What do I know about People' still hard to answer. The structural information required in an ER model can become too much, and is frequently oriented to a specific application and the designer's view of that application, not the users. The same database may be viewed in radically different ways by different users, but the SDM gives the designer's interpretation.

Another approach is to develop extensible relational database models, e.g. POSTGRES [11], or develop semantic data models that can be directly implemented, e.g. the functional data model [12], or the object-oriented model [13]. However, many relational databases are already in existence that do not have the benefit of a SDM and cannot be remodelled in a different representation. Yet they are still expected to be directly interacted with, and their schemas explored, by non-expert users.

Our approach is to recognise that there are plenty of databases without SDMs, that the users' viewpoints can differ radically between themselves and the designer, and that a structural model is a prescriptive one and not a descriptive one. In the same way as the SDMs, we enhance the relational model with a richer semantic model but instead of trying to reveal the database's logical structure we seek to eliminate it and make browsing conceptual and descriptive rather than structural. We what to support the question "What can I say about People" regardless of how many objects, roles or attributes represent "People". In this way we also make it straightforward to alter the conceptual model's (or 'world model') relationship with the best implementational model of the databases depending on user or application.

# 3  GUIDANCE Design—a Strategic Approach

The synthesis of a solution to the problems exposed by analysis depends on a set of disparate but related measures, that resolve into a common theme. There are 5 major threads:

1. The production of choices to solve articulatory problems in execution.
2. The production of examples to solve semantic problems in evaluation and subsequent execution.
3. The use of a 'model world' interface metaphor to increase semantic directness and user involvement.
4. The production of a full and relevant description of a query item, rather than a single value, to assist evaluation through interpretation.
5. The support of 'conceptual navigation' (non-structural navigation) for query refinement and multiple perspectives by use of a domain model.

The production of choices, rather than requiring a user to input the correct symbol, means that the articulatory gap is lessened for execution. The option to do so is a common strategy in many commercial and research systems. Kaleidoscope [14], for example, is aimed at a different user group, professional programmers with knowledge of SQL. It offers choices of commands, relation names and field names 'intra-query' to avoid syntactic and semantic errors, and is an aid to navigating around the structure of a database that is either unknown or partially known.

Producing example values as the results of an initial query enables the user to fix the domain of enquiry. Taking an example from Williams [15], if an interface offered a blank space following the field 'Manufacturer', what should be put into this field? A company name, a country name or a company site? At least some of this ambiguity can be removed by presenting a sample value and relying on the domain knowledge of the user. By applying context and an example to fix a domain we can go a long way to solving the naming problem, and substantially narrow the semantic distance for evaluation as well as subsequent execution. GUIDANCE uses this *retrieval by reformulation* technique, first introduced in the RABBIT system [16], as an aid to information retrieval. The idea is based on psychological theories of human remembering which states that people when attempting to bring something to memory first create a partial description of the class object, and then instantiate its slots with a set of values. If any of these values are wrong they are changed until the required set of values are obtained. This can be used to aid information retrieval, where slot values of a class object are returned and iteratively 'criticised' until the correct instance with the correct set of values is discovered, thus taking full advantage of the user's tacit knowledge of the domain and intention.

One of the assumptions made by the workers on the RABBIT system was that all queries to their system were under specified. If this is the case then the production of descriptions and example values act as 'signposts' to the intended data, and the process of query becomes a process of discovery and investigation. It is conceivable through allowing this kind of access to data that the user group would 'browse' the information source and discover information that they had no reason to believe was present, Clearly retrieval of information from a well-specified query does not suffer from this kind of presentation.

The use of a model world metaphor at the interface can substantially decrease semantic distance. An example of a direct manipulation system [17, p197] is Query-by-Example (QBE) [18] where the system shows the relations in tabular form on the screen, and allows the user to fill in example values, or orders to print a set of values. It is more 'direct' for the user to feel that she is directly manipulating the values, rather than having to formulate an expression like 'SELECT Staff FROM PersonTable WHERE RoomNo = CB2.92'.

The production of a full and relevant description of a query item is also attempted by QBE, but succeeds only as far as the relational model succeeds. It does not address whether the particular relation visualised is a complete or adequate description of the entity from the users point of view—the phrasing problem. This illustrates how structural exposure relies on the assumption that the representation in the model is coherent and sensible, whereas it may have been compromised by the normalisation process, and the lack of a generic/specific axis. For example, in a database there may be a relation 'Person' which contains all the information about the staff and students in a University department. In that relation there are fields for 'Room', 'Phone' and 'CourseNumber'. It is the case that the staff attend no courses, and the students have no phones or rooms. Similarly, information that may be considered essential to a complete description may be missing where such information has multiple values.

Although lessons can be learned from systems such as RABBIT, Kaleidoscope and Query-by-Example, fulfilling the aims of a full and relevant description if a query item and 'conceptual navigation' must be approached more radically by adding knowledge that does not exist or has been lost in translation from the ER model to the relational model. GUIDANCE thus uses an existing relational model as foundational, but imposes another conceptual layer which is further abstracted from the physical model. The imposition of a further conceptual level is achieved by including two models in the GUIDANCE architecture:

- A World Model containing conceptual knowledge—how concepts can combine and therefore how they can be described—that is similar to the users own.
- A Database Model to enable a mapping from these concepts to a specific database.

The approach taken here is to *conceal* the relational model in favour of the *exposure* of a conceptual model more like the users own. Communication with the user thus takes place via the medium of the system's 'richer' representation, the relational model becoming transparent to the user.

## 3.1 GUIDANCE Architecture

GUIDANCE was written in VisualWorks[6], and the World and Database Models were written in GRAIL[7] [19, 20], a member of the KL-ONE family of knowledge representation formalisms [21]. It is implemented by a semantic network in ObjectWorks/Smalltalk interfaced to the Sybase RDBMS.

GRAIL is a descriptive classification-based knowledge representation formalism developed by the University of Manchester for modelling medical terminology. It is generative, defining complex entities (called particularizations) in terms of complete descriptions made up of a limited set of elementary concepts place in a subsumption lattice, and bi-directional binary relations linking concepts. The particularizations are new composite concepts implied by the descriptive relationship and are assembled according to a system of sophisticated semantic sanctions. These are placed in the subsumption hierarchy by a classifier, and become a form of implied subtype of their base supertype, and inherit its properties. The relationships have cardinalities and qualifiers which ensure that the creation of only self-consistent and non-redundant particularizations.

The purpose of GRAIL is to represent statements about conceptual entities that allow the expression and validation of all and only semantically correct descriptions. The GRAIL classifier has two broad functions:

- Give a concept description X, is it sensible (i.e. can it be classified)?
- What is it sensible to say about X?

GRAIL is in some ways similar to other fact-based models, e.g. NIAM [9] except that it has a semantically constrained generative functionality.

The five basic modules of GUIDANCE are:

1. A World Model that can exist in its own right as a pure conceptual model, and is therefore strictly independent of the implementation of the database. It contains knowledge of terminology and concept combinations. This is modelled in GRAIL, so it is possible to express what it is sensible to say about any concept at this level—People can have Machines, People who have Machines are kinds of People who have Names, Machines have IDs.

2. A Database Model that determines the mapping between the concepts in the World Model and the relational model and contains database specific information used to perform the mapping—Information about People is held in the DeptPerson table, Surname maps directly to DeptPerson.SurnameColumn, LoginColumn is a kind of DatabaseColumn.

3. The GRAIL classifier which unifies the World and Database Models into a Concepts Model that contains all the information about concepts, how they

---

[6]VisualWorks and ObjectWorks/Smalltalk are products of ParcPlace.
[7]An earlier version of GRAIL is known as SMK.

combine, database entities and tables and columns. The classifier can accept new combinations of concepts as input, and classify and sanction them, ensuring that the combinatory and reference properties are correctly inherited.

4. A Query Architecture that consults the Concepts Model and the database on behalf of the user and sends results to the interface for display. This architecture implements three 'spaces' or levels at which consultation of the Concepts Model or interaction with the Interface takes place (see section 6). The Query Architecture can ask of the database questions such as "Find the value in DeptPersonTable.SurnameColumn when DeptPersonTable.ForenameColumn is 'Fred'", and of the Concepts Model questions like "What is sensible to say about Person?".

5. An Interface that deals with all communication with the user.

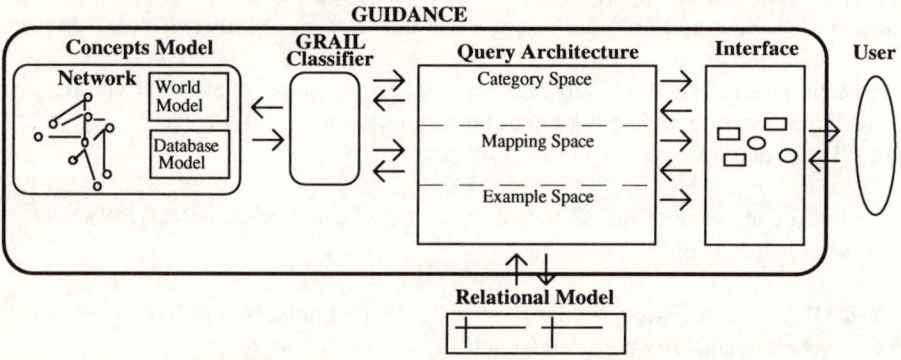

**Figure 3**. The full modular architecture of the GUIDANCE system.

The strategy of modularisation (see figure 3) is to produce a system of such a generalised nature that extended World and Database Models can be simply 'plugged in' to allow the accommodation of other databases and/or a larger Universe of Discourse.

## 4 The Interface

The interface is built using the 'model world' metaphor [4]. The entities are directly represented on the screen, and directly manipulated. The entities values can be viewed and investigated by using the buttons that occupy the same physical space. No 'command-line' style interaction is available. The information is visualised graphically by representing the category of the queried item in a central focus position in the window, with the attributes and example values that describe an instance of it surrounding this central position, as in figure 4.

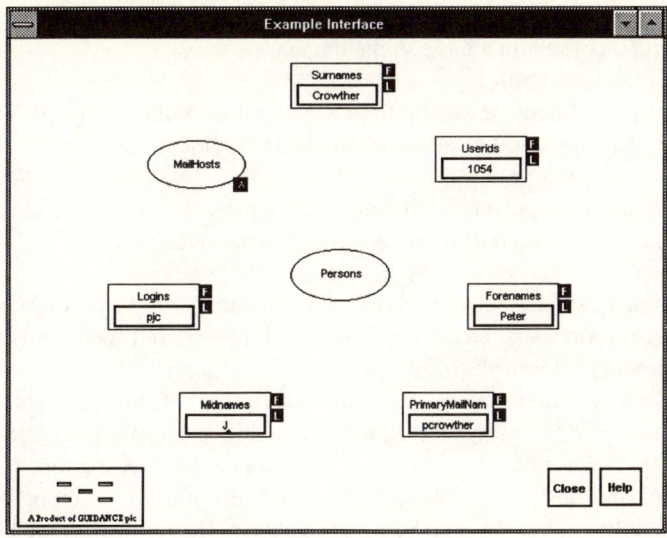

**Figure 4.** An Example Interface for a query on Persons.

A number of important points about this representation should be noted:

- The functionality of the interface is distinctly limited. The target user group's requirements of the system are that of simple data retrieval, and as long as the functionality is there to support this task there is no reason to add more just for the sake of it—or, to put it bluntly, to satisfy the developers ego.

- Attribute links are not named on the interface. It is considered that the user will be able to make the required inference as to what the link is. Effectively the examples are 'typed' by the attribute name on the box in which they appear. In the relatively simple domain used here the inferences are straight forward, and leaving the link names out avoids a cluttered interface. It is possible that in a more complex domain. it may be useful to include the link names when the link contains more semantic information than can be readily inferred from the objects at either end.

- The user is expected to be able to identify the instance of 'Person' shown in figure 4 by the values of the attributes that are written in the slot under the name of the attribute. The instance described in this case is a 'Natural Category' and it is considered here that instances of these special types of category cannot be uniquely identified by any *single* value of any of its attributes (see the following section). Therefore the central figure has no slot and no value within it.

- Instances of 'Value Categories' which in this case are all the attributes of the Person instance except MailHosts, can be uniquely identified, and therefore each have a value. In database terms these instances of Value Categories map 1:1 with a column in a table in the database.

- Whether the Focus or Attribute is a Natural or Value Category is dependant on the semantics of the category, not of its graphical position.

- The description presented on the interface is, by necessity, consistent, and may have been derived from a single or many relations.

Like 'Persons', 'MailHosts' is considered a Natural Category. Although it has no value itself, it represents an instance of a MailHost, but with only one of its attributes showing - the link to Person instance. It is possible by pressing the 'A' (for Add Focus) button to see the full description of the relevant 'MailHost' alongside the 'Persons' entity description, and this is shown in figure 5. By this method the user can navigate conceptually between entities that are linked in the World Model and answer questions like "What do you know about People?", or more specifically "What do you know about Alan Rector?" without knowing the relational or conceptual schema structures.

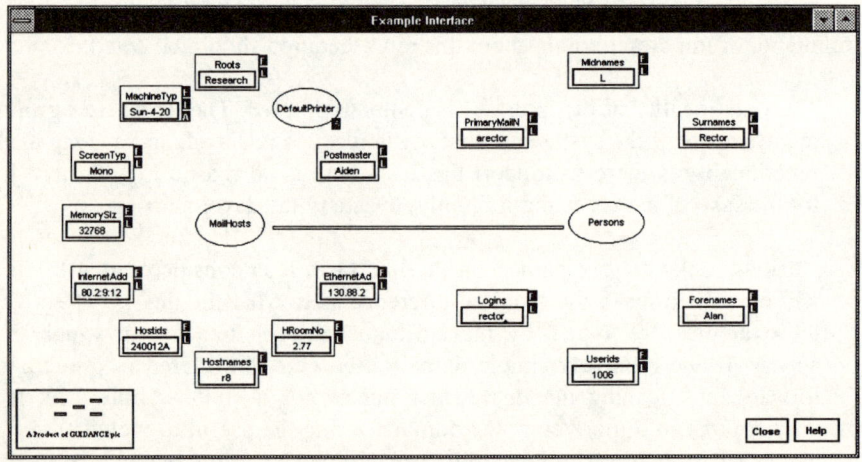

**Figure 5.** A Double Example Interface, with MailHosts added to Persons.

The 'F' for fix and 'L' for list provides the remaining functionality. The 'L' button when pressed will return a list of example values for the specific attribute instance, from which the user can choose. Note that the example values for an attribute are collected from all the set of all focus instances - pressing 'L' on the Forenames attribute for Person will produce a list of all possible forenames for all instances of Person. An example of this is shown in figure 6:

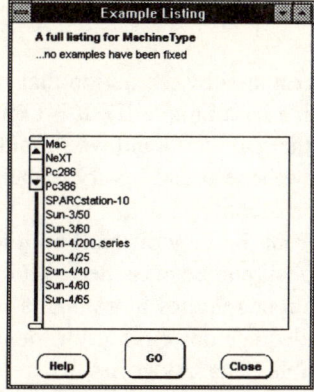

**Figure 6.** The listing produced by pressing 'L' on a MachineType attribute.

The making of a choice is equivalent to the setting of a constraint, and GUIDANCE will re-populate the slots of all the Value Categories displayed on the interface according to this constraint. The 'F' button is available to fix the slot value of an attribute, so that it is possible to investigate other descriptions of instances using the 'L' button that include that value for that attribute. For instance, pressing 'F' on 'Forenames' in figure 4 would mean that any listings of other attributes in the description will respect the fact that 'Peter' is the fixed value for 'Forenames'. Subsequently pressing the 'L' button on 'Surnames' will produce a listing of all surnames that are included in descriptions of Person instances that have 'Peter' as the value of 'Forename' (for an example see figure 7). Once an Item is fixed, the text 'Value Fixed' appears under the entity and the 'F' button changes colour and becomes an 'U' button for 'Unfix'.

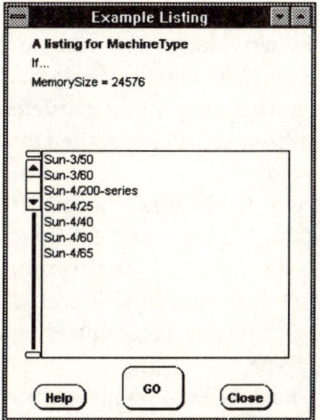

**Figure 7.** A listing for MachineType where the value of MemorySize has been fixed at '24576'.

## 5 The Use of Natural Categories

The relational model is underpinned by the notion that it is necessary that a record must be definitively identifiable by a unique ID. It is argued here that this is not the case with regard to things in the real world and we should not impose this constraint on our users allowing them the benefit and luxury of being able to make their own inferences about the nature and identity of data.

We do not pretend to confront the very difficult notion of whether a non-barking animal with three legs and no tail can be classified as a dog or not, but merely state that to make certain classifications requires more than a *single* piece of information, and therefore to provide an adequate description for identification requires as much relevant information as possible. The categories where this is the case are called Natural Categories. A similar concept is presented by Johnson-Laird who contrasts his *natural kind terms* (e.g. apple) with *constructive terms* (e.g. chair) [17].

For Natural Categories, therefore, no one particular feature is either necessary or sufficient for classification. For instance, being able to bark is neither a necessary or sufficient condition for being a dog. Secondly (and more pointedly for this system) there can be no single value of any one of its attributes (or set of values of a set of attributes) upon which an instance of it can be *definitively* identified. For example, we could identify one particular University by any of the following criteria:

The University that is outside Brighton.
The University called 'The University of Sussex'.
The University I graduated from in 1978.

It is argued that although all these descriptions describe the same place, none of them is a *definitive* description of it. Fogelin, referring to Wittgenstein [22] confirms this ideas:

> "We can say that the individual with the name "Moses" is both overdetermined in the sense that there is a superabundance of descriptive information available for a definition, but underdetermined since no one set of these characteristics has been actually specified as definitive" [23, p135]

We suggest that an instance of the Natural Category 'Person' cannot be uniquely identified by any (or all) of its features, and the burden of inference should be placed on the *user* to interpret the values of the descriptions by using their expertise in the domain. Instances of 'Value Categories' are more conducive to definitive interpretation—a particular machine can be uniquely and functionally identified by a particular name it has been given.

Arguments as to precisely *how* mental representations are stored (as a semantic network [24], as a cluster of instances at different semantic distance to a prototype [25], as a mental model [26]) are irrelevant - we have abstracted a simple and well-established fact and utilised it, to the benefit of the user, and implemented it in this system.

Practically, this confers advantages for the system because:

- Although the relational model must provide a unique identifier for an instance of 'Person', there is no *a priori* reason to do this at a more abstract conceptual level. Although the structural implementation in the relational model *requires* a unique and definitive identifier, GUIDANCE does not.

- To artificially designate a unique reference for an instance of a Natural Category would mean that a choice would have to be made as to which one. Again there is no good *a priori* reason to choose 'Surname' over 'Userid' or 'Login' or vice versa. It has been argued that no one value can definitively identify an instance of a Natural Category, and it is possible by this methodology to finesse the issue of which one to choose.

- Selecting a unique and definitive identifier involves a commitment to it over time. GUIDANCE is theoretically extensible to other domains and any choice could limit this. Choosing 'Login' could affect extensibility where the domain information included people but not computers. This confers great practical gain with regard to database integration.

Instances of Natural Categories are thus identifiable by the user from the set of attribute values presented in the description. An example of this is shown in figure 8.

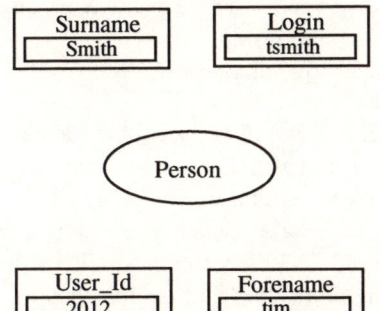

| Login | Surname | Forename | User_Id |
|---|---|---|---|
| aek | knowles | alan | 1756 |
| arector | rector | alan | 1016 |
| tsmith | smith | tim | 2012 |
| ⋮ | ⋮ | ⋮ | ⋮ |

Values in the columns in the relational model are used to provide descriptive information rather than to definitively identify.

**Figure 8.** A Natural Category is identifiable by the user by inference from the values of the features in its description.

The use of Natural Categories in this way is reminiscent of the non-lexical entity tokens of the functional data models where an entity token represents objects in the real world and not the numbers or identifiers associated with the objects, and hence the entities themselves cannot be printed [27]. It is similar to the idea that an object is not identified by its values captured in the object identity philosophy of the object-oriented models.

Whether or not a particular conceptual entity is designated as a 'Natural Category' or not is carried out in the Database Model, and thus these assumptions are part of the implementational strategy rather than being part of the pure knowledge representation coded in the World Model.

## 6 The Models and the Query Architecture

The Concepts Model, as the repository of information derived from the World and Database models, contains information about how concepts can be combined, and is consulted by the Query Architecture on behalf of the user. An in-depth description of how this is achieved is beyond the scope of this paper, and is to be presented in a future paper [28]. However, a brief indication of the principles can be given here. The aim is to produce a Concepts Model that contains information such that when presented with a query entity the Classifier can provide a description to the Query Architecture that is made up of 'all and only' those attributes that are relevant to the enquiry. By virtue of the Classifier, both models can be thought of as 'compressed data', and the GRAIL representation is an extended T-box [29].

### 6.1 The World Model

The World Model contains conceptual knowledge along three dimensions:

1. Generic/specific 'isa' relationships between concepts coded as a class hierarchy
2. Sanctioning constraints on binary 'fact-based' relationships that control the use of them in composing new, composite concepts. These constraints also deal with transitivity in part-whole structural relationships.
3. Constraints on the handling of tautologies and equivalencies

The latter are not true 'facts' but statements that it is *possible* that, for instance, a `Student takesCourse CourseNumber`. The model thus contains statements which positively state what is *allowable*, the default being that it is not. The GRAIL Classifier uses these sanctioning statements to assess whether a particular combination is permitted, if it is, then it is placed in its correct position in the subsumption lattice, if it is not, it is rejected. The word 'fact' is therefore possibly misleading—the composite concepts derived from this model are in truth "...determined by what it is possible to think." [26].

The World Model owes no allegiance to any particular database, or any particular structure or kind of database, it is purely a knowledge representation and is mapped by the use of the Database Model and other parts of the architecture to the relational model. It is therefore extensible outside the Universe of Discourse of the database, as it has no direct reference to it.

### 6.2 The Database Model

The Database Model is specific to the database, and provides the information to perform the mapping of the World Model to the relational model. As well as a generic/specific dimension which deals with tables and columns, this model has a set of referential links with very specific semantics that are encoded as assertional information, namely that:

- `containsInfoOn`—A particular table contains information about a particular conceptual entity.
- `isInfoOn`—that a particular column has a direct reference to a particular conceptual entity
- `isPrimaryKeyFor`—A particular table uses the value for a particular conceptual entity as its primary key.

These three classes of link 'join' the World to the Database model and operate on a referential dimension, the other two dimensions being thought of as generic/specific and fact. The Database Model thus contains meta-data—about conceptual entities in the World Model and about tables and columns in the Relational Model.

Whether or not a particular concept is designated as a Natural Category or not is determined by the lack of a `isInfoOn` link to it from the Database Model. Although these links are written from the databases point of view (with the database entity—table or column—as the topic of the statement and not the comment), it is worthwhile to consider what the inverse of the link means with respect to the mapping. For instance, it may be the case that values pertaining to the description of 'MachineType' may be held in two tables—the 'HostsTable' and the 'MachineTypesTable', and it may also be the case that the definitive identifier of 'MachineType' is held in a column called 'MachineTypeColumn'. This would be coded as three links:

1. `MachineType infoContainedIn HostsTable`
2. `MachineType infoContainedIn MachineTypeTable`
3. `MachineType infoIsIn MachineTypeColumn`

If 1 and 2 are considered first, what is being attempted here is to 'reinstate' the complete object that has been removed from the relational model, for all information pertaining to the description of 'MachineType' is contained within these two tables, and the values of the description of 'Machine Type' as determined by the World Model is required to be drawn from these two tables. As it is not necessarily the case that any set of tables represent the values for the description, the full set of columns in the tables will most probably be a superset of the data fields required to describe the object. The 'MachineTypeColumn' is likely to exist in both of these tables (if it is a foreign key, which in this case it is with respect to HostsTable), and the Query Architecture recognises this and has the capacity to perform the join.

With a Natural Category, this still the case—`infoContainedIn` links are made to tables such that the values of its description should be drawn from these tables, but the `infoIsIn` link is omitted. The Query Architecture can still use the information about where the information is held, but will not return a value for the entity itself.

## 6.3 The Query Architecture and the Concepts Model

When both the World and Database models are processed by the Classifier, the Concepts Model is loaded with knowledge about:

- What it is possible to say about an entity.
- The column name under which the value of an entity may be found.
- In which table or tables information about an entity may be found.
- Primary key information

The function of the Query Architecture is to consult both the Concepts Model and the database itself on the users behalf. All communication between the user and the Query Architecture is mediated by the Interface. The Query Architecture is divided in to three layers or spaces, and objects within each layer constrain the creation of objects in the next lowest one.

*Category Space:* Objects are concerned with deriving information concerning what attributes of the query entity are possible.
*Mapping Space:* Objects are concerned with determining meta-data about the reference of these objects.
*Example Space:* Objects retrieve values from the database, and do not consult the Concepts Model.

The Concepts Model thus provides the schemata for the instantiations that are carried out in two of the three spaces—Category Space and Mapping Space. The creation of Example Objects from Mapping Objects is a purely algorithmic operation, and Example Objects consult the database to determine values.

The main operation carried out in Category Space is the formation of a *saturated category*. When a query entity is received by the Query Architecture, the Concepts Model is asked for a full description—what is it possible for this entity to combine with? In the case that 'Persons' is the queried entity, it may be possible that it may combine with 'Logins', 'PrimaryMailNames', 'Surnames' and 'Forenames', and in that case a conceptual entity will be returned that contains all of these possibilities combined, and therefore can be said to be *saturated*. This entity is then sent to the Classifier to be placed in the subsumption lattice. The Saturated Category in this case would be:

```
Persons which <   hasLogin Login
                  hasPrimaryMailName PrimaryMailName
                  hasForename Forename
                  hasSurname Surname     >
```

In Mapping Space, this category object is further instantiated so that it contains database specific information about where information about all the concepts can be drawn from, and more closely resembles what is traditionally referred to in database terms as an 'intension'. It is important to note that this is not an artificially separated two stage process, but that due to the nature of the classificatory process information cannot be drawn on the individual parts of the objects in isolation—the information is included or not on the basis of the complete object. To put it more simply, the information derived from the Concepts Model on 'Login' as part of a description of 'Person' is different to the information derived from the Concepts Model on 'Login' as an individual non-composite entity—the entity inherits according to where it is placed in the subsumption lattice, and 'Login' on its own is in a very different place to the Login entity contained in 'Person which `<has Login Login>`'.

In Example Space, the mapping object is instantiated again to return values from the database. A flavour of how this is achieved was described in section 5. Basically, the focus entity is the lynch pin of the algorithm, as all the information about the focus entity must *by definition* come from the tables pointed to by the `infoContainedIn` links. The focus entities descriptive features have referential links to tables and columns too, but precedence is given to the table(s) that are determined by the focus entity, and a correspondence achieved. It can be seen that although the Natural Category entities have not in themselves any direct value, the values of their descriptive features are determined by the tables in which information about them are stated to be.

When considered in database terms, the objects in the Mapping Space and Example Space reflect reasonably standard notions of intension and extension. It is the contention here that the Category Space objects reflect a *class intension* where the Mapping Space object is its instantiation with reference to a particular database. This is consistent with the idea of the information in the Concepts Model derived from the World Model as being purely conceptual, and not database specific. This idea of a class intension appears very much in line with the notion of intension which is presented in philosophy and linguistics [30] where its context or 'possible world' can be seen as the specific database or databases specified in the Database Model. The conceptual entities in the World Model, therefore, have no 'meaning' (in the traditional linguistic sense) and are isolated from their reference until it is attributed to them by applying a context via a mapping to a possible world - their instantiation as an intension in a database. Other possible worlds or other contexts therefore become imaginable with different mappings and the semantics of a class intension becomes a function of the mapping to a database which enables a context within which to interpret it.

# 7 Evaluation

A qualitative study was carried out following the implementation of the system to get feedback on how users actually performed using the system. Full details of this evaluation and are presented in Haw [31]. The study was carried out in the style of Carroll and Mack [32], where an evaluator was present throughout the session to encourage discussion, as the main point of the exercise was to elicit criticism of the system rather than gather statistics.

It was generally considered to be a system that was easy to learn and use. This is objectively borne out by the fact that the sessions did not last more than forty minutes from start to finish, with some lasting only twenty. The only real problem that was encountered that was common to most participants was getting to grips with the 'fix' facility. Once the idea behind this was clarified by explanation and example, they had no further problems. A particular advantage with GUIDANCE is that there is very little functionality, and hence very little to master.

The representation was never criticised, and all considered it comprehensible and clear. A rather revealing problem emerged for one participant that supports the theoretical analysis of the problems of information retrieval presented earlier. When required to answer a query relating to the room number of a member of the department, she went unerringly to enquire on the entity 'Students'. In the World Model (and hence the interface representation), 'Students' do not have rooms or phones, but do courses, and 'Staff' have rooms and phones, but do not do courses. She was confused when 'RoomNo' was not included in the description for 'Students', and was asked why. She commented that she had been thinking of postgraduate students (she was one), and they *do* have rooms. Perhaps the GUIDANCE model may not be correct, but it is clear from this example that this user was consulting her own model of the world. The system does appear to have enabled the right kind of meaningful system/user communication, even if in this particular case the models did not match.

It was particularly encouraging that a number of participants noticed that multiple perspectives on data were available. That the participants realise this suggests that the World Model embedded in the system is matching with the participants model in a dynamic sense—the objects on the screen 'mean' what they mean in the world, and the participants are being directly engaged.

Although the representation of Natural Categories produced no obvious problems for the users, one or two problems did emerge. For example, the query which asked users to "Find all the people in the department whose middle name is David" does not explicitly say "Find all the *surnames* of people in the department whose middle name is David". As the use of a Natural Category representation does not provide a unique identifier to its instances, the participants had to choose themselves which value was appropriate as an answer. In this case the surname was probably the most appropriate, but other perspectives may have demanded others, say if the user wished to e-mail a person who she knew had the middle name David, she may consider that the PrimaryMailName was the better 'answer'.

## 8 Related Work

A good deal of attention has been paid to improving the interface between the casual user and the database. Broadly, three approaches appear in the literature:

1. 'intelligent systems' which use artificial intelligence to simulate a 'person-oriented' dialogue [16].
2. systems that use a natural language (usually domain specific) interface that maps to a database language [33].

3.   graphical systems which use icons, highlighting etc. and the 'natural' arrangement of objects [10, 34].

GUIDANCE falls into categories 1. and 2. Most graphical approaches expose the structure of the conceptual model through some sort of extended ER representation. Queries are constructed using the now visible relationships. Such systems take a different viewpoint to GUIDANCE which seeks to disguise the structure. which has the advantage of being schema independent—the structure of the model can change but such changes are hidden from the user, and just require some reconfiguration of the Database Model.

SIMS [35] and CANDIDE [33] have similar ideas in using a classification based knowledge representation to model the domain and extend the semantics of a relational model, but have not developed the user interface aspects (the Natural Categories and user-centred approach) to the same degree. Together with RABBIT [16] they also use the classification approach for querying, contrasted with the more operational approach such as the SQL-type query languages, requires the user to have a thorough understanding of the database schema; that they know all the names of the objects and attributes, specify the access paths and plan the joins. GEM [36] and ARIEL [37] are two such operationally-oriented data manipulation languages. GUIDANCE does interface to existing RDBMS, and so maps the classified queries into appropriate SQL queries (leaving the execution of such to the RDB's query optimiser) and uses the Database Model to map to the relations. CANDIDE and RABBIT are attempts to integrate the data with the KBS into a single uniform representation.

GUIDANCE is not a relationally complete language, and cannot handle, for example, recursive or aggregate queries. It was not designed as such; it is a 'conceptual navigation' tool for interrogating schemas rather than formulating large complex but well defined queries. As such it is a navigation aid along the lines of Kaleidoscope [14].

## 9   Conclusion and Future Work

We have presented a database user interface assistant—GUIDANCE—that enables that people who are not experts in computing but are experts in their own domain to use a relational database by concealing the logical structure of the database and using a technique of 'conceptual navigation' based on Natural Categories. The interface aims to support ill-formed or 'discovery based' enquiries about specific data rather than well-specified complex queries over sets of data instances. The user does not have to know anything about the structure of the database and are able to use their own domain knowledge to support the creation and interpretation of queries. Thus we have used GUIDANCE as an experiment in the understanding of the twin gulfs of execution and evaluation, and the ideas of semantic and articulatory directness.

GUIDANCE uses a three space model to represent the user's conceptual World Model and mappings to specific logical database representations of these concepts

(Database Model) and example instances. All models are presented in a descriptive subsumption-based classification formalism (GRAIL) which has a system of semantic sanctions to control the creation of implied concepts. Extending the World Model to a larger universe of discourse to cover the terminology used in many databases seems a natural progression - adapting and deriving a Database Model to map a number of local database schemas to this global schema. Work has begun on the application of the GUIDANCE architecture to mediate between heterogeneous semantic schemas and not just mediate between users and relational databases [35]. Work is also required to extend GUIDANCE to be relationally complete.

# References

1. Avison DE, Fitzgerald G. Information Systems Development: Methodologies, Techniques and Tools. Basil Blackwell, London, 1988.

2. Hull R, King R. Semantic Data Modelling: Survey, Applications and Research Issues. ACM Computing Surveys 19(1), 1987, pp 201-260.

3. Norman DA. Cognitive Engineering. In: Norman DA and Draper S (eds) User-centered system design: New perspectives on HCI. LEA Inc., Hillsdale, NJ, 1986, pp 31-62.

4. Hutchins EL, Hollan JD, Norman DA. Direct Manipulation Interfaces. In: Norman DA and Draper S (eds) User-centered system design: New perspectives on HCI. LEA Inc., Hillsdale, NJ, 1986, pp 87-124.

5. Furnas GW, Landauer TK, Gomez LM, Dumais ST. The Vocabulary Problem in Human-System Communication. Communications of the ACM 30, 1987, pp 964-971.

6. Bartlett FC. Remembering: A Study in Experimental and Social Psychology. CUP, Cambridge, 1932.

7. Motro A. Annotating Answers with their Properties. SIGMOD record, 21(4), 1992, pp 54-57.

8. Peckham J, Maryanski F. Semantic Data Models. ACM Computing Surveys. 20(3). 1988, pp 153-189.

9. Nijssen GM, Halpin TA. Conceptual Schema and Relational Database Design: a Fact Oriented Approach. Prentice-Hall, Sydney, 1989.

10. Rogers TR, Cattell RGG. Entity-relationship database user interfaces. Proc. 6th International Conference on Entity-Relationship Approach, New York, 1987 pp 323-336.

11. Stonebraker M, Kemnitz G. The Postgres Next-Generation Database Management System. Communications of the ACM 34(10), 1991, pp 78-92.

12. Shipman DW. The Functional Data Model and the Data Language DAPLEX. ACM Transactions on Database Systems 6(1), 1981, pp 140-173.

13. Atkinson M, Bancilhon F, DeWitt D, Dittrich K, Maier D, Zdonik S. The Object-Oriented Database Systems Manifesto. Proc. of the 1st International Conference on Deductive and Object-oriented Databases (DOOD). Kyoto, Japan. 1989, pp 40-57.

14. Cha SK. Kaleidoscope: A Co-operative Menu-Guided Query Interface (SQL Version). IEEE Transactions of Knowledge and Data Engineering. 3(1)1991, pp.42-47

15. Williams MD. What Makes RABBIT Run? International Journal of Man-Machine Studies 21, 1984, pp.333-352.

16. Tou FN, Williams MD, Filkes R, Henderson A, Malone T. RABBIT: an Intelligent Database Assistant. Proc. AAAI 1982 pp.314-318.

17. Shneiderman B. Designing the User Interface—Strategies for Effective Human-Computer Interaction. Addison-Wesley, Reading, Mass, 1992.

18. Zloof M.M. Query-by-Example. Proc. National Computer Conference, AFIPS Press, Montvale, NJ, 1975, pp 431-438.

19. Rector AL, Nowlan WA, Kay S. Conceptual Knowledge: The Core of Medical Information Systems. In: Lun KC, Degoulet WE, Pierre P, Reinhof O. (eds) MEDINFO 92 Proc. of the Seventh World Congress on Medical Informatics, Geneva, North-Holland, 1992, pp 1420-1426.

20. Goble CA, Glowinski AJ, Nowlan WA, Rector AL. A Descriptive Semantic Formalism for Medicine. In Proc. Ninth International Conference on Data Engineering, 1992, pp 624-632

21. Woods WA. The KL-ONE family. Computers and Mathematics Applications. 23, 1992, pp 133-177.

22. Wittgenstein L. Philosophical Investigations. Basil Blackwell, Oxford, 1953.

23. Fogelin RJ. Wittgenstein. Routledge and Keegen Paul, London, 1987.

24. Collins AM, Quillian MR. Retrieval Time from Semantic Memory. Journal of Verbal Learning and Verbal Behaviour, 8, 1972, pp 240-7.

25. Rosch E. Classification of Real World Objects: Origins and Representations in Cognition. In: Johnson-Laird PN, Wason PC. (eds) Thinking: Readings in Cognitive Science. CUP, Cambridge, 1977.

26. Johnson-Laird PN. Mental Models. CUP, Cambridge, 1983.

27. Gray PMD. The Functional Data Model related to the CODASYL model. In: Stocker P (ed.) *Databases: Role and Structure.* CUP, Cambridge, 1991, pp 57-59.

28. Haw DC, Goble CA, Rector AL. The Use of a Descriptive Terminology Formalism to Support the User Interface to the Relational Data Model. In preparation, 1994.

29. Brachman RJ, Filkes RE, Levesque H.J. KRYPTON: A Functional Approach to Knowledge Representation. In: Brachman RJ, Levesque HJ. (eds): Readings in Knowledge Representation. Morgan Kaufman, California, 1985 pp 411-429.

30. Kaplan D. Demonstratives: an essay on the semantics, logic, metaphysics and epistemology of demonstrative and other indexicals. Paper presented at the March 1977 meeting on the Pacific division of the American Philosophical Association, 1977.

31. Haw DC. Communicating with the User: An Intelligent System to Enable Relational Database Mediation. M.Sc. Thesis, University of Manchester, 1993.

32. Carroll J, Mack R. Learning to Use a Word Processor: By doing, by thinking and by knowing. In: Thomas J, Schneider M. (eds): Human Factors in Computer Systems. Ablex, Norwood NJ, 1984, pp 13-51.

33. Beck HW, Gala S, Navathe S. Classification as a query processing technique in the CANDIDE semantic data model. Proc. IEEE 5th International Conference on Data Engineering, Los Angeles, CA, 1989, pp 572-581.

34. Angelaccio M, Catarci T, Santucci G. Query by Diagram*: A Fully Visual Query System. In Journal of Visual Languages and Computing 1(3), 1990, pp.255-273.

35. Arens Y, Chee CY, Hsu C-N, Knoblock CA. Retrieving and Integrating Data from Multiple Information Sources. University of Southern California Information Sciences Institute Internal Report ISI-RR-93-308, 1993.

36. Zaniolo C. The database language GEM. Proc. of the ACM SIGMOD International Conference on the Management of Data, 1983.

37. MacGregor RM. ARIEL - A semantic front-end to a relational DBMSs, Proc 11th VLDB , Stockholm, 1985, pp 305-315

# HIBROWSE for Hotels: Bridging the Gap Between User and System Views of a Database

G P Ellis, J E Finlay, A S Pollitt
Centre for Database Access Research and Human Computer Interaction
Research Centre,
University of Huddersfield, UK

**Abstract.**

Database theory and technology has traditionally been concerned with issues such as consistency and efficiency rather than usability. This has led to interaction styles which focus on the structure of the database, which is system-based, rather than the user's view of its content. Therefore the problem that needs to be addressed is that of bridging the gap between the user's model of the data and that of the system. The system presented here approaches this problem by presenting the user with a domain oriented view of the database. Access is then achieved by manipulating the contents of the database rather than the structure.

## 1 Introduction

Database theory and technology has traditionally been concerned with issues such as consistency and efficiency rather than usability. This is important, particularly with large databases, but has led to interaction styles which focus on the structure of the database rather than its content.

Unfortunately the ideal structure from an implementational and theoretical viewpoint may not reflect the user's view or model of the data, which is governed by knowledge of the domain rather than of the database itself. Such a mismatch between user and system models can lead to problems in accessing the data, since access methods demand an understanding of the database structure in addition to domain knowledge.

The increasing reliance on databases as tools for use in diverse applications by a range of users has led to a recognition of the need to facilitate database access. Approaches to this vary. Some recent database systems, both commercial (such as Microsoft Access™ and Quest™ from Gupta Europe) and research systems [1, 2] employ graphical user interface techniques which have the advantage of providing the user with cues to understanding the structure of the database and composing queries. While an improvement on command style query languages such systems do not address the underlying problem of the focus on the system rather than the user view.

Approaches such as Query-by-Example begin to address this issue. Here the user is presented with a view of the database structure and is able to specify "example" values for particular fields as a means of accessing the data (Figure 1)

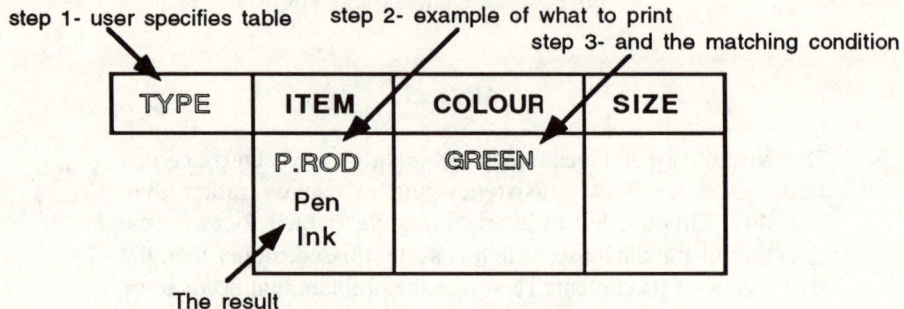

Figure 1: An example of Query-by-Example

This has proved to be successful for certain database applications but the approach still presents the user with the underlying structure of the database (which may not reflect the user's interests) and requires some understanding of this structure and of appropriate example values. This can be problematic if the user has insufficient knowledge of the database to select the necessary examples or tables or to evaluate the system's response.

In our view the problem that needs to be addressed is not simply that of making the interface more accessible or even the structure more explicit but that of bridging the gap between the user's view of the data and that of the system. HIBROWSE, the system discussed here, approaches this by presenting a view of the database which reflects the interests of the user. Access is achieved by manipulating the displayed database contents not by queries based on the structure. This approach has several advantages for the user. Access does not require an understanding of the structure of the database, making it more intuitive. Consequently queries can be produced far more quickly than with conventional access techniques and, additionally, the user is able to browse the database contents.

HIBROWSE is designed with the principle of interface separation in mind: the application is distinct from the interface and the two are linked by a dialogue controller. This architecture has a number of advantages:

- it allows the presentation of an alternative view of the database while retaining the database application unchanged;
- it supports reusability and portability;
- it allows continued use of the existing application facilities in parallel to the new functionality provided through HIBROWSE.

In the following sections we will explore the design and implementation of a prototype application of HIBROWSE, developed for the Hotel and Catering Research Centre at the University of Huddersfield, identifying issues associated with the interface, application database and dialogue control.

## 2  HIBROWSE for Hotels

HIBROWSE has its origins as Query-by-Menu, a system first described by Pollitt [4]. It was compared with Query-by-Example [5], and shown to be less complex for an end-user to employ in the specification of a search. The approach has been further developed and applied through a number of database applications, such as INSPEC [6] and the Hotels application considered here.

### 2.1  The Motivation

The Hotel and Catering Research Centre (HCRC) is based in the Department of Food, Nutrition and Hospitality Management and amongst other activities maintains a comprehensive database of up-to-date information on UK hotels and hotel companies. This includes details on over 3400 hotels which are owned by hotel groups or are members of one or more hotel consortia. A summary of the structure of the database is given in Figures 2 and 3. The HCRC publishes a paper directory, the UK Hotels Groups Directory, and also offers a consultancy service to companies with interests in the hotel industry. Clients are typically interested in receiving information on those hotels, groups or consortia which meet certain criteria (for example, 3 star AA rating and above with 200 or more bedrooms in North England and Scotland) or for information on a particular company which includes hotel details and summaries of the data by geographic region, star rating and number of bedrooms.

Prior to using HIBROWSE, the Hotels database was queried using SQL, a structured command language. This requires a knowledge of the database tables and associated fields in addition to experience of formulating queries obeying the SQL syntax. This placed an unnecessary burden on the staff, and although they usually managed to answer a client's request for specific information, the average time taken to undertake each request was half a day. Therefore the staff did not have sufficient time to process all the consultancy requests they received and it was actually considered uneconomic, in terms of the time taken, to process these requests using the existing system.

### 2.2  Requirements for HIBROWSE for Hotels

In addition to the primary requirement of supporting the consultancy task described above, other requirements were identified in consultation with the staff in the HCRC. One of these was for the research staff to be able to browse through the data to identify trends and statistical information. For example, an analysis of the hotel consortia based on the number of bedrooms. Another was to cater for the wide range of document and file formats requested by the clients. These include the ability to produce files for export to the client's own database, comprehensive sort and selection options and the production of cross reference data. Not only were these requirements difficult to meet using SQL but most of them required some form of post processing on the data.

### 2.3 The Database

The Hotels relational database is held on an ORACLE DBMS running on a Sun 670 server and is accessed over the University's campus network. The main structure and tables of the database are illustrated in Figures 2 and 3

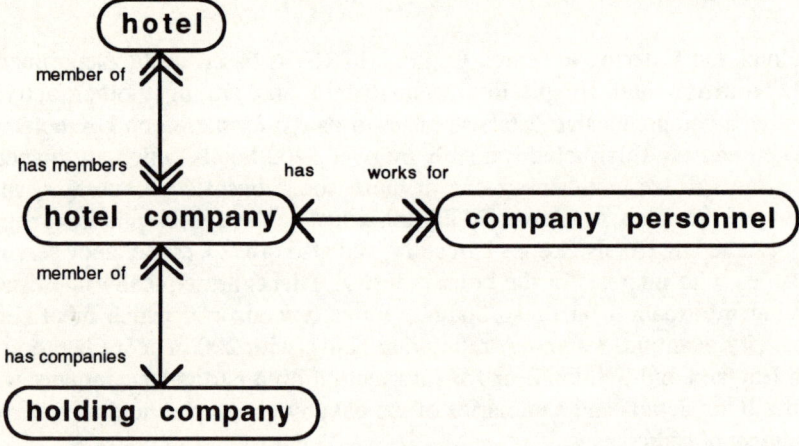

Figure 2:   Entity-Relationship diagram for the Hotels database

**hotel** (hotel_code, name, street, city, county, country, tourist_board_area, postcode, phone, telex, fax, aa_rating, rac_rating, rooms, hotel_type)

**hotel_company** (hotel_company_code, company_type, holding_company_no, name, street, city, county, country, postcode, phone, telex, fax)

**holding_company** (holding_company_code, name, street, city, county, country, postcode, phone, telex, fax)

**membership** (hotel_company_code, hotel_code)

**company_personnel** (hotel_company_code, name, position)

Figure 3:   The main tables in the Hotels database

## 2.4 A Typical SQL Query on the Hotels Database

As part of their consultancy, the HCRC may have a request from a client for information on hotels and the companies with interests in these hotels meeting the following criteria: "3 star AA rating and above with 200 or more bedrooms in North England and Scotland"

A) To retrieve the information on the hotels the following SQL query would be required:
   select name, city, rooms, aa_rating
   from hotel
   where aa_rating in ('3','4','5')
   and rooms >= 200
   and tourist_board_area in
   ('BOR','CEN','DUG','FI','GRA','HI','LOT','STR','TAY','NOR','CUM','IOM', 'NWE','YH')
   sort by name

B) To retrieve a summary of information on the hotel companies with interests in those hotels the following SQL query would be required:
   select hotel_company.name, count(*) hotel, sum(hotel.rooms) rooms
   from hotel_company, membership, hotel
   where hotel.aa_rating in ('3','4','5')
   and hotel.rooms >= 200
   and hotel.tourist_board_area in
   ('BOR','CEN','DUG','FI','GRA','HI','LOT','STR','TAY','NOR','CUM','IOM', 'NWE','YH')
   and company_type = 'C'
   and hotel_company.hotel_company_code = membership.hotel_company_code
   and hotel.hotel_code = membership.hotel_code
   group by hotel_company.name
   sort by hotel_company.name

It can be seen that even with this is a relatively simple query the researcher needs a good knowledge of the structure of the database (e.g.. the appropriate field and table names), the various coding scheme used in the database (e.g.. the tourist board area codes) and a good knowledge of formulating an SQL query (e.g.. the 'group' command used in example B for producing summary information).

Bearing in mind that the data retrieved by these query statements also requires editing on a word processor into the appropriate form for the client (this often took a significant time in the HCRC), the total effort required is considerable, even for this simple example.

## 2.5 The HIBROWSE Interface

Figure 4 shows the top level screen of the HIBROWSE interface for the HCRC Hotels database. The main characteristics of HIBROWSE are that it presents a view of the contents of the database to the user and allows the user to search and browse the database by selection of the contents. The presentation of this information is achieved using a number of windows, each one presenting either
i) raw data, as in the hotels window which shows the name, city, number of bedrooms and star rating values for each hotel
ii) summary information, as the AA star rating, rooms and tourist board areas windows
iii) related data, as in the companies window which shows those hotel companies which have interests in the hotels.

The summary information windows in HIBROWSE for Hotels present data from the database in different ways. The AA star rating window, shows a straightforward count of the number of hotels with each rating. The rooms window shows a count of the number of hotels within prescribed room ranges, aggregating the values in the database. The tourist board areas window presents the data based on the geographical location in the UK. This is a hierarchical view; at the top UK level it gives the number of hotels in each of the large regions such as South England, but allows the user to browse down to a lower level to get more information on the number of hotels in the actual tourist board areas (Figure 5). This presentation method is based on the MenUSE interface being developed at CeDAR [7].

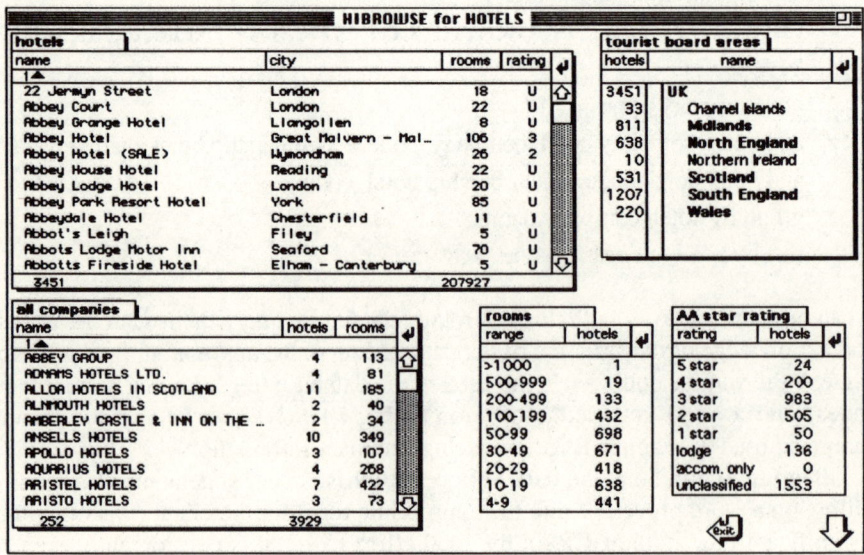

Figure 4: HIBROWSE for Hotels top level

It is clear from the top level screen (Figure 4) that a significant amount of information is presented to the user, without the user even asking a question of the system. For example, there is only 1 hotel with 1000 or more rooms; according to the AA star rating scheme there are 136 lodges and 24 5 star hotels; there are only 10 hotels in Northern Ireland which belong to hotel groups or consortia; and there is a hotel called "22 Jermyn Street" in London.

Additional functionality is provided by allowing the user to customise, where appropriate, the windows in order to alter the way the data is presented. For example, if the user is interested in seeing the largest hotels, according to number of bedrooms, then the user selects rooms in the hotels window and the data is sorted by rooms as shown in Figure 5. (The user could easily change the sort direction to ascending if the area of interest was in the smallest hotels). Similarly, Figure 5 shows the companies window sorted by number of hotels in the consortia, with a secondary sort on the total number of rooms (as indicated by the value 2 next to the sort direction indicator triangle). Figure 5 also shows that the summary information on star rating has been changed to RAC instead of AA. This illustrates another feature of HIBROWSE which, where appropriate, gives the user the additional flexibility of changing the view of the data.

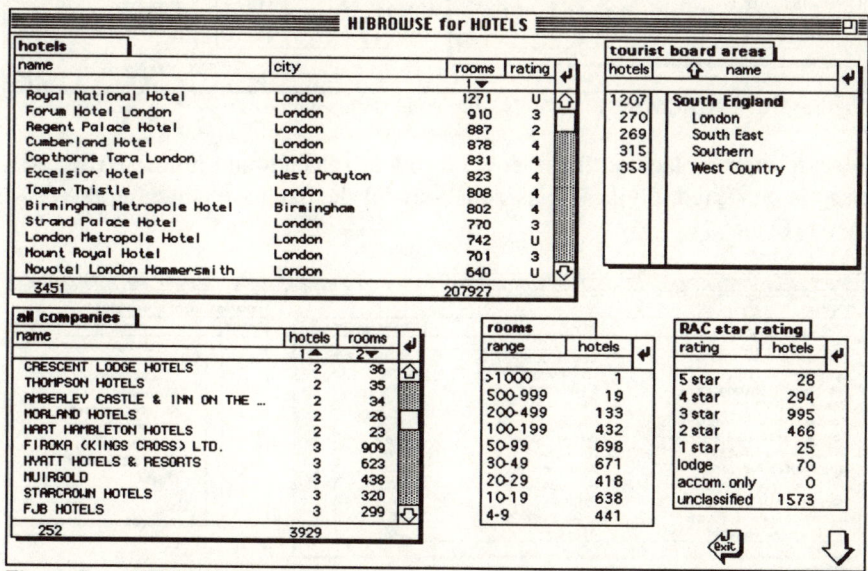

Figure 5: HIBROWSE for Hotels top level showing different sort criteria and also browsing the tourist board area window to show the South of England regions

## 2.6 Querying the Database

The previous section described the HIBROWSE interface and how the user can customise their view of the data. This section illustrates how the user queries the database in HIBROWSE and can be compared to the SQL query given earlier to retrieve those hotels matching particular criteria i.e.. "3 star AA rating and above with 200 or more bedrooms in North England and Scotland"

The user highlights the required star ratings and room ranges and selects North England and Scotland regions (Figure 6).

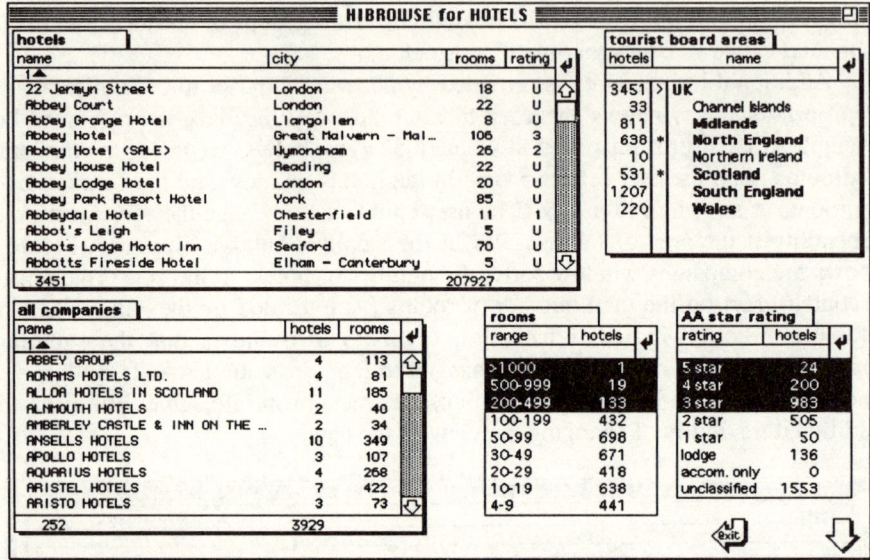

Figure 6: HIBROWSE for Hotels - top level with selections

No search takes place until the down arrow is selected and a new HIBROWSE screen is presented, giving the user the view of the database matching the chosen criteria (Figure 7).

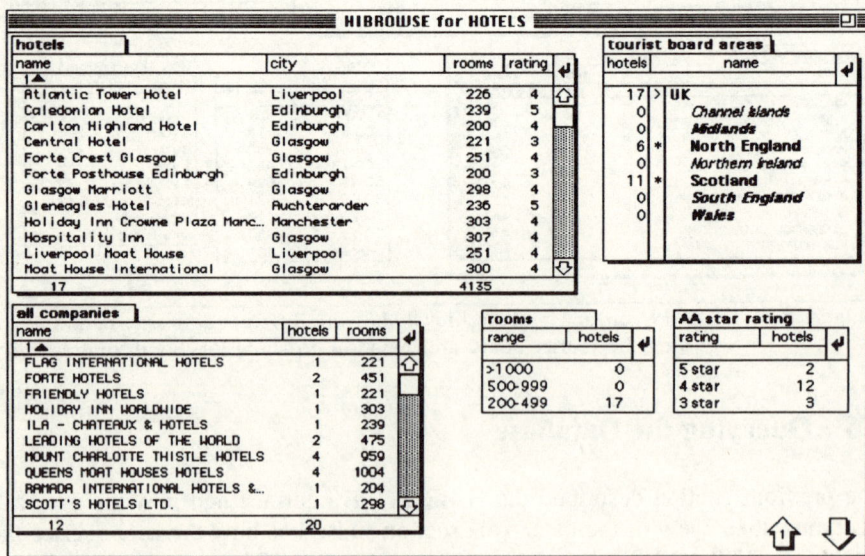

Figure 7: HIBROWSE for Hotels for 3 star AA rating and above with 200 or more bedrooms in North England and Scotland

All the windows are automatically updated to reflect this and the user is free to scroll through the lists of hotels and companies as well as sorting the order of the data as required.

With a minimum of effort on behalf of the user, both of the example queries have been answered. In addition a large amount of 'extra' information has been presented. For example, of the 17 hotels only 2 have a 5 star rating, 6 are in North England and there are no hotels with 500 or more bedrooms. To see the consortia to which the hotels belong, the companies window can be easily changed (Figure 8).

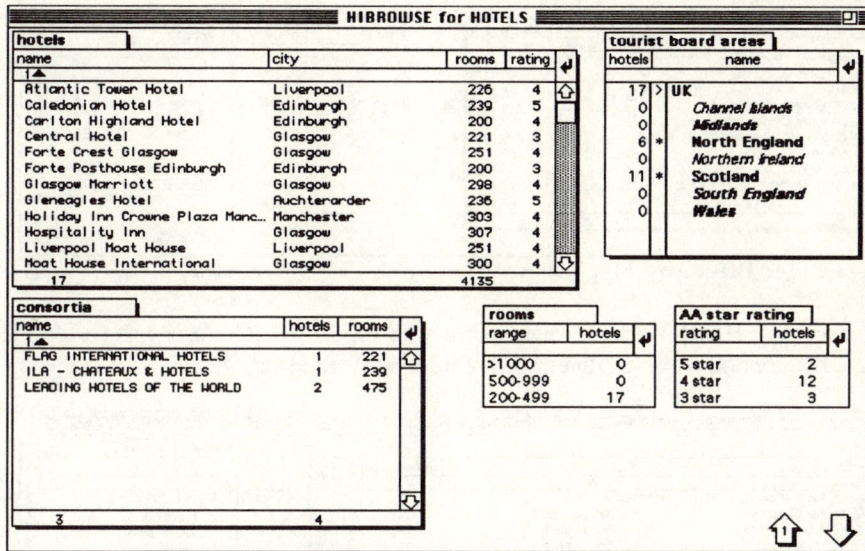

Figure 8: HIBROWSE for Hotels for 3 star AA rating and above with 200 or more bedrooms in North England and Scotland, showing information on the consortia with members in this range.

## 2.7 Browsing the Database

In the previous example the user was seeking specific information. HIBROWSE also permits the user to browse the database, gradually refining the query. At each stage the user is presented with an updated view of the database which both provides an intermediate result and serves as the source for selections at the next stage. This supports the principle of equal opportunity [8] to the extent that the distinction between input and output is blurred. Instead of being forced to cycle between request and result, the user can browse the contents of the database viewing any item as input or output.

This is best illustrated through a worked example. Our client is interested in hotels in Cumbria. The user selects North England from the region window and selects the 89 hotels shown to be in Cumbria (Figure 9).

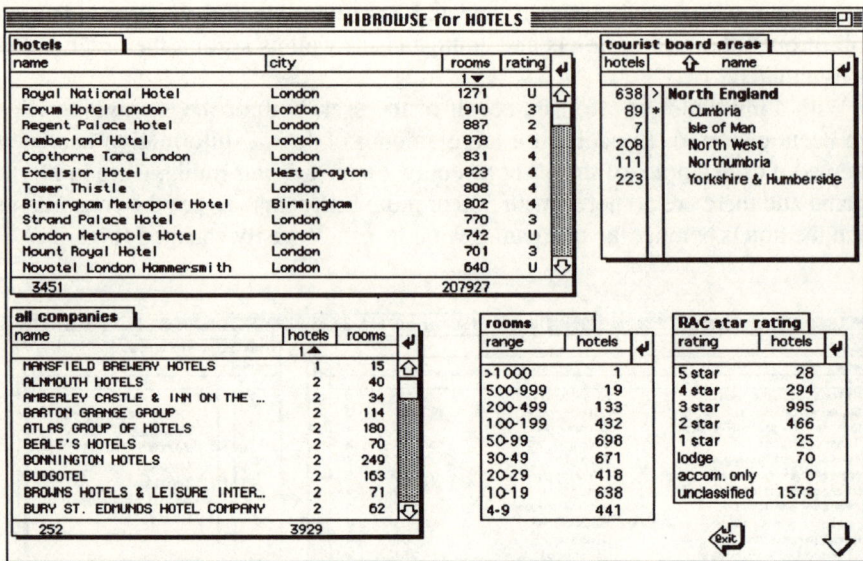

Figure 9: HIBROWSE for Hotels top level with Cumbria selected

The resulting HIBROWSE screen is shown in Figure 10. The user has sorted the hotels by city and observes that there are three in Ambleside.

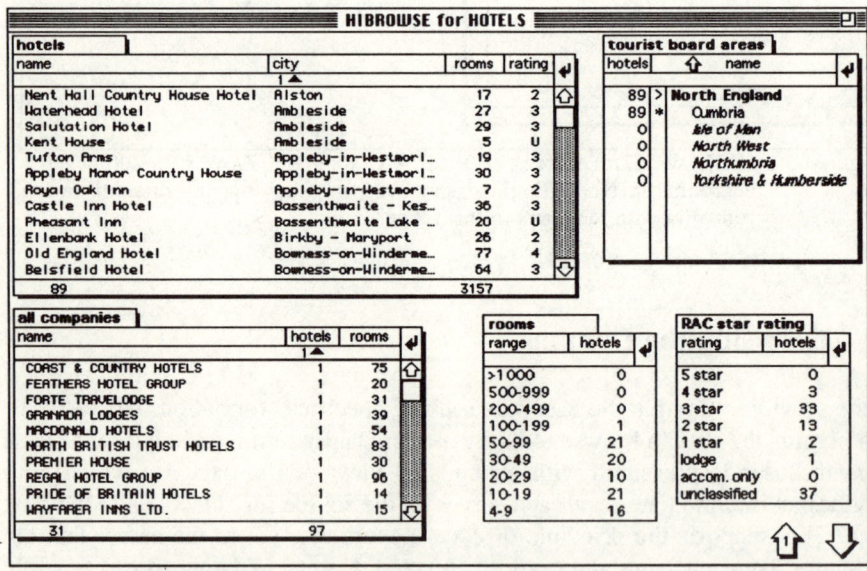

Figure 10: HIBROWSE for Hotels showing information on the hotels in the Cumbria tourist board area

Selecting one of these, the Waterhead Hotel, the user is presented with further information (Figure 11). It can be seen that this hotel is a member of ENGLISH LAKES HOTELS. To see what other hotels are in this company, the user simply highlights this from the list shown in the companies window and selects the down arrow to activate the search.

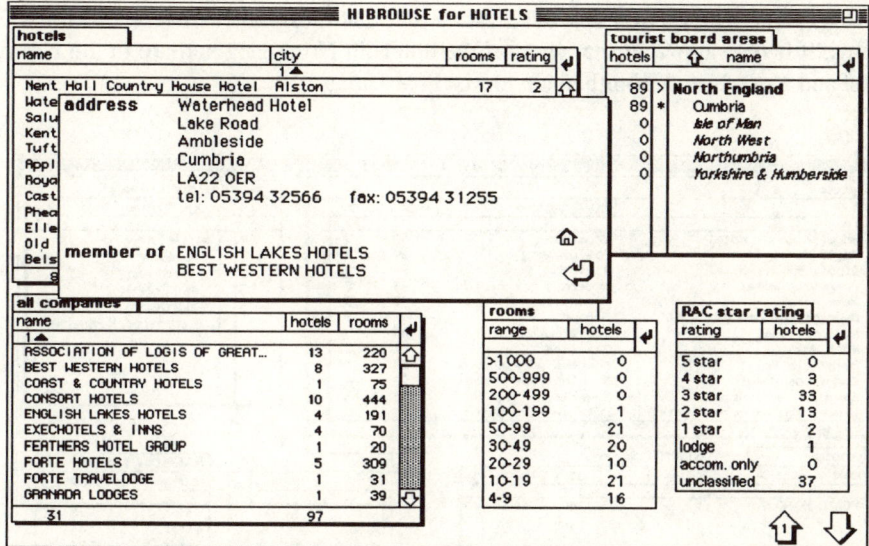

Figure 11: HIBROWSE for Hotels showing additional information for the Waterhead Hotel in Ambleside

The new HIBROWSE screen (Figure 12) shows the four hotels associated with the company. Note that three of these hotels are also members of BEST WESTERN HOTELS.

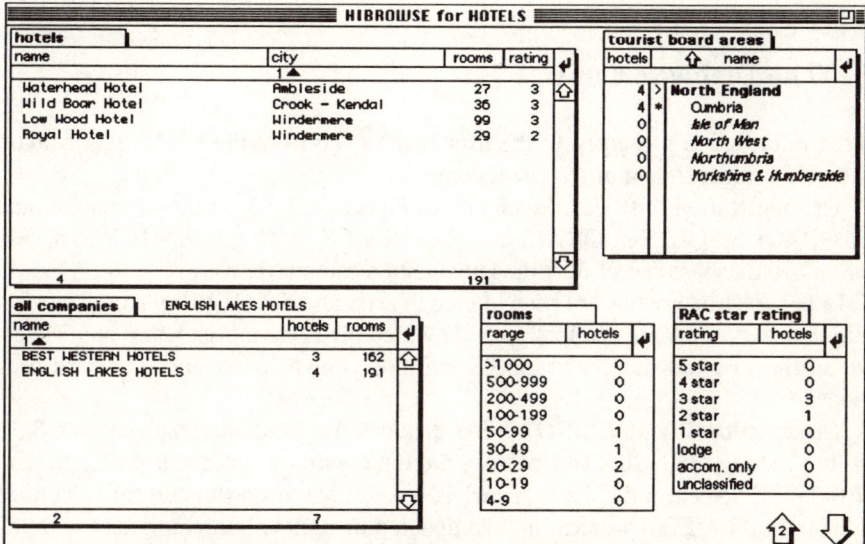

Figure 12: HIBROWSE for Hotels showing in Cumbria which are members of ENGLISH LAKES HOTELS

A valuable feature of HIBROWSE for Hotels is the ease with which a summary of information on a particular hotel company can be produced. Figure 13 shows information on FORTE HOTELS It can be immediately seen that the majority of FORTE HOTELS are of 3 star RAC rating and that most have between 50 and 200 rooms. It is also apparent that most of the hotels in North England are in the North West and Yorkshire & Humberside tourist board areas.

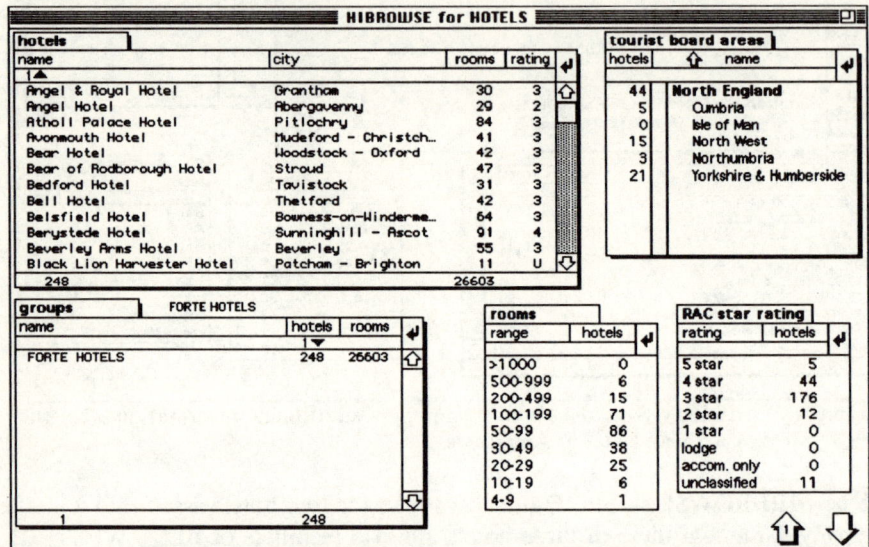

Figure 13: HIBROWSE for Hotels showing information on the hotels belonging to the FORTE HOTELS group

## 2.8 The Dialogue Control

All the information presented to the user is retrieved from the ORACLE database server and is independent of the client computer.

The application has been developed in HyperCard 2.1 on the Macintosh and uses ORACLE SQL*Net, ORACLE's HyperCard XCMD and MacTCP to access the Sun 670 database server over the University's campus network.

Database structure has not been altered to accommodate HIBROWSE. The only additional database table is a lookup table which gives the tourist board area codes, used in the original database, for the regions shown in the tourist board area window.

The functionality of HIBROWSE is achieved by generating and sending SQL type requests to ORACLE and parsing the data which is returned. For each new HIBROWSE screen, a database 'view' is created based on the current selections made by the user. Each window is then updated using this 'view' together with the current sort criteria for that particular window. This approach reduces the length of SQL queries which have to be sent to the DBMS.

## 2.9 The System in Practice

HIBROWSE for Hotels was developed with the cooperation of the HCRC. The system has been evaluated using an approach based on cooperative evaluation [9]. This has involved the users of the system "walking through" common tasks in HIBROWSE and "thinking aloud", describing their actions and their reactions to the new system. This led to the installation of the first version in March 1993 which has been used successfully since then with only minor modifications.

The main responses from the users can be summarised as follows:

i) The learning time was very short even for users with no previous knowledge of the Hotels database.
ii) The rapid response to consultancy requests was impressive. The substantial reduction in time even permitted the HCRC staff to respond immediately to requests over the telephone.
iii) The ability to browse the database was found very useful for the research staff especially when preparing commentaries on hotel companies.
iv) Users made far fewer errors than with SQL, where syntax errors were common. In HIBROWSE the user is protected from this type of error and any errors that occur in browsing are easily recovered from through altering the selections made and backtracking.
v) Although not illustrated in this paper, the flexible document production options associated with HIBROWSE for Hotels, used together with the sort criteria for the hotel and companies windows, provided the HCRC with an expanded consultancy market, as they could produce computer files in many different formats suitable for importing to the clients' own databases.

# 3 The Future for HIBROWSE

Response from users in initial trials and the longer term use of HIBROWSE for Hotels suggests that this mode of database access does bring substantial gains both in productivity and user satisfaction. The view the users have of the database reflects their existing domain knowledge and allows them to manipulate data and perform searches in terms of the domain rather than in terms of the underlying database.

Various usability issues have yet to be resolved including:

i) How the system should deal with the arrangement of windows, especially if there are too many to fit on the screen at one time.
ii) The problem of presenting many-to-many relationships in that it has to be obvious to the user that the contents of one window reflects the selections made in another.
iii) Direct access to a hotel by perhaps entering the first characters of its name. This also applies to regions when the user is not sure in which area of the UK it is located.

The use of separation as a paradigm for the design has been beneficial in a number of ways. It avoids the need to alter the underlying database application which means that existing databases can be provided with the functionality of HIBROWSE without modification. It also means that the approach is portable and can in theory be applied to any relational database. Other example HIBROWSE applications have been developed for various databases, for example INSPEC and EPOQUE (European Parliament Online Query System) to illustrate this principle [6]. Current work is concentrating on the development of a toolkit to support the rapid generation of HIBROWSE applications for relational databases.

## References

1. Weiland W, Shneiderman B. A graphical query interface based on aggregation/generalisation hierarchies. Info Systems 1993; 18; 4:215-232
2. Young D, Shneiderman B. A Graphical Filter/Flow Representation of Boolean Queries: A Prototype Implementation and Evaluation. JASIS 1993; 44; 6:327-339
3. Zloof M M. Query-by-Example. a database language. IBM Systems Journal 1977; 16; 4:324-343
4. Pollitt A S. Query-by-Menu: A novel DBMS query language, a description and comparison with QBE. 8th BCS IRSG Research Colloquium on Information Retrieval, University of Strathclyde, 1986
5. Zloof M M. Query-by-Example. In: Proceedings of the National Computer Conference, Vol44, pp431-438, Arlington, VA, AFIPS Press
6. Pollitt A S, Ellis G P, Smith M P. HIBROWSE - Adding the power of relational databases to the traditional IR architecture - the future for Graphic User Interfaces. 15th BCS IRSG Research Colloquium on Information Retrieval, University of Strathclyde, 1993
7. Pollitt A S, Ellis G P. Multilingual access to document databases CAIS/ACSI '93 Information as a Global Commodity - Communication, Processing and Use. 21st Annual Conference of the Canadian Association for Information Science, Antigonish, Nova Scotia, Canada, 1993, pp 128-140
8. Thimbleby H. User Interface Design, Addison Wesley, 1990
9. Monk A F, Wright P C, Davenport L and Haber J. Improving your human-computer interface: A practical technique. Prentice Hall Practitioner Series, 1993

Formal Approaches

# A Visual Approach to Multilinear Recursion[1]

Tiziana Catarci and Giuseppe Santucci

Dipartimento di Informatica e Sistemistica, Università degli Studi di Roma "La Sapienza"
Via Salaria 113, I-00198 Roma, ITALY
e-mail: [catarci/santucci]@infokit.dis.uniroma1.it

Abstract.

The problem of expressing complex queries in a friendly way is particularly relevant due to the growing diffusion of databases. However, the most significant proposals for extending the expressive power of the relational query languages are based on the logical paradigm. In particular, an extension of the Horn clause queries, i.e. the so-called stratified Datalog, yields stratified queries, that are a proper subset of fixpoint queries. It is a general opinion that logic is not a friendly interfacing medium for a casual user. As a consequence, other types of query languages, i.e. visual query languages, have been proposed, some of them having an expressive power higher than the relational algebra. Up to now, no visual query language has been proved to provide the expressive power of stratified Datalog. In this paper, we present QBD**, a visual query language, and show that it is able to express all stratified queries.

## 1 Introduction

"One key question concerning query languages is what power they should have...the role of a query language should be primarily the selection of data from a database, rather than arithmetic computation on this data. The computational capability, if desired, should be separate from the retrieval capability" [1]. Following Aho and Ullman we agree that the expressive power of a query system, i.e., the ability of the system to extract meaningful information from the database, is a basic aspect in query languages. Unfortunately, traditional query languages, based on relational algebra and calculus [12], have a limited expressive power, i.e. they can compute the class of first-order queries, while, as shown in [8] other more general classes of queries exist. In particular, an important extension of the class of first-order queries is obtained by adding to a relational query language some operators allowing for expressing some kind of recursion. A notable example of recursion is the transitive closure, but it has been proved that there exist several recursive queries which cannot be expressed using the transitive closure operator [8].

As a consequence, researches in the area of database querying are devoted to find query languages able to express notable classes of recursive queries. Relevant proposals in this sense are based on the logical paradigm, introducing the query languages known as *Datalog* and *stratified Datalog* (this is the case of the deductive databases [17, 27]). Stratified Datalog is obtained by augmenting the Horn clause

---

[1] Research partially supported by the EEC, under the Esprit Project 6398 VENUS.

programs with the use of stratified negation [27]. Stratified Datalog can express *stratified queries*, which include both the first-order queries and the transitive closure queries, and other interesting queries, such as those corresponding to the "path accessibility problem" on boolean circuit families, which is the prototypical logspace-complete problem in PTIME discovered by Cook ([14], see also [20]). Then, stratified Datalog seems to be largely considered as a new benchmark in the theory of the query language expressive power (as it was for the relational algebra in the recent past). However, it is also a general opinion that logic is not a friendly interfacing medium for non-expert users.

A more friendly approach is the one based on user-oriented interaction techniques, such as the direct manipulation in visual environments (see [26] for the definition of direct manipulation, and [5] for a survey on *visual query languages*). Unfortunately, visual query languages often suffer from a drawback in the lack of formalization and/or precise definition, notable exceptions are: [2, 13, 16, 22, 15]. In particular, in [13] the expressive power of the query language *GraphLog* has been studied, showing that such language can express, among the others, the *stratified linear queries*. This class of queries is a subset of those expressible by stratified Datalog, and is obtained by restricting stratified Datalog programs to have only *linear* recursion. This class of queries has been also proved to be equivalent to the class expressible by using relational algebra plus a transitive closure operator.

The work of Consens and Mendelzon concerns linear Datalog, together with its relationship with the transitive closure operator, and the definition of an equivalent visual query language. However, note that the query style of GraphLog is not based on direct manipulation of objects; on the contrary, queries have to be expressed building query graphs, labeled by complex literals. It is our opinion that an interesting research problem is to verify whether *stratified Datalog* programs (*removing the linearity constraint*) can be expressed using some direct manipulation visual query language. The definition of such a language, which will allow one to express in an easy way a large and "real life" class of recursive queries, is the main goal of this paper. It is worth noting that, when using the query language we propose, the user is unaware of the fact that s/he is expressing a certain kind of recursive query. What the user knows is that s/he is asking the system to perform some kind of recursion (either the user has to have the concept of recursion in mind, or the system can help her/him in learning it).

It is a theoretical result of this paper showing that the proposed visual query language has the same expressive power than stratified Datalog. From this point of view, the foundations of our proposal are in the extended closure operator introduced in [7], where it has been also proved that it is possible to express the class of stratified queries using the relational algebra plus such an extended closure operator.

In this paper we propose the visual query language QBD**, which is an enhancement of the language QBD* [2, 3]. Then, we show that QBD** can express all the stratified queries, since it provides the user with a visual mechanism isomorphic to the extended closure operator.

The paper is organized as follows. In Section 2 we informally introduce the query languages QBD* and QBD**. In Section 3 we recall some basic notions about both multilinear and bilinear recursion, and stratified bilinear Datalog programs. In Section 4 we first introduce a special relational operator, and, based on this operator, we define the notion of simple extended closure. We show that such an extended closure can capture the class of simple bilinear Datalog programs, studied in [28]. Then, we generalize the extended closure in order to capture the whole class of stratified bilinear Datalog programs. In Section 5 we discuss the expressive power of QBD**. Finally, in Section 6, we draw some conclusion.

## 2   QBD* vs QBD**

In this section we first recall the basic notions on the visual query language QBD* supporting the transitive closure, as introduced in [2], and then we show that an enhanced version of QBD*, namely QBD**, can express the same class of recursive queries computable through a stratified Datalog program. From the user point of view, QBD** offers a uniform means for expressing an interesting class of "real-life" recursive queries, representing a large subset of fixpoint queries, i.e., queries which can be computed augmenting the standard first order operators, $\forall, \exists, \wedge, \vee, \neg$, with fixpoints. Indeed, finding fixpoint queries that are not computable through a stratified Datalog program is a hard task. It seems that the only fixpoint queries (on finite structures, such as databases) which are not expressible by stratified logic programs are related with the need of taking fixpoints over universal quantifiers, as it happens in the problems of determining winning strategies between two or more players in a certain game [21], and this could be considered a marginal need from the point of view of a potential user of a query system.

We will see in the following that the intuitive meaning of the graphical mechanisms adopted in QBD** is quite simple. In fact, the system allows the user to express a query by first navigating on an Entity-Relationship diagram for selecting the concepts (entities and relationships) s/he is interested in, then the user can express conditions on the attributes by using a window, where the attribute names of different entities are listed on different columns. The user may link attribute names belonging to different columns by using edges labeled with comparison operators (e.g., "=", "<", ">") in order to specify the comparison conditions. The same mechanism is used for expressing the basic step of the closure (transitive or extended) operation. Indeed, considering, for instance, the operation of finding the kings' dynasties. The user typically does not know that this query contains a transitive closure. However, s/he can imagine that the query involves some kind of recursion on the entity KING, which contains the information KING_NAME and FATHER_NAME. Thus, it is reasonable to think that s/he will select the icon representing the recursion and the entity KING. At this point, the system knows that the user is asking a closure query, and shows a window containing two copies of the attributes of the entity KING on different sub-windows. Then, the user has only to specify the condition of the recursive step, i.e., to draw an edge labeled "=" between KING_NAME in sub-window one and FATHER_NAME in sub-window two. We will see that the same holds for the extended closure, which is the visual operator standing for the operation of performing some recursion on more than one entity.

Note that we made some experiments on QBD*, and its way of operating seemed to be easily understandable by most users, which were 90 non-experts in computer science. Also, since the system is equipped with a rich set of strategies and types of interactions available in all phases of query formulation, it addresses the needs of different classes of users. Novice users may both acquire information about the database schema and perform simple queries by navigating in a diagram. On the other hand, expert users may perform complex queries and have detailed knowledge about the available data.

In the following we give an informal description of the query language QBD*, and show how it evolves in QBD**. The expressive power of both the languages will be discussed in Section 5.

## 2.1 The Visual Query Language QBD*

QBD* is a graphical query language on the Entity-Relationship model [10]. The operations of the relational algebra can be directly expressed by picking up symbols (entities or relationships) and following links in the diagram. The general structure of the query is based on the location of a distinguishing concept, called *main concept*, that can be seen as the entry point of one or more subqueries; these subqueries express possible navigations from the main concept to other concepts in the schema. The attributes belonging to each subquery are determined by the following strategy: the attributes of the main concept are automatically considered (unless explicitly deleted by the user), while the other ones are shown in the result only if requested by the user. The presence of a main concept associates with each subquery a type: as an example, if the main entity is the entity person, the result of the query will be a set of persons (eventually enriched with attributes coming from other concepts), no matter what kind of subsequent operations the user performs to specify it.

The subqueries can be combined together by applying several set-oriented operators on two or more subqueries derived from the same entity. The structure of the involved subqueries being, in general, different, it is impossible to perform pure set-oriented operations, and a more general approach is needed (see [24] for the specific solution adopted within QBD* and [23] for a very general approach to this subject).

Once the main concept has been selected, two different types of primitives are available for navigating in the schema. The first one allows the user to follow existing paths on the schema; the other one, called BRIDGE[2], is used for comparing two concepts by building a new path (relationship) on the schema. Comparison conditions during a BRIDGE session, as well as generic conditions on the attributes, are expressed by means of a simple window mechanism including a suitable set of icons. The attributes of the two entities involved in a BRIDGE session are displayed in two different stripes of the window, and the comparison operators are specified as labels of edges connecting the involved attributes. Roughly speaking, we can say that a path on the schema corresponds to an ordered sequence of natural joins[3] among the pairs <entity, relationship> constituting the path, followed by a final selection and projection. The explicit presence of relationships releases the user from the need of looking for concepts like "foreign keys" and the system can perform in the right way the join operations. On the other

---

[2] QBD* is a visual language, so it is based on a graphical representation of the database (Entity-Relationship diagrams) and visual interaction mechanisms (the clicking of concepts along paths of the diagram, and the use of a window for specifying the attribute conditions). However, for the sake of simplicity, in order to denote the visual operations we use in the following a textual syntax, which is formally defined and shown to be equivalent to the visual operations in [2].

[3] We mean here the natural join and theta-join operators as defined in relational algebra [11].

hand, a BRIDGE corresponds to a theta-join between the two involved entities, and it is up to the user the specification of the theta-condition.

Queries involving transitive closure are expressed by a visual approach similar to the one adopted in the BRIDGE operation, the difference being the pre-selection of a particular icon, which signals the beginning of a recursive session. In this way the textual interaction is minimized, so reducing the complexity of the query from the user point of view. The main idea is to represent the generic step of recursion as a reflexive relationship, by displaying twice the list of the attributes of the involved entity. The user may specify the recursive comparison conditions on the attributes, and thus the system helps him/her in determining the attributes involved in the projection (evidentiated with black dots in Figure 2.1).

**Example 2.1**

Let us assume that the user is interacting with the entity FLIGHT[4], with attributes SOURCE_CITY, DESTINATION_CITY, DEPARTURE_TIME, ARRIVAL_TIME. The user wants to compute all the cities reachable by Rome either directly or through a sequence of "waiting less than one day" flights. More precisely, the user wants the sequence of flights connecting Rome to the destination satisfying the following two properties:
1) the destination of each flight (except the last) is the source of the next, and
2) the arrival time of each flight (except the last) occurs before the departure time of the next.

Such a query may be expressed as shown in Figure 2.1. The user specifies the generic element of the chain of flights selecting DESTINATION_CITY = SOURCE_CITY AND ARRIVAL_TIME < DEPARTURE_TIME. The attributes involved in the projection are DEPARTURE_TIME and SOURCE_CITY of the previous flight, and ARRIVAL_TIME and DESTINATION_CITY of the next flight. Moreover, the user specifies that the first flight must leave from Rome by writing the initial selection condition (SOURCE_CITY = "ROME") in the leftmost sub-window containing FLIGHT.

□

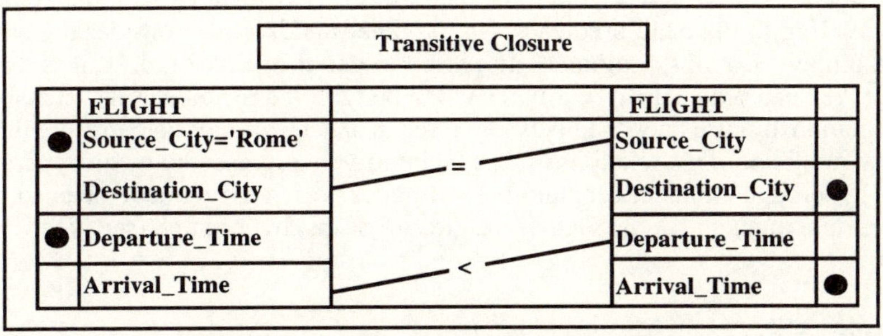

**Fig. 2.1.** An Example of Transitive Closure

The user is provided with an intuitive meaning of the recursive query s/he is performing: through the window mechanism described above, s/he builds a

---
[4]It can be considered either as an entity already belonging to the schema or as the result of a previous query

transitive relationship between various instances of an entity. Such a relationship may be thought as a graph, so that this query corresponds to the transitive closure of the graph. The precise semantics of the above graphical operator is given in terms of a closure operator [2], akin to the one presented in [25].

The expressive power of the query language underlying QBD* is noticeable, being able to express the class of queries computable by stratified linear Datalog, which in turn contains all the first order queries plus the transitive closure queries [13]. However, there still exist recursive queries worth to be considered that need more powerful operators in order to be computed by the query language. The next section describes a simple extension of QBD*, QBD**, which will be proved to be able to express the class of stratified queries (see next sections).

## 2.2 QBD**

The main problem we met when extending the QBD* query language was related to the question of which expressive power was reasonable to give to a graphical query language without loosing its graphical behavior (see [6]). Looking at the question from a different point of view, the problem is to find out an intuitive way in which it is possible to generalize the idea of recursively closing a relation. Incidentally, this generalization corresponds to expressing at least the queries which are computable by using a logic language such as stratified Datalog.

In designing QBD* we established a correspondence between transitive closure queries over a relation (i.e. Datalog linear recursion) and the transitive closure of a graph. An analogous relation can be established between closures involving more than one relation (i.e. Datalog bilinear recursion) and a particular closure of hypergraphs.

The transitive closure of a graph is usually computed by adding an edge between two nodes $x$ and $z$ if there exist two edges, one between $x$ and another node, say $y$, and the other between $y$ and $z$. It is worth noting that an edge always connects two nodes. This has a direct correspondence with a linear recursive Datalog rule, where the head predicate appears only once in the body of the recursive rule. In other words, there is a recursive relationship between two instances of the relations corresponding to the head predicate. On the other hand, let us consider the case of simple bilinear Datalog programs (discussed in detail in Section 4.1). It is easy to see that the head predicate appear twice in the body of the recursive rule. This means that a relationship is established between three instances of relation corresponding to the head predicate. This relationship can be intuitively represented by an hypergraph whose hyperedges link sets containing two nodes with a single node. The solution to the recursive query can be seen as the closure of this hypergraph (see [7] for more details).

**Example 2.2**

Let us consider an example based on the well-known problem of the electrical propagation in a circuit of AND gates (note that the following example corresponds to the Datalog program shown in Section 4.1, Example 4.2). Assume the structure of the circuit represented by the entity GATE with attributes INPUTPIN1, INPUTPIN2, OUPUTPIN, STATUSPIN1, STATUSPIN2. The user query is the following: "Given a set of AND gates in on state (both input pins are set on), find all the on gates (both those initially set on and those turned on through the circuit commutation). Such a query is similar to the one in Example 2.1, but a ternary instead of binary relationship has to be established among the instances of the entity GATE. Similarly to the previous case, such a query can be expressed by QBD** using the window shown in Figure 2.2. In particular, the user first specifies an entity and then defines a new ternary relationship on it.

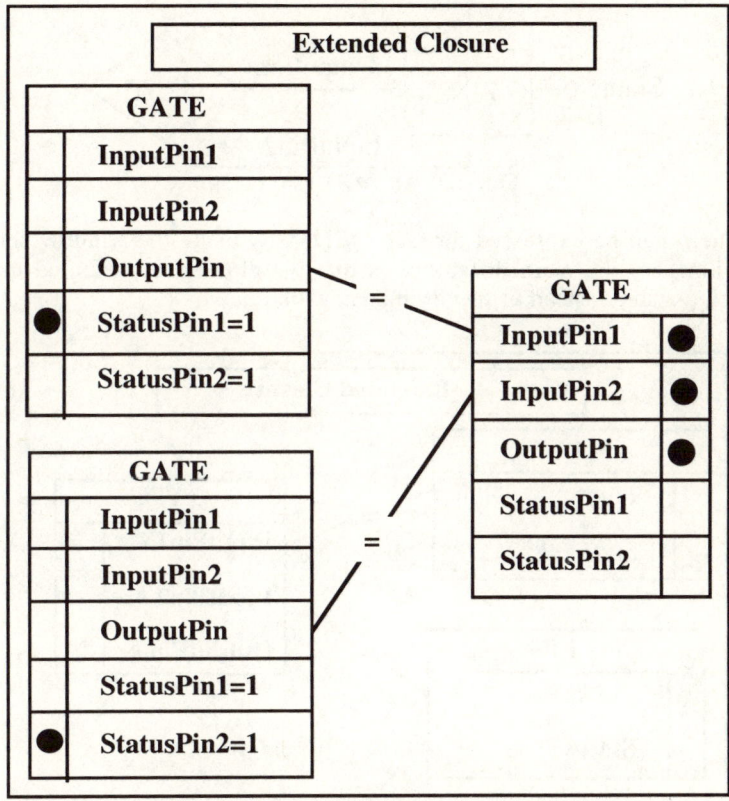

**Fig. 2.2.** An example of extended closure

□

The precise semantics of the above graphical operator is given in Section 5. Intuitively, it resembles the structure of a hyperedge of the hypergraph discussed above, and the visual placement of the three tables conveys the intuition that the recursion proceeds from the left to the right.

The above example is based on the particular case in which the relationship among the instances of the relation to be closed (i.e., GATE) is given by the structure of the relation itself. In other words, the computation of the closure starts from a subset of the instances of GATE (the initial gates set on), and finds a larger subset of the instances of GATE, including the gates which are reachable through the circuit starting from the initial subset. There are cases in which this is not true, as shown in the following variation of Example 2.2.

**Example 2.3**

Let us consider the schema shown in figure 2.3, representing again the topological structure of an AND gate circuit. The user query is slightly different from the previous one: "Given a set of pin placed on, find all the on pin (placed on and turned on by the circuit commutation)."

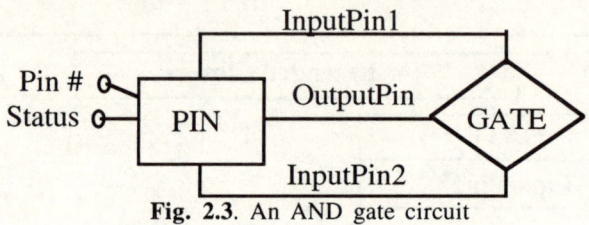

**Fig. 2.3.** An AND gate circuit

The query can be expressed through QBD** by using the window shown in Figure 2.4, where the main difference is that the closure is computed using an existing relationship instead of specifying a new one.

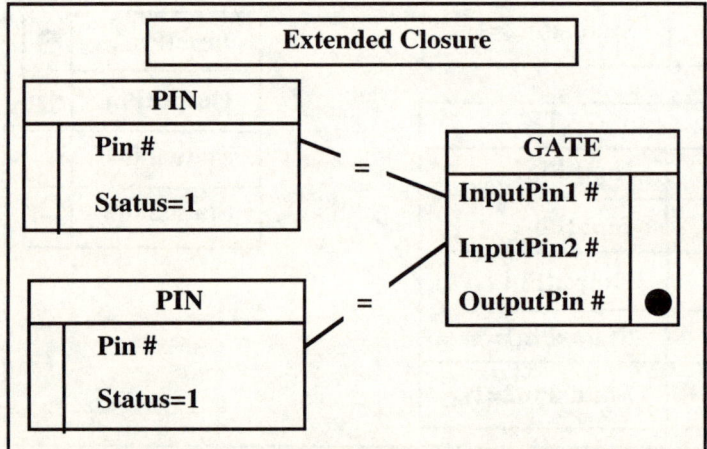

**Fig. 2.4.** A second example of extended closure

Similarly to Figure 2.2, on the left hand side we have two copies of the attribute names of the entity involved in the closure (PIN), and on the right the attribute names of the relationship (GATE) used for computing the closure. The attribute that has to appear in the relation resulting from the recursive step is marked with a black dot.

□

It is worth noting that we cannot have more than three columns containing attributes, since they represent the relations to be joined together in the extended closure (see Section 4). Moreover, each window is used only for specifying the recursive step of the extended closure, other operations are expressed by selecting elements in the Entity-Relationship diagram or using other windows, so avoiding window cluttering.

In the next sections 3 and 4 we will lay the bases for proving, in Section 5, that using the above simple visual mechanisms we can express all the stratified queries.

## 3 Linear, Bilinear, And Multilinear Recursion

In this section we clarify the distinction among linear, bilinear, and multilinear stratified Datalog programs, and show that it is possible to capture the expressive power of stratified Datalog by considering just bilinear programs. The content of this section summarizes some of the results obtained in [19] and in [7].

In [19] an algebraic framework for the study of recursion has been developed. For immediate linear recursion, a Horn clause is represented by a relational algebra operator. Regarding non linear recursion, it has been shown that Horn clauses always give rise to multilinear recursion, which can always be reduced to bilinear recursion. In [7] the results of Ioannidis and Wong have been extended by showing that *any multilinear stratified Datalog program can be reduced to a stratified Datalog program whose recursive rules are bilinear*.

In the rest of this section we briefly recall the above results. For the Datalog syntax and the basic definitions (e.g. Horn clause, recursive and nonrecursive rule, stratification) see [27].

The following definitions are presented in terms of Horn clauses and are direct consequences of the definitions given in [19] in algebraic terms.

**Definition.** Consider a set of Datalog rules consisting of both recursive and nonrecursive rules, and let $\{p_1, ..., p_n\}$ be the predicates appearing in the heads of the rules. The set of Datalog rules is called linear if each recursive Horn clause has at most one of $\{p_1, ..., p_n\}$ in its body[5].

**Example 3.1**

The following Datalog system is linear according to the above definition.
p(x,y):- p'(x, z) t(z, y)
p(x,y):-p(y,x)
p'(x,y):-p(z,x) s(z,z,y)
p'(x,y):- r(x,y)

The following Datalog system is not linear, because the head predicates are p and p', and the body of the first recursive clause contains both of them.
p(x,y):- p'(x, z) t(z, y) p(w,z)
p(x, y):- p(y, x)
p'(x,y):- p(z,x) s(z,z,y)
p'(x,y):- r(x, y)

□

**Definition.** Consider a set of Datalog rules consisting of both recursive and nonrecursive rules, and let $\{p_1, ..., p_n\}$ be the predicates appearing in the heads of

---

[5] As also remarked in [19], this definition of linearity is more restrictive than the one given in [4].

the rules. The set of Datalog rules is called bilinear if each recursive Horn clause has at most two of $\{p_1, ..., p_n\}$ in its body, and there exists at least one recursive clause having exactly two of $\{p_1, ..., p_n\}$ in its body.

**Example 3.2**

The following three Datalog systems are bilinear according to the above definition.
p(x,y,z):-q(x) s(y) t(x,y,z)
p(x,y,z):-p(a,b,x) t(x,y,z) p(c,d,y)

p(x,y,z):-p(a, b, x) p'(x,y,z)
p'(x,y,z):-p(y,b,x) s(x,y,z) t(x,y,z)

p(x,y,z):-p''(a,b,x) q(x,y,z)
p'(x,y,z):-p(y,b,x) s(x,y,z) t(x,y,z)
p''(x,y,z):-p'(a,y,x) r(x,w,z) p(y,z,w)
p''(x,y,z):-q'(x,y,z)
□

Ioannidis and Wong proved that any multilinear Horn clause system can be expressed in algebraic form as a set of bilinear equations. In [7] it has been shown that any stratified Datalog program can be rewritten as a stratified Datalog program whose recursive rules are bilinear. This result has been achieved by demonstrating that: 1) any Horn clause system can be written as a Horn clause system whose recursive rules are bilinear; 2) any stratified Datalog program can be rewritten as a stratified Datalog program whose recursive rules are bilinear. Also, since in a stratified Datalog program each stratum can be evaluated having already computed the relations corresponding to the predicates at lower strata, we can evaluate one single stratum at a time. Each single stratum contains a set of *directly recursive rules*, since it has been shown in [9] that mutual recursion can be always reduced to a recursion over a single relation.

All the above considerations allow us to limit our attention to *a single stratum of a bilinear Datalog program* (i.e., a Datalog program whose recursive rules are bilinear).

# 4 Extended Closure

In this section we introduce a special relational operator and show that the closure of this operator can express the bilinear Datalog programs. In other words, the relational algebra plus such an operator has the same expressive power than stratified Datalog. We proceed by first considering an interesting subclass of bilinear Datalog programs, namely the class of *simple bilinear Datalog programs*, and show how they can be expressed by the simple extended closure. Then, we generalize such a result to the class of bilinear Datalog programs.

Note that in the following we indicate with bold capital letters the relations corresponding to Datalog predicates, which in turn are indicated by plain lower case letters.

## 4.1 Simple Bilinear Datalog Programs and Simple Extended Closure

These programs consist of two rules, one non recursive, and the other direct recursive. We use the notation introduced in [28]. Let p be a predicate of arity n. The recursive rule defining p will involve n distinct universally quantified variables, denoted by $X = (x_1, x_2, ..., x_n)$. In the body of this rule there will be $p \geq 0$ distinct existentially quantified variables denoted by $E = (e_1, e_2, ..., e_p)$. A simple bilinear program is now written as:

$r_e$: p(X):- f(X)
$r_r$: p(X):- p((X,E)$Z^1$) q((X,E)W) p((X,E)$Z^2$)

where $r_e$ is the exit (or initialization) rule, $r_r$ is the recursive rule, f and q are base predicate, and $Z^1$, $Z^2$, W are selectors. In fact, for each predicate of arity $g$ in the body of the rule $r_r$, g arguments are selected from the variables in X and E. Such a selection is denoted by a matrix product

$$(X,E)H = (x_1, x_2, ..., x_n, e_1, e_2, ..., e_p)H,$$

where the selector H is a $(n+p) \times g$ matrix of 0's and 1's, with exactly one 1 in each column. If $x_j$ ($e_i$) is in the k-th argument position in the matrix product, we say that H selects $x_j$ ($e_i$) and places it at position k.

Let **R** and **S** be two finite relations, A a list of attributes of **R** and **S**, in such a way that the number of elements of A is equal to the arity of **R**, and let F be a set of conditions on attributes of **R** and **S**, where the elements of the set are intended to be in conjunction. In order to define the extended closure of **R** with respect to **S**, we introduce the operator $c_{A,F}$ defined as follows:

$$c_{A,F}(\mathbf{R,S}) = \mathbf{R} \cup \Pi_A \sigma_F(\mathbf{R} \times \mathbf{S} \times \mathbf{R})$$

where, as usual, $\Pi$ and $\sigma$ denote projection and selection respectively [27]. Notice that the result of applying $c_{A,F}$ to **R** and **S** is a new relation having the same arity as **R**.

Now, we use the $c_{A,F}$ operator for defining the i-th power of **R** w.r.t. **S** according to A,F as follows:

$$\mathbf{R}^2_{S,A,F} = c_{A,F}(\mathbf{R,S}) = \mathbf{R} \cup \Pi_A \sigma_F(\mathbf{R} \times \mathbf{S} \times \mathbf{R});$$

$$\mathbf{R}^3_{S,A,F} = c_{A,F}(\mathbf{R}^2_{S,A,F}, \mathbf{S}) = (\mathbf{R} \cup \Pi_A \sigma_F(\mathbf{R} \times \mathbf{S} \times \mathbf{R})) \cup$$
$$\Pi_A \sigma_F((\mathbf{R} \cup \Pi_A \sigma_F(\mathbf{R} \times \mathbf{S} \times \mathbf{R})) \times \mathbf{S} \times (\mathbf{R} \cup \Pi_A \sigma_F(\mathbf{R} \times \mathbf{S} \times \mathbf{R})));$$

Generalizing:

$$R_{S,A,F}^n = \begin{cases} R & n=0 \\ c_{A,F}(R_{S,A,F}^{n-1}, S) & n>0 \end{cases}$$

It follows from the definition that $c_{A,F}$ is monotone and $R, S$ are finite relations, therefore there must be some $n_0$ such that $R_{S,A,F}^{n_0} = R_{S,A,F}^{n_0+1}$. (i.e. there exists a least fixpoint).

As a notational convenience, when no ambiguity arises, we simply write $R_S^{n_0}$ instead of $R_{S,A,F}^{n_0}$.

**Definition.** Let $R$ and $S$ be two finite relations, A a list of attributes of $R$ and $S$, such that the number of elements in A is equal to the arity of $R$, and let F be a set of conditions on attributes of $R$ and $S$. Then, the *simple extended closure of $R$ with respect to $S$ according to $A,F$* is defined by:

$$R_{S,A,F}^+ = \bigcup_{i=0}^{\infty} R_{S,A,F}^i$$

□

It is worth noting that the simple extended closure is a generalization of the usual transitive closure of a binary relation (see [1]), as demonstrated in [7] and illustrated in the following example.

**Example 4.1**

The well known problem of finding a path in a graph can be written as a Datalog program as:

PATH(x,y):-ARC(x,y)
PATH(x,y):-PATH(x,z) ARC(z,y)

or as the equivalent:

PATH(x,y):-ARC(x,y)
PATH(x,y):-PATH(x,z) PATH(z,y)

The answer to such a query expressed in terms of our extended closure is $ARC_\emptyset^+$ where A={$1,$4}, F is $2=$3, and $\emptyset$ indicates the 0-ary relation {()}.

□

Our next goal is to show that the simple extended closure is able to capture the class of simple bilinear Datalog programs. Consider the simple bilinear program B:

$r_e$: p(X):- f(X)
$r_r$: p(X):- p((X,E)$Z^1$) q((X,E)W) p((X,E)$Z^2$)

Let **P** be the relation obtained by the evaluation of f(X), and let **Q** be the relation corresponding to the predicate q. It is easy to see that the solution to the query represented by B is:
$$\mathbf{P} \cup \mathbf{P}\mathbf{Q}\mathbf{P} \cup \mathbf{P}\mathbf{Q}\mathbf{P}\mathbf{Q}\mathbf{P}\mathbf{Q}\mathbf{P}\mathbf{Q}\mathbf{P} \cup \ldots\ldots\ldots^6$$
that may be written more concisely as:
$$\mathbf{P'} = \mathbf{P} \cup \mathbf{P}^2\mathbf{Q} \cup \mathbf{P}^4\mathbf{Q}^3 \cup \ldots\ldots \cup \mathbf{P}^n\mathbf{Q}^{n-1} \cup \mathbf{P}^{2n}\mathbf{Q}^{2n-1} \cup \ldots\ldots$$

**Theorem 1**

Let B be a simple bilinear Datalog program as specified above, and let
- $A = \{\$i_1,\ldots\$i_n\}$ such that $\$i_k \in A$ iff one of the $x_j$ is in position k in one of the selectors of the body predicates ($Z^1$, $Z^2$, or W);
- $F = \{\$i_k = \$i_j \mid [ (x_l\ (e_p)$ is in position k in $Z^1$ and in position j in $Z^2$ ]
    or [ $x_l\ (e_p)$ is in position k in $Z^1$ and in position j in W ]
    or [ $x_l\ (e_p)$ is in position k in $Z^2$ and in position j in W ] }.

Then $\mathbf{P}_\mathbf{Q}^+ = \mathbf{P'}$.

□

**Example 4.2**

The problem of the electrical propagation in a circuit of AND gates (already presented in Section 2) can be written as a simple bilinear Datalog program as follows

ONGATE(x,y,z):-IN(x) IN(y) GATE(x,y,z)
ONGATE(x,y,z):-ONGATE(a,b,x) GATE(x,y,z) ONGATE(c,d,y)
where
- IN(x) indicates that x is an initial input pin in the ON state;
- GATE(x,y,z) means that an AND gate exists with input pins x and y and output pin z;
- ONGATE(x,y,z) indicates an AND gate in the ON state, i.e. with the output pin z in the ON state.

The solution to such a query using the c operator is given by
$$\text{ONGATE}^+_{\text{GATE}}$$
where $A = \{\$4,\$5,\$6\}$ and $F = \{\$3=\$4,\$5=\$9\}$.

It is worth noting the importance of such a problem, and the fact that it can be expressed through the simple extended closure, since it corresponds to the "path accessibility problem", which is the prototypical logspace-complete problem in PTIME discovered by Cook ([14], see also [20]).

□

---

[6] More precisely, **PQP** means $\prod_A \sigma_F(\mathbf{P} \times \mathbf{Q} \times \mathbf{P})$, as results from the algorithms 3.1 and 3.3 in [26].

## 4.2. The General Form of the Extended Closure

In this section we generalize the simple extended closure introduced in Section 4.1 in order to capture the whole class of stratified bilinear Datalog programs. From the definition of bilinear recursion (see Section 3) and the results in [7], we have that the general case corresponds to a set of Datalog rules that, for at least one predicate p includes a certain number of pair of rules as follows[7]:

p:- p p qp
p:- qp'

Without loss of generality we can restrict ourselves to the case where two such pairs exist, and concentrate on the Datalog program B:

p:- $q_1$'
p:- p p $q_1$
p:- $q_2$'
p:- p p $q_2$

Let us consider the $c_{A,F}$ operator introduced in Section 4.1.

We recall that if there is more than one definition of a predicate in a stratified Datalog program, then the set of tuples in the corresponding relation is the union of all the tuples provided by each definition [18]. Thus, we can answer the query represented by the above Datalog program computing the extended closure of **P** (as proved in [7]). Such a closure is actually composed by the union of two closures, so we use the shorter notations **P**$^+$ for indicating the following expression:

$$\mathbf{P}^+ = \bigcup_{i=0}^{\infty} \mathbf{P}^i$$

$$\text{with } \mathbf{P}^n = \begin{cases} \mathbf{P} & n = 0 \\ c_{A,F}(\mathbf{P}^{n-1}, \mathbf{Q}_1) \cup c_{A',F'}(\mathbf{P}^{n-1}, \mathbf{Q}_2) & n > 0 \end{cases}$$

## 5 The Expressive Power of QBD**

In this section we show that the visual query language QBD** can express the class of stratified queries. To achieve this aim we start briefly recalling the formal syntax and semantics of QBD*.

In formalizing QBD* the semantics of the language is expressed through a navigational operator $v$, defined in terms of relational algebra expressions. Moreover, transitive closures are expressed as closures of navigations. In order to do this, a mapping is defined between databases expressed in the Entity-Relationship

---

[7] Recall that that mutual recursion can be reduced to a recursion over a single relation [9].

model and Relational databases. However, since in the rest of this paper we will concentrate on operations involving only entities, which are mapped into relations, we do not deal with such a mapping, and we consider the QBD* operators directly acting on relations (in other words, in the rest of this section we will not distinguish between entities and relations).

The semantics of a single navigational step is given in terms of the algebraic operator $V$, that we now describe. Let r, s be two relations corresponding to relational schemata R and S, let $K \subseteq R \cup S$, and let H,G,J be boolean conditions involving attributes of R, S, and $R \cup S$ respectively. The *navigational operator* $V_{K,H,G,J}$ applied to r and s is defined as

$$V_{K,H,G,J} = \Pi_K\left(\sigma_{H \wedge G \wedge J}(r \times s)\right)$$

Each query in QBD* can be interpreted either as an application of the navigational operator or as a closure of navigational expressions. In particular, the expression giving the semantics to the BRIDGE construct (introduced in Section 2) in terms of the navigational operator is:

$$V_{K,H,G,J}(\mathbf{E}_1, \mathbf{E}_2) = \Pi_K\left(\sigma_{H \wedge G \wedge J}(\mathbf{E}_1 \times \mathbf{E}_2)\right)$$

where
- $\mathbf{E}_1, \mathbf{E}_2$ are the entities involved in the application of BRIDGE;
- K is the attribute set obtained by all the attributes of $\mathbf{E}_1$, but those explicitly deleted (denoted with D in the following), plus some added attributes belonging to attr($\mathbf{E}_2$) (denoted with B in the following), i.e. K= attr($\mathbf{E}_1$) - D $\cup$ B;
- H is the condition on attr($\mathbf{E}_1$);
- G is the condition on attr($\mathbf{E}_2$);
- J is the comparison condition.

The semantics of the closure operator is specified in terms of closure of navigational expressions as follows (we denote TRUE by T):

$$\left(V_{(attr(\mathbf{E}))-D \cup B, T, T, C}\right)^+(\mathbf{E}, \mathbf{E})$$

where

$$-\left(V_{(attr(\mathbf{E}))-D \cup B, T, T, C}\right)^+(\mathbf{E}, \mathbf{E}) = \bigcup_{i<\infty}\left(V_{(attr(\mathbf{E}))-D \cup B, T, T, C}\right)^i(\mathbf{E}, \mathbf{E})$$

$$-\left(V_{(attr(\mathbf{E}))-D \cup B, T, T, C}\right)^1(\mathbf{E}, \mathbf{E}) = \mathbf{E}$$

$$-\left(V_{(attr(\mathbf{E}))-D \cup B, T, T, C}\right)^{i+1}(\mathbf{E}, \mathbf{E}) =$$

$$V_{(attr(\mathbf{E}))-D \cup B, T, T, C}\left(\mathbf{E}, \left(V_{(attr(\mathbf{E}))-D \cup B, T, T, C}\right)^i(\mathbf{E}, \mathbf{E})\right)$$

In other words, $\left(V_{(attr(\mathbf{E}))-D \cup B, T, T, C}\right)^+(\mathbf{E}, \mathbf{E})$ corresponds to the generalized transitive closure of $\mathbf{E}$ introduced in [25] with respect to the navigational operator $V_{(attr(\mathbf{E}))-D \cup B, T, T, C}$.

Note that we can express the semantics of the closure operator in terms of the simple extended closure introduced in Section 4, as follows:

$$\mathbf{E}^+_{\emptyset, A, F}, \text{ where } A = (attr(\mathbf{E})-D) \cup B \text{ and } F=C.$$

The graphical realization of the closure operator has been already shown in Figure 2.1, and it is recalled in Figure 5.1, which is an abstraction of a real situation, where instead of considering every single attribute of **E**, they are divided into two sets, namely $Att_1$ and $Att_2$. The attributes evidentiated with a black circle have to appear in the result of the recursive step, while the others have to be projected out. Moreover, the comparison conditions are globally represented by the label "C" of the edge connecting the two copies of the **E** attributes (the letters we use in the figure, namely B, C, D, can be retrieved in the ∨ expression with the same meaning).

In [13] it has been proved that the set of queries expressed by stratified linear Datalog programs is the same as that expressed by the relational calculus extended with the transitive closure operator (transitive closure queries). Since in [2] it is shown that QBD* can express transitive closure queries, it follows that its expressive power is at least that of *stratified linear Datalog*. In such a paper we show how to extend QBD* in such a way to express stratified queries, i.e. QBD** has the same expressive power of stratified Datalog. We recall that QBD** is obtained by extending QBD* with a graphical mechanism generalizing the operation of transitive closure. Now we show that this simple mechanism visualizes the extended closure introduced in Section 4. In Figures 2.2 and 5.2 we present the extended closure window of QBD**. Analogously to the transitive closure case, Figure 5.2 is an abstraction of a real situation. We evidentiate with a black circle the attributes to be included in the final result, and link the attributes to be compared by means of labeled edges.

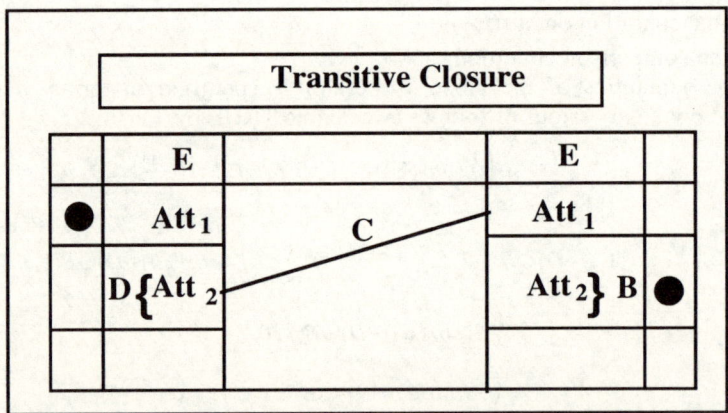

**Fig. 5.1.** Graphical realization of the closure operator

The semantics of the above graphical operator is specified in terms of the simple extended closure introduced in Section 4, as follows:

$$E^+_{Q,A,F},\text{ where } A=(attr(E) \cup attr(E)-D'-D'') \cup B \text{ and } F=C' \wedge C''.$$

Following the notation introduced for the transitive closure, we denote with A the attributes to be included in the final result. In particular, A is composed by twice the attributes of **E** (assuming a positional approach for the attributes), $attr(E)$, minus certain sets D' and D", which are subsets of $attr(E)$, plus a set $B \subseteq attr(Q)$. The selection condition are specified by the union of the set of conditions on $attr(E)$ vs $attr(Q)$, namely C', and the set of conditions on $attr(Q)$ vs $attr(E)$, namely C".

It is easy to see that the same visual approach can be followed for visualizing the general case of extended closure operator. The realization of the extended closure window is based on the same graphical choices of the simple extended closure window, using different colors for evidentiating different recursive rules: selection conditions are expressed by drawing colored labeled edges between involved attributes and attributes to be included in the final result are marked with colored dots.

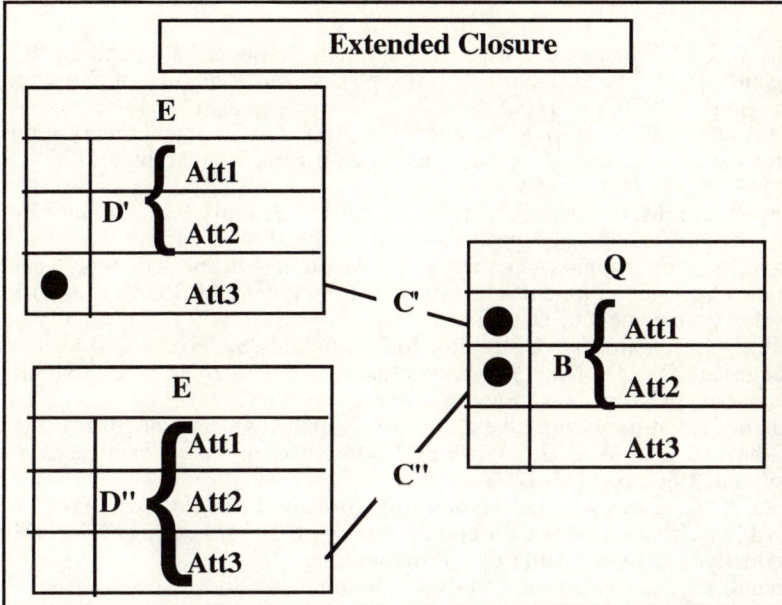

**Fig.5.2**. Graphical realization of the simple extended closure operator

# 6 Conclusions

In this paper we have described a visual query language QBD** which exhibits a high expressive power while retaining the easy of use. In particular, QBD** has been proven to be (at least) equivalent to stratified Datalog in terms of expressive power. This result has been obtained by first introducing the notion of extended closure as a uniform and elegant way for expressing stratified queries, and then using the extended closure operator for giving a formal semantics to the QBD** recursive queries.

A prototype of QBD* has been implemented using the C language under MS-DOS operative system. The current version of this prototype allows for retrieving and manipulating a stored Entity-Relationship schema and for graphically expressing a query on it. It is possible to browse the top-down refinement chain of the current schema, to extract a subschema, modify a concept or a portion of the schema, and save the resulting view of the schema. All types of queries can be expressed in the visual query language (including recursive queries). All the activities, but the schema transformation, can be fully intermixed, resulting in a very flexible user interaction. A metaschema describing the structure of the whole set of schemata which are available to the user can be queried with the same mechanisms. Such a meta-querying allows the user to quickly locate the schema s/he is looking for.

We are currently working on an extended version of the prototype, namely QBD**, including the feature of expressing generalized closure queries.

# References

1. Aho A.V., Ullman J.D. Universality of Data Retrieval Language. In: Proc. of the 6th ACM SIGACT-SIPLAN Symposium on Principles of Programming Languages, 1979, pp. 110-120.
2. Angelaccio, M. Catarci T., Santucci G. QBD*: A Graphical Query Language with Recursion. IEEE Transactions on Software Engineering, 1990, 16, 10: 1150-1163.
3. Angelaccio, M. Catarci T., Santucci G. QBD*: A Fully Visual Query System. Journal on Visual Languages and Computing, 1990, 1, 2: 255-273.
4. Bancilhon F., Ramakrishnan R.. An Amateur's Introduction to Recursive Query Processing Strategies. In: Proc. of the 1986 ACM-SIGMOD Conference on the Management of Data, 1986.
5. Batini C., Catarci T., Costabile, M.F. Levialdi S. Visual Query Systems. Technical Report N.04.91, Dipartimento di Informatica e Sistemistica, Università di Roma "La Sapienza", 1991.
6. Catarci T. On the Expressive Power of Graphical Query Languages. In: Proc. of the 2nd IFIP W.G. 2.6 Working Conference on Visual Databases, North-Holland, 1991, pp. 411-421.
7. Catarci T., Cruz I.F. On Expressing Stratified Datalog. In: Proc. of the ICLP'94 (International Conference on Logic Programming) Workshop on Deductive Databases And Logic Programming, 1994.
8. Chandra A.K. Theory of Database Queries. In: Proc. Symp. Principles of Database Systems, 1988.
9. Chandra A.K., Harel D. Horn Clause Queries and Generalizations. Journal of Logic Programming, 1985, 1, 1: 1-15.
10. Chen P.P. The Entity-Relationship Model toward a Unified View of Data. ACM Transactions on Data Base Systems, 1976, 1, 1.
11. Codd E. F. A Relational Model for Large Shared Data Banks. Communication of the ACM, 1970, 13, 6.
12. Codd E.F. Relational completeness of database sub-languages. In: R.Rustin (ed.): Data Base Systems, Prentice Hall, Englewood Cliffs, 1972, pp. 65-98.
13. Consens M., Mendelzon A.O. Graphlog: A Visual Formalism for Real Life Recursion. In: Proc. of the ACM Symp. on Principles of Database Systems, 1990, pp. 404-416.
14. Cook S.A. A taxonomy of problems with fast parallel algorithms. Information and Control, 1985, 64: 2-22.
15. Cruz I.F. DOODLE: A Visual Language for Object-Oriented Databases. In: Proc. of the ACM SIGMOD Conf. on Management of Data, 1992.
16. CruzI .F., Mendelzon A.O., Wood P.T. G+: Recursive Queries Without Recursion. In: Proc. of the 2nd International Conference on Expert Database Systems, 1988, pp. 355-368.
17. Gallaire H., Minker J., Nicolas J.M. Logic and Databases: A Deductive Approach. ACM Computing Surveys, 1984, 16, 2: 153-185.
18. Henschen L.J., Naqvi S.A. On compiling Queries in Recursive First-order Databases. Journal of the ACM, 1984, 31, 1: 47-85.

19. Ioannidis Y.I., Wong E. Towards an Algebraic theory of Recursion. Journal of the ACM, 1991, 38, 2: 329-381.
20. Kanellakis P.C. Elements of Relational Theory. In: J.van Leuween (ed.): Handbook of Theoretical Computer Science, Elsevier Science Pub, 1990.
21. Kolaitis P.J. The Expressive Power of Stratified Logic Programs. Information and Computation, 1991, 50-66.
22. Paredaens J., Peelman P., Tanca L. G-Log: A Declarative Graphical Query Language. In: Proc. of the Second International Conference DOOD'91, 1991, pp. 108-128.
23. Rundensteiner E.A., Bic L. Set Operations in Object-Based Data Models. IEEE Transactions on Knowledge and Data Engineering, 1992, 4, 4: 382-398.
24. Santucci G., Sottile P. A. Query By Diagram: a Visual Environment for Querying Databases. Software Practice and Experience, 1993, 23, 3.
25. Sippu S., Soisalon-Soininen E. A Generalized Transitive Closure for Relational Queries. In: Proc. of the International Conference on Principle of Database Systems, 1988.
26. Shneiderman B. Direct Manipulation: A Step beyond Programming Languages. IEEE Computer, 1983, 16: 57-69.
27. Ullman J.D. Principles of Database and Knowledge-Base Systems, vol. I. Computer Science Press, Rockville, MD, 1988.
28. Zhang W., Yu C.T., Troy D. Necessary and Sufficient Conditions to Linearize Doubly Recursive Programs in Logic Databases. ACM Transactions on Database Systems, 1990, 15, 3: 459-482.

# Database Querying by Hypergraph Manipulation

Tiziana Catarci and Laura Tarantino

Dipartimento di Informatica e Sistemistica, Università degli Studi di Roma "La Sapienza"
Via Salaria 113, I-00198 Roma, ITALY
catarci@infokit.dis.uniroma1.it

Dipartimento di Ingegneria Elettrica, Università degli Studi di L'Aquila
Poggio di Roio, I-67040 L'Aquila, ITALY
tarantino@vaxaq.cc.univaq.it

**Abstract.** In this paper we propose a theoretical framework for visual interaction with databases, having a particular kind of hypergraph, the Structure Modeling Hypergraph (SMH), as a representation tool able to capture the essential features of existing data models. Notable characteristics of SMHs are: uniform and unified representation of both intensional and extensional aspects of databases, direct representation of containment relationships, and immediate applicability of direct manipulation primitives. In particular, we define some basic direct-manipulation primitives (IPs), which can be composed and sequenced to build meaningful queries. The interpretation of well-formed IP sequences is given in terms of an operational semantics. Note that the result of querying an SMH is still an SMH, (i.e., the model is closed under the query operations). Finally, by specializing our approach to the relational data model, we show that it is possible to express at least all the first order queries by sequences of IPs.

## 1. Introduction

Visual Languages [9, 3] are languages that systematically use visual structures (such as forms, diagrams, icons) to convey a meaning in a friendly and effective way, and direct manipulation mechanisms [19] to interact with such visual structures. A particular kind of visual languages is emerging in the database area, namely Visual Query Languages, VQLs, (see [3] for a survey on them), which are part of friendly visual interfaces to database systems.

One of the basic drawbacks of existing VQLs is the lack of a syntactic and semantic formalization, in contrast to the well-established traditional query languages. As a consequence, while traditional query languages have been normally compared with each other in terms of their expressive power, a similar analysis has rarely been performed for VQLs. Just a few attempts of comparison have been made in this direction (see for example [1] and [12]); however, these studies are not aimed at defining a general framework where any VQL can be formally characterized to evaluate its expressive power; rather they are limited to specific comparisons between individual languages. A more general approach should provide a single formal framework able to visually represent intensional and extensional aspects of databases, while providing a set of basic interaction primitives suitable for being the formal counterpart of visual primitives of existing VQLs.

An attempt at defining a general data representation structure is presented in [16], where a graph-based data model is proposed which shares many features with existing data models. An associated graph transformation language is presented, discussing how it is suitable for graphically describing querying, browsing, restructuring and updating databases. However, the paper is focused on the object-oriented data model and it is difficult to use this structure (and the corresponding interaction primitives) for non network-based data models. In fact, while graphs are a natural mathematical tool for representing models based on objects and binary relationships between them, it is not equally suitable for modeling different kinds of interdependencies (e.g., schemata in the relational data model).

Hypergraphs, on the other hand, offer richer modeling capabilities, and may therefore be a natural mathematical counterpart of arbitrarily complex visual structures. Hypergraphs have been extensively used in the field of relational databases (see, e.g., [15] and [18]).

A particular kind of hypergraphs, namely the *recursive label-node hypergraph*, was proposed in [6] as a tool for knowledge representation systems. In particular, [6] discusses the equivalence of this kind of hypergraph with several knowledge representation formalisms (functional programming, logic programming, and conceptual languages). In [17] the *higraph*, a diagrammatic formalism suitable for various kinds of applications, is presented. Higraphs combine a form of Euler/Venn diagrams, suitable for representing collection of sets and the notion of inclusion, with edge relations typical of graphs and hypergraphs. However these two papers ([6, 17]) are more concerned with modeling and representation issues rather than with interaction issues. An hypergraph-based system that deals also with interaction can be found in [13], where a Hygraph-based query and visualization approach is presented.

In this paper we propose a theoretical framework for visual interaction with databases, based on a particular kind of hypergraph, called *Structure Modeling Hypergraph* (*SMH*). SMHs are a representation tool able to capture the essential features of the existing data models and offering a set of interaction primitives. We want to point out that our aim is to provide a framework where (existing or new) visual languages can be represented and evaluated. The user will not interact with the database by acting directly on SMHs, but by acting on a visual user-friendly interface where SMH concepts are mapped. In this respect our proposal differs from [13] where the query primitives proposed are the actual interface.

SMHs profit from the basic property of diagrams (i.e., the unambiguous representation of relationships) while overcoming their limitations. Notable characteristics of SMHs are: uniform representation of both intensional and extensional aspects of databases (advantageous both in navigation and querying activities), direct representation of containment relationships (e.g., set-subset relationships) and immediate applicability of direct manipulation primitives [19]. While representation capabilities of SMHs have been discussed elsewhere [7], in this paper we show how SMHs can be queried by formal systems closed under queries (the result of querying an SMH is still an SMH). In particular, we introduce the basic interaction primitives (IPs) that, suitably composed, allow one to express queries against a database represented by an SMH. Furthermore, we introduce a query strategy that defines correct compositions and sequences of IPs corresponding to meaningful queries, and we provide an operational semantics for the interpretation of well-formed IP sequences. Finally, by specializing this approach to the relational data model, we prove that the basic interaction primitives we introduce allow us to formulate at least all first-order queries.

The remainder of the paper is organized as follows. In Section 2, we introduce the SMHs, and we show how this class of hypergraphs may be further specialized for representing the relational data model. In Section 3, after having introduced the main issues of database querying, we formally describe the basic interaction primitives and the adopted query strategy. In Section 4 we evaluate the expressive power of the proposed query system. Finally, conclusions are drawn in Section 5.

## 2. Structure Modeling Hypergraphs and their Application

In this section we first recall the definition of Structure Modeling Hypergraph (SMH) introduced in [7]. Then, we show as an example of SMH data model representation, how to map to an SMH a database expressed in the relational model [13].

### 2.1 SMH Definition

SMHs represent in a uniform way both intensional and extensional aspects of a database. Generally speaking, an SMH consists of a set of labeled nodes, representing distinguishable concepts of the real world and their properties, and a set of (undirected or directed) hyperedges used to describe their structure. Formally:

**Definition 1** A Structure Modeling Hypergraph is a 7-tuple $< \mathcal{N}, \mathcal{A}, \mathcal{H}, \mathcal{L}, \lambda_1, \lambda_2, \mathcal{C} >$, where $\mathcal{N}$ is the set of (labeled) nodes, $\mathcal{A}$ is the set of arcs, $\mathcal{H}$ is the set of hyperedges, $\mathcal{L}$ is the set of labels, $\lambda_1$ and $\lambda_2$ are two node-labeling functions, $\mathcal{C}$ is a set of constraints. More particularly:
- $\mathcal{N}$ is partitioned into two subsets $\mathcal{N}_I$ and $\mathcal{N}_U$, where $\mathcal{N}_I$ is the set of identifiable nodes, i.e., nodes which are uniquely identified through the associated label, and $\mathcal{N}_U$ is the set of unidentifiable nodes, i.e., nodes for which the above property does not hold.
- $\mathcal{A} \subseteq \mathcal{N} \times \mathcal{N}$ is the set of admissible directed arcs.
- $\mathcal{H} = \mathcal{H}_U \cup \mathcal{H}_D$, where $\mathcal{H}_U \subseteq \mathcal{P}(\mathcal{N})$[1] is the set of admissible undirected hyperedges (shortly hyperedges) and $\mathcal{H}_D \subseteq \mathcal{N} \times \mathcal{P}(\mathcal{N})$ is the set of admissible directed hyperedges (also called hyperarcs). More in detail:
  - $\mathcal{H}_U = \mathcal{H}_S \cup \mathcal{H}_E \cup \mathcal{H}_G$, where a generic hyperedge $h \in \mathcal{H}_U$ is either a non empty set of nodes in $\mathcal{N}$ or a non empty set of hyperedges. Admissible hyperedges fall into three categories, namely *structure hyperedges* ($\mathcal{H}_S$), *extension hyperedges* ($\mathcal{H}_E$), and *group hyperedges* ($\mathcal{H}_G$), satisfying constraints in Definition 2.

---

[1] $\mathcal{P}(\mathcal{N})$ is the powerset of $\mathcal{N}$.

- An admissible hyperarc $h \in \mathcal{H}_D$ is a pair $< i, h_U >$, where $i$ is a node in $\mathcal{N}$ and $h_U$ is an hyperedge in $\mathcal{H}_U$.

- $\mathcal{L} = \mathcal{L}_I \cup \mathcal{L}_U$, where $\mathcal{L}_I$ and $\mathcal{L}_U$ are disjoint sets of labels, used to label nodes in $\mathcal{N}_I$ and in $\mathcal{N}_U$, respectively.

- $\lambda_1 : \mathcal{N}_I \rightarrow \mathcal{L}_I$ is a total labeling function such that $\forall\ n_1, n_2 \in \mathcal{N}_I, n_1 \neq n_2 \Rightarrow \lambda_1(n_1) \neq \lambda_2(n_2)$

- $\lambda_2: \mathcal{N}_U \rightarrow \mathcal{L}_U$ is a total labeling function.

- $\mathcal{C} = \mathcal{C}_G \cup \mathcal{C}_{DM}$, where $\mathcal{C}_G$ is the set of "general" constraints independent of the data model (given in Definition 2), which limit the hypergraph structure, and $\mathcal{C}_{DM}$ is the set of constraints dependent of the data model, which force an SMH to be a representation of an admissible database for the data model DM. Note that $\mathcal{C}_{DM}$ may be empty if no particular data model is considered.

**Definition 2** The set of general constraints $\mathcal{C}_G$ is specified as follows:

$\mathcal{C}_G^1$: an SMH either is empty or contains at least one node in $\mathcal{N}_I$.

$\mathcal{C}_G^2$: a *structure hyperedge* $h_S \in \mathcal{H}_S$ is a non empty set of nodes in $\mathcal{N}_U$ such that for each $n_U \in h_S$ there exists either exactly one arc $< n_U, n_I > \in \mathcal{A}$ with $n_I \in \mathcal{N}_I$, or exactly one hyperarc $h_D = < n_U, h_G >$, with $h_D \in \mathcal{H}_D$. Also, for each pair of distinct nodes $n_U', n_U'' \in h_S, \lambda_2(n_U') \neq \lambda_2(n_U'')$.

$\mathcal{C}_G^3$: each $h_G \in \mathcal{H}_G$ is a non empty subset of nodes in $\mathcal{N}_I$. For each $h_G \in \mathcal{H}_G$ there exist $h_D \in \mathcal{H}_D$ and $n_U \in \mathcal{N}_U$ such that $h_D = < n_U, h_G >$.

$\mathcal{C}_G^4$: for each $n_I \in \mathcal{N}_I$ there exists at most one hyperarc $h_D = < n_I, h_S >$, with $h_D \in \mathcal{H}_D$ and $h_S \in \mathcal{H}_S$ (*structure uniqueness*).

$\mathcal{C}_G^5$: for each $n_U \in \mathcal{N}_U$ there exists exactly one $h_S \in \mathcal{H}_S$ such that $n_U \in h_S$.

$\mathcal{C}_G^6$: an *extension hyperedge* $h_E \in \mathcal{H}_E$ is either a set of nodes in $\mathcal{N}_I$ or a multiset of structure hyperedges in $\mathcal{H}_S$, satisfying the *compatibility* constraints given in $\mathcal{C}_{DM}$, if any.

$\mathcal{C}_G^7$: for each $h_S \in \mathcal{H}_S$ there exists either exactly one $h_E \in \mathcal{H}_E$ such that $h_S \in h_E$, or exactly one $h_D \in \mathcal{H}_D$ and an $n_I \in \mathcal{N}_I$ such that $h_D = < n_I, h_S >$.

$\mathcal{C}_G^8$: for each $n_I \in \mathcal{N}_I$ there exists at most one hyperarc $h_D = < n_I, h_E >$, with $h_D \in \mathcal{H}_D$ and $h_E \in \mathcal{H}_E$ (*extension uniqueness*).

$\mathcal{C}_G^9$: for each $h_E \in \mathcal{H}_E$ there exists exactly one hyperarc $h_D = < n_I, h_E >$, with $h_D \in \mathcal{H}_D$ and $n_I \in \mathcal{N}_I$ (*extension ownership uniqueness*).

$\mathcal{C}_G^{10}$: constraints $\mathcal{C}_G^1$ to $\mathcal{C}_G^9$ define all the admissible $h_D \in \mathcal{H}_D$ and all the admissible $a \in \mathcal{A}$.

It is easy to see how the above concepts allow for representing the various aspects of the existing models, as it will be shown for the relational model in the next subsection. Here we briefly illustrate, by means of a simple example, an admissible SMH (together with a possible semantics) without any concern for the data model.

The SMH in Figure 1 represents a simple database, containing information about persons. We note that nodes in $\mathfrak{N}_I$ (filled in black in Figure 1) represent the distinguishable objects in our reality of interest, whereas nodes in $\mathfrak{N}_U$ (filled with an orizontal texture in Figure 1) represent the properties that describe them. As for the hyperedges, those in $\mathfrak{H}_S$ (ovals with grey texture) are used to associate to nodes in $\mathfrak{N}_I$ the description of their structure in terms of a set of properties, while hyperedges in $\mathfrak{H}_E$ (ovals with white texture) represent the extension of nodes in $\mathfrak{N}_I$. The link between nodes and hyperedges is realized in both cases by an hyperarc $h_D \in \mathfrak{H}_D$ (all the $h_D$ are represented by arrows in Figure 1). Finally, an arc connects each node belonging to a structure hyperedge to the value of the associated property.

Although in the above example we only use strings as labels, the SMH definition does not force any particular label domain to be adopted. For example, icons, pictures or even earcons in case of multimedia databases may be used as well, for augmenting the metaphorical power of the representation and achieving a more effective representation of the database. Furthermore, our approach better exploits the potentiality of diagrams. In fact, we propose a uniform representation of both the intensional and the extensional level of the database, while in existing systems diagrams are generally adopted for representing either one of the two database levels. Moreover, we adopt diagrams in which containment relationships may be directly displayed (in the sense of [4,5]), differently from the majority of proposals, where what is actually used is a network, in which connections are the only admitted relationships.

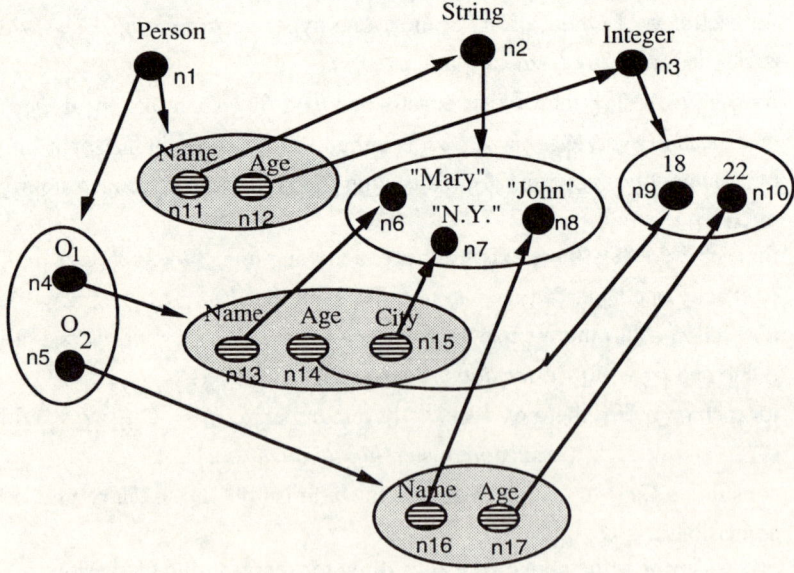

**Fig. 1.** A simple example SMH

## 2.2 SMH Relational Model Representation

The structure modeling hypergraph, as defined above, is a general mathematical tool consisting of nodes, links, and semantics for each node. However, traditional data models, which we want to represent in terms of such a structure, are characterized by precise constraints, both from an intensional and an extensional point of view. Therefore, depending on the data model, we must define suitable constraints in $\mathcal{C}_{DM}$.

In the following we show how to map to an SMH a database expressed in the relational model by defining a suitable set of constraints. In [7] it is shown how to represent object-oriented and semantic databases by SMHs.

The relational model represents data in a database as a collection of relations. Informally, each relation resembles a table, and each row in the table represents a collection of related data values (Figure 2 depicts a very simple relational database).

*Employees*

| Name | Company |
|------|---------|
| Mary | IBM |
| John | Apple |
| Phil | IBM |

*Companies*

| Company | City |
|---------|------|
| IBM | San Jose |
| Apple | Boston |

**Fig. 2.** An example of relational database represented by tables

More formally, a relational database can be defined as follows:

**Definition 3.** Let $D = \{D_1,..,D_n\}$ be a family of (finite) *domains*, each composed by a set of *values*; let $U = \{A_1,..,A_m\}$ be the *universe* of *attributes*, and let $dom : U \rightarrow D$ be a function that associates a domain $dom(A)$ to each $A \in U$. A *tuple* on $R$, with $R \subseteq U$, is a function $\tilde{t} : R \rightarrow \cup_{D_i \in D} D_i$, which associates to each $A \in R$ a value in $dom(A)$. Let $RN = \{rn_1,..,rn_k\}$ be a set of *relation names*, let $\tilde{attr} : RN \rightarrow \mathcal{P}(U)$ be a function which associates to each $rn \in RN$ a non empty set $\tilde{attr}(rn)$ of attributes, called *relation scheme*, and let $\tilde{inst} : RN \rightarrow \mathcal{P}(\tilde{t}(U))$ be a function, which associates to each $rn \in RN$ a finite set $\tilde{inst}(rn) \subseteq \tilde{t}(\tilde{attr}(rn))$, called *relation instance*, (where $\tilde{t}(R)$ denotes the set of all possible tuples on $R$). A *relation* is a triple $r = <rn, \tilde{attr}(rn), \tilde{inst}(rn)>$, with $rn \in RN$. A *relational database* $DB = \{r_1,..,r_k\}$ is a set of relations with different names.

The constraints in the following definition specialize the SMH components given in Definition 1 to represent the relational data model. In particular, we describe how the above concepts of the model are mapped into the basic components of a generic SMH $hg$. For the sake of simplicity, in the following we assume that identifiable nodes are referred to by their labels.

**Definition 4**

$C_{dm}^1$: the set $\mathcal{N}_I$ is partitioned into three subsets $\mathcal{N}_D$, $\mathcal{N}_V$ and $\mathcal{N}_{RN}$, where $\mathcal{N}_D = \{d_1,...,d_n\}$, $\mathcal{N}_V = \{v_1,...,v_l\}$, and $\mathcal{N}_{RN} = \{rn_1,...,rn_k\}$;

$C_{dm}^2$: $\mathcal{L}_U = \{A_1,...,A_m\}$;

$C_{dm}^3$: the set of arcs $\mathcal{A}$ is partitioned into two subsets $\mathcal{A}_{Dom}$ and $\mathcal{A}_{Val}$, with $\mathcal{A}_{Dom} \subseteq \mathcal{N}_U \times \mathcal{N}_D$, and $\mathcal{A}_{Val} \subseteq \mathcal{N}_U \times \mathcal{N}_V$;

$C_{dm}^4$: the set of hyperarcs $\mathcal{H}_D$ is partitioned into three subsets $\mathcal{H}_{Attr}$, $\mathcal{H}_{Inst}$ and $\mathcal{H}_{Val}$, where $\mathcal{H}_{Attr} \subseteq \mathcal{N}_{RN} \times \mathcal{H}_{Sch}$, $\mathcal{H}_{Inst} \subseteq \mathcal{N}_{RN} \times \mathcal{H}_{Ext}$, $\mathcal{H}_{Val} \subseteq \mathcal{N}_D \times \mathcal{H}_{Set}$;

$C_{dm}^5$: the set of structure hyperedges $\mathcal{H}_S$ is partitioned into two subsets $\mathcal{H}_{Sch}$ and $\mathcal{H}_{Tuple}$; nodes in $\mathcal{H}_{Sch}$ (resp. $\mathcal{H}_{Tuple}$) have an outgoing arc in $\mathcal{A}_{Dom}$ (resp. $\mathcal{A}_{Val}$);

$C_{dm}^6$: the set of extension hyperedges $\mathcal{H}_E$ is partitioned into two subsets $\mathcal{H}_{Ext}$ and $\mathcal{H}_{Set}$ where each $h_{ext} \in \mathcal{H}_{Ext}$ is a set of hyperedges in $\mathcal{H}_{Tuple}$ and $\mathcal{H}_{Set} \subseteq \mathcal{P}(\mathcal{N}_V)$.

Nodes, labels, arcs, hyperarcs and hyperedges, as introduced in constraints from $C_{dm}^1$ to $C_{dm}^6$ are associated to the concepts of the relational model recalled in Definition 3 in the following way:

$D$ is represented by the set $\mathcal{N}_D = \{d_1..d_n\}$, where each $d_i$ represents a domain $D_i$. Nodes in $\mathcal{N}_V$ represent the (active) values of the domains. $RN$ is represented by the set $\mathcal{N}_{RN} = \{rn_1,...,rn_k\}$, where each $rn_i$ represents a relation name $rn_i$. There exists a one-to-one correspondence between attributes $A_1,...,A_m$ and labels in $\mathcal{L}_U$ (hence $U$ is represented by $\mathcal{L}_U$). The function $dom$ is represented by arcs in $\mathcal{A}_{Dom}$. The function $attr$ is represented by hyperarcs in $\mathcal{H}_{Attr}$. A tuple on $R$ is represented by a hyperedge $h_{tuple} \in \mathcal{H}_{Tuple}$ such that $\lambda_2(h_{tuple}) = R$. The function $inst$ is represented by hyperarcs in $\mathcal{H}_{Inst}$. A relation is represented by a triple $r = <rn, h_{attr}, h_{inst}>$, where $rn \in \mathcal{N}_{RN}$, $h_{attr} \in \mathcal{H}_{Attr}$, $h_{inst} \in \mathcal{H}_{Inst}$, with $h_{attr}$ and $h_{inst}$ originating from $rn$.[1]

Figure 3 illustrates the SMH representation of the relational database depicted in Figure 2. A comparison between the two figures reveals the different power of the two representation languages: the SMH representation embodies all the different (intensional and extensional) components of the relational database, while the tabular representation does not include, e.g., the information on the attribute domains. The comparison here is not done on the friendliness of the representation (the table being obviously winning for this aspect), but on the capacity of the representation language for uniformly representing all the components of the database (the SMH being winning for this aspect).

---

[1] In Section 4 we will use the notation $hg = \mathfrak{M}(db)$ for specifying that the database $db$ is represented by the hypergraph $hg$, conformingly to the above correspondences.

## 3. Interacting with SMHs

A *query language* is a set of formally defined operators that, suitably composed, allow one to express requests to a database; the execution of the query produces the extraction, from the database, of data that are consistent with the meaning of the request. The set of operators, along with the data model, constitutes the *query model*, which is, in turn, presented to the user in terms of a *query representation*. The query model and the query representation are the two component parts of the query language, as introduced above. In the following, we will use the term query language when we are not interested in distinguishing between such two components.

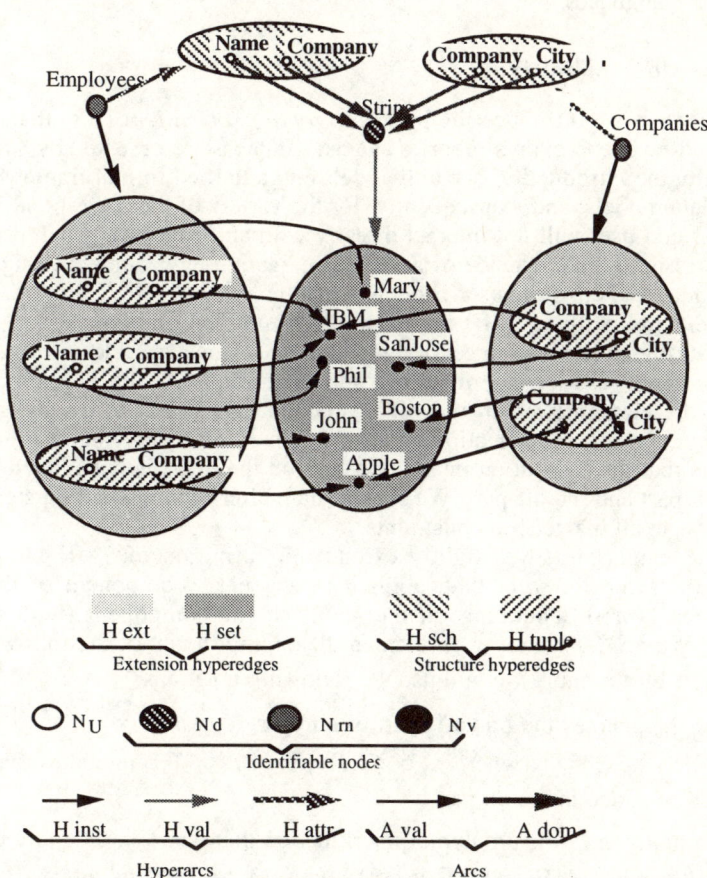

**Fig. 3.** An SMH representation of a relational database

A relevant example of query model is the relational algebra [10], to which several query representations have been associated so far: such representations may be textual (as in SQL [20]), form-based (as in QBE [21]), graphical (like in G$^+$ [14]).

Several query languages have been proposed in the literature, which are strongly influenced by the corresponding data models, and typically do not adopt friendly representations. In any case, independently of the adopted data/query model, the process of database querying can be seen as composed by three phases: the first phase selects which parts of the database we should operate on (*structure definition*); the second phase defines the relations within the part to produce the query result (*extension definition*) and the third phase operates on the query result, if necessary (*testing*). For instance, the phase of structure definition is accomplished by the specification of the SELECT-FROM clauses in SQL [20], by the specification of the P. operator in QBE [21], and by the selection of schema concepts in semantic and object-oriented languages [2]. On the other hand, in the phase of extension definition, relations among concepts of the database are defined by the WHERE clause of SQL, by example variables in QBE, and by condition specifications in semantic and object-oriented query languages.

### 3.1 Interaction primitives

In this subsection we introduce the basic *Interaction Primitives* (IPs) that, suitably composed, allow one to express queries against a database represented by a SMH. As pointed out in the introduction, we aim at defining a unified formal framework for a variety of data models, and, consequently, for the variety of the corresponding query models. The end-user will not interact directly with an SMH using such primitives. Rather, we assume the existence of a visual interaction environment designed as a mapping from SMHs to more user-friendly structures.

The interaction with an SMH is carried on by simple primitives acting on SMH elements. During an interaction session the entire SMH is available and its elements may switch their status from **on** to **off** and vice versa. At the beginning of the session all the elements are in the **off** status and may be set to **on** by graphical selection (conversely, the selection of an element in **on** status puts it in **off**). The basic idea is that throughout an interaction session the SMH is partitioned into two parts: the **on** part and the **off** part. We require that, after each interaction step, the **on** part conforms to all the general constraints.

To achieve this aim, we slightly extend the definition of SMH by adding a *polymorphic status function* that, applied to a generic component of the SMH, returns either 1 or 0 depending on the status of the component (with the term *component of an SMH* we mean an element belonging to any of the following sets: $\mathcal{N}, \mathcal{C}, \mathcal{H}, \mathcal{I}$)[1]. Furthermore we will use the following notations:

- $hg_{on}$ ($hg_{off}$) denotes the **on** (**off**) part of a hypergraph $hg$;
- $hg_{on} \cup \{x_1, \ldots, x_n\}$ (where $x_i \in X$, $X=[\mathcal{N} / \mathcal{C} / \mathcal{H} / \mathcal{I}]$) indicates that each $x_i \in X$ is to be added to the on part of X.

More formally, an IP is a polymorphic function that when applied to a pair $<hg, e>$ (where $hg$ in an SMH and $e$ is a component of $hg$) returns an SMH $hg'$ that differs from $hg$ only in the values of the status function.

---

[1] We assume that any hyperedge may be **on** independently of the status of its components. Conversely it suffices that one of its component be **on** for forcing the hyperedge to be **on**.

The following rules define the modifications of the values of the $hg$ status function when the **on** IP is applied to the different components of $hg$. Notice that, since the **on** and **off** parts are disjoints, any adding of an element to one of them implies its removal from the other.

Let $hg$ be an SMH.

1) for each $n \in \mathcal{N}_I$ on$(hg, n)$ => $hg_{on} := hg_{on} \cup \{n\}$

2) for each $n \in \mathcal{N}_U$ on$(hg, n)$ => $hg_{on} := hg_{on} \cup \{n, \text{on}(hg, h_S), [\text{on}(hg,a) / \text{on}(hg, h_D)]^1\}$ where $h_S$ is the structure hyperedge $n$ belongs to, $a \in \mathcal{Q}$ ($h_D \in \mathcal{H}_D$) is the arc (hyperarc) outgoing from $n$.

3) for each $a = <n_1, n_2> \in \mathcal{Q}$
$$\text{on}(hg, a) => hg_{on} := hg_{on} \cup \{a, \text{on}(hg, n_1), \text{on}(hg, n_2)\}$$

4) for each $h_S \in \mathcal{H}_S$
$$\text{on}(hg, h_S) => hg_{on} := hg_{on} \cup \{h_S, [\text{on}(hg, h_E) / \text{on}(hg, h_D)]\},$$

where $h_E \in \mathcal{H}_E$ (resp. $h_D \in \mathcal{H}_D$) is the extension hyperedge $h_S$ belongs to (resp. is the hyperarc incoming in $h_S$)

5) for each $h_E \in \mathcal{H}_E$
$$\text{on}(hg, h_E) => hg_{on} := hg_{on} \cup \{h_E, \text{on}(hg, h_D)\},$$

where $h_D \in \mathcal{H}_D$ is the hyperarc incoming in $h_E$

6) for each $h_D = <n, h_U> \in \mathcal{H}_D$, with $n \in \mathcal{N}$ and $h_U \in \mathcal{H}_U$
$$\text{on}(hg, h_D) => hg_{on} := hg_{on} \cup \{h_D, \text{on}(hg, n), \text{on}(hg, h_U)\}$$

7) for each $h_G \in \mathcal{H}_G$
$$\text{on}(hg, h_G) => hg_{on} := hg_{on} \cup \{h_G, \{\text{on}(hg, h_{Di})\}\},$$

where $h_{Di} \in \mathcal{H}_D$ are hyperarcs incoming in $h_G$

8) for each $l \in \mathcal{L}_I$ on$(hg, l)$ => $hg_{on} := hg_{on} \cup \{l, n\}$, where $n = \lambda_1^{-1}(l)$

9) for each $l \in \mathcal{L}_U$ on$(hg, l)$ => $hg_{on} := hg_{on} \cup \{l, \{\text{on}(hg, n_i) \mid n_i = \lambda_2^{-1}(l)\}\}$

Concerning the **off** operation, it is intuitive that switching an element off should imply a propagation of the **off** operation to the subhypergraph rooted at such element. Actually, the situation is slightly more difficult since checks must be performed in order to maintain **on** those elements of a subhypergraph that are shared by other subypergraphs rooted at other **on** elements (in other words, they play some roles in the description of other components of $hg_{on}$).

In Section 4 we illustrate how the semantics of the **on/off** operations may be imposed by the represented query model, by showing how the **on/off** operations are used to represent the relational algebra.

---

[1]We use the common notation [a / b] to mean that either a or b must be considered.

## 3.2 Query Strategy in SMHs

The **on/off** operations are the basic interaction primitives for querying SMHs. We have now to introduce a "query strategy" that defines the correct way for composing and sequencing IPs, in order to have meaningful queries. We also provide an operational semantics for the interpretation of well-formed IP sequences, in terms of transformation of the SMH representing the query result.

The main issues to be faced for the definition of the query strategy are: the formulation of a query and the extraction/reuse of the query result. The idea is that each query interaction is regarded as a two-phases session (leaving out the testing): a first phase is devoted to the definition of the schema of the result, while a second phase is aimed at defining the rules for populating the extension of the result (as a matter of fact, a *phase 0* has also to be considered, where the user communicates the system the intention of issuing a query). Generally speaking, when a query session is started, the SMH query system automatically creates an identifiable temporary node, leaving its structure and extension empty (the structure and the extension will be filled with appropriate components during subsequent phases). During the structure definition phase, a number of **on** operations will be performed on the original SMH; the query system automatically adds unidentifiable nodes to the structure hyperdge owned by the result together with their outgoing arcs (or hyperarcs). During the second phase, a number of **on** operations are performed on the database extension; the system automatically inserts new elements in the result extension. In the following we denote by $hg$ the original (i.e., the queried) SMH, and by $hg'$ the SMH representing the query result. It is important to point out that $hg$ and $hg'$ are not disjoint (links will be created among components of the two hypergraphs, as it will be clarified by the operational semantics).

The query formulation is composed by the following sequence of phases:

0) query activation
1) structure definition
2) extension definition

For each phase we consider the user's action and the associated system's action.

*Phase 0.* We assume the user has a way for communicating the system s/he is going to start a query session (s/he will also specify the query name). The system triggers the following macro, which initializes the components of $hg'$ to be filled with the intentional and extensional parts of the query results:

@*initQuery(queryName)*
    $hg' := \emptyset$
    add($hg'$, $n_q$);
    $\lambda_1(n_q) := query\mathcal{N}ame$;
    add($hg'$, $h_{Sq}$);
    add($hg'$, $h_{Eq}$);
    add($hg'$, $<n_q, h_{Sq}>$);
    add($hg'$, $<n_q, h_{Eq}>$);
@*end*

where **add** is a polymorphic function that takes as parameters an SMH and an element of any of the following types: $\mathfrak{N}, \mathfrak{A}, \mathfrak{H}, \mathfrak{E}$. It is used for augmenting the SMH by adding the specified element. Notice that one application of **add** does not guarantee the achievement of an SMH, rather a transaction (i.e., a series of **add** applications) is needed for defining an admissible SMH. In particular, the semantics of the above macro in terms of its effect on $hg'$ is the following:

$hg' := <\{n_q\}, \{\}, \{\{\{h_{Sq}\}, \{h_{Eq}\}, \{\}\}, \{<n_q, h_{Sq}>, <n_q, h_{Eq}>\}\},$
$\{queryName\}, \{<n_q, queryName>\}, \{\}, \mathfrak{E}_G>,$

where the components of $hg'$ are listed following the order of Definition 1.

*Phase 1.* The user selects (by **on** operations) a number of unidentifiable nodes belonging to structure hyperedges of $hg^1$. The system activates the following macro:

@*createSchema*
    **for each** $n_U \in hg_{on}$ **do** copy($hg, n_U, hg', h_{Sq}$)
@*end*

where copy is a polymorphic function that takes as parameters an SMH source, a component of the SMH source, an SMH target, and an hyperedge of the SMH target.

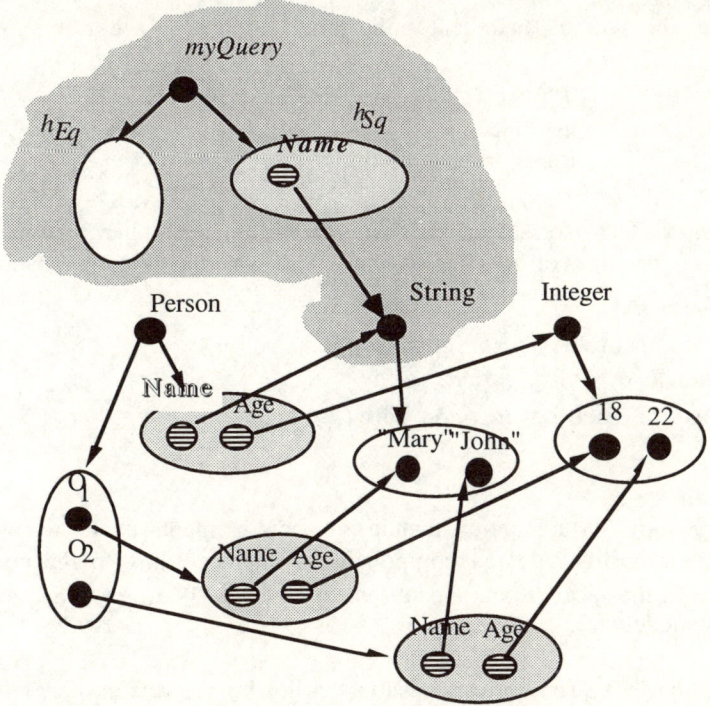

**Fig. 4.** Example situation for the application of @createSchema

---

[1] At this point we do not make any constraint on the "selectable" nodes. Once $hg$ represents a database by a particular data model, this phase will conform to the rules of the associated query model.

It is used for augmenting the SMH target by including in the target hyperedge the root of a subhypergraph $sh$. $sh$ is obtained by duplicating the subhypergraph of $hg_{on}$ rooted at the specified component, without duplicating identifiable nodes (this is a first case in which links may be created between $hg'$ and $hg$). Figure 4 illustrates the situation at the end of Phase 1 during the formulation of a query against the SMH described in Figure 1. In particular, the structure hyperedge of $hg'$ is obtained by selecting the unidentifiable node labeled $\mathcal{N}ame$ in the structure hyperedge belonging to $\mathcal{P}erson$ (the selected node is characterized by a shadowed label, while $hg'$ lies on a grey background).

Note that it is possible to select several unidentifiable nodes with the same label. Since maintaining such label for each of these nodes within a single structure hyperedge would violate constraint $\mathcal{C}_G{}^2$, the used approach is to suffix all labels with unique codes. A mapping table is handled by the system for retaining the correct correspondence between nodes in $hg$ and $hg'$ (this is necessary during the extension population).

The semantics of the macro $@createSchema$ in terms of its effect on $hg'$ is the following (if $e$ is a component of $hg$, we use the notation $e'$ for indicating its duplicate; the symbol $\cong$ indicates the label conformity according to the above rewriting rule):

$hg' := hg' \cup \{n_{U'} | n_U \in hg_{on}, \lambda_2(n_U) \cong \lambda_2(n_{U'})\}$
$\cup \{ <n_{U'}, n_I> | <n_U, n_I> \in hg_{on}\} \cup \{ h_G' | <n_U, h_G> \in hg_{on}\}$
$\cup \{ <n_{U'}, h_G'> | <n_U, h_G> \in hg_{on}\}$

*Phase* 2. The user selects (by **on** operations) a number of components of extension hyperedges of $hg$[1]. The system will activate the following macro:

$@retrieveResult$
    **if** compatibilityConstraint $\in \mathcal{C}_{DM}$
    **then** copy\*($hg_{on}, hg', h_{Eq}$)
    **else for each** $e \in hg_{on}$ **do** copy($hg, e, hg', h_{Eq}$)
$@end$

where copy\* is a function that inserts new elements in the result extension suitably composing selected component of $hg$, according to the compatibility constraint of the specific data model (an example will be given in Section 4 for the relational model).

In summary, a query corresponds to the following sequence, where # is the prefix for user's actions, and @ is the prefix for system actions.

---

[1] The specific query model will impose restrictions on the selectable components.

```
#start(<queryName>)
@query
      @initQuery
      #structureDefinition
      @createSchema
      #extensionDefinition
      @retrieveResult
@end
```

## 3.3 Example Application

SMHs can be regarded as a formal background to be used in the design of new visual interfaces. Actually, the end-user would not interact directly with an SMH using its primitives, but through a visual interaction environment designed as a mapping from SMHs to user-friendly structures. Also, a relevant application for SMHs is to have a formal tool in terms of which existing VQLs could be expressed and possibly compared. In the following we give an example which illustrates how a direct manipulation user interface can be associated with our notation.

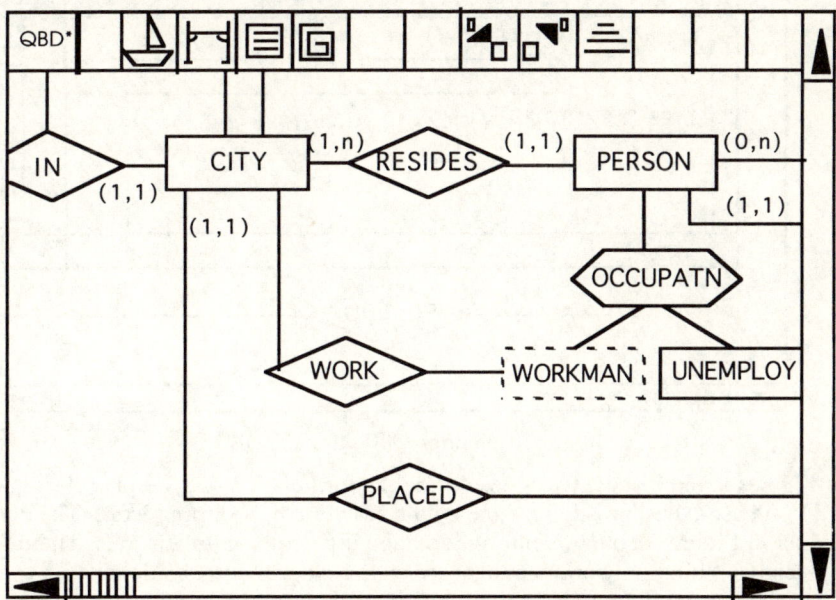

**Fig. 5.** Selection of the main entity in QBD*

The interface we illustrate adopts the well known diagrammatic representation of the Entity-Relationship model. In particular, we show some aspects of the QBD* query language [1]. QBD* is mainly a navigational language on Entity-Relationship diagrams, which as usual represent conceptual schemata. The user first interacts with the conceptual schema to understand its information content, and extracts the subschema of interest containing the concepts involved in the query, then, during the "navigation" activity, s/he may express the query, defining all its procedural characteristics. First a central concept, called *main concept,* is chosen, that can be seen as the entry point of the query, then two different types of primitives are available for navigating in the schema. The first one allows the user to follow paths of concepts, the other one is used for comparing two concepts which are not directly connected to each other. Conditions on the attributes are expressed by means of a window, where the list of the attributes is shown together with the elements involved in the comparison (i.e. constants, other attributes, etc.), and a set of icons suitable to formulate conditions on the attributes. Conditions are expressed selecting the attributes and the icon corresponding to the required operator.

The mapping between SMH and the semantic data models, such as the Entity-Relationship, has been formally defined in [7]. Roughly speaking, entities are associated with identifiable nodes, while entity attributes and relationships are associated with unidentifiable nodes collected in structure hyperedges.

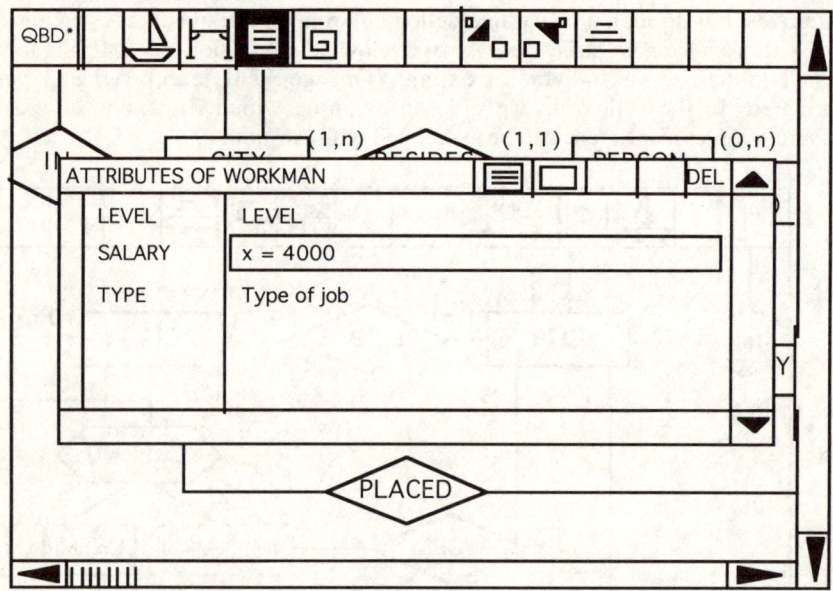

**Fig. 6.** Condition definition in QBD*

Figures 5 and 6 show two steps during the formulation of a simple select query in QBD* (Phase 0 has already be done by the selection of a starting icon). The database schema in Figure 5 contains information about persons and their jobs. The query to be issued is: "Find all workmen that earn exactly four thousands dollars". As we said before the crucial step is the selection of the main concept, i.e. the entity WORKMAN. The selection is performed by clicking the rectangle respresenting the entity on the screen, which gets highlighted (shown in dashed lines in Figure 5). In terms of our IPs, this action corresponds to Phase 1, in which all the nodes of the structure hyperedge representing the entity attributes are put on. The next step is the condition definition (Figure 6): the user types the desired constant in the SALARY field of the window containing the attributes of WORKMAN. In terms of IPs, this corresponds to Phase 2, in which all the nodes of the extension hyperedge connected to WORKMAN are put on if they verify the selection condition. Notice that in semantic models the extension hyperedge of an entity is a collection of identifiable nodes owning a structure conforming to the entity structure. In our example, an object in the extension hyperedge of WORKMAN will be put on if the unidentifiable "SALARY" node of its structure is connected to the identifiable node labeled 4.000.

## 4 Evaluation of the expressive power

In this section we show how a representation based exclusively on combination of **on/off** operations can be associated to the relational algebra [11]. The main issue to be faced for the definition of such representation is the formulation of single-operator queries, while complex queries may be formulated in an incremental way as a series of single-operator queries[1]. Hence, we will show in the following how each relational algebra operator can be expressed by a sequence of IPs (we denote with $-, \cup, \times, \Pi_A, \sigma_F$ the basic relational algebra operators, see [20]).

In the case of the relational model, we assume the database is represented by an SMH $db$ conforming to Definition 4. To force a generic SMH to be a representation of a relational database we need an additional set of constraints $\mathcal{C}'_{dm}$, presented in [8] and not listed here for the sake of brevity. We only need to say that a *compatibility constraint* ensures us that a tuple conforms to its relation schema, and a *set constraint* ensures us that no identical tuples belongs to the same extension hyperedge. The copy* function populates the extension of the result by copying (combinations of) $h_{tuple}$ set to **on** in $db$, in such a way that all the constraints of $\mathcal{C}'_{dm}$ are satisfied. In particular, the compatibility constraint and the set constraint make the resulting extension correct and complete, i.e., the resulting SMH is the correct representation of the expected result.

The simplest relational algebra expression is the single operand $r$, where $r$ is a relation of the database, that is a triple $r = <rn, h_{attr}, h_{inst}>$ in $db$, where $rn \in \mathcal{N}_{RN}$, $h_{attr} \in \mathcal{H}_{Attr}$, $h_{inst} \in \mathcal{H}_{Inst}$, with $h_{attr}$ and $h_{inst}$ originating from $rn$. In this case, the actions described in the above section are specialized into:

#structureDefin: on($db, n$), for each $n \in h_{Sch}$, with $h_{attr} = <rn, h_{Sch}>$;

#extensionDefin: on($db, h_{tup}$), for each $h_{tup} \in h_{ext}$, with $h_{inst} = <rn, h_{ext}>$;

and the effect of copy*($db_{on}, hg', h_{Eq}$) is:

**for each** $h_{tuple} \in db_{on}$ **do** copy($db, h_{tuple}, hg', h_{Eq}$).

Consider now a relational algebra expression $E_i$ whose outermost operator is one of union, difference, projection, selection, and product ($E_i$ can refer to both a relation of the database and the result of a previously formulated query). As already stated in Section 2.2, we use the notation $r_i = \mathcal{M}(E_i)$ for denoting the SMH representation of $E_i$. We recall that a relation is represented by a triple $r = <rn, h_{attr}, h_{inst}>$, where $rn \in \mathcal{N}_{RN}$, $h_{attr} \in \mathcal{H}_{Attr}$, $h_{inst} \in \mathcal{H}_{Inst}$, with $h_{attr}$ and $h_{inst}$ originating from $rn$.

---

[1] This choice derives from the "closure under queries" property of the relational model [20]

*Case 1*: The expression is $E = E_1 \cup E_2$. Let $r_1 = \mathfrak{M}(E_1) = \langle rn_1, h_{attr1}, h_{inst1}\rangle$ and $r_2 = \mathfrak{M}(E_2) = \langle rn_2, h_{attr2}, h_{inst2}\rangle$. The above actions are specialized into:

#structureDefin: on($db$, $n$), for each $n \in h_{Sch1}$, with $h_{attr1} = \langle rn, h_{Sch1}\rangle$;

#extensionDefin: on($db$, $h_{tuple}$), for each $h_{tuple} \in h_{ext1} \cup h_{ext2}$,

with $h_{inst1} = \langle rn, h_{ext1}\rangle$ and $h_{inst2} = \langle rn, h_{ext2}\rangle$;

and the effect of copy*($db_{on}$, $hg'$, $h_{Eq}$) is:

**for each** $h_{tuple} \in db_{on}$ **do**

$h_{Eq} := h_{Eq} \cup h'_{tuple}$, such that $h'_{tuple} \approx h_{tuple}$[1], $h'_{tuple}$ satisfies the compatibility constraint and $h_{Eq}$ satisfies the set constraint.

*Case 2*: The expression is $E = E_1 - E_2$. Following the same reasoning line we have:

#structureDefin: on($db$, $n$), for each $n \in h_{Sch1}$, with $h_{attr1} = \langle rn, h_{Sch1}\rangle$;

#extensionDefin: on($db$, $h_{tuple}$), for each $h_{tuple} \in h_{ext1} - h_{ext2}$,

with $h_{inst1} = \langle rn, h_{ext1}\rangle$ and $h_{inst2} = \langle rn, h_{ext2}\rangle$;

and the effect of copy*($db_{on}$, $hg'$, $h_{Eq}$) is:

**for each** $h_{tuple} \in db_{on}$ **do**

$h_{Eq} := h_{Eq} \cup h'_{tuple}$, such that $h'_{tuple} = h_{tuple}$, $h'_{tuple}$ satisfies the compatibility constraint and $h_{Eq}$ satisfies the set constraint.

*Case 3*: $E = \Pi_A(E_1)$. Let $r_1 = \mathfrak{M}(E_1) = \langle rn_1, h_{attr1}, h_{inst1}\rangle$. In this case, we have:

#structureDefin: on($db$, $n$), for each $n \in X$, where $X \subseteq h_{Sch1}$, with $h_{attr1} = \langle rn, h_{Sch1}\rangle$, and $X$ is the set of nodes corresponding to attributes in $A$;

#extensionDefin: on($db$, $h_{tuple}$), for each $h_{tuple} \in h_{ext1}$, with $h_{inst1} = \langle rn, h_{ext1}\rangle$;

and the effect of copy*($hg_{on}$, $hg'$, $h_{Eq}$) is:

**for each** $h_{tuple} \in hg_{on}$ **do**

$h_{Eq} := h_{Eq} \cup h'_{tuple}$, such that $h'_{tuple} \subseteq h_{tuple}$[2], $h'_{tuple}$ satisfies the compatibility constraint and $h_{Eq}$ satisfies the set constraint.

---

[1] Given $h$ and $h' \in \mathcal{H}_{Tuple}$, we say that $h' \approx h$ when $|h| = |h'|$, $\lambda_2(h) = \lambda_2(h')$, and for each pair $n$, $n'$ such that $n \in h$, $n' \in h'$, and $\lambda_2(n) = \lambda_2(n')$, it holds that $n$ and $n'$ are connected to the same $v \in h_{set}$.

[2] Given $h$ and $h' \in \mathcal{H}_{Tuple}$, we say that $h' \subseteq h$ when $|h'| \leq |h|$, $\lambda_2(h') \subseteq \lambda_2(h)$, and for each pair $n$, $n'$ such that $n \in h$, $n' \in h'$, and $\lambda_2(n) = \lambda_2(n')$, it holds that $n$ and $n'$ are connected to the same $v \in h_{set}$ and $h_{set}$ is connected to $d \in \mathfrak{N}_D$, which is in turn connected to $n$.

*Case 4*: $E=\sigma_F(E_1)$. Let $r_1 = \mathcal{M}(E_1) = \,<rn_1, h_{attr1}, h_{inst1}>$. Following Ullman (Lemma 3.5 in [20]), we may assume that $F$ is a simple selection either of the form $a_1 \Theta v$ or of the form $a_1 \Theta a_2$, where $a_1$ and $a_2$ are attributes of $E_1$, and $v$ is a value in $dom(a_1)$. In this case:

#structureDefin: on($db$, $n$), for each $n \in h_{Sch1}$, with $h_{attr1} = \,<rn, h_{Sch1}>$;

#extensionDefin: on($db$, $h_{tuple}$), for each $h_{tuple} \in h_{ext1}$ (with $h_{inst1} = \,<rn, h_{ext1}>$) which verifies the selection condition, specialized into:

    a) there exists an arc $<n, v'>$, where $n \in h_{tuple}$, $\lambda_2(n) = a_1$, and $v'$ represents a value for which $\Theta\, v$ is true;

    b) there exist $<n_1, v'>$ and $<n_2, v''>$, where $n_1, n_2 \in h_{tuple}$, $\lambda_2(n_1) = a_1$, $\lambda_2(n_2) = a_2$, and $v'$ and $v''$ represent two values $v'$ and $v''$ such that $v' \Theta v''$.

and the effect of copy*($db_{on}$, $hg'$, $h_{Eq}$) is:

**for each** $h_{tuple} \in db_{on}$ **do**

    $h_{Eq} := h_{Eq} \cup h'_{tuple}$, such that $h'_{tuple} \approx h_{tuple}$, $h'_{tuple}$ satisfies the compatibility constraint and $h_{Eq}$ satisfies the set constraint.

*Case 5*: The expression is $E = E_1 \times E_2$. Let $r_1 = \mathcal{M}(E_1) = \,<rn_1, h_{attr1}, h_{inst1}>$ and $r_2 = \mathcal{M}(E_2) = \,<rn_2, h_{attr2}, h_{inst2}>$. In this case we have that:

#structureDefin: on($db$, $n$), for each $n \in h_{Sch1} \cup h_{Sch2}$, with $h_{attr1} = \,<rn, h_{Sch1}>$ and $h_{attr2} = \,<rn, h_{Sch2}>$ (notice that name duplications in the two schemata are automatically solved by suffixing);

#extensionDefin: on($db$, $h_{tuple}$), for each $h_{tuple} \in h_{ext1} \cup h_{ext2}$, with $h_{inst1} = \,<rn, h_{ext1}>$ and $h_{inst2} = \,<rn, h_{ext2}>$;

and the effect of copy*($db_{on}$, $hg'$, $h_{Eq}$) is:

**for each** pair $h_{tuple1}, h_{tuple2} \in db_{on}$, with $h_{tuple1} \in h_{ext1}$ and $h_{tuple2} \in h_{ext2}$, **do**

    $h_{Eq} := h_{Eq} \cup h'_{tuple}$, such that $h'_{tuple} = h_{tuple1} \times h_{tuple2}$[1], $h'_{tuple}$ satisfies the compatibility constraint and $h_{Eq}$ satisfies the set constraint.

Summarizing, the above result shows that the IPs, applied to an SMH representing a relational database, allows us to express at least the first-order queries, as the relational algebra do.

---

[1] Given $h_1$, $h_2$ and $h' \in \mathcal{H}_{Tuple}$, we say that $h' = h_1 \times h_2$ when $|h| = |h_1| + |h_2|$, $\lambda_2(h') \cong \lambda_2(h_1) \cup \lambda_2(h_2)$, and for each pair $n'$, $n_1$ such that $n' \in h'$, $n_1 \in h_1$, it holds that $n'$ and $n_1$ are connected to the same $v \in h_{set}$, and for each pair $n'$, $n_2$ such that $n' \in h'$, $n_2 \in h_2$, it holds that $n'$ and $n_2$ are connected to the same $v' \in h_{set}$.

## 5. Conclusions

In this paper we proposed the Structure Modeling Hypergraph as a database representation tool usable as a formal counterpart for visual interfaces. We showed how SMHs can be queried by formal systems closed under queries (the result of querying an SMH is still an SMH). Towards this aim we introduced a basic direct manipulation IP, namely the selection of an SMH element. A precise semantics is given to well-formed sequences of IPs, which can express a large set of meaningful queries. In particular, it has been proven that the IPs, applied to an SMH representing a relational database, allow us to express at least all the first-order queries.

## References

1. M. Angelaccio, T. Catarci, G. Santucci: QBD*: A graphical query language with recursion. IEEE Trans. on Software Engineering, 16, 1150-1163 (1990).
2. P. Atzeni, P.P. Chen: Completeness of query languages for the entity relationship model. In: P.P. Chen (ed.): Proc. of the 2nd Intl. Conf. on the Entity Relationship Approach to Information Modelling and Analysis, Washington D.C., North Holland, 111-124 (1981).
3. C. Batini, T. Catarci, M. F. Costabile, S. Levialdi: Visual query systems. Technical Report, No. 04.91, Dipartimento di Informatica e Sistemistica, Università di Roma "La Sapienza" (1991).
4. J. Bertin: Graphics and graphic information processing, Berlin: Walter de Gruyter & Co. 1981.
5. J. Bertin: Semiology of graphics, London: The Univ. of Wisconsin Press 1983.
6. H. Boley: Directed recursive labelnode hypergraphs: a new representation language. Artificial Intelligence, 9, 49-85 (1977).
7. T.Catarci, L.Tarantino: Structure modeling hypergraphs: a complete representation for databases. In: Proc. of the 3rd Intl. Conf. on Database and Expert System Applications - DEXA'92, Valencia, Spain (1992).
8. T.Catarci, L.Tarantino: A hypergraph-based framework for visual interaction with databases. Technical Report, Dipartimento di Informatica e Sistemistica, Universita' di Roma "La Sapienza", in printing (1994).
9. S. K. Chang: Principles of pictorial information systems design. Englewood Cliffs, NJ: Prentice-Hall 1989.
10. E. F. Codd: A relational model for large shared data banks. Communication ACM, 13, 6 (1970).
11. E. F. Codd: Relational completeness of database sub-languages. In: R.Rustin (ed.): Data Base Systems, Englewood Cliffs, NJ: Prentice-Hall 1972, pp. 65-98.
12. M.P Consens, A.O. Mendelzon: Graphlog: a visual formalism for real life recursion. In: Proc. of the ACM Symp. on Principles of Database Systems, pp. 404-416 (1990).
13. M.P Consens, A.O. Mendelzon: Hy+: A hygraph-based query and visualization system. (also video presentation). Proc. of the ACM SIGMOD International Conference on Management of Data, pp. 511-516 (1993).
14. I. F. Cruz, A.O. Mendelzon, P. T. Wood: $G^+$: Recursive queries without recursion. In: Proc. of the 2nd International Conference on Expert Database Systems, pp. 355-368 (1988).
15. A. D'Atri, P. Di Felice, M. Moscarini: Dynamic query interpretation in relational databases. Information Systems, 14, 3, 195-204.

16. M. Gyssens, J. Paredaens, D. Van Gucht: A graph-oriented object model for database end-user interfaces. In: Proc. ACM SIGMOD Conference on the Management of Data, Atlantic City, USA, pp. 24-33 (1991).
17. D. Harel: On visual formalism. Comm. of the ACM, 31, 514-530 (1988).
18. D. Sacca': Closures of database hypergraphs. Journal of the ACM, 32, 4, 774-803 (1985).
19. B. Shneiderman: Direct manipulation: a step beyond programming languages. IEEE Computer, 16, 57-69 (1983).
20. J. D. Ullman: Principles of Database and Knowledge-Base Systems, Vol. I. Rockville, MD: Computer Science Press 1988 .
21. M. M. Zloof: Query-by-Example: a database language. IBM Syst.Journal, 16, 4, 324-343 (1977).

# SFQI: Semi-Formal Query Language Interface to Relational Databases

M.N. MdSap

Department of Computer Science, University of Strathclyde

Glasgow, United Kingdom

D.R. McGregor

Department of Computer Science, University of Strathclyde

Glasgow, United Kingdom

### Abstract

Semi-Formal Query Language Interface (SFQI) is a user interface for interaction with database systems. SFQI is based on a Semi-Formal Query Language (SFQL) which is an enhancement of SQL. SFQI provides facilities for guiding users in performing database querying, such as formulating a valid database query, refining user-misconceptions and modifying database query misconstructions. The syntax of SFQL is not as rigid as in most database query languages. The system provides logical database navigation and users are not required to know, in detail, the structure of the database being queried.

## 1 Introduction

Providing sufficient system resources on the technical side is not enough - a system must be designed to match the needs and the abilities of its end-users. A successful computer system, targetted for end-users, must have an easy-to-use and powerful user interface. This is an important criterion for establishing the system's acceptability by the end-users, since they judge the system's capabilities while interacting with the database system via the user interface.

In order to find another method of providing an interface which is as powerful as formal database query languages, while remaining easy to learn and use, we developed a Semi-Formal Query Language Interface (SFQI). SFQI is a cooperative interface which relieves users of the impedence mismatch that they experience in interacting with database systems. It supports SFQL, an English-like query language allowing users to phrase queries in formal language with restricted English expressions.

The remainder of this paper is organised as follows: Section 2 highlights the motivation for the development of the interface. Section 3 describes the interface's philosophy. Section 4 gives the overview of the system. Section 5 gives examples of using the interface to access data from a sample database. Section 6 describes, in general, the implementation of the interface. Section 7 briefly explains the evaluations of SFQI. Section 8 relates the work on the interface with other works toward developing an easy-to-use interface to databases. Section 9 explains future research work to be carried out. Section 10 summarises the paper. The outputs of the queries in section 5 and the sample database are given in Appendices 1 and 2 respectively.

## 2 Problem Requirements

One of the problems facing the end-users of a database system is to gain a competent understanding of the associated query languages. In order to help end-users, database management systems (DBMS's) provides a user-friendly interface such as QBE [27] and a non-procedural data manipulation language such as SQL [1]. However, several human factors studies [22, 24] have found that end-users still find these languages very difficult to use for querying databases. Formulating a query with SQL is often time consuming and susceptible to errors. It requires skills and knowledge about the syntax and semantics of the language, as well as the structure of a database. Consequently, fast and easy access to a database can only be achieved either if the users are database experts or if they are supported by a powerful access tool.

A new database query language using natural language has been introduced. An interface system, i.e Natural Language Interface (NLI) has been developed to use natural language as a query language. To help the end-users of the database systems, many facilities have been incorporated into the NLI systems.

Looking at the work on NLIs and the conventional database query languages like QUEL and SQL, we can see that some of the techniques that have been implemented in NLIs can also be implemented in Formal Query Languages (FQL). Many of the shortcomings of FQLs can be overcome by extending them, by giving more intelligence to the parser and incorporating much knowledge into the interface.

The system can be developed to incorporate interactive query facilities, with a query language that resembles natural language, or one which is at least easy to learn and use. This means furnishing the system's users with a powerful yet simple to use language for information retrieval. Artificial languages, like SQL, would have tremendous potential if some of the features of natural language systems were added. For example, SQL could be improved by providing automatic logical navigation, spelling correction, spelling guide, name completion, synonyms, concepts, improved editing (eg. with a mouse), advance help facilities, ellipsis query and semantic checking. In this way, less experienced users would be served much better without losing the reliability of an artificial language.

## 3 The Interface

### 3.1 The Motivations

The motivations behind the Semi-Formal Query Interface are as follows:

1. Many of the problems users experience with FQLs appear to arise from the following issues:

    (a) The user does not understand the context and semantics of the data available. Thus, for example, a user who is fully competent in the

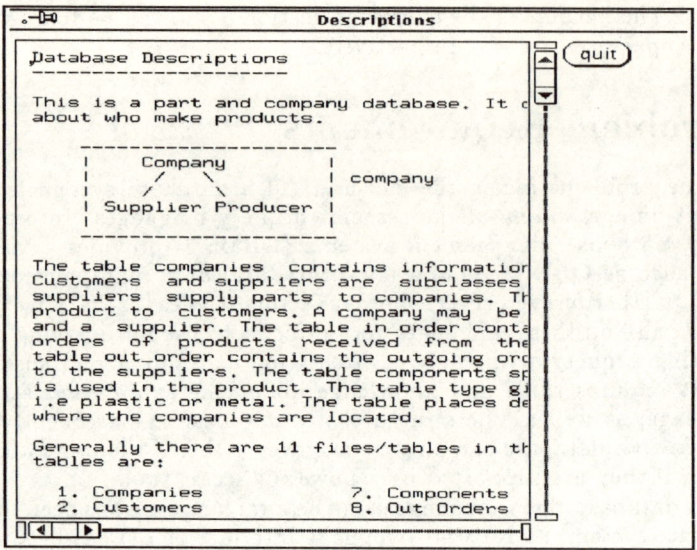

Figure 1: Database Descriptions

general syntax and semantics of the query language, often may not be able to proceed.

The interface has to assist the user by providing this missing domain metadata.

(b) The user may understand the domain semantics and the general syntax and semantics of the query language but may, nonetheless, be unsuccessful in acquiring information because of a mismatch of data vocabulary.

The interface has to assist by providing appropriate lexical matching and synonym information and possibly meta data to the user.

(c) The user may understand both the previous areas (items a and b) but may be unfamiliar with the language itself. A simplified language may be provided for the interface.

2. If an FQL is provided with many guiding facilities, as in NLI systems, users can still effectively interact with database systems using the language. In addition, the expressive power of the FQL is retained.

## 3.2 Querying A Database

In SFQI, a user who is unfamiliar with the current database can obtain a description (Fig. 1). Following this, the user can obtain the database graph (Fig. 2). This shows the structure graph of the database. By 'clicking' on the various relation names etc., the user can obtain a simple view of the database contents. For example, if the user clicks on 'suppliers', a suppliers table is displayed. In principle, any other words can be activated in this way.

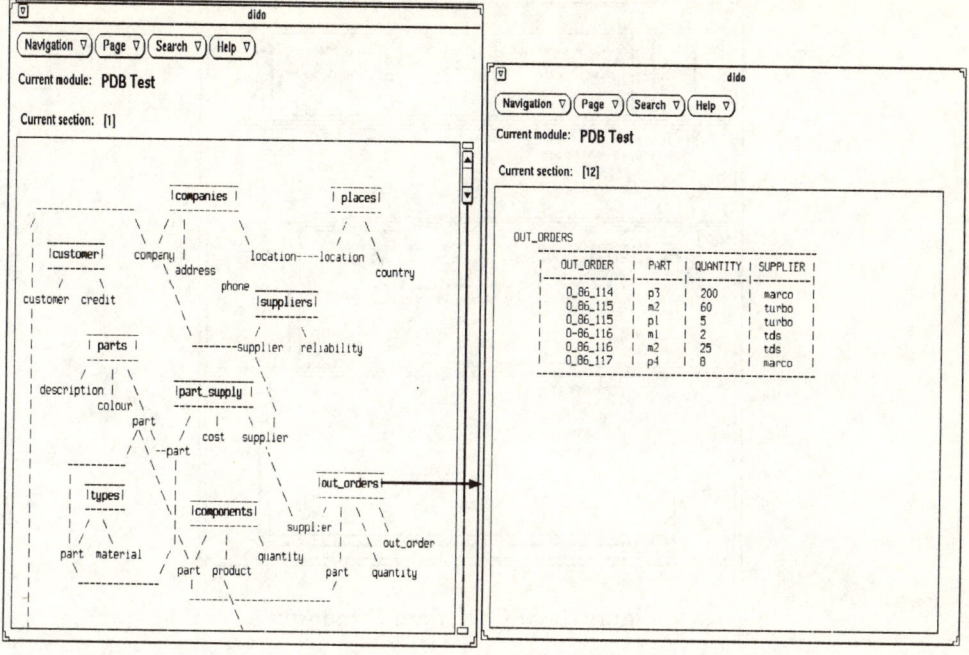

Figure 2: Database Graph

This is a simple dynamic approach which enables the novice user to begin interrogating the system.

Where the query is more complex, the user can initiate a dialogue in the provided query language (Fig. 3). A query is formulated by typing the query into the User Query Window. This typing activates the "Spelling Guidance" popup window, indicating the available vocabulary compatible with the user's typing so far.

The user indicates that the query formulation is complete by 'clicking' the Process button in the adjacent window. The query is processed, and, if successful, its translation is output in the target database query language window (Fig. 3). Finally, the corresponding output from the database is displayed in the output window (Fig. 3).

Thus, in summary, the philosophy is to continue where possible to make use of the formal query language (with its advantages of unambiguous interpretation), but to provide facilities by adding 'syntactic sugar' or 'semantic sugar' to sweeten the user's task. One advantage of this operation is that the user may decide what type of and amount of sugar he requires in order to complete the task. Further the quantity of user-controlled sugar can vary as the user becomes more competent with the system. Other important features (like spelling correction, syntax and semantic corrections, logical database navigation and modifying database query misconstruction) have also been integrated into the system to further enhance the query formulation.

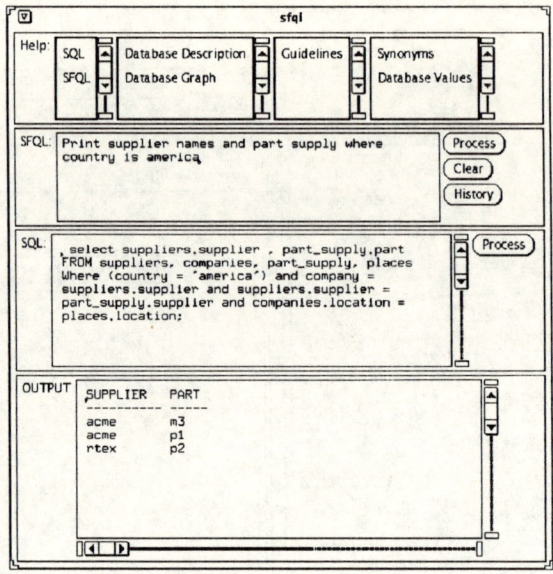

Figure 3: SFQI's Main Window

## 4 Overview of SFQI

In implementing SFQI, we have aimed to make the system as easy to use as possible. To achieve this, wherever possible, we follow the techniques used in NLI. While SFQI is an easy to use tool, it maintains the full features and power of the language, i.e. SQL.

Wherever possible, users are allowed to use noise words to allow a more natural query formulation and to make queries self-explanatory.

Also, as users often violate the syntax and semantics of a query language, in SFQI we detect the syntax and semantic errors and whenever possible correct them.

In this section, a brief description of the system is presented. A detailed description of the SFQI architecture and implementation is given in [18].

### 4.1 SFQI Architecture

Fig. 4 shows the architecture of SFQI. As depicted in the figure, the main component of SFQI is the User Interface Window, the Parser, the Dictionary and the Query Generator.

Arrows indicate the direction of information flow. A user's query is passed to the Lexical Analyser, Syntax Analyser, Semantic Analyser and Query Generator prior to the DBMS's Access Mechanism. In parsing the query, the parsers perform their operations with the knowldge given by the Dictionary. The Steiner Tree mechanism is used to navigate through the database relations and to find tables relevant to the query.

Readers who are interested in the architecture of SFQI are referred to [18].

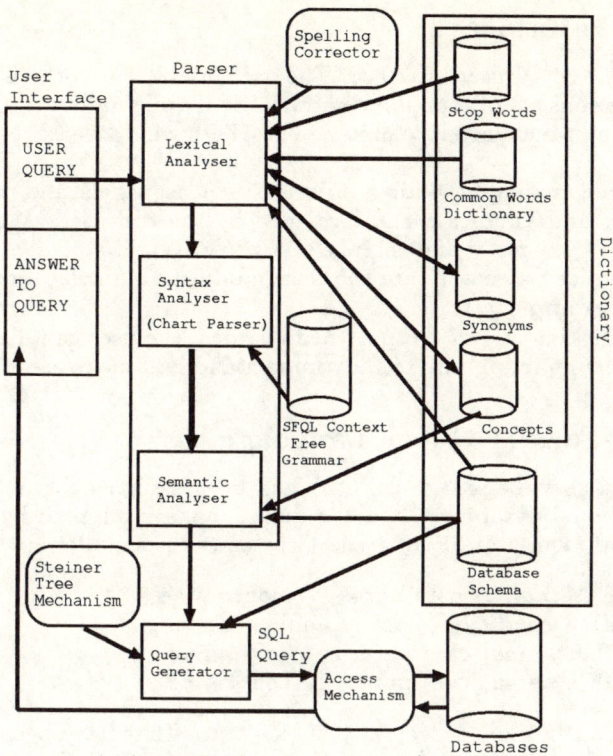

Figure 4: SFQI Architecture

## 4.2 The Data Model

The implicit semantics of the system are that the user is engaged in querying a Relational Database. Although in this paper we focus on the Relational Ratabase, the basic idea can also be extended to other data models as well.

In defining the data model, we use exactly the same definition as in the Relational Data Model (RDM). A database is composed of a collection of relations that contain tuples representing real-world entities or relationships. A relation has attributes of fixed types that represent properties of the entities and relationships and a primary key. A candidate key is a sequence of attributes of the relations which, when taken together, uniquely identify each tuple. A primary key is a single set of attributes that is used to uniquely identify instances of a relation. If there is more than one candidate key, then one of them is arbitrarily chosen as the primary key.

Each attribute has an associated domain and each domain has an associated type. Names of relations, attributes, and domains must all be distinct. This means that the same name cannot be used for a relation and an attribute, or a relation and a domain, or an attribute and a domain. However, attributes in different relations may use the same name if they are in the same domain. In this paper we shall consider only two types, STRING and NUMBER.

## 4.3 User Interface

Fig. 3 shows the SFQI user interface. The user interface is composed of a main window which consists of four subwindows: the Help Window, SFQL Window, SQL Window and the Output Window. The SFQL window accepts user queries in SFQL.

This module manages window objects, such as panels and buttons, and their contents, and handles events provided by the end-user. When the user operates the SFQI window and enters a query in SFQL, it activates the analyser modules. Users can also activate the help modules to display the contents of the database, examples, etc.

Thus, by clicking any of the provided buttons, the user can display various guiding facilities enabling him to fully understand and make use of the system.

## 4.4 Semi-Formal Query Language

Semi-Formal Query Language (SFQL) has been designed as a language for querying relational databases. It is the main language adopted by SFQI.

The general format of SFQL's select statement is as follows:

> SELECT $name_1$ conj $name_2$ ...conj $name_m$
> WHERE $condition_1$ conj ...conj $condition_n$
> GROUP $name_1$ conj $name_2$ ...conj $name_r$
> ORDER $name_1$ conj $name_2$ ...conj $name_s$

SELECT can be replaced by any of the words that have been assigned as synonyms for the word select. Some of the words are Get, Find, List, Display and Retrieve.

WHERE can be replaced by any of the words that have been assigned as synonyms to the word where. Some of the words are in, for, when, and if.

$name_1, name_2, ......, name_n$ can be the attribute name, synonym or concept. Values can be either character or numeric. $<condition>$ is in the form of $name_1 <comp> name_2$, or $name_1 <comp> value_1$, or a combination of such terms with the logical connectors 'and' and 'or'. The comparator $<comp>$ can be one of the following words or phrases: is equal, is not equal, is greater, is less, is greater or equal, is less or equal, or a synonym of one of these.

As in SQL, the answer to this query is defined by a product of all the relations named in the From clause (the relevant tables for the query being derived using Lin Dekang's approximation algorithm [12] for finding the connection between the tables involved in the query being posed), followed by a selection according to the condition in the Where clause, followed by a projection onto the attributes named in the Select clause.

## 4.5 Spelling Correction

Composing a syntactically correct query is one of the common problems in SQL. Since SQL will only accept correct commands, a user of SQL must spell all words in a query correctly. Even simple errors require re-keying the entire query.

Like many NLIs, SFQI provides spelling correction. Spelling error detection and correction is essential, since SFQL relies on user input, where typing mistakes can occur quite frequently. Querying databases to obtain information requires the user to have knowledge of a query language and underlying data. However, due to the inevitable unreliability of human memory [3], user queries are subject to various types of failure. These often include spelling mistakes.

In SFQI, the type of errors covered include omission (customr, custmer), insertion (customerr), replacement (castomer) and change of position (customre). The spelling correction is based on Owolabi's algorithm [20] for spelling correction.

SFQL also provides a guiding facility for word spelling. It will display in the "Spelling Guidance" popup window the correct spelling for a word that a user has begun to type. In this way the user will be aware of the correct spelling of the word that the system understands.

## 4.6 Syntactic Correction

In any query language, users frequently make small syntactical errors. SQL studies of syntactic and logical errors, over the years, have shown that the percentage of incorrect SQL queries have varied from 12% to 75% [7, 21, 26]. Most prevalent among these were simple mistakes.

To provide maximum assistance in query formulation, there must be a mechanism which detects and reports syntactic errors in the most convenient way(s). In SFQL the Syntactic Corrector employs its knowledge of syntax to assist the user in making a syntactically correct query before the query is passed to the parser.

Syntactic correction is performed on the different parts of the query statement: Select Clause, Where Clause, Order Clause and Group clause. Most syntactic correction is done to the Where clause. Such corrections include:

1. Insert the default comparator "=" where a comparator is expected, i.e. between two attributes or between an attribute and a value.

2. Insert the default connecter "and" where a connecter is expected, i.e. between two subexpressions.

3. Discard certain bad input words.

Syntactic correction for the Select clause includes:

1. Insert "," between the attribute names.

2. Discard bad input words.

In effect, the aim of the syntactic correction is to coerce the input query into the syntax of the SFQL and, as a result, enhance the parsing process. With this capability, the user is also free to act in an exploratory way, trying out potential words, without being committed to them.

## 4.7 Semantic Correction

Another type of mistake users often make is violation and misconception of the entities and relationships in a database. For example, within the Where Clause, users often give incorrect conditions, or assign a wrong value to an attribute.

SFQL will detect this error, and display to the users which value should be assigned to the attribute, or which attribute should be assigned to the value stated in the query. This means that a value being assigned to an attribute in all conditions of a Where clause must be from the domain of the attribute, and the value must also be available in the column of the attribute.

Specifically, the Semantic Corrector will verify that any condition of the form $a_1 < comp > a_2$ where $a_2$ can be a value or an attribute-name, the domain of attribute $a_2$ must be the same domain with the domain of $a_1$. In addition, if $a_2$ is a value, it must be available in the column of the attribute $a_1$. This is important to ensure that the result of the condition is valid.

Generally, if there is any mismatch, our approach has been to notify users of the problem, i.e. 1) Which constraint was violated and 2) Which attribute the value should belong to.

Since users are given immediate feedback and a means of correcting errors, this provides a valuable service in constructing a valid query. Also, this kind of arbitrary error recovery can greatly enhance the usability of the system. The user no longer needs to fear the catastrophic consequences of mistakes and the system can be much more tolerant of human error.

## 4.8 Null Answer

In querying a database, there is always a chance that a user's query will produce a null answer. The main reason for this is that there is not enough checking of the conditions in the Where Clause. As an example, consider the following conditions.

```
where country = England
  and company = Marco
```

These conditions can result in a null answer because of one of the following reasons:

1. There is a country called England but there is no company called Marco.

2. There is no country called England but there is a company called Marco.

3. There is no country called England and there is no company called Marco.

4. There is a country called England and there is a company called Marco but Marco is not in England.

Now, suppose a user gets a null answer. The user will easily understand that there is a company called England and there is a company called Marco stored in the database but Marco is not located in England. This can be concluded because during the semantic processing, the parser will first check whether there is a country called England and whether there is a company called Marco. The parser will popup a "Check-Value" popup window if the data is not in the database or the value is not found in the column of the specified attribute name.

The following example shows SFQL's technique of tracking a null answer. Suppose the user gives conditions:

where country = China and
company = Marco

where actually there is no country called China stored in the database.

When the semantic parser is processing the condition "country = China", it will ask the user to modify this condition. While asking for a new country, the system will display all the countries that are available in the column of attribute name country (Fig. 5). In other words the system guides the user towards choosing a country that is available in the database.

In this way, in SFQI, if the query will result in a null answer, the user can easily conclude that Marco is not located in that country (i.e. the new country given by the user for correcting the condition "country = China").

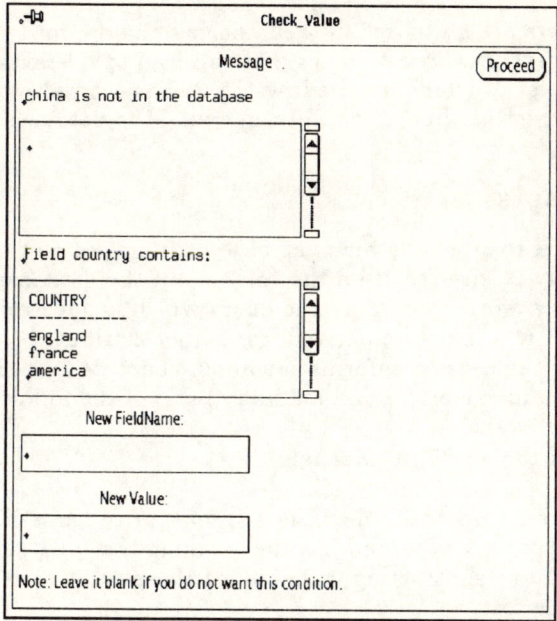

Figure 5: "Check-Value" Popup Window

## 4.9 Synonyms

The main reason for providing synonyms is to allow the user to create a synonym which gives a table, an attribute or a value an alternative name. They may want an alternative name that is more suitable in their understanding of the global concept.

The Synonym table stores information about synonyms. It is implemented as an auxiliary table of the following form:

Synonym table=(Word, Synonym)

During initial parsing the parser will detect any word or combination of words that is not in the system. The user is required to tell the system whether or not these words refer to a synonym. In doing so, the system offers a list of names (synonyms of the attribute names) and values that are available in the database, to guide the user in creating a new synonym.

Since users can define their own synonyms, there is a possibility that a defined synonym refers to two or more attributes in the database. For example, salary may be defined as a synonym for both gross_salary (as expressed in units of currency) and salary_level (as expressed by a code). During the lexical analysis, when the system detects that there is more than one attribute referred to for a given synonym, it will display a "Multiple Meaning" popup window, listing all the words (i.e. attributes) that have been assigned for the synonym. Users are required to select the appropriate attribute according to their intentions.

In SFQL, users are quite free in their choice of names for tables, attributes and values. However, awkward names that can lead to mistakes are not advisable. The extra set of words required by the user is entered into the synonym table via an interactive window or while querying the database.

### 4.10 Concepts

A concept is used to store the meaning of a word or group of words where its meaning can only be derived from the contents of the database. For example the user can list a word "profit" in the query which is not explicitly stored in the database but which can be derived from other attributes.

The Concept table stores information about concepts that the word can be related to. It is implemented as an auxiliary table of the following form:

Concept table=(Word,Meaning)

An example of a Concept table tuple is (profit, price - cost) which states the word profit is a concept word and has the meaning that $profit = price - cost$, i.e. it is calculated by subtracting values in attribute name price with the value in attribute name cost.

Users can define concepts via an interactive window or while querying the database. In defining the concept, the system will highlight to the users what attributes are available in the database. The system will also provide a mechanism to detect whether the concept has been correctly formulated. In doing this the system stores a number of formulae in the concept table.

The notion of concept in SFQI is quite similar to views in many database systems. However, SFQI stores world concepts and provides a mechanism to check that the user-defined concept is in accordance with the world concepts.

### 4.11 Ellipsis

One of the important features of SFQI is Ellipsis. It is a phenomenon in natural language where there is a possibility of omitting information where it can be recovered by the context. This allows complex and long statements to be expressed concisely and provides continuity of dialogue. This phenomenon, which may significantly shorten a dialogue sequence, is handled by most of today's NLIs.

Users can combine or replace part of the previous query, either in the Where clause or Select clause, by stating to SFQI that it is of type ellipsis [16, 17]. This is done by giving a special symbol i.e. #, at the beginning of the query and SFQI will be notified that it is an ellipsis query. When SFQI discovers #, it will process the query and fill in any missing information by referring to the query which has preceeded it.

At the present implementation, the system only pointing the last query that was issued for processing ellipsis. The reason for this is that we want to minimise the use of storage for keeping the clause that has been parsed. At present the newest query will replace the query stored.

The examples in section 5 show several forms of ellipsis query that the user can use in SFQI.

## 4.12 Ergonomic And Cognitive Considerations

A fundamental consideration in designing interfaces in general and SFQI in particular is the ergonomic and cognitive aspect of the interface. The interface should provide many facilities in helping and guiding users to formulate queries.

With regards to these factors, in designing and implementing SFQI we have taken, amongst others, the following aspects into consideration:

1. SFQI should require the minimun amount of time to learn by users.

2. The expected rates of errors committed by users are minimum.

3. Users can easily understand and remember the syntax and semantics of SFQL.

4. SFQI should be able to satisfy users subjectively. This can be achieved, for example by providing on-line help facilities, etc.

5. SFQI should provide facilities for spelling correction, syntax correction and semantic corrections.

6. Users should be freed from knowing the physical and logical structure of the database.

7. SFQI should provide users with meta-level information.

8. The format of displayed information should be clear, yet simple and easy to understand. SFQI should allow users to use a mouse, pointing devices, etc. to help them in performing their tasks.

This means that as far as possible SFQI has minimised the memory load that users have to bear. Users of SFQI are not required to remember the contents of databases. They can easily refer to the meta-level information, before, during or after formulating their queries.

# 5 Examples

## 5.1 A Sample Database

For the purpose of giving examples of querying a database using SFQI, we used a database of companies and parts.

The semantic interpretation of this database is as follows:

Customers and suppliers are subclasses of companies. The supplier supplies parts to companies. The company sells products to customers. A company may be both a customer and a supplier. The table *in_orders* contains the incoming orders of products received from the customers. The table *out_orders* contains the outgoing orders of parts sent to the suppliers. The table *components* specifies which part is used in the product. The table *types* gives the type of part, i.e. plastic etc. The table *places* describes the country where the companies are located.

The schema of the database are as follows.

> companies(**company**, address, phone, location)
> customers(**customer**, credit)
> suppliers(**supplier**, reliability)
> products(**product**, cost)
> parts(**part**, colour, description)
> in_orders(**in_order, product**, quantity, customer)
> out_orders(**out_order**, part, quantity, supplier)
> part_supply(**part, supplier**, cost)
> components(**product**, part, quantity)
> types(**part**, material)
> places(**location**, country)

The fields in bold font are key fields.

Fig. 8 in Appendix 2 shows the contents of the sample database.

## 5.2 Querying The Database

Suppose a user wants to get information about customer name and customer address for company acme or marco. In SFQI he can input the query as:

> $SFQL_1$ : List customer name and customer address
>     where company name is acme or marco
>   or
> $SFQL_2$: List customer name and address for acme
>     and marco

Supposing the user input the first query, i.e. $SFQL_1$. Next suppose the user wants to know the country as well. He can do this by typing another query as:

> $SFQL_3$: List customer name, customer address
>     and country where company name
>     is acme or marco

or, since the last query is just to get extra information from the previous query, he can use SFQI's ellipsis facility by just typing:

$SFQL_4$: # and country

If the user inputs query $SFQL_4$, the system will know that it is an ellipsis query for the Select Clause. In generating the SQL query, the generator will concatenate this ellipsis query with the previous query, i.e. the system will consider "# and country" as part of the previous query.

Next, say the user also want to know the address of a customer whose name is tds. Using the ellipsis query, he can type in the query as:

$SFQL_5$:# or company = tds.

In $SFQL_5$, the parser will understand the query as an ellipsis and it will be used in the Where Clause. During query generation, the query generator will concatenate $SFQL_5$ with the conditions already existing in the Where Clause. This means that the last ellipsis query is equivalent to: "List part supply where company name is acme or marco or tds".

The outputs for these queries are shown in Appendix 1. Other examples of querying the database are shown in [16, 17].

# 6 Implementation

Most of the components of our current prototype are implemented in Objective-C. The system runs under UNIX environment. The spelling corrector for detecting and correcting mispelled words is implementent in C++. The user interface's windows have been developed on X-Windows.

# 7 System Evaluations

As to date, a set of users trials has been carried out to evaluate SFQI. The interface has been evaluated through on-line interaction with users.

In the experiment, thirty one users (post-graduate and undergraduate students) were asked to evaluate SFQI as compared to SQL and BNQL (Basic Natural Query Language) developed at IKBS's research group, University of Strathclyde. They were grouped into two types of users: i) Novice end-users - Users who did not know SQL and ii) Database end-users - Users who already knew SQL. They were given a set of questions to query a database using the three languages.

At the end of the experiment, they were given a set of questionnaires to evaluate the languages. For evaluation purposes, we also considered the effort required by subjects to learn these languages. The amount of help required by users serves as a measure of the difficulty of learning the language. Less need for help indicates that an interface is more intuitive. The better interface would be the one on which more subjects were able to complete the tasks.

The results of this experiment showed that in general BNQL was strongly preferred by novice end-users and SQL was strongly preferred by database end-users. On the other hand both groups of end-users considered SFQL was an average language, i.e. the difficulties and ease-of-use was between SQL and BNQL.

One of our conclusions from this experiment is that a carefully designed English-like query language has a tendency to improve the efficiency of user-system communication significantly. Although we have only implemented parts of the features, the system has already achieved good results.

## 8 Related Work

Many new graphical interfaces and query languages have been invented to help end-users in querying databases. These include Graphical Query Language (GQL): QBE [27], QPE [4, 5], PICASSO [11]; Natural Language Interfaces (NLIs): INTELLECT [9, 10], TEAM [8, 15], LOQUI [23], Kaleidoscope [2]; and formal query languages (FQL): FLEX [19]. SFQI can be categorised under FQL but provides many enhancements to the present SQL.

Like most NLIs (interfaces based on natural language), SFQI also provides users with meta-level information. This is important since as found by [25], users who did not know the stored data might have queried the wrong information from the databases. As in PICASSO and QPE, in SFQI, attributes of the database are displayed on the screen. SFQI's users, at any time can refer to the database graph to look at the data and meta-data of the database being queried.

Similar to FLEX [19] SFQI is based on a Formal Query Language (i.e. SQL). However, to suit the end-users we have modified the language, so that the language does not have the FROM clause. As in the Universal Relation Model (URM) [14], users of SFQI are freed from logical database navigation. In doing this we used Lin Dekang's approximation algorithm for steiner problems in graph [12, 13].

As in many NLIs (eg. INTELLECT, TEAM and LOQUI), SFQI also provides a mechanism for processing synonyms, concepts, ellipsis and allows a word to have many meaning and categories. The ellipsis mechanism allows users to pose a query which can refer to the context of the previous query.

As in Kaleidoscope, FLEX, the approach in SFQI also tries to resolve the user's misconceptions before query failure. This means that the query that is sent to the database processor is free from syntax and semantic errors. In doing this, we believe that in resolving query failures the system should first guide the user away from the query failure. Previous research, [6, 19] has provided a range of options for such query generalizations.

In contrast most research in natural language processing and NLIs have proposed postquery cooperation to increase the usability of the NLI systems. When queries fail to produce results because of the user's misconception, the system asks the user to resolve specific causes of failures.

## 9 Future Research

Although the present system has incorporated many of the features for good user interfaces and the results of the experiment were quite promising, there are still many ways to enhance the present system. These include:

1. In implementing the prototype, the relational model and SQL were used as vehicles. The ideas should be applied to other formal query languages and database models as well.

   In fact, one of the main purposes of the current implementation is to provide solid foundation for further development.

2. Another important extension is the inclusion of heuristic rules for validation and integrity checking.

   Better still, the conceptual model of SFQL can be made to contain extra rules and meta knowledge, thus providing SFQL with effective reasoning and deduction mechanisms.

3. The works on enabling the system to fully handle linguistic phenomena; ellipsis, synonyms, concepts etc. should be continued. This can be achieved for example by the expansion of the grammar and parser.

4. SFQI can and should be extended to be as near to a natural language query system as possible.

   This can be achieved by expanding the parser, grammar and word dictionary that it currently uses.

# 10 Summary

In this paper, a high-level query language interface to relational databases has been presented. The paper has highlighted that:

1. A high-level formal query language can also be designed which:

   (a) Is easy to use by novice and experienced users.

   (b) Retains the advantages of a formal query language such as SQL for experienced users.

2. The improved ease of use can be achieved by adding syntactic, semantic and interaction features to the user interface.

3. Facilities which provide the user with meta-level information are vital to effective use by database users.

4. Freeing users from the logical database structure can significantly reduce a user's difficulties in formulating queries.

5. "Proactive is better than reactive".

SFQI provides an English-like query language for users to phrase queries in formal language with restricted English expression. SFQI provides various degrees of freedom in query formulation. Since the objective is to develop a powerful and easy-to-use interface, SFQL has been implemented as an easily-used query language.

In developing SFQI, one of our aims is to show that a carefully designed English-like query language interface can also improve the efficiency of man-computer interaction. In achieving this, many of the features that have been made available in NLI, are incorporated into SFQI.

When SQL is taken as a reference, queries written in SFQL are significantly much easier than and as powerful as SQL. In querying a database, users do not have to remember many details, such as the names of relations and attributes in a database schema. Since SFQL is reminiscent of formal queries, the formulated queries are unambiguous and always produce the desired results.

To date, the first prototype has been implemented. Although the present prototype system has produced interesting results, there is still a lot of room for improvement.

# References

[1] Astrahan M.M., Chamberlin D.D. Implementation of a structured English query language. Communications of the ACM 1976, 18, pp 580-587

[2] Cha S.K. Kaleidoscope: A Cooperative Menu-Guided Query Interface (SQL Version). IEEE Trans. on Knowledge And Data Engineering 1991, 3, pp 42-47

[3] Cha S.K., Wiederhold G. Kaleidoscope Data Model for An English-like Query Language. In Proc. 17th Int. Conf. on Very Large Data Bases, pp 351-361. Lohman G.M., Sernadas A., Camps R. (ed), Morgan Kaufmann Publ., 1991

[4] Chang N.S., Fu K.S. Query-by-Pictorial-Example. IEEE Trans. on Software Eng. 1980, 6, pp 519-525

[5] Chang N.S., Fu K.S. Picture Query Languages for Pictorial Data-Base Systems. IEEE Computer 1981, 11, pp 23-33

[6] Chaudhuri S. Generalization and a framework for query modification. In Proc. IEEE Data Engineering Conf., pp 138-145. IEEE Computer Society, 1990

[7] Greenblatt D., Waxman J. A study of three database query languages. In Databases: Improving Usability and Responsiveness, pp 77-97. Shneiderman B.(ed), Academic Press, 1978

[8] Grosz B.J., Appelt D.E., Pereira F.C.N. TEAM: An Experiment In The Design of Transportable Natural-Language Interfaces. Artificial Intell. 1987, 32, pp 173-243

[9] Harris L.R. Experience with Robot in 12 Commercial Natural Language Data Base Query Applications. In Proc. 6th Int. Joint Conf. on Artificial Intell., pp 365-368. Int. Joint Conf. Publ., 1979

[10] Johnson T. Natural Language computing: the commercial applications. Ovum Ltd., London, 1985

[11] Kim H.J., Korth H.F., Silberschatz A. PICASSO: A Graphical Query Language. Software Practice and Experience 1988, 18, pp 169-203

[12] Lin D. Automatic Logical Navigation Among Relations Using Steiner Trees. In 5th Int. Conf. On Data Engineering, pp 582-588. ACM Press, 1989

[13] Lin D. Parsing semantic dependencies in associative networks. In Proc. 3rd Int. Conf. on Industrial and Eng. Appl. of Artificial Intell. and Expert Syst., pp 467-471. ACM Press, 1990

[14] Maier D. and Ullman J.D. Maximal objects and the semantics of universal relational databases. ACM Trans. on Database Systems 1983, 8, pp 1-14

[15] Martin P., Appelt D.E., Grosz B.J., Pereira F. TEAM: an experimental transportable natural-language interface. In: Proc. Fall Joint Computer Conf., pp 260-267. Stone H.S. (ed), IEEE Computer Society, 1986

[16] MdSap M.N., McGregor D.R. SFQI: An English-Like User Interface to Relational Databases. Technical Report IKBS-14-93, Department of Computer Science, University of Strathclyde, U.K, 1993

[17] MdSap M.N., McGregor D.R. A High Level Query Language Interface: An Alternative Approach. In Proc. 7th Int. Conf. on Industrial and Eng. Appl. of Artificial Intell. and Expert Syst., pp 97-116. Anger F.D., Rodriguez R.V., Ali A. (ed), Gordon and Breach Science Publ., 1994

[18] MdSap M.N., McGregor D.R. SFQI: An English-Like User Interface to Relational Databases. Technical Report in preparation, Department of Computer Science, University of Strathclyde, U.K, 1994

[19] Motro A. FLEX: A tolerant and cooperative user interfaces to databases. IEEE Trans. On Knowledge And Data Engineering 1990, 2, pp 231-246

[20] Owolabi O., McGregor D.R. Fast Approximate String Matching. Software Practice and Experience 1988, 18, pp 387-393

[21] Reisner P. Use of psychological experimentation as an aid to the development of a query language. IEEE Trans. on Software Engineering 1977, 3, pp 218-229

[22] Reisner P. Human factor studies of database query language: A survey and assessment. Computing Surveys 1981, 13, pp 13-31

[23] Ridder D.D. An open natural query system, general description. BIM Information Technology, 1989

[24] Shneiderman B. The Future of Interactive Systems and the Emergence of Direct Manipulation. In Designing the User Interface: Strategies for Effective Human Computer Interaction, pp 1-27. Addison-Wesley, Reading MA, 1986

[25] Small D.W., Weldon L.J. An Experimental Study of Natural Language and Structured Query Languages. Human Factors 1983, 25, pp 253-263

[26] Welty C. Correcting User Errors in SQL. Int. Journal of Man-Machine Studies 1985, 22, pp 463-447

[27] Zloof M. Query-by-example: a database language. IBM System Journal 1977, 16, pp 324-343

# Appendix 1: Query Outputs

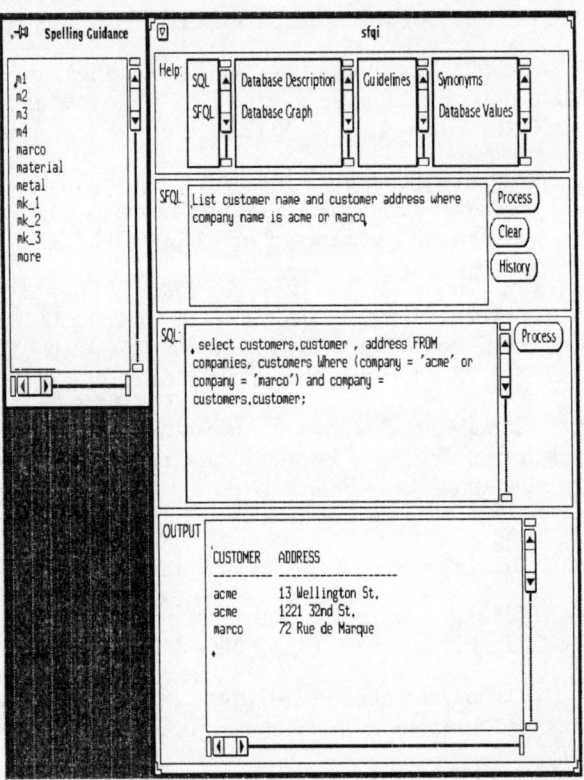

Figure 6: $SFQL_1$: List customer name and customer address where company name is acme or marco

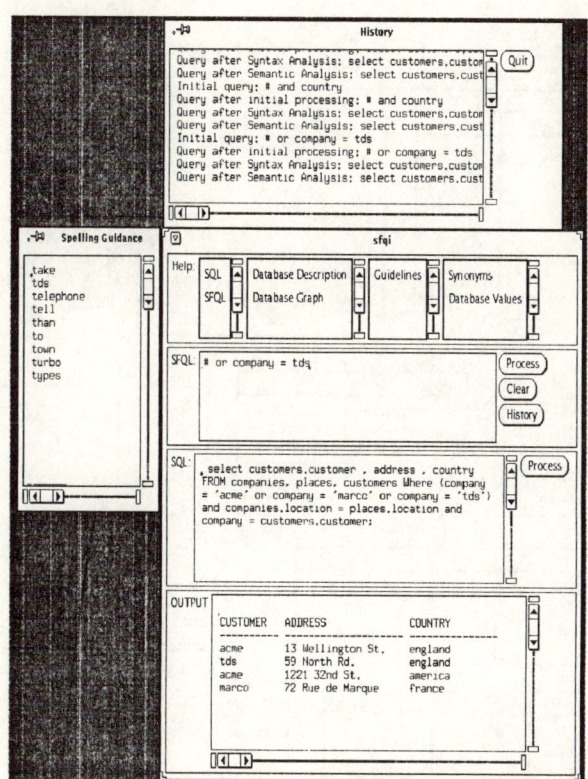

Figure 7: $SFQL_5$: # or company = tds

# Appendix 2: Contents of the Sample Database

COMPANIES

| COMPANY | ADDRESS | PHONE | LOCATION |
|---|---|---|---|
| acme | 13 Wellington St. | 01-993-9734 | london |
| acme | 1221 32nd St. | 010-1212-247351 | new york |
| wellgo | 47 High St. | 01-248-1234 | london |
| ged | 352 Newbury Ave. | 010-1212-124444 | new york |
| marco | 72 Rue de Marque | 010-331-7552212 | paris |
| tds | 59 North Rd. | 01-458-1132 | london |
| turbo | 12 Victoria St. | 01-334-2222 | london |
| rtex | 994 First St. | 010-1212-554156 | new york |

SUPPLIERS

| SUPPLIER | RELIABILITY |
|---|---|
| acme | good |
| tds | good |
| rtex | poor |
| marco | |
| turbo | |

CUSTOMERS

| CUSTOMER | CREDIT |
|---|---|
| wellgo | 1200 |
| ged | 900 |
| marco | 0 |
| acme | 2500 |
| tds | 0 |

PARTS

| PART | DESCRIPTION | COLOUR |
|---|---|---|
| m1 | support | grey |
| m2 | nut | green |
| m3 | bolt | grey |
| m4 | base | grey |
| p1 | frame | red |
| p2 | casing | red |
| p3 | washer | black |
| p4 | frame | blue |

PART_SUPPLY

| PART | SUPPLIER | COST |
|---|---|---|
| m1 | tds | 10 |
| m2 | tds | 0 |
| m2 | turbo | 0 |
| m3 | acme | 0 |
| m4 | tds | 24 |
| p1 | acme | 12 |
| p1 | turbo | 12 |
| p2 | rtex | 14 |
| p3 | marco | 0 |
| p4 | marco | 13 |

PRODUCTS

| PRODUCT | COST |
|---|---|
| mk_1 | 116 |
| mk_2 | 125 |
| mk_3 | 139 |

TYPES

| PART | MATERIAL |
|---|---|
| m1 | metal |
| m2 | metal |
| m3 | metal |
| m4 | metal |
| p1 | plastic |
| p2 | plastic |
| p3 | plastic |
| p4 | plastic |

PLACES

| LOCATION | COUNTRY |
|---|---|
| birmingham | england |
| london | england |
| paris | france |
| california | america |
| new york | america |

COMPONENTS

| PRODUCT | PART | QUANTITY |
|---|---|---|
| mk_1 | p3 | 6 |
| mk_1 | m2 | 12 |
| mk_1 | m3 | 12 |
| mk_2 | p3 | 8 |
| mk_2 | p4 | 1 |
| mk_2 | m1 | 1 |
| mk_2 | m2 | 15 |
| mk_2 | m3 | 15 |
| mk_3 | p3 | 8 |
| mk_3 | p4 | 1 |
| mk_3 | m1 | 2 |
| mk_3 | m2 | 18 |
| mk_3 | m3 | 18 |

IN_ORDERS

| IN_ORDER | PRODUCT | QUANTITY | CUSTOMER |
|---|---|---|---|
| I_86_12 | mk_1 | 1 | ged |
| I_86_13 | mk_1 | 3 | marco |
| I_86_13 | mk_2 | 1 | marco |
| I_86_14 | mk_3 | 1 | acme |

OUT_ORDERS

| OUT_ORDER | PART | QUANTITY | SUPPLIER |
|---|---|---|---|
| O_86_114 | p3 | 200 | marco |
| O_86_115 | m2 | 60 | turbo |
| O_86_115 | p1 | 5 | turbo |
| O_86_116 | m1 | 2 | tds |
| O_86_116 | m2 | 25 | tds |
| O_86_117 | p4 | 8 | marco |

Figure 8: Parts-Database

3-Dimensional Visualisation and Virtual Reality

# Design of a 3D User Interface to a Database

John Boyle[1,2], John E. Fothergill[2], and Peter M.D. Gray[1]

Dept. of Computing Science[1], King's College,
Dept. of Molecular and Cell Biology[2], Marishal College,
Aberdeen University
Aberdeen, UK

**Abstract**

A new revolution is occurring in graphical interface design with multimedia and virtual metaphors taking their place beside menus and dialogue boxes. Nowhere is such a paradigm shift more needed than in visual query systems for databases.

Previous studies in visual query languages for database management systems have attempted to use solely the desktop metaphor. We have used three dimensional graphical techniques to construct an interface for our object oriented database. Interactive animated 3D graphics have been embedded inside a standard menu driven framework. 3D representations for both query construction and result representation have been developed. This paper will discuss our approach and the design of our interface AMAZE.

The upsurge in the number of casual users and the general acceptance of computer technology has shown that the principal driving force in software engineering is shifting from functionality to usability. It has also become evident that the Xerox Star interface and its whole related genre do not provide the modern interface designer with the expressive power that is needed. As the desktop metaphor popularised document management, so the new generation of interfaces will take database access out of the hands of a select few and give it to the many.

## 1 Introduction

This paper discusses the use of three dimensional high performance graphics in the construction of an advanced user interface, which will enable users to interact more readily with complex computer systems. A number of interfaces have been developed which use three dimensional graphics as a integral part of the interaction [1]. The use and power of the WIMP system has led to a generation of users who would otherwise have remained completely computer illiterate. We believe that while the WIMP system still has a lot to offer, in some cases it should be extended to encompass 3D interactions. Whilst the use of the desktop metaphor allows easy interaction with word processing packages, spreadsheets and other menu-driven processes, it does not always lend itself kindly to a user who wishes to interact with a database management system, particularly when query specification and result visualisation are important. Interfaces for database systems usually fall into one of two categories, form based or graph based. Form based interfaces rely on a table based approach for their expressive power: there are numerous examples of these including QBE [2], CUPID [3], QBPE [4], SBA [5], ABE [6], GQBE [7], Formmanager [8], G-Whiz [9], QBSRT [10], OBE [11], NFQL [12], Pasta 3 [13], STBE [14] CARD [15], TBE [16], GRADI [17]. Graph based interfaces use a pictorial representation of the conceptual schema as the basis for interactive querying, examples include GUIDE [18], LID [19], ISIS [20] , SNAP [21], KiView [22], VILD [23] , OdeView [24].

Recently other metaphors have been used to construct interfaces, which rely on good visual representations to help the user. Some of these use 3D graphics (TripleSpace [25], LyberWorld [26], Amaze [27]), while others use complex 2D visualisations (InfoCrystal [28], Sketch [29]).

We have constructed a working environment which relies on three dimensional graphics to supply the extra visualisation power that is lacking in the normal flat 2D designs. The ease of integration of interactive 3D graphics inside a WIMP framework, and the resulting expressive power, make such systems a valuable tool for interface designers.

## 2 Background

The database management system, P/FDM [30], is an implementation of the functional data model [31] with object-oriented extensions, written in Prolog. The functional data model is a form of semantic data model in which attributes of, and relationships between, entities are viewed as the results of applying functions to that entity. A high level query language, based on Daplex [31], has been implemented which fulfills the role of SQL. We have developed two graphical user interfaces for P/FDM. One is based on QBE [2] and has evolved from an earlier version [15]. Our second interface makes use of animated interactive three dimensional graphics [27].

Our graphical interface to P/FDM uses a client-server model. The client processes reside on an SGI Indigo. The graphical interface process, which is implemented in C, uses the X11 Windowing System, with the OSF/Motif toolkit. Extensive use is also made of the API to the IrisGl 3D graphics routines. The server processes reside on a SUN 4 workstation, and network communication is managed by the use of RPCs.

Our main application database uses protein structure data [32]. This data is used by biochemists when attempting to understand the complex structures of large macromolecules. Biochemists are familiar with 3D graphic manipulation, as molecular display packages are commonplace in the computational biology laboratories. The interface has been designed to be highly generic, while allowing for customisation for specific groups of users.

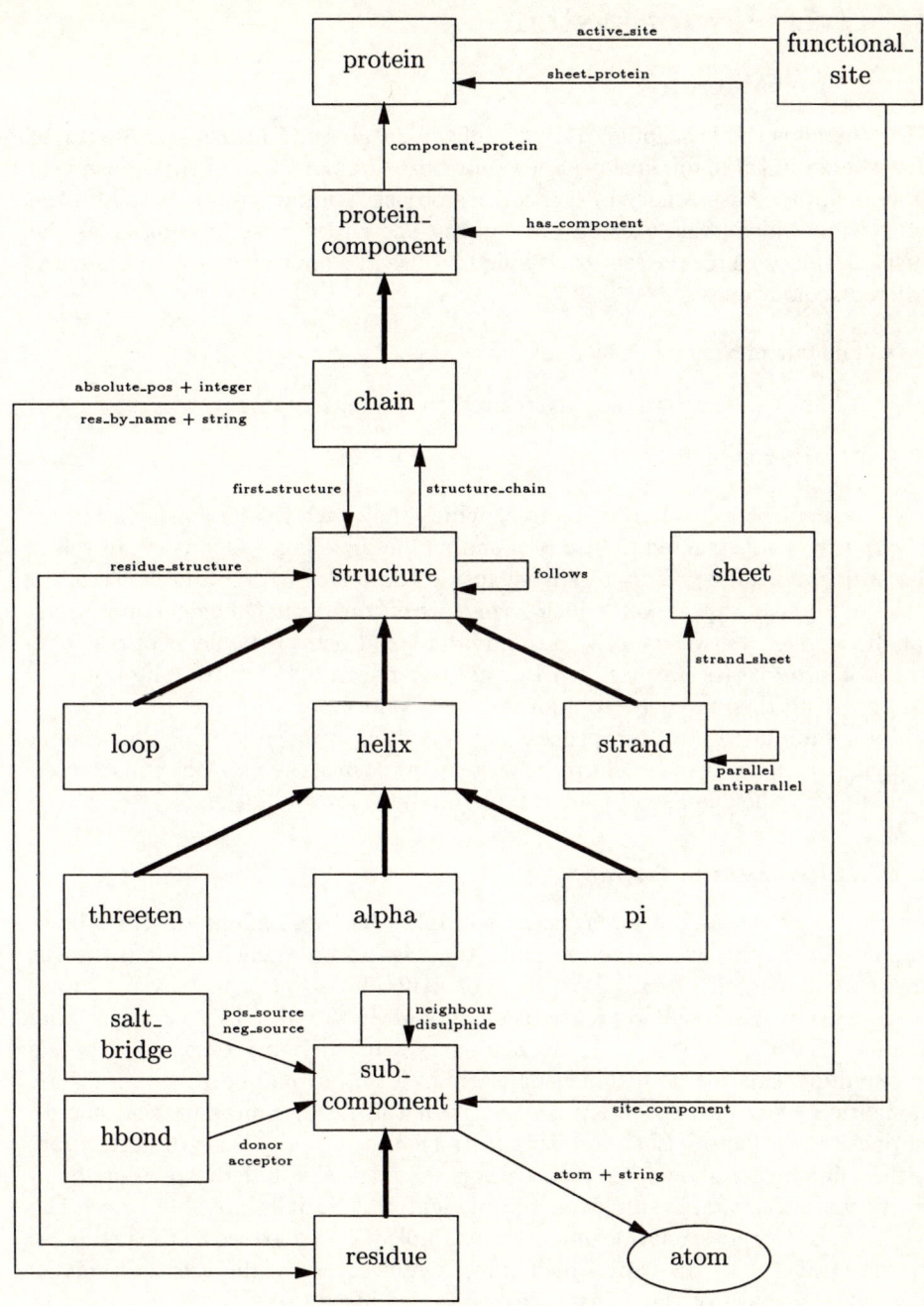

Figure 1: Diagrammatic representation of the Protein Database schema

## 3 Overview of system

### 3.1 The Schema

The schema is the basis of all querying of the database **(Figure 1)**. The use of the schema in three dimensions allows for both the portrayal of the conceptual schema and the user query in one concise object. All querying is based on the navigational idea. The user navigates from one entity class to another as the query develops. This navigation is aided by use of colour cues - there are three different colour cues.

- The current entity of interest
- All entities that are directly related to the current entity
- All other entities

The users initially choose an entity which they wish to start querying from. The query is constructed by use of a simple dialogue box. The user can select the scalar attributes of interest from inside the dialogue box and construct a series of boolean expressions which form a set of constraints. Logical operations can be applied between both the individual and sets of boolean operations. Trees of sub-queries are built up by the user beneath the entity class object. The user can then navigate to another entity and repeat the querying process. So by a simple step by step process it is possible to move around the schema applying constraints to build up the large query. Once the user has constructed such a query they can send it off to the database for evaluation.

### 3.2 The Result Maze

For the result representation a 'maze' metaphor has been adopted. This allows the user to see the size of the returning data set and how each of the instances are related to each other. As query construction is performed by a process of navigation, the result representation should be visualised in a navigational manner. Each entity visited during the query construction process corresponds to one dimension in the result visualisation. If we have a query with only one navigation between two entity classes, then the result representation should emphasise this factor. Each resulting instance is represented as a discrete cube, with a link being shown between each entity instance and the related set of entity instances that result from the navigation. So it is possible to see the results and their interrelationships. For example if we ask to see all the instances in the entity class **protein** which have a molecular weight greater then 10 kDa, and for each of those instances we would like to see all the instances of their **sheets**, and also all the **strands** associated with the **sheets**- this can be visualised simply **(Figure2)**, with one dimension showing the number of proteins, and the second dimension showing the number of protein components for each of the separate instances of protein.

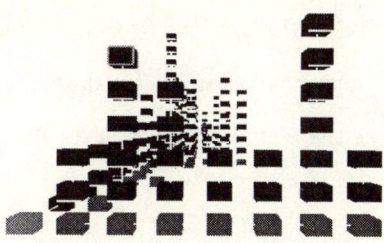

Figure 2: Result maze showing discrete blocks for each of the results obtained from the query.

The use of a three dimensional visualisation for the results allows the user to see the size of the data set that has been returned as well as how the sets of data are interrelated. This feature means that it is easy for the user to actually see the results. Each result is returned as a unique instance, and is represented as a cube, which the user can select if they wish to query further. The result 'maze' also allows the user to visualise more than the normal 3 related sets of results (as constrained by 3 dimensions) by the use of a 'turning the corner' analogy - as the user progresses through the results one set of results is faded out, as the next set is faded in.

## 3.3 Result Visualization

The user is presented with a collection of cubes in the results maze, each of which represents an abstract token. When the user wishes to uncover more information about that abstract they select an abstract and choose a visualisation method. In our application database a number of different display actions are defined in the database. These are responsible for the instance result to visualisation mappings. Specifically four different display visualisations are being designed for the customisation of our interface for protein chemists.

- Basic textual display of all scalar values.
- A 3D molecular displayer - displaying the structure.
- A phi/psi angle graph plotter - displaying a plot of the dihedral angles.
- Sequence displayer - displaying the amino acid residues.

Three display actions, the textual, molecular and sequence displayers, have been fully implemented.

# 4 Functionality

To better explain the concepts behind this interface a brief description of the functionality is given. The functionality has been divided into three subsections.

- Querying, description of the aids the user has when constructing a query
- Results, shows how a user can examine the data obtained from the database.
- Graphical, describes the visual interaction itself.

## 4.1 Querying

A visual representation of the conceptual schema is used to portray the information to the user about the entity classes and their relationships. The user can apply queries to an entity class, forming a subset of the entity class. The user can connect any number of queries to an entity class. Each query is represented as a tree beneath the relevant class.

**The root** node of a query tree is represented as a cube hanging directly beneath the entity class. This is a visual representation of a subset the user is interested in. It is from this box that the user will be able to project out results so they can be used as values in other query trees.

**The leaves** of the tree are constraint boxes. These represent the sets of boolean expresssions the user wishes to use to form the subset of instances. A dialogue box is used to aid the user in the construction of these boolean expressions.

**The nodes** of the tree represent logical operations between the constraint boxes. This allows the user to perform conjunction or disjunction operations between the sets of boolean expressions.

Once the user has constructed the query s/he activates the **evaluate query** button and the query is sent off to the remote database. The query is translated into daplex and piped to a remote process which handles the traffic to and from the database. The traffic is kept to a minimum to improve performance.

The user can restart the query at any time. Additional functionality will be added which will allow the user the power to load in and save queries. Also the user should be able to load in parts of saved queries.

## 4.2 Results

The data is displayed to the user as a token abstract - represented as a cube. When the user wishes to materialise the abstract they select a display action. The default display action, the data action, will materialise all the scalar attributes associated with that instance of the entity class.

We have tailored our interface for biochemist users by adding an additional display action. e.g. a protein molecule displayer(**Figure 6.b**). A display action is stored in the database, that will return the three dimensional coordinates of the atoms. The displayer is relatively primitive. When a user selects a part of the 3D representation of the protein a dialogue gives the user information about the atom they have chosen and the amino acid name from which it comes.

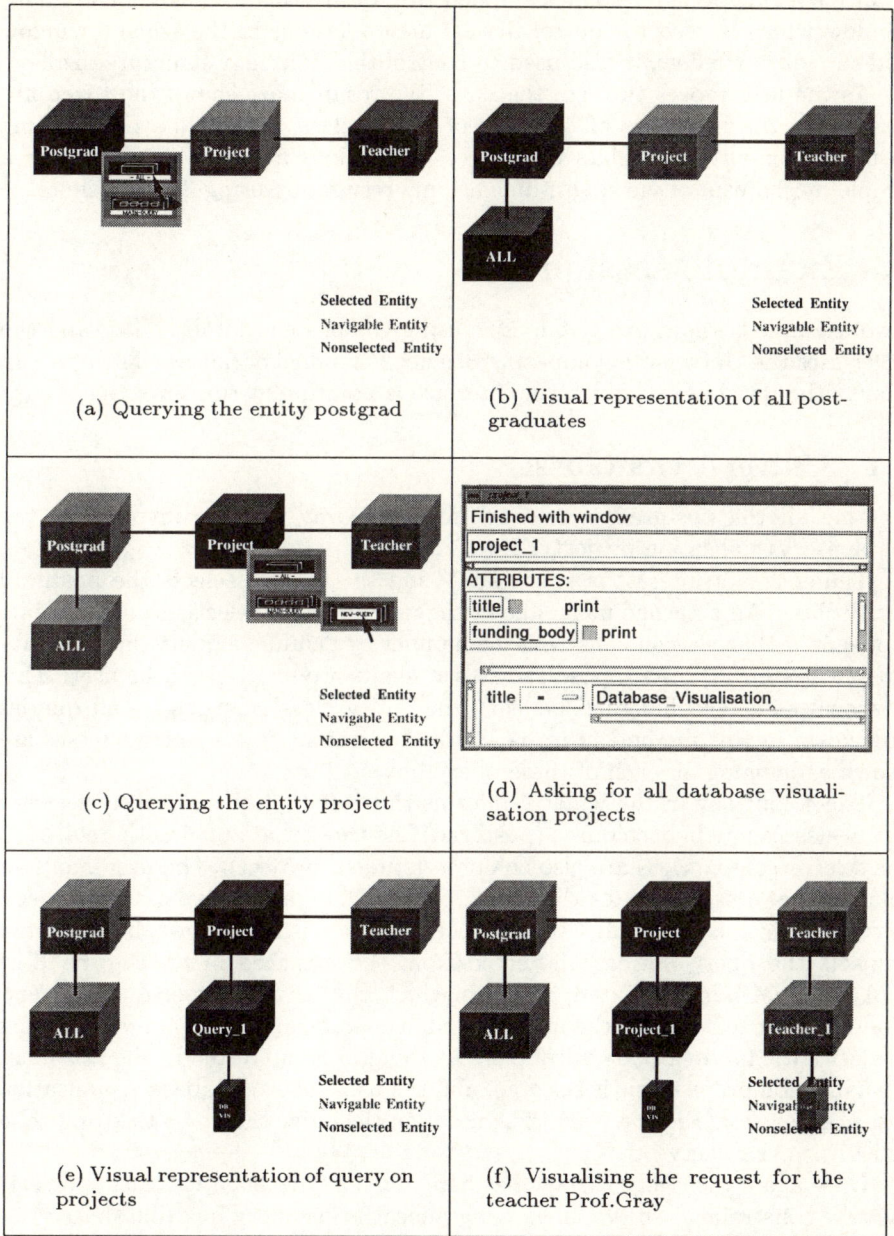

Figure 3: Step by step construction of the query for all postgraduates students who work under the supervision of Prof.Gray on the Database Visualisation project.

Additional functionality could be added to improve this displayer. The 'dials' window which is used to control the 3D manipulations in the schema window and the maze window, is also used to control the molecular structure display.

As the user moves through the data, the result maze shows the token abstracts for the instances of the current entity class, as well as the resulting instances for an entity class up to two navigations away. This allows for a simple mechanism of viewing n-dimensional results, by using 3D snapshots.

## 5 Example session

Two example sessions are given. One using the protein database [32] and the other uses the University Computing Science Personnel database. The user can change the database to which the interface is pointing at run time.

### 5.1 University database

Get me all the postgrads who work for Prof.Gray and are involved in the Database Visualisation project**(Figure 3)**.

The entity of interest is postgrads - and so the user selects the postgrad entity class. An attached menu allows the user to either select all postgraduate students or the user can constrain the number by defining a query on the entity class**(Figure 3.a)** . ALL postgraduate students are selected by the user. This is shown as a box 'hanging' beneath the entity class **postgrad** - all queries are shown in this method **(Figure 3.b)**, constraints on the entity classes are shown as hanging off each of these query boxes.

The colour key in the window informs the user that the currently selected entity class is uniquely coloured (postgrad) and those that are directly related to the selected entity class are also coloured (student,project). The user wants to know all the postgraduates that work on the Database Visualisation project, and so project is selected. As the user doesn't wish to know about all the projects the query option is selected from the attached menu**(Figure 3.c)** . A dialogue box is created, through which the user can specify the query. The user can select from the scalar attributes associated with the entity class project (title,funding body,duration). As the user is interested in the Database Visualisation project title is selected, and the user enters database visualisation into the text box**(Figure 3.d)**. The user can then give the box a title and then finish with the query box.

Once again the query is shown as hanging beneath its entity class (project) and the constraint is shown as hanging beneath this query box (database visualisation)**(Figure 3.e)**.

The user then selects the entity class **teacher** and enters the query that the name of the supervisor must be Gray**(Figure 3.f)**.

The user can then browse the results as they wish - in fact a glance at the results maze shows the user that there are in fact only two postgraduates who work on the database visualisation project under the supervision of Prof.Gray.

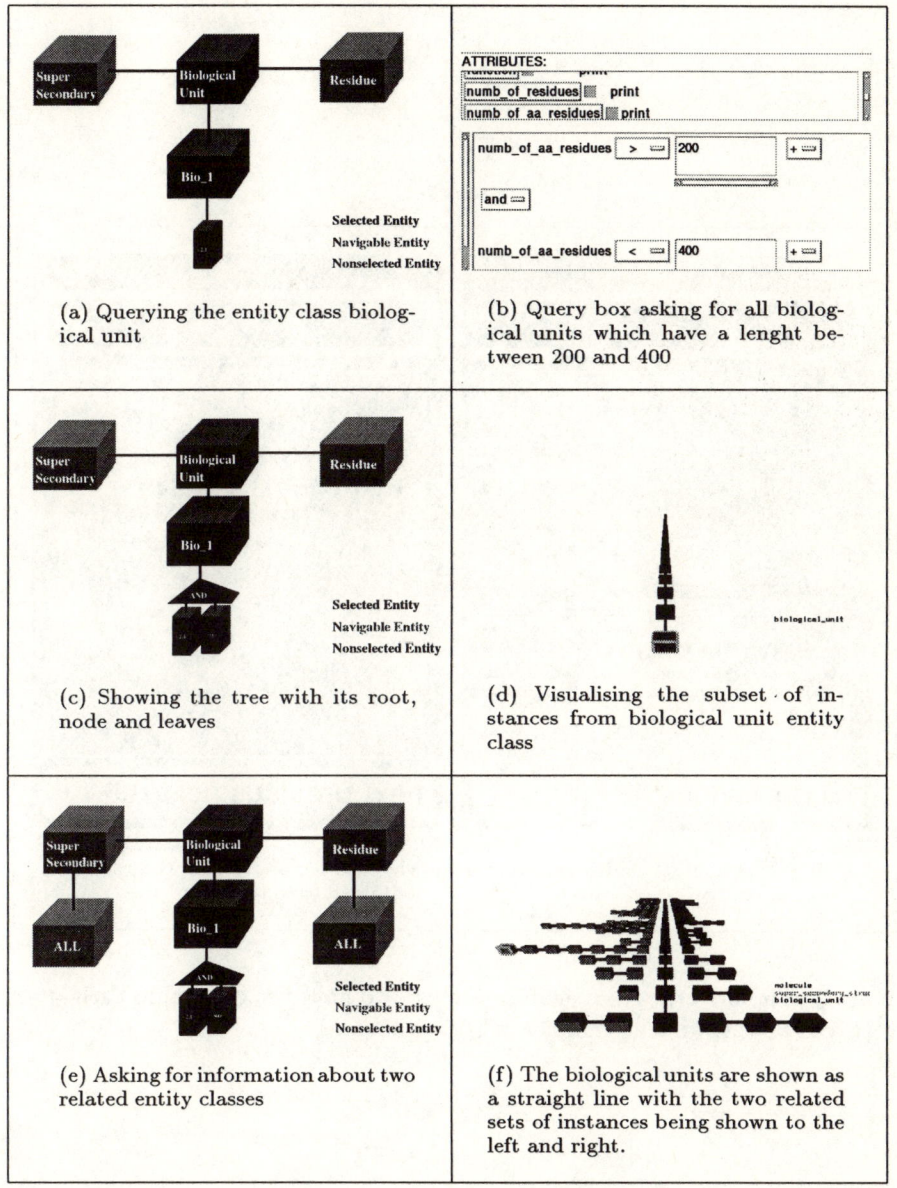

Figure 4: Showing the user using the database to explore the maze to discover information about protein structure.

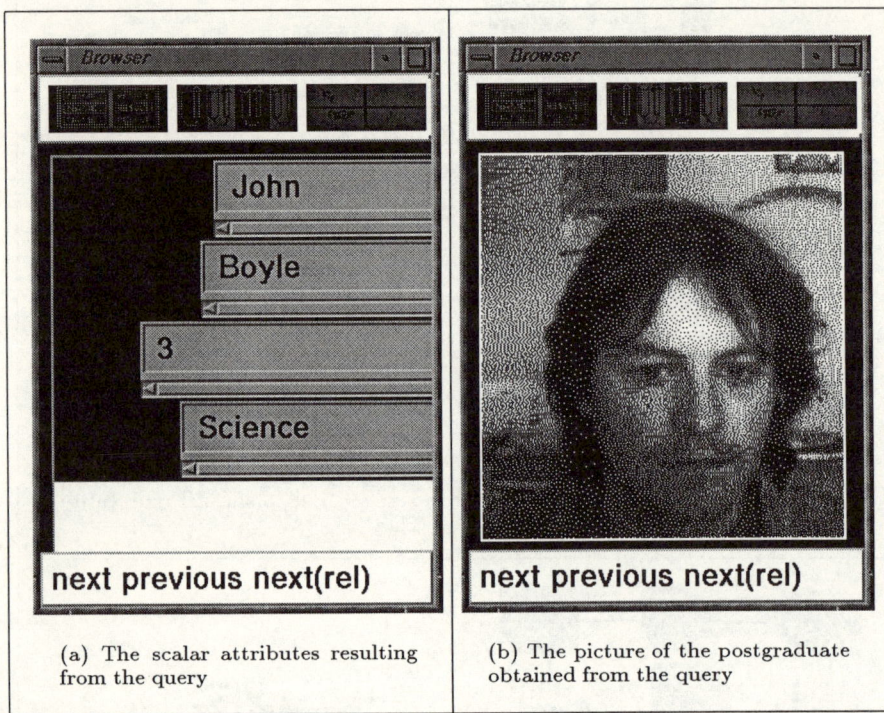

(a) The scalar attributes resulting from the query

(b) The picture of the postgraduate obtained from the query

Figure 5: The browsing tool enables the user to have the data from their query portrayed to them in the manner of there choosing.

The browsing tool allows the user to examine the scalar results. The user can also choose to have a picture of the person extracted from the database and displayed in the browser.

Once the query has been performed a visualisation of the results is available, through which some idea of the quantity of results and how they are interrelated can be obtained **(Figure 2)**.

The user can get information by clicking on any of the result representations **(Figure 5)**. The display of results is not limited to text format only**(Figure 5.a)**, the database interface can be customised to supply other means of visualising the data. In the specific case of the university database a picture displayer has been added **(Figure browser.b)**

## 5.2 Protein database

If the user is interested in finding out about protein structure then they can select the entity class biological unit, and ask for all proteins for which well determined data is available**(Figure 4.a)** - for example all the proteins which have had their structures resolved to a resolution less than 2.1. The number of results can be seen in the results maze**(Figure 4.d)**.

The user could then decide to restrict the number of proteins they are interested in to those that are made up of between 200 and 400 amino acids**(Figure 4.b)**. This can be shown graphically as being part of the query tree structure - with two constraint boxes being linked by a conjugation**(Figure 4.c)**

The user can then use the database to explore other aspects of protein structure such as its supersecondary structure or its constitutive molecules**(Figure 4.e)**. Once again the result maze is used to visualise the results**(Figure 4.f)**.

The user can visualise the abstract information from the result maze in a number of ways**(Figure 6)**

# 6 Further Work

## 6.1 Evaluations

Our system evaluations are planned on a three stage approach.

**The usability study** will help analyse the 'look and feel' of the interface. It will identify inconsistencies and help improve the user interaction. This is a very subjective study involving basic observation of and dialogue with the users to find what methods of interaction they prefer. This was performed as the interface was being designed and developed, by asking for user input where it was felt it was needed.

**The task study** is planned for the next few months. This involves giving the users a selection of tasks with varying complexity. How easily and quickly the users move through the tasks, and at what levels they find problems will help establish the limits of our interface. The tasks will have to be

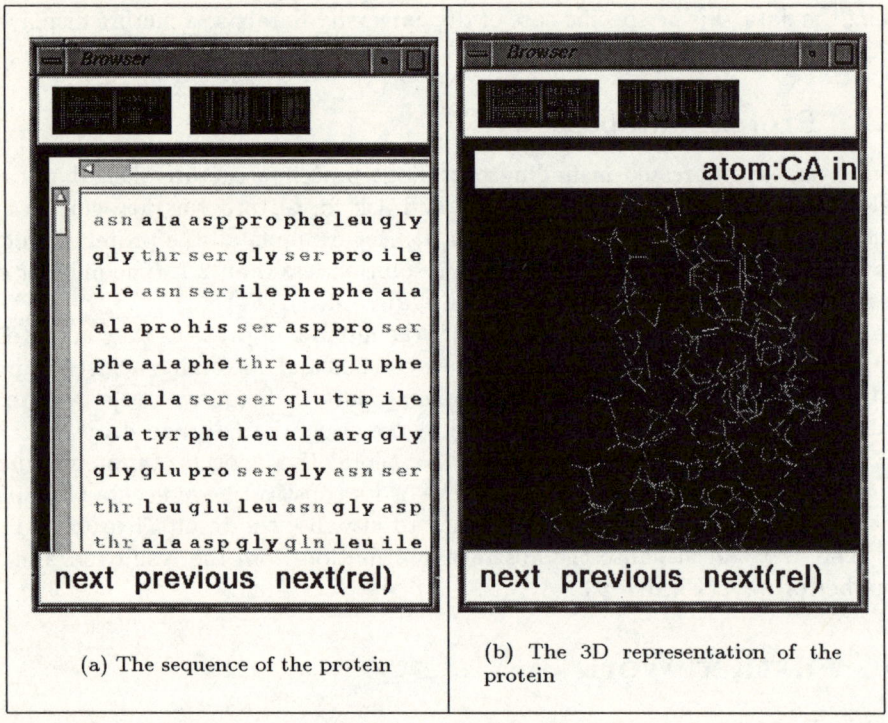

Figure 6: The browsing tool has been customised for protein structure information.

chosen carefully to introduce new concepts as the user progresses through them. So the first few tasks will be restricted to a single entity class, and the next will introduce the idea of navigation and relations between entity classes. In this way the evaluation can also be seen as a teaching exercise.

**The empirical study** is a full blown evaluation which will attempt to derive some statistics from the user interaction with interface. It will record timings and user interaction, by simply keeping a log of the user input events, as well as user successes and failures. Such a study would evolve groups completing tasks over several sessions, presumably measuring their knowledge acquisition('power law of practice'). There are no detailed plans about this stage.

The feedback generated from these studies will help improve the dialogue between the user and the interface, and will guide further directions of research as the more successful ideas behind our designs are exploited. Preliminary observation show that the use of the three dimensional representions is certainly entertaining and enjoyable to use.

## 6.2 Extensions

Because response time for any user interface is important, we have used simple renderings. We have avoided the lag caused when generating complex three dimensional mapping. Animation can thus occur in real time. Some more advanced graphical features, (lighting, 3D fonts and use of spheres) are available - but have to be explicitly asked for by the user. Numerous further extensions are planned to improve the usability of Amaze: most importantly we wish to allow the user to perform querying from inside the result maze.

# 7 Conclusion

A working environment has been constructed which relies on three dimensional graphics to supply the extra visualisation power that is lacking in the normal flat 2D designs. Ideas and designs for a new generation of user interfaces are proposed, specifically for database access using novel features for both query construction and result representation

The problem of graphical interface design for database systems has been with us for over 20 years. One of the reasons for this is that the basis of interface design is a 'desktop metaphor' which is not suited to the representation and abstraction needed for the portrayal of 'information'.

# Acknowledgements

The authors would like to acknowledge the value insights and help given by Suzanne Embury, Graham Kemp and Scott Leishman. John Boyle is funded by the Science and Engineering Research Council.

# References

[1] G. Robertson, S. Card and J. Mackinlay: *Information Visualization using 3D Interactive Animation*, Communications of the ACM, 36, 4, 57-71.

[2] M. Zloof: *Query by Example*, National Computer Conference, 431-437, 1975.

[3] N. McDonald and M. Stonebraker: *CUPID - The Friendly Query Language*, TODS, 5, 127-131.

[4] N.S. Chang and K.S. Fu: *Query-by-Pictorial-Example*, IEEE Trans. on Software Eng., 14, 5, 630-638.

[5] M. Zloof and P. deJong: *The System for Business Automation*, Comm. ACM, 20, 6, 385-396.

[6] A. Klug: *ABE: a query language for constructing aggregates by example*, Proc. Int'l Workshop on Statistical Database Management, 190-205, 1981.

[7] B.E. Jacobs and C.A. Walczak: *A Generalized Query-by-Example Data Manipulation Language Based on Database Logic*, IEEE Trans. on Software Engineering, 9, 1, 40-57.

[8] S. Yao, A.R. Hevner, Z. Shi and D. Luo: *FORMANAGER: AN Office Forms Management System*, ACM Trans. on Office Information Systems, 2, 3, 235-262.

[9] S. Heiler and A. Roseenthal: *G-WHIZ, a Visual Interface for the Functional Model with Recursion*, VLDB, 209-218, 1985.

[10] A.U. Tansel, M.E. Arkun and G. Ozsoyoglu: *Time-by-Example Query Language for Historical Databases*, IEEE Trans. on Software Engineering, 15, 4, 464-478.

[11] K.Y. Whang: *Office-by-Example: An Integrated Office System and Database Manager*, ACM Trans. on Office Information Systems, 5, 4, 393-427.

[12] D.W. Embley: *NFQL: The Natural Forms Query Language*, ACM Trans. on Database Systems, 14, 2, 168-211.

[13] , M. Kuntz and R. Melchort: *Pasta-3's Graphical Query Language: Direct Manipulation, Cooperative Queries, Full Expressive Power*, VLDB, 97-105, 1989.

[14] S.P. Ghosh: *Statistical Relational Tables for Statistical Database Management*, IEEE Trans. on Software Eng., 12, 12, 1106-1116.

[15] G.L. Kemp and D.G. Melvin: *A graphical interface for an object-oriented database*, Hypermedia/Hypertext and Object Oriented Databases, 307-322, Chapman and Hall, 1991.

[16] A.U. Tansel, M.E. Arkun and G. Ozsoyoglu: *Time-by-Example Query Language for Historical Databases*, IEEE Trans. on Software Engineering, 15, 4, 464-478.

[17] D. Keim and V. Lum: *GRADI: A Graphical Database Interface for a Multimedia DBMS*, The 1st International Workshop on Interfaces to Databases (IDS92), Springer-Verlag, 1992.

[18] H. Wong and I. Kuo: *GUIDE: Graphical User Interface for Database Exploration*, VLDB, 22-32, 1982.

[19] D. Fogg: *Lessons from a Living in a Database Graphical User Interface*, SIGMOD, 1984.

[20] K.J. Goldman, P.C. Kanellakis, S.A. Goldman: *ISIS: Interface for a Semantic Information System*, SIGMOD, 1985.

[21] D. Bryce and R. Hull: *SNAP: a graphics-based schema manager*, Proc. Int'l Conf on Data Engineering, 1986.

[22] A. Motro, A. D'Atri and L. Tarantino: *The Design of KIVIEW: An Object-Oriented Browser*, Proc. 2nd Intl. Conf. Expert Database Systems, 1988.

[23] M. Leong, S. Sam and D. Narasimhalu: *Towards a Visual Language for an Object-Oriented Multi-Media Database System*, Visual Database Systems, Elsevier Science Publishers B.V.(North-Holland), 1989.

[24] R. Agrawal, N.H. Gehani and J. Srinivasan: *OdeView: The Graphical Interface to Ode*, ACM-SIGMOD, 34-43, 1990.

[25] J. Mariani and R. Lougher: *TripleSpace: an experiment in a 3D graphical interface to a binary relational database*, Interacting with Computers, 4, 2, 147-162.

[26] M. Hemmje: *LyberWorld: A 3D Graphical User Interface for Fulltext Retrieval*, Proc. Workshop on Database issues for Data Visualization (forthcoming), Springer-Verlag, 1993.

[27] J.Boyle, J.Fothergill and P.Gray: *Design of a 3D user interface to a database*, Proc. Workshop on Database issues for Data Visualization (forthcoming), Springer-Verlag, 1993.

[28] A. Spoerri: *InfoCrystal: A Visual Tool for Information Retrieval*, IEEE Visualization, 150-157, 1993.

[29] B. Meyer: *Beyond Icons*, The 1st International Workshop on Interfaces to Databases (IDS92), Springer-Verlag, 1992.

[30] P. Gray, K. G. Kulkarni and N. W. Paton: *Object Oriented Databases - A Semantic Data Model approach*, Prentice Hall, 1992.

[31] D. W. Shipman: *The functional data model and the data language DAPLEX*, ACM TODS, 6, 140-173.

[32] P. M. D. Gray, N. W. Paton, G. J. L. Kemp and J. E. Fothergill: *An object-oriented database for protein structure analysis*, Protein Engineering, 3, 235-243.

# Three Dimensional Interface for an Object Oriented Database

Martin H Rapley and Jessie B Kennedy
Computer Studies Dept., Napier University
219 Colinton Road, Edinburgh EH14 1DJ

**Abstract**

An experimental 3D interface to an object oriented database is described. It is hoped that using such techniques will help make complex data structures more comprehensible and easier to navigate. A number of 3D visualisation techniques are used to encourage exploration of the data space. The visualisations inform users about the structure and contents of the database by showing classes, objects, and relationships between objects. A discussion of related work is presented followed by a description and initial evaluation of WINONA a prototype 3D interface to an OODB.

## 1 Introduction

The user interface is a neglected part of most database systems. Object oriented databases (OODB) have a particular need for high quality interfaces as they are used to store diverse types of data, and often have complex schemas which reflect the nature of the real world data. The types of data which have to be handled include graphical images and sounds. Graphical interfaces are the obvious solution as they provide a simple way of interacting directly with the data. The system described here uses three dimensional computer graphic techniques to present a number of different visualisations of the contents of an OODB. Three dimensional graphics are used because this allows a greater density of information to be presented in the limited screen area. The visualisations have been designed to help users better understand the structure and relationships within the database, and to more easily navigate the data. Ease of use is further enhanced by allowing direct manipulation of the visualisation to access further information.

### 1.1 Why visualise?

Visualisation encompasses a wide variety of real world application areas with one goal in common, to make some set of abstract data more comprehensible. It is known that a picture can convey a large amount of information in a clear and simple way. Generally, visualisation has been used to make very abstract numerical information much easier to understand. Now the same ideas are being used to help in understanding all sorts of processes such as computer programming and project management. In addition graphical user interfaces can be considered a form of visualisation as they provide a graphical representation of abstract operating system functions such as file management and program execution.

OODBs are suited to visualisation as they have a complex underlying model and structure which can be better explained using graphical representations. Though the concepts of class hierarchies, aggregation, and relationships are fairly simple in themselves it is when they are combined in a highly connected network that even those most comfortable with the concepts have difficulty in understanding all the intricacies.

The aim of visualisation in this project is to remove the need for the user to conceive and maintain a complex mental model of the OODB. This can be achieved by giving an explicit representation of the structure of the database. However, the problem is finding an effective representation that can either be directly mapped to the real structure or make use of a relevant and easily understood metaphor

## 1.2 Interfaces to Databases

Database systems are only just starting to take full advantage of graphical interfaces. In particular, those promoting object oriented databases are beginning to realise that to gain greater acceptance for their systems they must provide easy to use graphical software tools. Databases are highly interactive and therefore require good interfaces. Interactions take many forms, from designing and creating schemas to querying, browsing, and manipulating database contents. Barclay and Kennedy [1] have shown the advantages of providing a graphical interface to an ecological database.

The complexity of a graphical user interface can be directly related to the expressiveness and complexity of the underlying data model. The highly expressive nature of an OODB comes at the cost of complexity, therefore it is much more difficult to produce a good interface. Whilst there is no definitive definition of an OODB it is recognised that there are some core features which every OODB should have, such as complex object modelling, encapsulation and inheritance [2,3].

Examining both commercial and research systems [4] it is possible to conclude that most effort so far has been in the areas of structural schema design and database browsing although some work has been done on visual querying (GEMSTONE and GOOD) and visual manipulation (ObjectStore and $O_2$). Schema design follows the same approach as most object oriented design tools in providing a graphical editor for placing classes and relationships. The browsers tend to use the form metaphor showing information textually rather than graphically. These are usually difficult to navigate, often requiring tedious backtracking if the wrong option is chosen. One proposed solution to this is to browse using 'information spaces' [5] where objects are placed in a multi-dimensional space according to their attributes and their relationships to each other.

Designing interfaces for an OODB holds a number of challenges [6]. Complex data held in OODBs such as bitmaps, structural relationships, and sounds require more complex interfaces than the simple tabular data of relational systems. They need standard mechanisms for displaying and interacting with object oriented data that have no special representation of their own. Some OODBs already supply 4GL type forms interfaces. Different views of the same data may be required, e.g. data relating to a building might be seen by those working in it as simple floor plans, while maintenance staff require technical data such as wiring to be shown, and a heating engineer wants to see airflow's.

The OODB also has HCI implications. Objects can store their own interface, so you can tell them to display themselves rather than being reliant on a representation given to the object by the system (this depends on the ability of database to hold such information) and OODBs have complex schema which require clever graphical tools to create them.

Standard interfaces could be provided in several ways. Each class could inherit its user interface from the superclass [7], i.e. all objects in that class will be shown in this way. Then it is simply a matter of calling the display method of the class to see its visual form. Another advantage of this approach is that the interface is easy to extend using standard inheritance and overriding. The visualisations in this case are two dimensional graphs showing the schema, with nodes, which represent the different classes, displayed as icons. These visualisations were evaluated [8] and it was found that the graph representation was not necessarily the best one to use. Alternatively, there could be a separate display handler which takes data from the database server and displays it in a standard way. Finally, there could be display objects which deal with many classes of object by using rules for displaying given objects, e.g. if it is text, show it as a grey rectangle with black text. This option has the advantage that you can provide more than one display object for a given class allowing the user to choose which one is most suitable. Also it allows for portability between interface systems - it is only necessary to re-implement these object display classes.

It has been suggested [9] that using three dimensional displays in conjunction with the standard 'desktop' metaphor would be a good approach to building a database interface. The idea is that users will respond more favourably to something which has some familiarity rather than a completely new concept. It is also suggested that the user can be encouraged to interact more freely with the database if presented with an interesting and stimulating interface. Although the implementation is for a specific application, that of protein chemistry, the same methods could be used for any type of data.

The three dimensional information system (3DIS) [10] takes a completely different approach by allowing all objects and relationships to be seen at the same time. This is an experimental system which represents data and mappings between data in a simple three dimensional form. All information is treated uniformly with every data item an object in the system. The aim to provide a simple formal geometric representation for databases. There are three orthogonal axes: Range,

Mapping, and Domain. If there is a mapping from a domain object to a range object this is represented by an "on-point" at a position defined by the triple (domain Object, mapping, range Object). Lines on the graph parallel to one of the axes can show a full range of domain, mapping or range objects. Similarly a plane can represent all objects in two dimensions of the database. The point, line, and plane are representations of queries and answers to queries. Subsets are represented by sublines or subplanes.

## 1.3 Visualisation

In the past five years there has been an explosion in the amount of research work in the area of data visualisation [11]. This has been prompted both by the requirements of users and by the wide availability of computer graphics hardware powerful enough to produce good results quickly. The aim of this research is to make abstract data more comprehensible by showing it in graphical form. There are a number of techniques which can be employed to produce a useful visual representation. These include animation, 3D graphics, and rendering. One of the challenges of visualisation is to find the best way of representing the data, because each type of data has its own particular characteristics, so that although one technique may work well for one type of data it may not be applicable to another. The visualisation process has to involve the colours, textures, and animation's that make the data easiest to understand. This is especially difficult when there are many dimensions to the data, which have to be shown on a 2D display. The usefulness of a representation is determined by its descriptive capacity, potential for comparison, aid in focusing attention, and versatility.

By combining volume visualisation with hypermedia, a high quality graphical interface to an educational medical database was developed [12]. The data had to be divided and labelled, for example picking out the skull and brain as two separate parts of a head. These labels could then be used as hypertext to point out differently coloured areas in the volume. The user is provided with various types of tool which can be used to explore the image and consult the knowledgebase.

Moving from 2D visualisations of electronic charge density to 3D volumetric renderings, [13] presented the benefits of the third dimension in aiding comprehension. Far quicker and better understanding of the processes at work resulted. It was also found that depth was easier to perceive in stereoscopic views of still images than in non-stereoscopic animated images.

The main process in visualisation is creating a mapping from the data to the graphical representation. There are two complementary approaches to this, a special purpose language which provides flexibility at the cost of a longer learning process, and visual dataflow programming which is more restrictive but easier to learn.

A new language for molecular visualisation called Pdbq [14] has been developed. It is an interpreted language based on C, providing data types, control structures, operators, and built-in functions appropriate to the task. The aim was to provide a powerful and flexible language capable of handling low and high level objects of interest fast enough to encourage experimentation and improve productivity while remaining easy to use. Making the language interpreted provides the speed but there is a steep learning curve. Once a program is perfected it can be incorporated into the more usable dataflow programs.

The dataflow technique is a toolkit approach, using the visual programming idea of having graphical symbols to represent program elements, for example, AVS [15] and AVE [16]. The dataflow is an attractive abstraction as it highlights the mapping of data to representation and allows for interactive exploration of different mapping methods. AVS was designed to make the development of interactive scientific visualisations much easier. The concept was to have software building blocks which could be interconnected to form the required application. The dataflow technique suffers in that it is not a true visual programming environment, is often inefficient when handling large amounts of data, and can lead to complex networks of modules.

## 1.4 Three dimensional interfaces

The current generation of graphical user interfaces have taken on a standard look and feel, with windows, menus, and mouse pointer helping create the metaphorical desktop environment. This approach has taken hold because it is very much easier for novice users. However, as this form of user interface has become universally accepted it has also been quite thoroughly examined and found wanting in a number of respects [17]. One problem is that a screen full of windows can become difficult to manage. This results from the user wishing to take advantage of the friendlier interface by working on more than one thing at a time, and also from having to handle larger volumes of information. A solution has been to move from the two and a half dimensions of windows environments to fully three dimensional interfaces by introducing depth to the display.

Navigating in the 2D space of the windows type interface has been made very easy by the use of mouse and pointer. The success of the mouse as an input device is a result of the direct and immediate response that it provides. The introduction of a third dimension adds a complication to the interaction when using a mouse. The problem is that the mouse only returns two dimensional movement information so there is no way that it can be used in the same direct way for three dimensional interaction. The solution is a new input device such as a spaceball or dataglove but as yet these are expensive and thus rarely available. Even with a suitable input device the interaction is more complex because it will probably be necessary to use a 3D cursor, i.e. a cursor which moves in and out of the 3D space. Another problem is navigating in what will very likely be a very large 3D space. Moving between distant points would be tedious and/or difficult. A three dimensional display introduces hidden information because any object shown will have a rear view which is not visible. Thus it is also necessary to have some means of rotating the viewpoint.

An experimental user interface [18,19,20,21,22] has been created which copes with the demands of large amounts of information. The graphical power of today's technology is used to introduce new ways of visualising information. A number of visual abstractions are used to help the user comprehend the information presented. A linear abstraction called the Perspective Wall is used to overcome the problem of large flat workspaces which cannot be accommodated on a single screen in a readable form. Usually a subpart of the space is shown full-size and an overview shows how it relates to the whole. The Perspective Wall distorts the information by folding the 2D information onto a 3D wall which has a central area of interest and two perspective areas on either side which show the context. If something in the contextual area is selected the wall smoothly scrolls the area of interest to the centre. Hierarchical data, for example directory structures or class hierarchies, is made more comprehensible by using the Cone Tree. These are 3D representations that give a uniform layout to the data, with each level represented by a cone. The cones are drawn in such a way as to not obscure those behind. Selecting a node on a cone causes it to rotate so that the selected item is at the front. If a child item is selected then its parent cone is also rotated to the front of that level. It is difficult to show a large wide hierarchy in 2D on a single screen unless scaled down to a point where individual elements are difficult to distinguish, whereas it can be shown quite easily in 3D cone form without loss of information.

Robertson et al investigate the advantages and challenges of three dimensional interfaces. A range of techniques are used to increase information processing capabilities. Firstly an effort is made is to enlarge the workspace available to the user. This is achieved in two ways, firstly by introducing their own version of the rooms concept where there are multiple 3D workspaces which users can move through, and secondly by using animation and 3D perspective to increase the density of information shown on one screen. The introduction of 3D workspaces requires new navigation and manipulation techniques. Users can walk through the workspace by using special on screen controls worked by mouse clicks. This allows general exploration but to move to particular areas of interest in a 3D display is quite difficult, especially with 2D pointing devices, and it is for this reason a technique called logarithmic motion was devised where a target point is specified and a ray created between the current view direction and target point, along which the user can move, either towards or away from. Similarly objects can be moved along such rays. The rooms can be navigated either by clicking on door objects or by using the overview which shows all the 3D workspaces, and which even allows rooms to be reached into and manipulated. A Governor mechanism is used to maximise human interaction rates, i.e. the Interactive Objects are scheduled to be in tune with human reactions. An example of this is to complete any animation in about a second, which is fast enough to be usable but not so fast as to disorientate the user.

The Cone Tree has been used to good effect in another interface [23]. In the "Viznet" system it is used to show hierarchical part-of relationships in a multi-media database. However, the main focus of this system is the use of "Fisheye" views of information, i.e. using exaggerated perspective to look at an object of greatest interest whilst maintaining a less detailed view of other available information. A spherical representation is used in a similar way to the "perspective wall" described above. Here, an object is represented by an icon on the surface of a sphere. Directly related objects are shown together on one surface, the closer two icons are the closer the relationship. The sphere can be rotated and by clicking on a particular icon it is possible to move down to a level which shows objects which are related but indirectly, through another object.

An experimental 3D interface developed at Apple Computers [24] uses a combination of 3D mouse and 3D cursor to provide direct manipulation of 3D objects. The aim was to find a way of matching the performance of the two dimensional mouse so that three dimensional interaction would be made just as easy. The results of user observations have shown the promise of such an approach.

The use of three dimensional interfaces is supposed to take advantage of the users everyday skill in working with spatial information. Some research, however, has shown that using spatial information does not necessarily help and can sometimes introduce complications to what should be a simple interaction. One test of spatial versus symbolic representation [25] found that performance was better using symbolic information rather than two or three dimensional spatial information.

## 1.5 Summary

Graphical schema design and browsing are now common, while querying and manipulation are still to receive the attention they deserve, as they would benefit greatly from an interactive graphical interface. There is still a need for research into the provision of graphical interfaces to databases, and most particularly object oriented databases.

It is difficult to provide flexible representations of complex semantically rich objects. Each of the different mechanisms for providing visualisations of objects offer advantages and disadvantages therefore the choice is dependent on the type of application. If a portable application is to be provided then classes of display objects may be the answer, whereas if extensibility is more important, then inheriting visualisations may be the best approach.

Graphical representation such as 3DIS may have appeal for those with mathematical backgrounds but for others it is extremely difficult to understand. The more complex a relationship being modelled the harder it is to comprehend. This shows that it is quite easy to design a three dimensional interface which is theoretically attractive but too difficult to use in practice. Users evaluation of prototype interfaces should help prevent this situation.

A special visualisation language, perhaps in the form of a library of classes, is one possibility that so far has not been used on C++ based object oriented databases but might be worth consideration. Clearly the best approach to creating graphical visualisations would be a graphical interface that allowed different aspects of the visualisation process to be controlled. The dataflow technique is an example of this but is perhaps not directly relevant to working with the more general information stored in an OODB.

The Cone Tree and Perspective Wall are a good starting point for developing visualisations as both are successful when used for particular types of data. The Cone Tree is good for hierarchical relationships but cannot cope with the possibility of overlapping subtrees, for example the case of the subpart which is used by two superparts. The Perspective Wall is effective when displaying a high density of information but is restricted in the visibility of contextual information, i.e. the two side walls are more difficult to read than the centre wall. The "fisheye" view could be useful in providing focus in a display which holds a large number of objects, and the use of a degree of interest function would help in this process. The idea of having many representations of differing levels of detail could also be useful, especially in controlling the complexity of a visualisation.

As 3D input devices are rare it is necessary to find a way of using the 2D mouse for 3D work. It may be possible to use the 3D cursor method even with the 2D mouse. Care must be taken that spatial information will actually provide benefits in terms of comprehension and ease of use. Three dimensional graphics will be presented as a part of a normal windows type interface as this evolutionary rather than revolutionary approach is more likely to succeed in attracting users. It would be too easy to design and implement a fantastical three dimensional interface which no one would want to use as it bore no relation to current working practices.

## 2 WINONA

The WINdows Object Navigation Application (WINONA) described, displays three dimensional visualisations of the contents of an object oriented database which allow the user to interact directly with the database. This experimental system is being used to investigate how three dimensional graphics can be used to visualise the contents of a database and thus help the user fully understand the database in terms of the structures, the types, and the objects which it holds.

The following criteria were addressed in the design of the system. The display should be designed to encourage users to explore the information. This would entail using representations which make interaction much easier than in current textual or two dimensional graphical interfaces. Perspective would be used to enhance the illusion of depth while colour and other means would be used to highlight the objects of interest within the display. It should be possible to manipulate the views by rotating, translating, and zooming. Different visualisations would be used to show different aspects of the database by displaying different subsets of the following elements: classes, objects, object attributes, object methods, and links between related objects. It should be possible to tailor the display to show only those elements of interest to the user. Standard dialog boxes and menus would be used to provide a familiar method of interaction when dealing with more detailed information about objects and classes. It should be possible to save the state of visualisations so that the user can return to a previously created visualisation.

## 2.1 Prototyping

An iterative development process was followed whereby a sequence of prototype interfaces were produced, each of which was evaluated and the results used to improve the subsequent prototype.

Basic elements of an OODB could be shown in a visualisation. Classes could be displayed either in relation to other classes or in relation to their own object instances. The relationships could be hierarchical, e.g. 'part-of', or simple associations, and could be one to one, one to many, or many to many.

To encourage users to explore the data, visualisations of a database were devised which would make interactions as easy as possible. By producing attractive and exciting visualisations it was hoped that the interactive process would be made more stimulating than the standard form type of interface used at present. Numerous ideas were sketched to see how a three dimensional space might be used to both aid understanding of the database and show a higher density of information. Trying to invent good three dimensional display ideas through working in a two dimensional space is rather difficult, requiring a highly developed mental modelling capability.

At first the idea of using metaphors was appealing, i.e. to use something in the real world as a metaphor for the computer model, a widely used example being the 'desktop' environments. One example of a metaphor, relating to nature, was that of seeing the classes as trees in a forest, objects as fruit on those trees, and vines between trees representing relationships. This forest could be explored, trees climbed and fruit picked. (See Fig. 1)

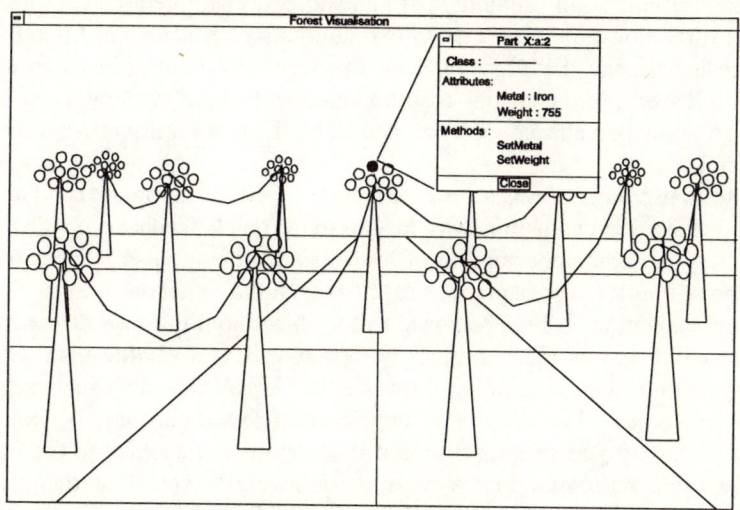

Fig. 1. Forest metaphor

Another natural world metaphor saw classes as mountains of objects that could be flown over and around. The library metaphor had classes as subject areas and objects as individual books. The user could walk round the library picking books off the shelves, looking inside for detailed information, and perhaps following references to related books. The Universe metaphor had classes as stars around which orbited the object planets. These metaphors were attractive as ideas but would be difficult to implement, so simpler geometrical representations were then devised. The idea was to combine a set of simple geometrical shapes so that they represented a logical visualisation of the structure and contents of an OODB. There were three elements, each of which could have a different representation. The class was seen as something which would contain its instances. The instances would be smaller elements, placed inside the class representation. The third element was the link which was most simply represented by a line between two instances. These elements were combined in a way that gave a true representation of the underlying structure.

A number of simple database schemas were designed in order to find out what types of structure were possible. There were two obvious hierarchical structures, the inheritance and aggregation relationships. Other relationships might be hierarchical or simple mappings. An example of a hierarchical relationship which depends on the semantics of the relationship is the manager (staff class) who manages (relationship) other staff. In the real world this would be seen as a hierarchical relationship from the overall manager, down through middle managers, to the non-management staff, but in the schema it is simply a one to many relationship. There is no way this sort of implicitly hierarchical relationship can be recognised unless it is explicitly labelled. This calls into question the current standard notations for representing relationships which are implicitly hierarchical.

The visualisation should distinguish between hierarchical and non-hierarchical relationships. There were two alternatives considered. Links could be drawn in such a way that they indicate the type of relationship as in standard graphical notations, or the spatial positioning could be used to show the difference. The latter option was chosen as it seemed to be a more intuitive use of the three dimensional space.

The first prototype was a set of drawings of visualisation ideas. The aim of presenting these for evaluation was to get some quick feedback on the quality, applicability, and comprehensibility of the approach being taken. There follows a description of the five representations together with the actual designs.

**1.** The representation in Fig. 2 shows a root object pointing to a disc containing subpart or child objects. Each subpart is represented as a smaller disc within the main disc. Within the subdiscs are even smaller discs which represent the subpart objects of that object - i.e. how many subparts the selected part has. To look further down the hierarchy you select a disc and its contents are zoomed to the next disc where the same representation is used, so allowing traversal of the hierarchy. Objects in the selected hierarchy are labelled suitably and the details of one object are shown in a popup window.

**2.** The representation in Fig. 3 is similar to the first except a rectangular representation is used and the number of subparts is represented by the "vertical" height of the bar or line. Again this can be used to navigate a hierarchy.

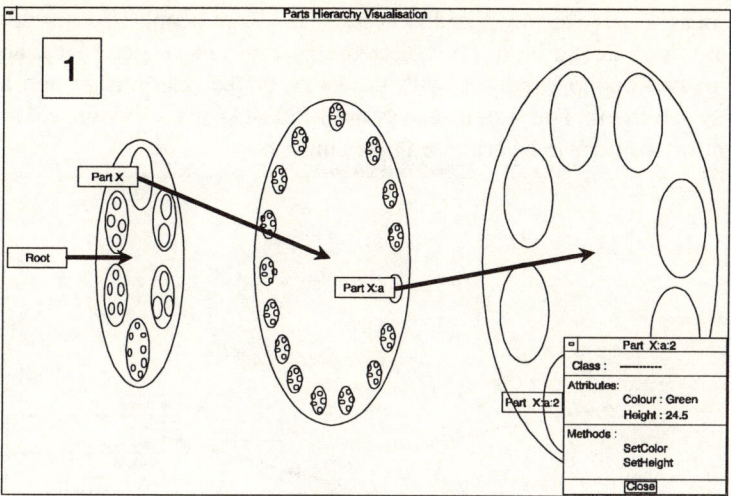

Fig. 2. Visualisation design 1

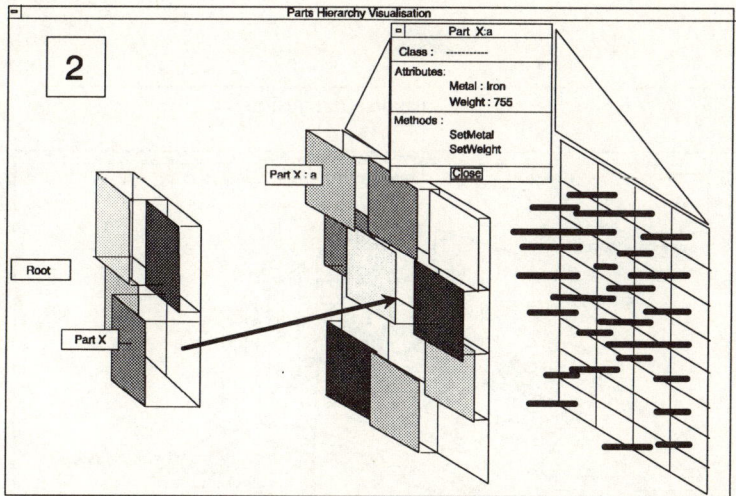

Fig. 3. Visualisation design 2

**3.** Fig. 4 shows another variant on the first which uses a pie representation to show the number of subparts - the bigger the slice the greater the number of subcomponents. It is possible that the size representations could be of a subcomponent of an object, for example to represent its weight attribute if it were a machine component, rather than the number of subparts. To see details of an instance you select a slice.

**4.** Fig. 5 shows a version of the 3DIS representation of a database which instead of trying to display every object on the axes shows only the instances of given classes and their related classes. For example the domain is of parts and the range is of subparts. The way this is presented is somewhat cluttered but has possibilities, especially for representing overlapping data, e.g. where workers can have more than one boss. It may however be too abstract for most people. To see details of a relationship you select a blob. The selected object and its related object are shown in detail in two popup windows, with the name of the relationship and an arrow drawn between them. This example was used to test if what was considered a bad representation would also be criticised by evaluators.

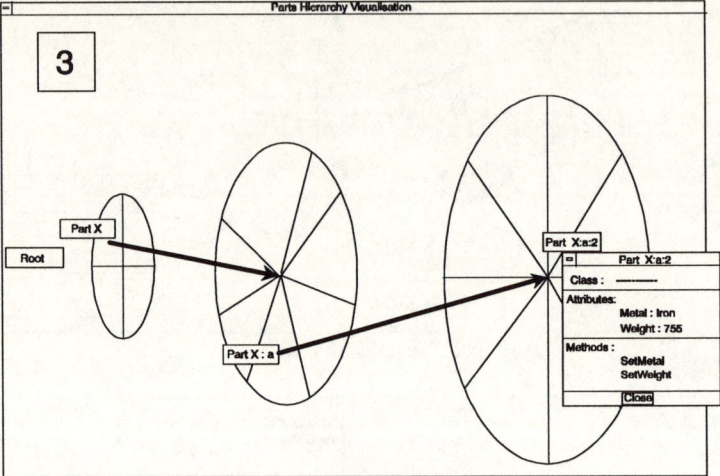

Fig. 4. Visualisation design 3

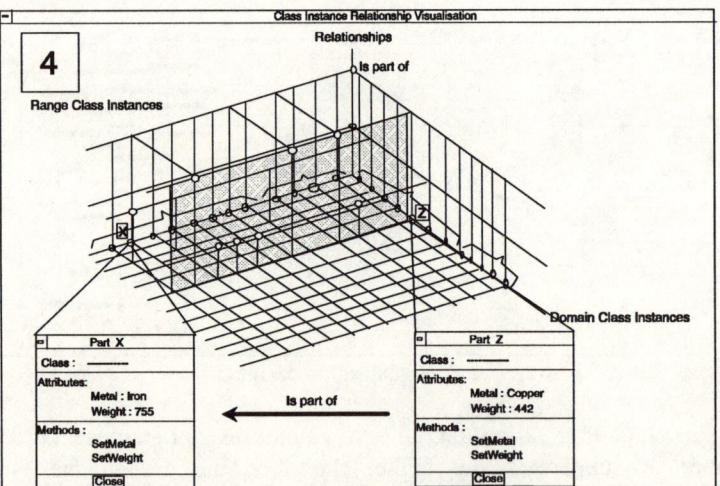

Fig. 5. Visualisation design 4

**5.** Fig. 6 is yet another hierarchical visualisation which borrows from 3DIS the use of points on a grid. Each plane is one class in the hierarchy - each blob representing an instance. An object in a higher plane which is related to an object in the next lower plane has a line drawn between it. This allows representation of intersecting sets of sub objects as they will have more than one connection with the upper plane. To see details of an object, including the related objects, you select a blob.

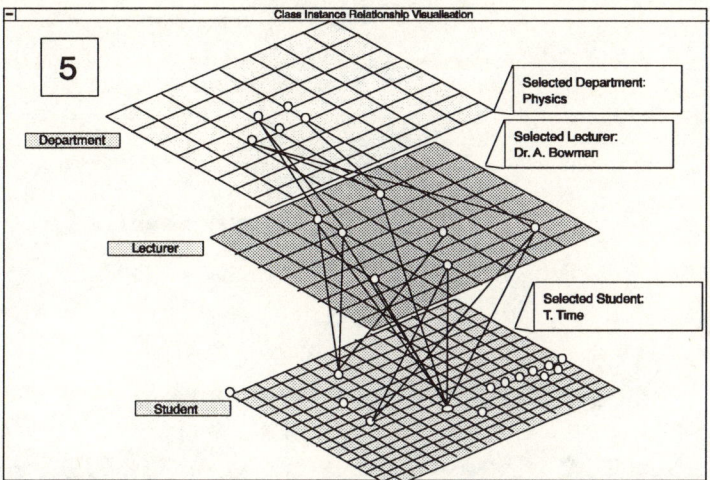

Fig. 6. Visualisation design 5

The designs were shown to a number of people who had knowledge of object-oriented databases and interface techniques. In general the designs were looked upon favourably, all except the 3DIS type display which was universally condemned as incomprehensible (even in this simplified form).

The prototype displays provided a useful means of finding problems and inspiring suggestions for improvements. A number of possible difficulties were discovered. For example, in the hierarchical displays it is impossible to select a sub-instance and move up the hierarchy. Another problem with the hierarchical displays is that they do not cope with the possibility of one object lower down in the hierarchy being connected to different objects above. The grid visualisation does handle this sort of relationship as every object in a class is shown. It was thought that the ability to represent information such as the number of related instances, or the size of a particular object attribute, e.g. weight, would be useful. Feelings about the methods of representation varied. The bar chart idea was easily understood and easy to judge but the pie chart approach was thought less easy to understand. The circles within circles was also thought difficult to judge, and was anyway seen as problematic for showing numbers higher than about twenty.

As a result of the prototypes it was decided to develop the interface based on visualisation number 5. Four further prototypes of increasing functionality were developed resulting in the version being reported here.

## 2.2 Present Interface

Currently two types of visualisation are provided. Fig. 7 depicts the hierarchical visualisation and Fig. 8 the circular wall.

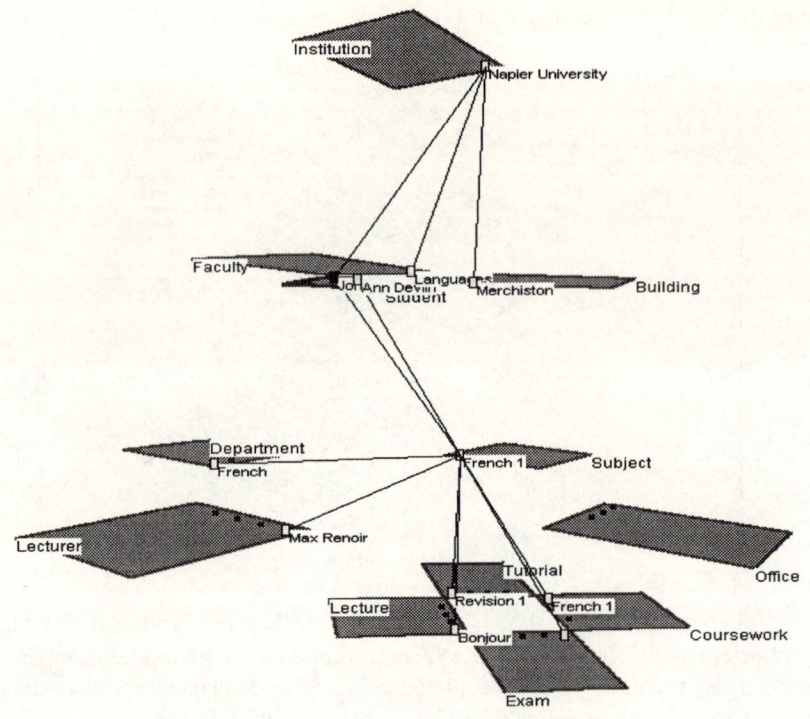

Fig. 7 . Hierarchical Visualisation

The hierarchical display shows database classes as equally sized squares arranged on a number of levels. The positioning of class squares reflects their position in the class hierarchy of the database schema. The proximity of one class to another implies the closeness of the relationship between those classes. Within each class square are the much smaller object visualisation squares, each representing one object of that class. These are arranged so that they always remain within the class boundary square. The density of object squares in a class square thus indicates the number of instances there are of that class.

The circular wall of classes visualisation was based on the perspective wall and sphere ideas described earlier. The idea was that selecting an object would cause directly related objects to be highlighted on the other classes. The wall can then be rotated to see those related objects. The interior of the cylinder shows link lines between related objects. This combines some of the perspective or fisheye effect with a more general relationship visualisation. Hierarchical relationships are not represented therefore the hierarchical visualisation aids in a fuller understanding of the database schema. The circular display represents database classes as fixed width rectangles with variable length. The length changes according to the number of instances there are of that class. The class rectangles are arranged in a ring, each one perpendicular and touching its neighbours. This arrangement allows each class rectangle to grow to any length. Again, each instance of the class is visualised as a small square within the class rectangle.

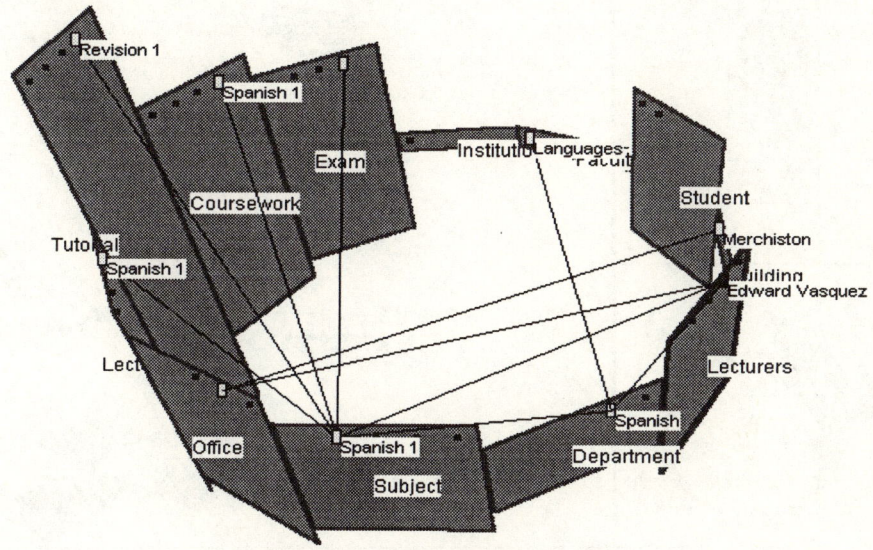

Fig. 8 . Circular wall visualisation

The visualisations have been incorporated into a standard Microsoft Windows style application with title and menu bars at the top, status bar at the bottom, and work area in the centre. The work area can hold many visualisation windows which are organised using the standard Windows multiple document interface technique. Each visualisation window is divided into three viewing areas (viewers), one large square viewer takes up two thirds of the screen to the right, and two equally sized smaller viewers are at the left. Each of these viewers is used to display a visualisation, appropriately scaled. It is intended that the user will work mostly on the visualisation in the large work viewer, with occasional interactions in the smaller viewers. If the visualisation in a smaller viewer becomes of most interest it can be swapped into the large viewer.

Figs. 9 -11 show the current prototype in use. Apart from the different structures, the visualisations show exactly the same sort of information. Each class has a label which is displayed beside the relevant class visualisation. An iconic representation can be used in conjunction with the class label or on its own, as a more visual indication of the class type. Both icons and labels can be toggled on and off when required.

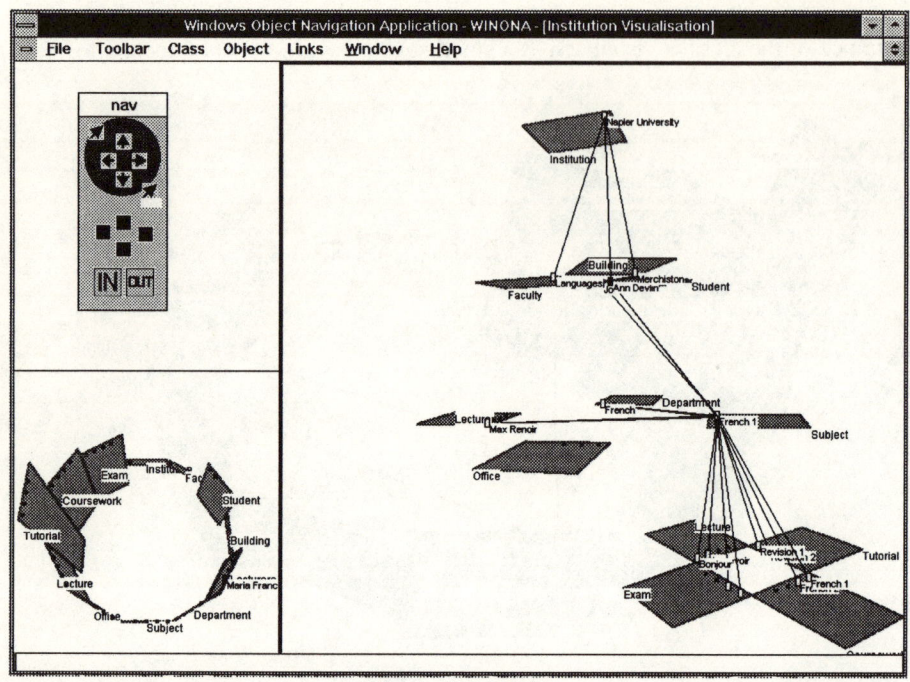

Fig. 9 . WINONA

The object has four different representations, each showing more information. The visualisation starts off by showing only that objects exist, using a small square within the class visualisation. When the object is selected the square is enlarged, given a different colour, and labelled. If there is a bitmap image to go with the particular object then the user can choose to show it, by itself or with the label. The most detailed view of object information can be chosen by double clicking on an object. This causes a popup window to appear which shows the objects attributes and methods in the form of scrollable lists. Relationships between objects are also visualised, and again the visualisation can be user-customised. When no relationships are to be shown only the selected object is highlighted, in red, and labelled. If direct relationships are to be shown then directly related objects are highlighted in yellow, and labelled. A further level of connection can also be shown, so that objects related via some intermediary object are also highlighted and labelled. If highlighting of related objects is not clear enough, then it is also possible to have linking lines drawn between each related object.

Users can directly interact with the visualisation in a number of ways. The mouse pointer is used to select objects of interest. When the left mouse button is pressed the system automatically detects which viewer, class and object are being selected. These are then highlighted as described above. Relationship lines are drawn if required.

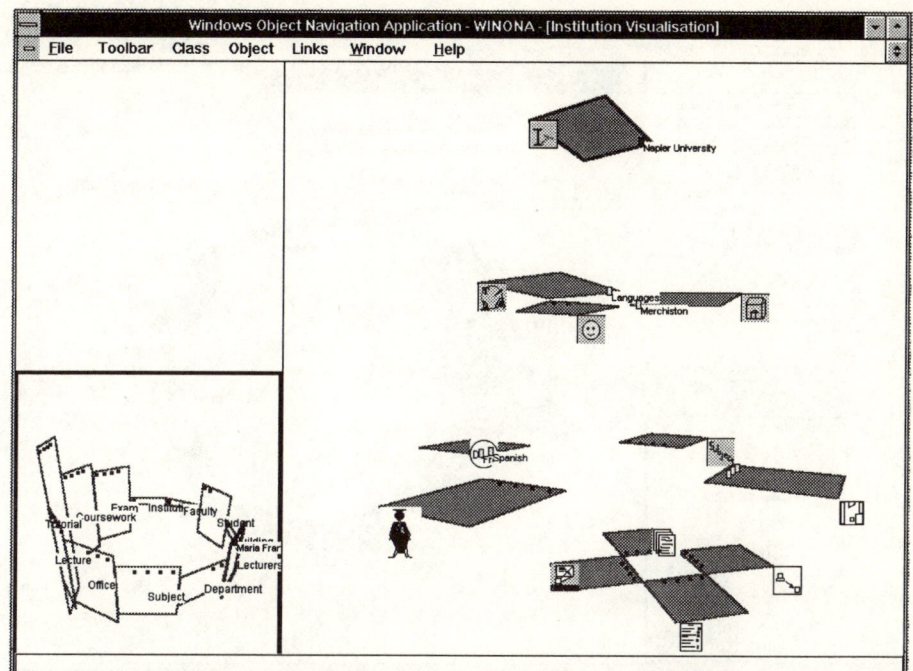

Fig. 10. WINONA - iconic representation of classes

As previously mentioned, double clicking on an object causes a popup window of detailed information to be displayed. However, this popup has two buttons, 'next' and 'previous', which allow all the object instances to be navigated by moving backwards or forwards through the instances of the class. For example, when 'next' is pressed the attributes values in the window are changed accordingly, and the related visual object is highlighted as though it had been chosen using the mouse. Thus it is possible to quickly move through the set of objects examining the attributes, and seeing relationships between that object and other objects. This popup also handles simple querying of the database for objects in that class. By double clicking on an attribute, another window appears where a query can be selected. This facility is currently limited, only allowing simple string searches, e.g. select objects whose labels begin with the letter 't', but it would be fairly easy to extend it to handle all sorts of queries. The important aspect of the query is that the results cause the popup to display only those objects matching the query, so pressing next and previous shows the next or previous object which matches the query, and again the attributes and relationships are shown.

By depressing the control key while selecting objects, either with the mouse or using the 'next' and 'previous' buttons, the previous selection will be retained. This allows the user to view many objects and their relationships together. In conjunction with the query facility it is possible to highlight in the visualisation all those objects matching the query.

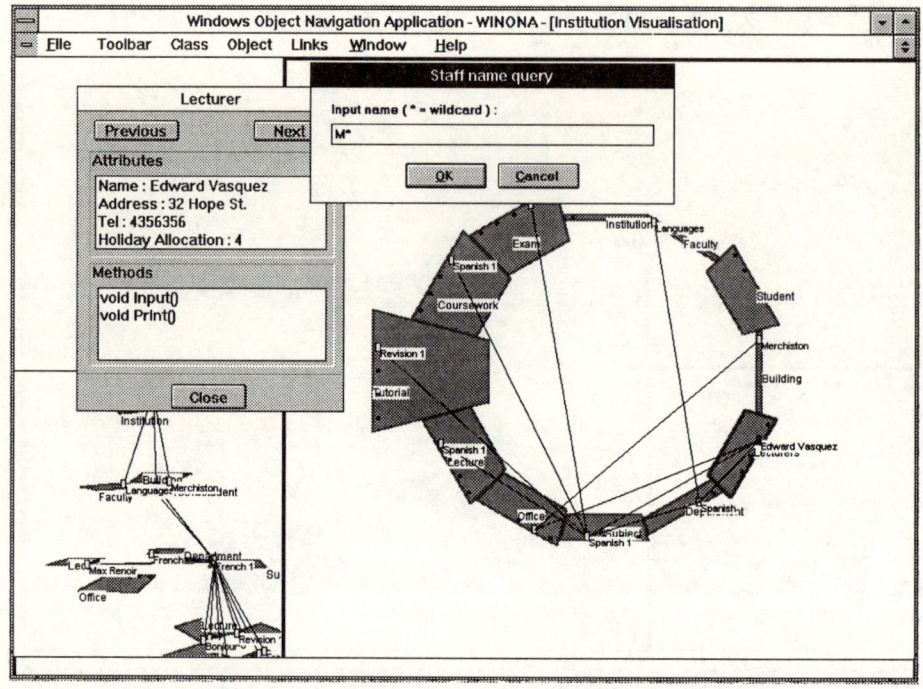

Fig. 11. WINONA - querying

A floating toolbar is provided for manipulating the visualisation displays. Six arrow buttons allow the display to be rotated around each of the x, y and z axes. Each visualisation is treated as a single object so that the whole of the selected visualisation will be rotated together. Two buttons, 'in' and 'out', can be used to increase or decrease the size of the visualisation. Finally, four other arrow type buttons can be used to move the visualisation up, down, left, or right.

Originally the visualisation system was intended to read from any OODB, transform the data to some intermediate form, and then visualise it. Thus there would be two separate phases to the process. The pre-processing stage would, over time, be developed so that it was capable of handling the data storage formats of all the major object oriented databases. Pre-processing would involve finding out the structure of the data held in the database, i.e. what classes were used and how were they related, so that an intermediate version of the schema could be created. Then it would be necessary to navigate this structure to access the data and transform that to a suitable form. The visualisation process would then be a simple matter of interpreting the intermediate form of the data and displaying it in the chosen graphical form. The database for which the pre-processor was written was POET, an OODB running on PCs. However, version 2 of POET has no data dictionary facilities for accessing the database structure, although this facility is expected in a future version. It was therefore decided that a specific example database would be developed and used. The data structures would be known and therefore could be directly accessed using normal methods and this restriction would not affect experimentation with visualisations.

# 3 Discussion

## 3.1 Challenges

The design and building of an effective, interesting, and easy to use three dimensional interface to an object oriented database has proved a difficult problem. In the end a reasonably useful experimental interface has been created but the most important results of the project are the insights that have been gained into the challenges this type of work offers:
- it is very difficult to find three dimensional representations that are simple, work for all structures, and can display large volumes of data in a comprehensible way
- there are issues relating to how the visualisation is created, totally automatically, part automatic/part user defined or totally user defined
- how does the user specify what is to be visualised, the whole database or just a small part
- the visualisations can be either dependent or independent of the information that is being visualised
- using three dimensional graphics introduces perceptual problems that are absent when working in only two dimensions
- navigation of a two dimensional space is much easier to handle than moving about in three dimensions
- the capabilities of the databases themselves have a bearing on the work that can be done, particularly in terms of making the interface non-application specific
- implementing this type of interface is affected very much by the hardware and software being used

## 3.2 Database visualisation

Visualisation can use metaphorical representations, which take a familiar real world structure as their basis, in the hope that the user will transfer their knowledge of the real world and apply it to understand the visualisation. The alternative approach, as used in the experimental interface, is to construct an abstract representation which relates well to the data being visualised and is easy to understand. The latter approach was taken because the implementation looked to be less difficult.

In an OODB there are two basic types of relationship that can be visualised, the hierarchical and non-hierarchical. The first problem is thus to find a way of showing the difference between these two types of relationship. The hierarchical relationship was divided into three types, i.e. inheritance, part-of, and implicit. Inheritance and part-of are recognisable as standard elements of object oriented design but the implicit hierarchy is a relationship specific to the data, i.e. the role of the specific data element affects how it should be shown. An example of implicit hierarchy is the manager employee relationship which the real world sees as hierarchical, and so should be visualised as such to make sense, but it is not represented as hierarchical in standard object oriented design techniques. The experimental interface does not show this type of hierarchical relationship.

In Winona only the part-of hierarchical relationship is represented, and in the most obvious way, by having a direct correspondence between the spatial positioning of a class in the visualisation and its position in the schema , i.e. containers are placed above their constituent classes in the representation. The relation of sub parts of a hierarchy to their super part is also be indicated by spatial positioning, i.e. constituent classes are not only placed below, but also in close proximity to, their containers. The problem is that it is possible for one class to be a sub part of many classes and so it would have to be shown in close proximity to all of them. Again, it would have been possible to use symbols and connecting lines to indicate relationships, as in two dimensional object oriented designs, but this would have moved away from the aim of using only three dimensional spatial positioning and so was not used. The experimental interface relies purely on spatial positioning to indicate part-of hierarchies. This is partly successful in that users can see that certain classes contain other classes but it requires explicit representation of object relationships for the user to gain full understanding of the relationships between classes.

Non-hierarchical relationships are also shown in Winona, and also cause problems in terms of spatial positioning. Directly related classes are shown on the same level in the hierarchical visualisation to show the relationship is non-hierarchical. However, it is possible for classes involved in different hierarchical relationships, and so perhaps on different levels, to be directly related in a non-hierarchical way. The visualisation can thus cause confusion, indicating hierarchy where there is none. This highlights the difficulty of providing a meaningful representation of the database structure using only spatial positioning. The difficulties described in finding representations that give a valid view of a whole database might be lessened if it was made possible to visualise only a small subset of classes at one time.

The objects or instances of a class have to be given some visual form. In the experimental interface a very simple approach is taken. Each object is given a direct representation as a small square within the relevant class square. This indicates both the presence of objects in that class, and the number of objects. In order to avoid information overload, no other information is provided unless the object is selected or is involved in a selected relationship. Most relationships will involve a small subset of objects and therefore giving them a more detailed visualisation should not cause a problem. This gradual revealing of more detail confirms to the idea of degree of interest. Only when the user indicates an interest in a particular object is that object shown in more detail. The experimental interface has four levels of detail, the square indicating existence, the label, the icon, and the popup information window. Each one allows the user to get more and more information about the object of interest.

Even though the lowest level of detail takes up very little screen space there are still problems in trying to show very large numbers of objects. The hierarchical visualisation has fixed size class squares into which any number of object squares must fit. Eventually it will be impossible to distinguish individual objects as they are packed closer and closer together. One way of overcoming this is shown in the circular wall where each class is represented by a rectangle which grows in size to accommodate more objects. It is also possible that objects need not be shown at all, unless involved in a selected relationship, but this would mean finding another way of representing class size information.

Visualisation of objects can be somewhat dependent on the type of data. Some data is inherently visual, e.g. photographs, so there is scope for showing that data directly within the visualisation but another piece of data may just be stored as text and so the only way to show it is to show the text. Abstract numerical data could be given as just numbers but would be more effectively presented in graphical form, e.g. a bar graph. The experimental interface provides the four standard representations which don't take into account the special needs of the different types of data being viewed. It would have been necessary to provide some mechanism for users to specify how each type of data was to be visualised, if each type of object was to be displayed differently. If each class provided their own visual representation this would not be required.

## 3.3 Working in three dimensions

Though we all inhabit the three dimensional world there are still relatively few people who are used to thinking and working with three dimensional representations in a computer display. Users of computer aided design packages and molecular modelling packages become familiar with the requirements of three dimensional work but the average user is more used to looking at flat pages of text. This general unfamiliarity means that when three dimensional displays and interfaces are used they must try and exploit all the available techniques to aid perception and understanding of the three dimensional space.

The experimental interface is relatively poor in helping the user to understand what they are seeing. Perspective projection is used to foreshorten objects, meaning that the nearer the object is the larger it is, and a form of hidden line removal is provided which adds to the users understanding because nearer objects hide farther away ones. Other techniques such as shading, transparency, and casting shadows would all add to the users perception of the three dimensional space.

Even when the image is understood it can still be difficult to position it in such a way that it reveals exactly the information you want to see. It is possible to bring one object of interest to the front and find that another one is then hidden or too far away.

A three dimensional graphical representation involves more complicated interactions than are present with two dimensional systems. These interactions relate to navigation and selection. Navigation of the experimental interface visualisations takes a very primitive form, working in much the same way as most computer aided design systems. The visualisation is treated as a single object which can be rotated around any axis, translated along any axis, and made larger or smaller. This has the advantage of familiarity but for larger visualisations it would be better to have some finer control, such as rotating one level, or even one class, at a time.

Selecting objects of interest within a three dimensional space also throws up challenges. In the experimental interface the mouse pointer selection technique is maintained because it is familiar to most users but in some cases this is not the best approach. The true feeling of direct manipulation is lost because the users cannot move their cursor about in the 3D world to select the object of interest.

## 3.4 Future directions

This work has revealed many areas suitable for future research:
1. There is enormous potential for the use of metaphors in this type of work. Some possible ideas have been discussed previously but there are no doubt many others that could be tried.
2. Other visual cues, such as colour and shape, for distinguishing between hierarchical and non hierarchical relationships could be tried. For example, the superclass(es) of a class could be shown as blue and subclass(es) shown as red whenever a class is selected.
3. With an inheritance hierarchy the challenge is how to represent relationships that can involve members of the generic or special type, both of which might be useful to the user at some stage in the interaction. An example of this is when you have a teacher, who is a special type of person. A user might wish to see which people (including teachers) read a particular newspaper, or see which teachers teach a certain subject. The interface has to handle showing the data as either type and must provide a way for the user to specify which one they wish to see at any one time. Should general and specialised classes be shown at the same time? The answer is probably not, because the user will be interested in relationships involving either the general or specific classes but not both. One way of dealing with the visualisation and interfacing problems this involves would be to show only the most general class at first and allow the user to indicate in some way that the specialised subclasses should be shown instead. There must therefore be an indication in the visual class that shows it has subclasses or a superclass so that the user sees a choice can be made. An alternative approach would be to show all subclasses in a hierarchy with a symbolic representation to show their exact relationships to each other. Only when a subclass was selected or involved in a selection would the irrelevant classes be removed from the visualisation. This is a reasonable approach but there may be structures which cause conflicts in terms of

placement, e.g. something many levels down in an inheritance hierarchy may be at the top of a part-of hierarchy. The complexity of relationships in the schema of an OODB make it difficult, perhaps impossible, to predict all the structures that the visualisation process will have to cope with, and so it may be impossible to make it completely generic.

4. The realm of implicitly hierarchical relationships needs to be investigated to see if there are many such real world relationships which will cause problems. In the type of relationship it is possible for recursion so that it will be necessary to show one class many times, taking different positions in the hierarchy, or there will have to be some sort of graphical representation linking objects within one class that shows their relative positions in a hierarchy.

5. The visual representation of large numbers of objects needs to be studied. Possible solutions include forcing a query to be performed on very large classes so that only subsets are shown, or alternatively, putting objects that have common attribute values into grouped objects which are then visualised (the grouped object may indicate in the visualisation how large the group is).

6. The experimental interface works only with a specific database whose structures are known. This information is used to hardcode the visualisation layout into the program. Any real system would have to include an automatic layout algorithm. Having laid out one small database by hand, and thought about how this may be done automatically, it was concluded that this would be a difficult task to achieve quickly. The difficulty stems purely from the complexity of an OODB schema, with multiple hierarchies and inter-relationships possible. The alternative to automatic layout is to allow the user to create their own. It is envisaged that power users would create these layouts, perhaps only showing part of a database, using their expert knowledge of the schema. These would then be made available to other users in a similar way to relational database 'views'. It may be possible to allow the user to create an initial layout and then use an algorithm which tidies it up in such a way that relationships are shown in as simple a way as possible. These ideas and others should be investigated.

7. A more effective approach to navigation could be investigated. One idea would be to make the visualisation a virtual world which can be explored. The user could then move about within the world as though inside that space. Walking in such a virtual world is not the best means of moving from one point of interest to another, especially if they are far apart, as the user would find passing through masses of uninteresting data very tedious. Techniques such as moving along lines of interest have proved successful but other navigation methods need to be found. It is also possible that for some visualisations it is necessary to restrict the user's ability to manipulate the scene. For example, in the experimental interface it would be quite valid to stop the user from rotating the hierarchical visualisation in such a way that the sense of what is above and below in the hierarchy is lost.

8. The usefulness of a three dimensional input device, such as a space ball, should be examined, together with a 3D cursor, as the combination might improve usability.

9. The informal user evaluations have shown that even a relatively primitive interface that makes use of three dimensional graphics has advantages over a

standard two dimensional interface. It would be useful to take a number of three dimensional visualisation approaches and perform a careful study of how performance compares with a conventional two dimensional interface.

10. Having tried to find a good three dimensional graphics library written in C++ and conforming to object oriented standards there is clear scope for such a library to be written. For this type of work it is particularly important that interactive functions are provided, e.g. what object is the mouse pointer nearest to.

11. There is obvious potential in three dimensional visualisations of object oriented databases for the creation of visual queries and to carry out visual manipulation. For example, in the experimental interface simple manipulations such as deleting an object could have been implemented relatively simply by adding a mechanism, such as pressing the delete key, to delete the selected object. Querying is a much more challenging prospect, however if all object attributes were given a visual representation then it would seem to be an easy further step to provide a way of selecting ranges of values for an attribute visually, perhaps using direct manipulation with the mouse. It is possible that current research is concentrating too closely on trying to find visual equivalents of the old textual query rather than using visual techniques to devise completely new ways of querying.

# Bibliography

1. Barclay, P. and Kennedy, J., 1992, Using a Persistent System to Construct a Customised Interface to an Ecological Database, in R.L. Cooper (ed), proc. of *First International Workshop on Interfaces to Database Systems*, Springer-Verlag (Workshop in Computer Science Series).
2. Atkinson M et al, 1990, The object-oriented database system manifesto, in *Deductive and Object-Oriented Databases*, Elsevier Science, Amsterdam, Netherlands
3. Atwood, T., 1993. ODMG 93: The Object DBMS Standard, *Object Magazine* Vol. 3 No. 3 September-October, pp 37-44
4. Kapel, G & Min Tjoa, A., 1992, State of the Art and Open Issues on Graphical User Interfaces to Databases, *Information and Software Technology*, Vol. 34, No. 11, pp. 721-730
5. Caplinger, M., 1986. Graphical database browsing, *3rd ACM SIGOIS Conference OIS C.Hewitt and S.Zdonik (eds)*, pp 113-121
6. Sawyer, P., Colebourne, A., Somerville, I., and Mariani, J., 1992. Object oriented database systems: a framework for user interface development, *Proceedings - International Workshop on Interfaces to Databases, Glasgow*
7. Paton, N., al-Qaimari, G., Kilgour, A., 1992. An Extensible Interface to an Extensible Object-Oriented Database System, *Proceedings - International Workshop on Interfaces to Databases, Glasgow*
8. Paton, N., al-Qaimari, G., 1993. Visualising Advanced Data Modelling Constructs, *Dept of Computing and Electrical Engineering, Heriot-Watt Univ.*
9. Boyle, J., Fothergill, J.E., & Gray, P.M.D., 1993. Design of a 3D user interface to a database, *Database Issues for Data Visualisation Workshop*

10. Afsarmanesh, H. & McLeod, D., 1989. The 3DIS: An Extensible Object-Oriented Information Management System, *ACM Transactions on Information Systems* Vol. 7 No. 4 October, pp 339-377
11. Pickover, C. A., 1991, *Computers and the Imagination*, Alan Sutton Publishing, UK.
12. Hohne, K.H., Bomans, M., Riemer, M., Schubert, R., Tiede, U. and Lierse, W., 1992. A Volume Based Anatomical Atlas, *IEEE Computer Graphics and Applications*, Vol. 12 No. 4, pp. 72-77
13. Wolfe, R. H., Needels, M., Arias, T., Joannopoulos, J. D., 1992. Visual Revelations from Silicon Ab Initio Calculations, *IEEE Computer Graphics and Applications*, Vol12 No4, pp.45-53
14. Palmer T. C., 1992, A Language for Molecular Visualisation, *IEEE Computer Graphics and Applications*, Vol.. 12, No. 3, pp23-32
15. Upson, C., Faulhaber, T., Kamlins, D., Laidlaw, D., Schlegel, D., Vroom, J., Gurwitz, R., van Dam, A., 1989. The Application Visualization System : A Computational Environment for Scientific Visualization, *IEEE Computer Graphics and Applications*, Vol.9 No.4, pp. 30-42
16. Dyer, D.S., 1990, A Dataflow Toolkit for Visualization, *IEEE Computer Graphics and Applications*, Vol.10 No.4. pp. 60-69
17. Shneiderman, B., 1992, *Designing the User Interface*, Addison-Wesley, USA
18. Robertson, G.G., Card, S.K., and Mackinlay, J.D., 1991. Rapid Controlled Movement through Virtual 3D Workspaces, *Proceedings of ACM CHI'91 Conference on Human Factors in Computing Systems* pp 461-462
19. Robertson, G.G., Card, S.K., and Mackinlay, J.D., 1991. Cone Trees: Animated 3D Visualisation of Hierarchical Information, *Proceedings of ACM CHI'91 Conference on Human Factors in Computing Systems* pp 184-194
20. Robertson, G.G., Card, S.K., and Mackinlay, J.D., 1991. The Perspective Wall : Detail and Context Smoothly Integrated, *Proceedings of ACM CHI'91 Conference on Human Factors in Computing Systems* pp 173-179
21. Robertson, P.K., 1991. A Methodology for Choosing Data Representations, *IEEE Computer Graphics and Applications*, Vol. 11 No. 3, pp. 56-67
22. Robertson, G.G., Card, S.K., and Mackinlay, J.D., 1993. Information Visualization using 3D Interactive Animation, *Communications of the ACM*, Vol. 36 No. 4, pp. 57-71
23. Fairchild, K.M., Serra, L., Hern, N., Hai, L.B., Leong A.T., 1993, Dynamic Fisheye Information Visualisations, In R.A.Earnshaw, M.A.Gigante, H.Jones (Eds.) *Virtual Reality Systems*. London: Academic Press
24. Venolia, D., 1993, Facile 3D Direct Manipulation, in proceedings of ACM CHI'93 Conference on Human Factors in Computing Systems
25. Dumais, S.T., & Jones, W.P., 1986. The Spatial Metaphor for User Interfaces: Experimental Test of Reference by location versus Name, *ACM Transactions on Information Systems*, Vol. 4 No. 1, pp 42-63

# Virtual Environments for Data Sharing and Visualisation -- Populated Information Terrains

Steve Benford

Department of Computer Science, The University of Nottingham,
Nottingham, NG7 2RD, UK
Phone: +44 602 514203   Email: sdb@cs.nott.ac.uk

John Mariani
Computing Department, Lancaster University,
Lancaster, UK
Phone: +44 524 593797   Email: jam@comp.lancs.ac.uk

**Abstract**.

The Concept of Populated Information Terrains (PITS) aims to extend database technology with key ideas from the new fields of Virtual Reality (VR) and Computer Supported Cooperative Work (CSCW). PITS are virtual data spaces which support visualisation of, and cooperative work within, shared data. This paper identifies key techniques for building PITS for various types of database, including multi-dimensional visualisation, statistical approaches, graph drawing techniques and human centred approaches. We then discuss issues concerned with populating such terrains including communication between users, embodiment of users, peripheral awareness of others and the relation to database concurrency control. Finally, we describe a prototype implementation that demonstrates the concept of PITS and which helps clarifies key design issues for future full-scale implementations.

KEYWORDS: Data Visualisation, Virtual Reality (VR), Computer Supported Cooperative Work (CSCW).

# 1. Introduction

The concept of Populated Information Terrains (PITS) aims to extend database technology with key ideas from the new fields of Virtual Reality (VR) and Computer Supported Cooperative Work (CSCW). We define a PIT to be a virtual data space that may be inhabited by multiple users. The underlying philosophy of PITS is that they should support people in working together within data as opposed to merely with data.

The requirement for PITS stems from two key observations about current database technology (our use of the term database is quite general and includes both general DBMS and also less structured collections of data such as filestores and electronic document repositories). First, traditional databases provide extensive support for structured querying but have tended to provide much less support for human browsing. This is where virtual reality might help. VR provides the ability to visualise information in three-dimensional space, to move through it and to interact with it. At the extreme, users might be immersed within the data through the use of head-mounted displays and related technology. Second, although many databases provide concurrent multi-user access, they do not support true *sharing* of data as part of cooperative work. Sharing and cooperative work demand an awareness of the presence and activity of other people as well as an ability to communicate with them. It has been argued that, by focusing on issues of access transparency and serialisability, existing databases actually seek to hinder cooperative work, not support it [14]. As a further example, a database which promotes awareness of others might allow the development of complementary forms of access management such as "social locking" where access is directly negotiated with others (in much the same way as we negotiate access to real world resources through behaviours such as queuing or scrumming).

Our aim is therefore to explore this notion of PITS both as a means of improving the way in which users browse and interact with data and also as a means of actively supporting cooperative data sharing.

Section two of our paper focuses on the construction of the base Information Terrains and identifies four key techniques applicable to a range of databases. Section three focuses on the population of these base terrains with multiple users, considering issues of communication, embodiment, awareness and concurrency control. Section four then describes an early virtual reality concept demonstrator which helps explore design issues for future full-scale implementations of PITS.

This work has been carried out as part of the COMIC project, the European ESPRIT Basic Research Action into CSCW, sponsored by the Commission of the European Communities.

## 2. Constructing Information Terrains

First we consider the problem of constructing the base information terrains. This involves processing data to arrive at a spatial configuration where the properties of and relationships between data are intuitively obvious from their position and presentation. We identify four broad approaches to this problem and subsequently argue that these are applicable to different types of data

*"Benediktine" Cyberspace and TripleSpace* : In his work on the structure of Cyberspace, Michael Benedikt argues that the attributes of an object may be mapped onto *extrinsic* and *intrinsic* spatial dimensions [1]. Extrinsic dimensions specify location in space (e.g. x, y, z co-ordinates). Intrinsic dimensions determine characteristics of the resulting point in space such as colour, shape, size, spin, texture, vibration and sound quality. Using Benedikt's approach, we might extend database schema notations to specify which attributes map to which intrinsic and extrinsic

dimensions. An example of an early "Benediktine" cyberspace, TripleSpace [12], has already been built on top of a triple store or binary relational database.

*Statistical clustering and proximity measures* : Statistical methods have been used to analyse collections of data (often documents) in an attempt to group objects together according to some measure of semantic "closeness" (i.e. do they logically belong together). The resulting proximity measures are typically scaled and returned as numerical values that are then used to cluster the objects in a data space. Systems adopting this and similar approaches include VIBE [13] and BEAD [5] (both for visualising collections of documents).

*Hyper-structures*: Some databases support the notion of explicit relations or links between objects (e.g. schema based on entity-relationship models or hyper-media and Network Information Retrieval systems such. Gopher, ARCHIE, WAIS and World Wide Web). The resulting structures might be visualised by applying three dimensional graph drawing techniques. In turn these might be extended through visualisation techniques such as fish-eye views, cone-trees and perspective walls [4, 10].

*Human centred approaches.* This final approach relies on users or system implementors designing appropriate visualisations. The first approach is to use real-world metaphors. Examples might include fly-through *library* interface for a document store; *cities, buildings* and *rooms* for organisational information in Directory services; and *maps* of the physical world for geographical information. A second approach is to allow humans to construct and organise the information terrain themselves on an ad-hoc basis (effectively how files are organised under the desktop metaphor). This approach might also extend previous work on rooms metaphors in user interfaces [9].

It may be possible to combine the "Benediktine" and human centred aspects by allowing the user to choose the mapping from attribute to dimensions, following the approach taken by Gray et al. in the Iconographer project [8].

## 2.1. Comparison and Applicability

The major difference between these approaches is in how they determine the spatial location of data. The Benediktine approaches determines location according to the values of three attributes. In the statistical approach, location is determined by some weighted combination of possibly many attribute values in relation to those of other objects. The hyper-structure approach relies on the presence of pre-existing (authored or computed) links which indicate which data objects are neighbours to which others. Finally, users get to chose locations under the human centred approach.

Early experiences suggest that each approach is suited to a different kind of database.

The Benediktine approach relates best to data which is naturally ordered and scaled. Numeric attributes work well. Text may be ordered alphabetically, but this is only useful if this ordering has a semantic meaning to the user. For example, an ordered list of names in a register might be useful for browsing whereas alphabetic ordering of document keywords is unlikely to aid browsing (it doesn't help that "zebra" is next to "yellow"). The Benediktine approach also has problems with multi-valued attributes. In short, this approach may be most applicable to well structured, ordered and often numeric data collections such as are often managed by relational DBMS.

In contrast, the statistical approach is more suited to data that is less well structured and often highly textual. In particular, this approach aims to uncover important semantic relations between objects that are not known in advance and have therefore not been incorporated into some pre-defined database schema.

Hypermedia structures fall somewhere between the previous two approaches in that they require that relations between objects are made explicit (and therefore at least a basic notion of schema). On the other hand, these relations may be between large often textual data objects. Good examples of suitable applications might be visualising hypertext or filestores.

Finally, the human centred approaches may be useful for particular niche applications.

## 2.2. Data Manipulation

We identify two approaches to data manipulation within PITS - *direct* and *indirect*.

The direct approach involves changing the attributes of an object via the representation. For example, simply moving an object in space could change the values of the extrinsic attributes. This idea highlights the notion of the granularity of space. In a Benediktine PIT, each spatial dimension may have a grain or minimum spatial measurement, which is defined by the values it represents. Thus, if a dimension represents an integer domain, it will not be possible to move objects to a position between two integer points. The notion of changing attribute values through movement in space actually points towards a deeper relationship between state and movement. In essence, any change of state is a movement along some combination of extrinsic and intrinsic dimensions and vice versa.

Indirect manipulation involves formulating queries to the underlying database which result in restructuring of the PIT. For example, a modification operation may move a set of objects closer to the user or may alter their representations. This also supports the idea of "action at a distance" where a query to the database may affect may objects in the PIT.

## 2.3. Keys, Exclusion and Browsing

The database concept of a *key* can be directly related to visualisation. If we can find a mapping between a database key and the set of three extrinsic dimensions (X,Y,Z), then we know that each object will appear in a given space and furthermore, that it will occupy a unique position. In essence, this is what Benedikt proposes in this principles of exclusion and maximal exclusion for cyberspace [1]. First, the Principle of Exclusion:

> *"Two non-identical objects having the same extrinsic dimensions and dimension values, whether at the same time, or including time as an extrinsic*

*dimension from the outset, is forbidden, no matter what other comparisons may be made between their intrinsic dimensions and values."*

In other words, you should not have two different things in the same place at the same time. Second, the Principle of Maximal Exclusion :

*"Given any N-dimensional state of a phenomenon, and all the values - actual and possible - on those N-dimensions, choose as extrinsic dimensions - as "space and time" - that set of (two, or three, of four) dimensions that will minimise the number of violations of the Principle of Exclusion."*

In other words, chose your extrinsic dimensions so that different objects are spatially separated as much as possible. This avoids the information loss that occurs when multiple objects collapse onto a single point of space.

However, the use of a key as the basis for locating objects in space may not actually be the most appropriate for aiding browsing. For example, what if, as in many cases, the key is some arbitrary reference or identification code? It will often be the case that those attributes which are best suited for browsing are those that don't form a unique key (e.g. keywords on a document). In opposition to Benedikt, we therefore argue that in many cases, one should avoid mapping the key onto extrinsic dimensions and that instead, spaces where multiple objects collapse onto a common point and where objects appear and disappear as extrinsic dimensions are changed may be better suited to browsing and therefore PITS as a whole.

### 2.4. Schema

The final issue for this section is that of a schema notation. Most databases involve some schema mechanism for specifying the meta-structure of their data. Such notations need extending to incorporate visualisation information. For example, following the Benediktine approach, the definition of an attribute may include a statement of which intrinsic or extrinsic dimension it is to be mapped into and how this mapping is to be achieved (e.g. scaling). Furthermore, this mapping should be dynamically configurable from within the PIT.

## 3. Populating Information Terrains

The population of information terrains with multiple users centres on the idea that users are as much a part of the database as is the data. Put another way users should be *directly visible* as objects within a shared database and should not be relegated to the status of external agents whose presence is merely implied as a side effect of their actions. Population raises a host of further issues.

### 3.1. Communication Between Users

First, PITS should support direct communication between their inhabitants, allowing them to discuss and negotiate access to data. Such communication should be both real-time, involving the possible use of audio, video and text channels, and asynchronous, such as the ability for inhabitants to annotate data with messages for other people (e.g.

a kind of "post it" note facility). In turn, this requires techniques for initiating, managing and terminating communication. One approach for densely populated PITS is to initiate direct communications whenever two users enter close proximity to one another. This supports the notion of bumping into people who are working with the same data as yourself. Of course, it should also be possible to communicate with other more distant users if required.

## 3.2. Awareness

Beyond direct communication, we need to consider the notion of *awareness* [7]. Peripheral awareness of other people plays a vital and subtle supporting role in cooperative work, enabling ad-hoc interaction, promoting knowledge of the state of activity, and supporting important behaviours such as monitoring and overseeing. PITS should automatically and continuously provide awareness of the presence and actions of other inhabitants. Awareness of action involves showing what data inhabitants are accessing and also what kind of access is being made (thus, reading might be distinguished from deletion). In the long term, a range of more sophisticated CSCW awareness mechanisms such as [2, 3] might be used to allow people to control their levels of awareness of others.

This notion of awareness should also apply to past action. Thus, not only should one be made aware of what changes have taken place in a database since last access, but one should also know who was responsible for these changes. Put more generally, in order to support cooperative data sharing, databases must notify users of the presence, location, ongoing activity and past activity of other users. This represents a direct challenge to the traditional view of database access transparency.

## 3.3. Embodiment

Awareness of presence raises the further issue of embodiment; that is, users need to be directly represented in the space alongside the data. This requires the provision of *appropriate* body images. The design of these virtual bodies may be constrained by a variety of factors, a few of which we list here:

- body images should convey presence, location and orientation.
- body images should convey identity.
- body images should convey activity and availability for communication.
- body images should support voluntary gesture and perhaps even involuntary expression.
- body images should be personalisable (i.e. tailorable by users).
- body images should reflect the capabilities of the users (e.g. "ears" suggest that they can receive audio messages).
- body images should be truthful - that is they should not lie about the above (especially identity).

### 3.4. Awareness and Access Transparency

Next, we consider awareness in relation to the database concept of access transparency. A central goal of multi-user databases has been to maintain data consistency. This has usually involved the introduction of concurrency control mechanisms which enable the serialisation of transactions. Serialisation gives each user of the database the impression that they have sole access to the data. Previous CSCW research has already pointed out that this is in direct conflict to the CSCW goal of awareness [14]. We argue that, by encouraging awareness of others, PITS may encourage the development of new "social locking" mechanisms to complement the more traditional approaches. Such mechanisms may be explicit, based on negotiation over direct communication channels, or implicit, based on positioning and social spatial behaviours such as queuing, jostling and scrumming.

Our hypotheses (yet to be proved) is that, only by promoting awareness of others, will databases allow such social mechanisms to come into being. However, we don't propose that social locking can replace existing techniques. Indeed, in some cases it will be a most unsuitable approach (e.g. controlling access to financial or safety critical data). The use of spatial proximity to indicate an interest in data also runs into problems when large sets of data are being manipulated at a time. In spite of these problems, we propose that there will be cases, such as access to documents, where social locking based on awareness may prove to be a more flexible and lower cost (in terms of system overhead) alternative to traditional approaches.

## 4. Implementation

We now describe the implementation of a prototypical PIT as a vehicle for exploring some of the issues raised above. The current demonstrator, Q-PIT, follows the "Benediktine" approach and has been implemented on a SUN 10 workstation using both the World ToolKit virtual reality library and the DIVE (Distributed Interactive Virtual Environment) distributed multi-user virtual reality system. We are currently implementing the other approaches as preparation to a more formal evaluation of PITS). The software is written in 'C' and runs under X-windows on the UNIX operating system.

Currently, Q-PIT can process a simple database containing a number of named tuples, display them within a three dimensional space and then allow this space to be shared and manipulated by multiple users.

### 4.1. Attribute Mapping and Schema in Q-PIT

Q-PIT maps tuples onto graphical objects according to an extended schema notation. As an example, we will consider a database which contains tuples representing people with the following domains: (name, age, gender, location, occupation). For each domain in the database, we build and maintain a list of values appearing within that domain. Each domain list is then sorted into alphabetical order. An attribute mapping file might then be created containing the following additional schema information:

```
extrinsic location x
extrinsic occupation y
extrinsic name z
intrinsic age spin_speed
intrinsic gender shape male cube female cone
```

We can see the mappings from the attributes location, occupation and name onto the extrinsic (x, y, z) axes. At the moment, these mappings are linear, being based on the ordering of the domain list. So, for example, if the name list is (Adrian, Bruce, Gordon...), then the tuples containing "Bruce" as the value of their name field are mapped onto co-ordinate 2 of the z axis. The intrinsic mappings currently supported are **shape**, **height** and **spin_speed**. Current shapes include cubes, spheres, diamonds, pyramids, cones, cylinders and hemispheres. We can associate a field and a field value with a shape; this dictates the shape of the graphical object which represents the tuple. In our simple example, we have associated the field "gender" with the shape mappings, followed by a list of (field value, shape) pairs. If a field value does not appear in the mapping, the shape defaults to a cube. It is possible to have as many (field value, shape) pairs as required, with duplication of shape mappings if necessary. If the tuple has the value "male" for field "gender", then the matching graphical object has a cube shape. Similarly, if the tuple is "female", the object is cone shaped.

Spin_speed dictates whether the object should rotate, and if so, how quickly. In the example, we map the integer value of a person's age onto the speed. Similarly, height dictates the height of an object. We could, for example, map age onto height; thus, the taller the object, the older it is.

## 4.2. Data Manipulation in Q-PIT

Data may be manipulated in a number of ways. First, by selecting an object via the mouse, the underlying tuple is displayed. Second, by issuing a query, all objects "hit" are automatically selected and highlighted. Thirdly, a user can update the values of the underlying tuple by engaging in an interactive sequence of textual instructions. Once an update has been completed, not only is the underlying tuple updated, but so is the corresponding graphical object. This may entail alterations to both intrinsic and extrinsic attributes, the latter taking the form of a *smooth animation* of the object moving to the new position. We believe that the display of smoothly animated changes in position as opposed to instant repositioning to be particularly effective at providing people with peripheral awareness of changes to nearby data. Lastly, again through textual interaction, a brand new tuple can be added to the data. This is matched by the creation of a new graphical object.

## 4.3. Populating Q-PIT

In the World Tool Kit implementation, a user is directly embodied as a "monolith" (a large, thin cuboid). Associated with each user is a unique colour, currently specified in their "user.profile" file. When two or more users are sharing a Q-space (the space defined by a Q-PIT), they see the others as differently coloured monoliths. In the DIVE implementation, a user is represented by a DIVE "blockie" (see figures 2 and 3).

Whenever a Q-PIT session is commenced, the users start in the same location, but are subsequently allowed to change position freely and independently of each other, so that everyone will eventually have a distinct view of the shared Q-space. Users may either use a Spaceball (an input device for movement with six degrees of freedom) or the more conventional mouse to navigate. By selecting a monolith, a user can obtain information about the other user. Direct communication currently has to be achieved though external applications including text and audio conferencing.

This simple visualisation of fellow users immediately provides an awareness of presence which is not normally available in traditional databases. Moreover, by their positioning within the Q-space, it is possible to identify the areas or clusters of data in which other people are currently interested. To provide awareness of activity, whenever the user selects an object, the object changes to the selecting user's colour. This allows other users to see what objects are currently in use and by whom.

### 4.4. Screen Images

We include three captured screen images from Q-PIT to give a flavour of how a simple Benediktine PIT might appear to a user in a two user occupied space at the same instant in time. Figure 1 (from the World Tool Kit implementation) shows a PIT of 130 objects and gives the current view of the "red" user (ourselves). We can see a variety of data objects of different shapes and sizes at different locations. Some foreground objects that we have selected have changed colour to red (the contents of the objects will be displayed in a separate window). In the distance we can see the "green user" located near to a row of cubes. We can also see at a glance that the green user is accessing some of these distant cubes. Notice that the PIT includes a fixed light source which aids basic orientation (thus the green user has the sun behind them and the red user is facing towards the sun). We would like to stress that the use of these relatively low quality static images fails to capture the full effect of animation (e.g. spinning objects) and the ability to smoothly adjust the user's perspective. Video or a demonstration are required to appreciate the full effect.

The next figure (2) shows a Q-space of people in the DIVE implementation. Here, the Q-space is occupied by three users, the observer and the two DIVE "blockies". One has a T-shape whilst the other has a round head. These are two possible embodiments of Q-PIT users.

Other points to notice are the provision of a ground grid to assist with basic orientation and the use of text to label the displayed objects. Many VR systems are poor at handling the display of text yet this seems essential for our application.

Figure 3 shows a Q-space populated by examination data. The data involved is based on exam marks and degrees awarded. In this example, shape was dictated by degree awarded. The positional attributes were based on the results of the final year project, the database exam, and type of major. In the example data, there were only three types of major so this produces an almost 2-D display.

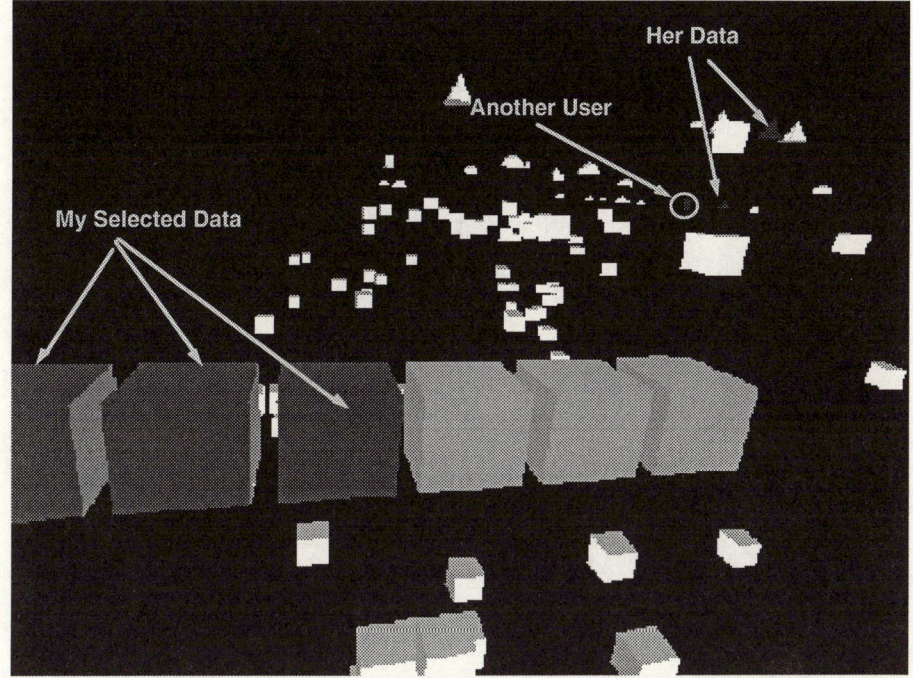

Figure 1 : The "red" user's view

This example highlights the power of different mappings. For example, we could have used three exams for all three axis and achieved a wider spread. We could use degree awarded as one positional axis and shape to reflect type of major. It seems clear that we should improve the potential for dynamic mapping and also for user-specified mapping functions (i.e. take the average mark for a group of related exams and use that as a positional attribute).

We can readily envision a number of examiners co-habiting this Q-Space to analyse, discuss, and modify marks. The external examiner could indeed be operating from their home university.

### 4.5. Immediate Reflections

The current early prototype is sufficient to demonstrate the basic principles of PITS in a tangible form; further development is required before more meaningful evaluation can be made. However, even at this early stage, we can make a few observations about the design of PITS.

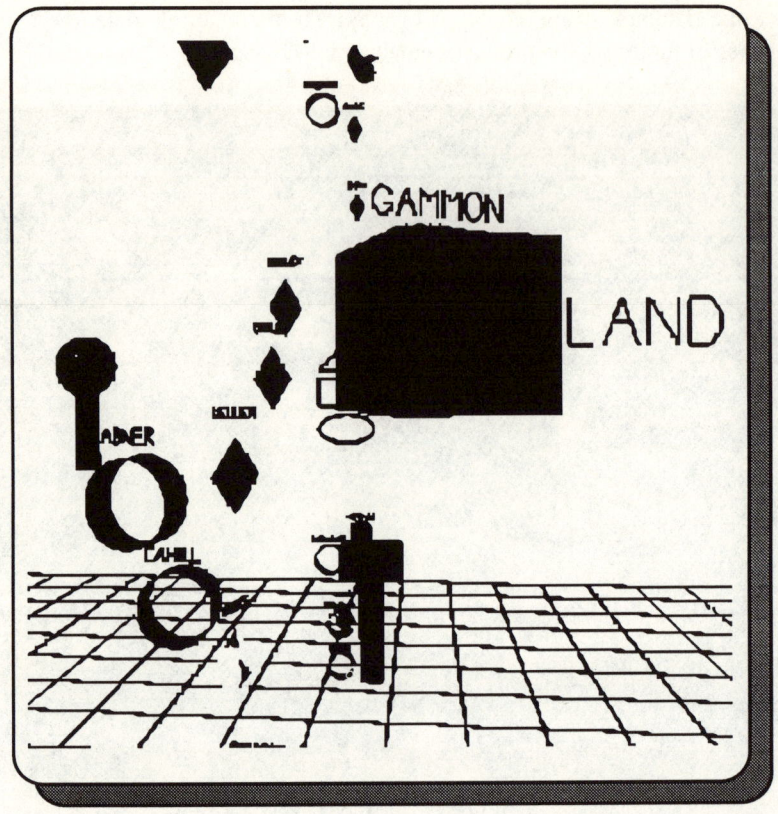

Figure 2 : Multi-users in a DIVE Q-Space

First, the lack of spatial cues other than the use of the light source make it easy to lose a sense of position. Basic cues might include a ground plane to aid orientation and also labelled axes showing the extrinsic directions X,Y,Z and their mappings. We would also like to label objects with some more meaningful information (in spite of the fact that VR systems are notoriously bad at displaying textual data).

Second, the current user embodiment (a simple coloured monolith) is too crude and easily becomes confused with the data objects. In fact we only currently meet the first of the factors listed previously. A few simple steps would overcome some of these problems including the use of a slightly more humanoid shape (the DIVE distributed VR systems shows just how simple such a shape can be and yet still convey the impression of representing a human [6]).

### 4.6. Some Longer Term Issues

Our current plans also include a number of longer term developments.

First and foremost, we aim to carry out an evaluation of PITS as a means of supporting data visualisation and sharing. This will include a comparison of the different visualisation approaches described previously (we are currently implementing statistical and hyper-structure versions of Q-PIT) followed by a series of experiments with different databases.

Figure 3 : a small group of examiners

Considering the current Q-PIT demonstrator, the mapping of attributes to dimensions could be far more powerful. Extrinsic dimensions could utilise decreasing and inverse orderings as well as non-linear scales (e.g. exponential and logarithmic). We believe the provision of configurable intervals is also necessary. Users may also wish to impose their own ordering on a domain. Extensions could also be made to the intrinsic mappings. Whole new intrinsic dimensions might be introduced such as the use of texture and sound.

We also propose the implementation of a dynamically configurable schema mechanism from within the PIT, allowing users to re-configure attribute mappings as they work within the data. Eventually this may include mixing and swapping visualisation approaches dynamically.

The current Q-PIT implementation uses colour to show which users are accessing which objects. We propose that future versions of Q-PIT should support "two-tone" or graduated colouring to identify both the person making the access and the kind of access being made. Future implementations could also support direct manipulation of objects, so that if an object is selected and moved, the extrinsic attributes will be updated to match the new location (the inverse of the usual visualisation process).

The current facility for selecting other users to obtain personal descriptions could be extended to initiate (if desired) direct communication amongst users. Initially, we envisage this will be a simple audio link or UNIX text-based "talk", but we hope to expand this by also adding communications information to the "user.profile". Further work is also required in the area of personalisation of user representations.

The work discussed seeks to add several new features : representation of users in the information space, mechanisms for communication between users, and, of course, a third dimension. If the aims of the project are successful, it will be difficult to discover which aspect was crucial. To this end, we have designed and are implementing a 2D desktop interface to a shared OODBMS with user awareness [11] which will provide a 2D PIT for evaluation and comparison.

## 5. Summary

A Populated Information Terrain is an abstract data space that allows multiple inhabitants to visualise and jointly manipulate the contents of databases. Our paper has explored theoretical issues concerned with how PITS might be constructed and then populated for a range of database types. It has also described an early concept demonstrator, Q-PIT, implemented as a vehicle for exploring some of these issues.

We identified four broad approaches to constructing PITS: *Benediktine*, following on from Michael Benedikt's work on the structure of Cyberspace; *statistical*, related to information retrieval systems; *hyper-structured*, relating to hyper-media systems and *human centred*. We also introduced a number of population issues including the need for direct communication, appropriate embodiment of users and the relationship between awareness of the presence and actions of others and more traditional database concurrency control.

Q-PIT, an early PIT implementation using the World ToolKit Virtual Reality library, adopts the Benediktine approach and allows a user to configure a PIT from a collection of tuples via an extended schema notation. Q-PIT currently represents data using three extrinsic dimensions (x,y,z) and three intrinsic dimensions (shape, height and spin-speed). The system supports multiple-users who are associated with different colours. This principle extends to using their colour to show other people which data they are currently accessing. Q-PIT also allows data to be manipulated through a simple query facility. Furthermore, any resulting positional changes in the data are smoothly animated so as to convey peripheral awareness of updates to other users.

Although Q-PIT still requires further work, we believe that it demonstrates the potential of the PITS concept to transform current databases into more powerful environments for data browsing, sharing and cooperative work.

Acknowledgements : we would like to thank the referees for their valuable comments and insights to both this paper and the direction of our research.

# References

1. Benedikt, M., Cyberspace: Some Proposals, in Cyberspace: First Steps, Michael Benedikt (ed.), , pp 273-302, MIT Press, 1991
2. Benford, S., Bullock, A., Cook, N., Harvey, P., Ingram, R. and Lee, O., From Rooms to Cyberspace: Models of Interaction in Large Virtual Computer Spaces, in Interacting with Computers, Vol. 5, no 2, pp 217-237, Butterworth-Heinemann, 1993.
3. Benford, S. and Fahlén, L.E., A Spatial Model of Interaction in Large Virtual Environments, in Proc. Third European Conference on Computer Supported Cooperative Work (ECSCW'93), Kluwer, 1993.
4. Card, S. A., Robertson, G.G., and Mackinlay, J.D., The Information Visualiser, an Information Workspace, in Proc. CHI'91, Human Factors in Computing Systems, ACM SICGHI, pp 181-188, May 1991
5. Chalmers M. and Chitson, P., Bead: Explorations in Information Visualisation, in Proc. SIGIR'92, published as a special issue of SIGIR forum, ACM Press, pp. 330-337, June 1992.
6. Fahlén, L. E., Brown, C. G., Stahl, O., Carlsson, C., A Space Based Model for User Interaction in Shared Synthetic Environments, In Proc. InterCHI'93, ACM Press, 1993.
7. Gaver, W., Moran, T., MacLean, A., Lovstrand, L., Dourish, P., Carter, K., and Buxton, W., Realising a Video Environment: EuroPARC's RAVE System, In Proc. CHI '92 Human Factors in Computing Systems, Monterey, Ca., USA, May 1992.
8. Gray, P.D., Waite, K.W. and Draper, S.W., "Do-It-Yourself Iconic Displays", Human-Computer Interaction -- INTERACT '90, D. Diaper et al (Eds)., Elsevier Science Publishers B.V. (North-Holland), pp. 639 - 644, IFIP, 1990
9. Henderson, A.J., and Card, S.A., Rooms: The Use of Multiple Virtual Workspaces to Reduce Space Contention, ACM Transactions on Graphics, Vol. 5, No. 3, July 1985.
10. Mackinlay, J.D., Robertson, G.G. and Card, S.K., Perspective Wall: Detail and Context Smoothly Integrated, in Proc. CHI'91, Human Factors in Computing Systems, ACM SICGHI, ,pp 173-179, May 1991
11. Mariani, J.A., "Design of a 2D PIT", COMIC Internal Report, Computing Department, Lancaster University, 1994

12   Mariani, J., and Lougher, R., TripleSpace: an Experiment in a 3D Graphical Interface to a Binary Relational Database, Interacting with Computers, Vol. 4, No. 2, pp 147-162., 1992

13   Olsen, K.A., Korfhage, R. R., Sochats, K. M.., Spring, M. B. and Williams, J. G., Visualisation of a Document Collection: The VIBE System, Information Processing and Management, Vol. 29, No 1, pp. 69-81, Pergamon Press Ltd, 1993.

14   Rodden, T., J.A. Mariani and G. Blair, Supporting Cooperative Applications, the International Journal of Computer Supported Cooperative Work (CSCW), Vol. 1, Nos. 1-2, Kluwer, 1992.

Data Model Issues I

# A Graphical User Interface for Schema Evolution in an Object-Oriented Database

Simon Monk

Department of Computing, University of Central Lancashire[*],
Preston, U.K.
srm@uk.ac.lancs.comp

## Abstract

This paper describes work carried out to prototype a GUI to support schema evolution using class versions. Class versions used for schema evolution require a more sophisticated GUI than schema editors (for schema design), because the database is populated an because support is required to browse and maintain the class versions. Current systems for class versioning require exception handlers or conversion functions to be defined as part of the schema evolution process and thus the GUI must provide support for these operations.

A number of desirable properties for such a GUI are discussed and illustrated with examples from the GUI developed by the author.

## 1 Introduction

The schema of a database is often considered to be static. In reality, this is not usually the case [14]. In fact from the time that a database is brought into use until it eventually becomes redundant, the structure of that database is likely to evolve as new requirements and flaws in the old structure are discovered. Mechanisms have been developed that ease the difficulties in allowing a schema to change. Some of these mechanisms use versions of class definitions [2, 3, 4]. Such versions have many similarities with views of class definitions, [5, 6, 7, 8] which afford the facility for users to have personal views of the database. It is the GUI used to define class versions that is the subject of this paper.

The author has implemented, as a prototype, a mechanism that can be applied both to the versioning of class definitions and the creation of views in a system called CLOSQL [9, 10]. This system also realises some earlier work on schema evolution that uses exception handlers [3]. The GUI to CLOSQL is used as an example and as a vehicle for the analysis of the special requirements for supporting schema evolution.

---

[*] The work described in this paper was carried out while the author was working at Lancaster University, Lancaster UK.

Although this work has some features in common with GUIs to support schema design [6, 12], there is a fundamental difference in that schema design is carried out on an empty database, where as schema evolution by its nature is something that happens to databases containing data.

## 2 Schema evolution and class versions

The motivation for using class versioning to support schema evolution arises because of the need to keep 'old' external programs running on new data. In order to discuss the GUI used for class versioning and views, it is first necessary to briefly explain the rationale for class versioning.

In most deployed systems that use a database, a number of external programs are acting with the assumption that the database conforms to an expected schema. In a traditional database system, these programs cannot be guaranteed to function after the schema is changed - since the data created to the changed schema may be incompatible with the old schema which the programs were expecting[1]. This problem can be addressed if the class definitions that comprise the schema are versioned rather than modified. The CLOSQL system uses such a mechanism to ensure backward compatibility of data created in a changed schema.

Every time a change is made to the schema, a new version of the class, or classes on which that change has an effect, is created. This results in a linear series of class versions corresponding to successive changes in the schema (figure 1).

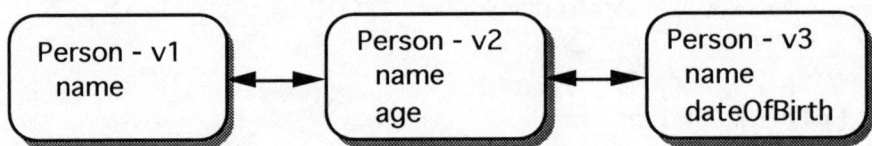

Figure 1. Class versions for schema evolution.

It is important to bear in mind that these versions are versions of the meta-data and not the data itself. The data itself (the instances) will exist in the format of one of the versions of the class definition. To allow programs assuming one version of the class definition to continue to work with data in another version, CLOSQL relies on user created 'update' and 'backdate' functions to convert instances of one version to another version in such a way that these changes can be reversed without loss of information. This mechanism is called dynamic instance conversion.

In figure 2 (which shows the second schema change of figure 1), a number of external programs are seen as operating on version 1 of the class definition which has three instances. However one instance of the class also exists in version 2. When the

---

[1] These programs need not be external; they may in fact be methods attached to one part of the schema acting on the part of the schema being the subject of the schema change.

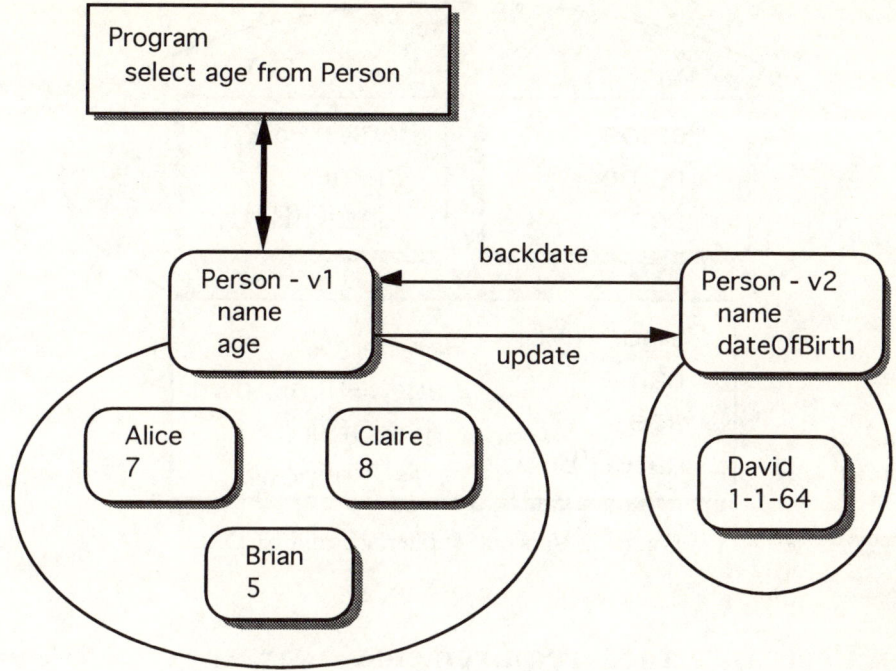

Figure 2. Dynamic instance conversion.

program acting on version 1 issues a query, the system determines the version of the class required by the query (in this case version 1) and converts any instances in the other version that may be of use to the query into instances of version 1. So in this case the instance 'David' of version 2 of 'Person' is converted into an instance of version 1, 'dateOfBirth' being converted to 'age' by a backdate function which the user created at the time the schema change was made.

Should the need subsequently arise to access the instance from version 2, the instance can be changed back into an instance of version 2 using the update method of version 1 of the class definition. For further detail on dynamic instance conversion see [MonkSom93].

CLOSQL also implements a system for supporting schema evolution first developed in the ENCORE system [3]. In this mechanism a version set interface (VSI) is created for the set of versions of each class definition. As well as containing class versions, the VSI also contains exception handlers that supply default values for attributes not present in a particular version that are, none the less, required by a query.

For example, in figure 3, handlers are provided for 'age' and 'dateOfBirth' that return simple default values. Note that these values are read only. That is, queries acting on these emulated values cannot change their values.

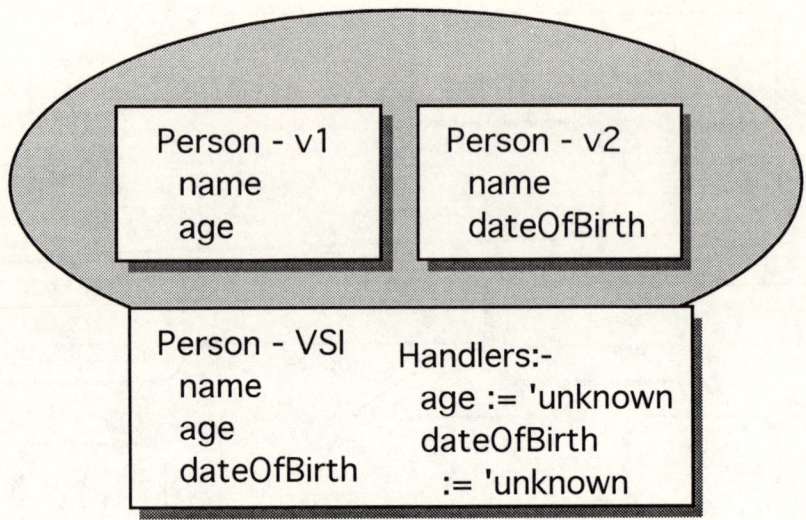

Figure 3. Version Set Interfaces in ENCORE

## 3 User Interface requirements

The user interface requirements for systems that support schema evolution can be discussed under the following three categories.

### 3.1 Ease of use

Since schema evolution can have an impact on all users of the system, it is expected that this will mostly remain the province of the database administrator and not the end-user. However it is unwise to use the database administrator's extensive conceptual model of the system as an excuse for not providing a usable interface. Indeed, it was the difficulty in using the textual format for specifying schema changes that prompted the development of a GUI to support the task.

### 3.2 Support for the evolution process

Defining a schema evolution can be semantically complex. This is particularly true both for dynamic instance conversion, where it is necessary to define update and backdate methods for the changed class, and for ENCORE's approach which requires the definition of handlers.

A good GUI should be able to supply some support for the process of changing the schema. For example by generating default update and backdate functions that can be altered by the user as required.

There are certain rules that govern the schema evolution process and these can be incorporated into the GUI. For example, in the ENCORE system, a handler must be defined for every attribute that is not present in every class in the version set. The GUI can enforce this rule, not as a simple validation, but by deciding which attributes require handlers and presenting them as a list for the user to interact with.

## 3.3 Information accessibility

A schema change may not be limited to a single class. Indeed, with inheritance in OODBs schema changes can propagate out to the leaves of the superclass/subclass tree. This means that the GUI must have good 'visibility'. That is, the user must be able to browse the schema structure quickly and easily.

The browsing of a schema becomes more difficult where there are class versions. In this case, another dimension is introduced to the class lattice. Figure 4 shows an extra dimension of class versions extending back from the class lattice. In this example we have assumed shallow versioning. That is, the creation of a version in a class does not automatically result in corresponding new versions being created in all the subclasses of that class. This simplifies the user interface by reducing the number of nodes in the lattice.

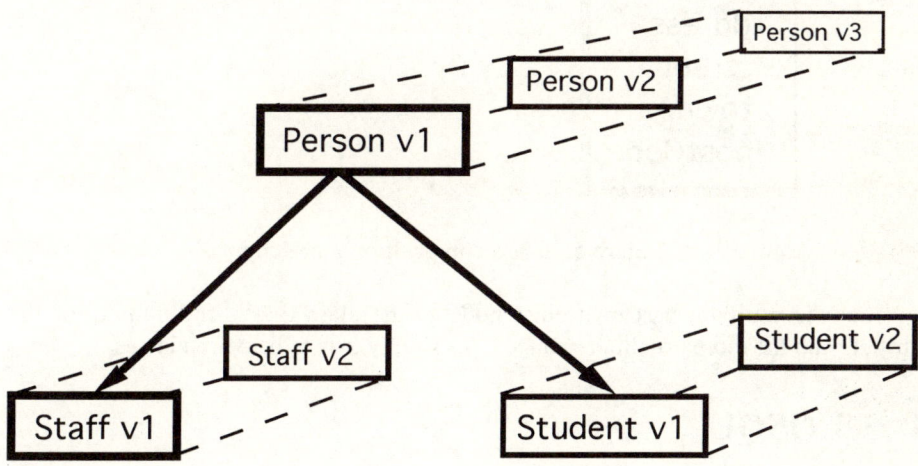

Figure 4. Versions and inheritance hierarchy.

There is yet another dimension to the schema which is neglected in many schema GUIs - that is the class composition network. This is the network formed by the domains of attributes referencing other classes whose attributes also have domains [13] (figure 5).

Techniques that can help represent these complex and interconnected networks include perspective views [14] and switchable views which allow the user to switch easily between dimensions (versions, inheritance and composition) whilst still focusing on the same part of the schema.

This issue of information accessibility is one that is addressed in the systems developed for schema design, since that process too requires good browsing facilities. The GS Designer [11] incorporates a tool for browsing both the class composition and inheritance networks. Unlike CLOSQL, this system represents classes as a complex node in the diagram showing the attributes of the class as well as its name.

This allows both networks to be displayed on the same graph, with different arc types indicating the links in the two hierarchies. The class composition links extend

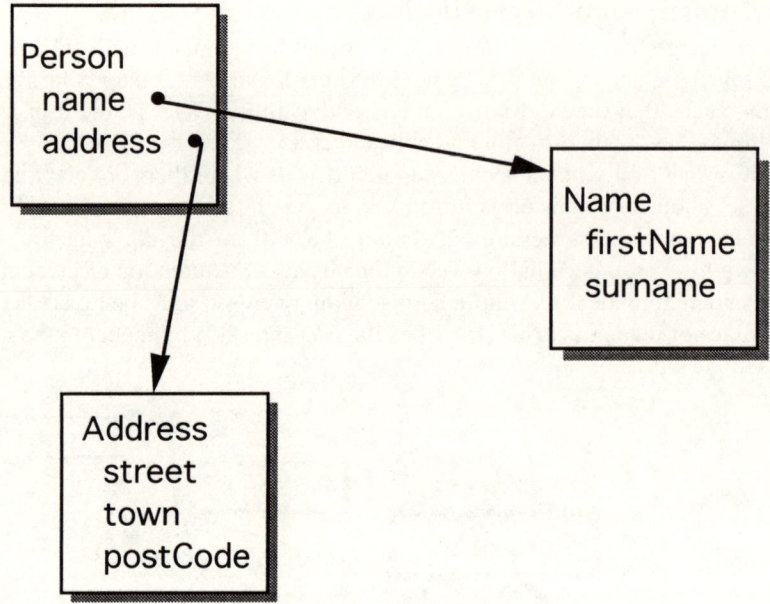

Figure 5. Class composition hierarchy.

from the attribute part of a class node to the class that is the domain of the attribute and the more usual inheritance links simply extend between classes.

## 4 CLOSQL

This section describes the GUI to CLOSQL and uses its example to justify the abstract requirements of the previous section. Since this paper is primarily about the user interface to the schema evolution system and not the system itself, a small simple example is given rather than a more complex example as can be found in [10].

CLOSQL was implemented to prototype the use of dynamic instance conversion for schema evolution. In implementing this test-bed another system of class versioning based on ENCORE's approach was also developed. It became apparent that the mechanism of dynamic instance conversion was equally applicable to the creation of class views and this was added to the system.

### 4.1 Architecture of CLOSQL

CLOSQL has been developed in CLOS, the object-oriented extension to common LISP [15, 16]. A graphical tool-kit provided with Harlequin LispWorks [17] was used to develop the X-windows GUI code.

CLOSQL was built in a layered manner (figure 6) with a combined DML (data manipulation language) and DDL (data description language). All GUI functionality maps down onto this 'database interface language' (DIL). Where the DIL lacked facilities required by the GUI, those feature were added to the language rather than by-passed by the GUI. The advantage of such a layered architecture is that other GUIs

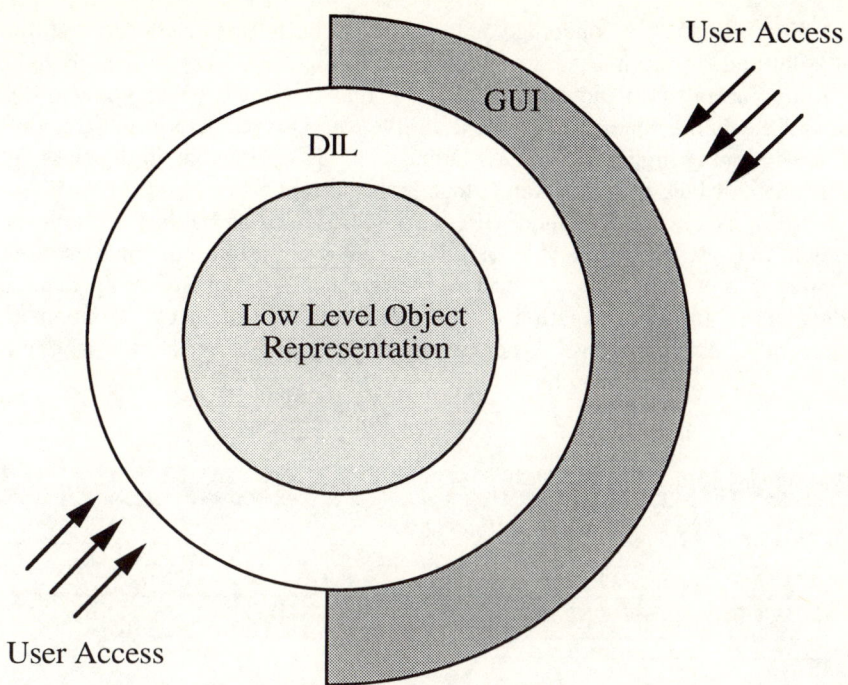

Figure 6. The architecture of CLOSQL.

could be developed without the need to modify the lower layers. At the same time this also allows the possibility of replacing the object-representation layer should the need arise.

## 4.2  GUI for CLOSQL

The two approaches to schema evolution contained in CLOSQL (dynamic instance conversion and ENCORE) each have their own GUI. These GUIs are based on form filling and are supported by a general schema browser that allows the inheritance and version networks to be traversed. In the graphical representation, the inheritance and class version networks are combined into one network with a 'surrogate class' used to represent the position of the set of versions in the inheritance hierarchy. The individual versions are represented as branches of the surrogate class. In the dynamic instance approach the surrogate class always represents the most recently created version of the class. In ENCORE's approach it represents the VSI.

Using the schema browser, class definitions can be inspected and created; instances created and viewed and methods written or edited. The class versioning and viewing operations are also initiated from this window. Figure 7 shows the schema browser with class and instance windows.

New classes are created by selecting a parent class on the graph and then pressing the 'subclass' button. A class window (figure 7.ii) is then created to which attribute and method definitions can be added.

The class window (figure 7.ii) has two sections. The top half is concerned with the instances. That is, editing, creating copying and deleting entities. The bottom half of the class window is concerned with the class definition itself. To distinguish locally defined from inherited attributes, inherited attributes are shown greyed out. This is important, as it indicates to the user that if those attributes are to be the subject of a schema change it may be desirable (but not mandatory) to carry out the schema versioning higher in the class lattice. That is, at the node in the class lattice in which the attribute is defined rather than in the current class.

Where instances have methods, these are represented as buttons in the instance window. Similarly, where the value of an attribute is an instance of some other class, that value is represented as a button which when pressed opens the instance in a window. This allows navigation of the class composition network albeit at an instance rather than class level. Where a method has parameters, the user is prompted to enter the values in a dialog box.

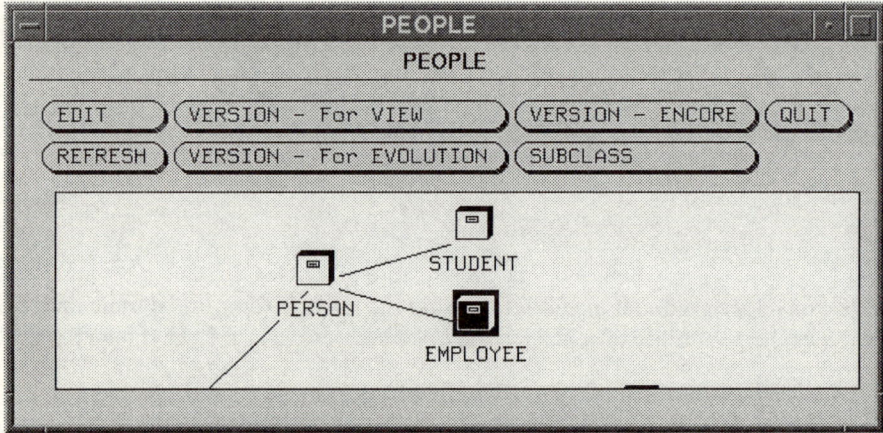

Figure 7.i. Schema Browser.

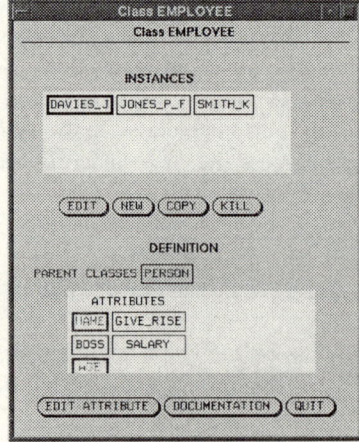

Figure 7.ii. Class Window.

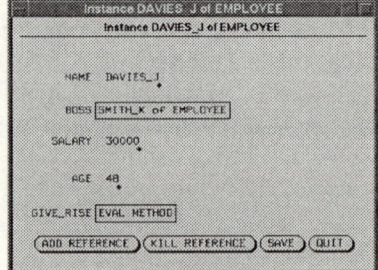

Figure 7.iii Instance Window.

In the example of figure 7.iii, clicking on the value of the attribute BOSS would open another instance window on the instance SMITH_K of the class EMPLOYEE. Clicking on the 'eval method' button next to the 'give-rise' method would result in 10% being added to the value of the 'salary' attribute of the instance.

*4.2.1 Dynamic Instance Conversion*

When a new version of a class is created, in order to effect some change to a schema, the window shown in figure 8 is opened. The two columns of window list the attributes of the old (left) and new (right) class versions. Initially, the right hand column is empty and attributes that are to be retained, in the new version, are selected and the COPY ATTRIBUTES OVER button pressed. This has the effect of copying the attribute selected into the right-hand column to indicate that those attributes are to be unaffected by the schema change.

An update function must be created for each of the attributes on the left, to express how instances of that version should be converted to the new version. Similarly backdate functions must be defined for each of the right hand attributes. Here the GUI provides a useful default, automatically generating functions for the attributes that were copied over. It is not always the case that these automatically generated functions will remain unchanged - for example where changing units of measurement for an attribute, in which case the user can edit the functions.

In this example, where the attribute 'age' is being replaced by 'date_of_birth', methods need to be written. This is accomplished using the editor window in figure 8 which shows the update function required to derive a value for 'date_of_birth'. This is in prefix notation because of the use of CLOS to implement the system.

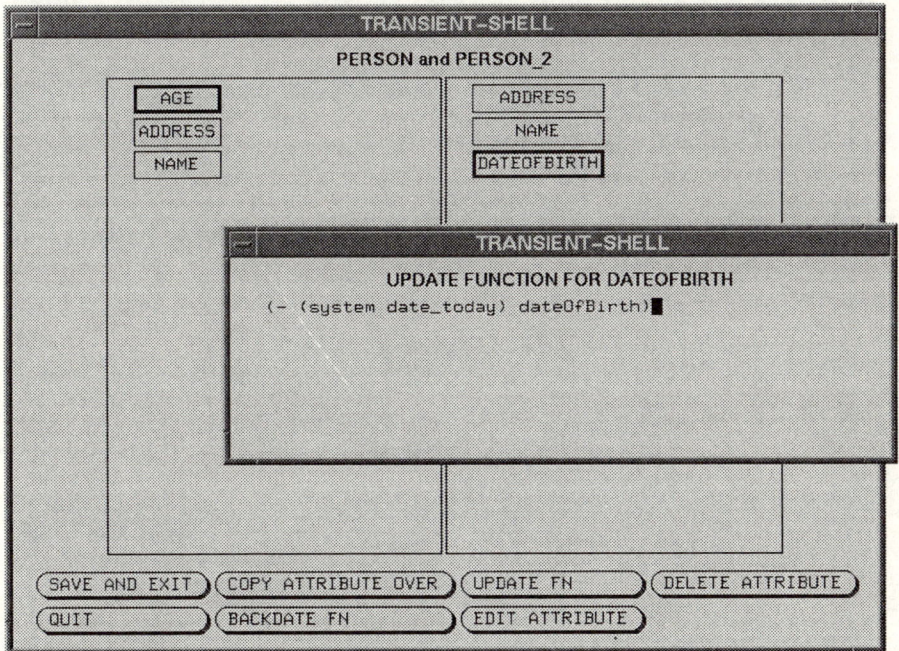

Figure 8. Schema change window for dynamic instance conversion.

To summarise, the important points for this interface are that :-
- The attributes for which some action is required are listed in the left-hand column.
- Default update and backdate functions are automatically generated for those attributes which the user specifies as not changing by copying them over.
- The functions can be edited and new attributes for the new version created.

### 4.2.2 *The ENCORE approach*

In ENCORE's approach, new versions are created with respect to the VSI rather than the previous version of the class. Here we need three columns (see figure 9).

The left hand column lists the attributes of the VSI, the centre column the attributes of the new version and the right hand column the attributes for which handlers must be defined. The contents of this last column are generated automatically and dynamically as the set symmetric difference of the other two columns. The user then creates handlers in the same way as update and backdate methods are defined for views and dynamic instance conversion. In this way, the GUI supports the process of schema evolution by ENCORE's methodology, ensuring that all the required handlers are written.

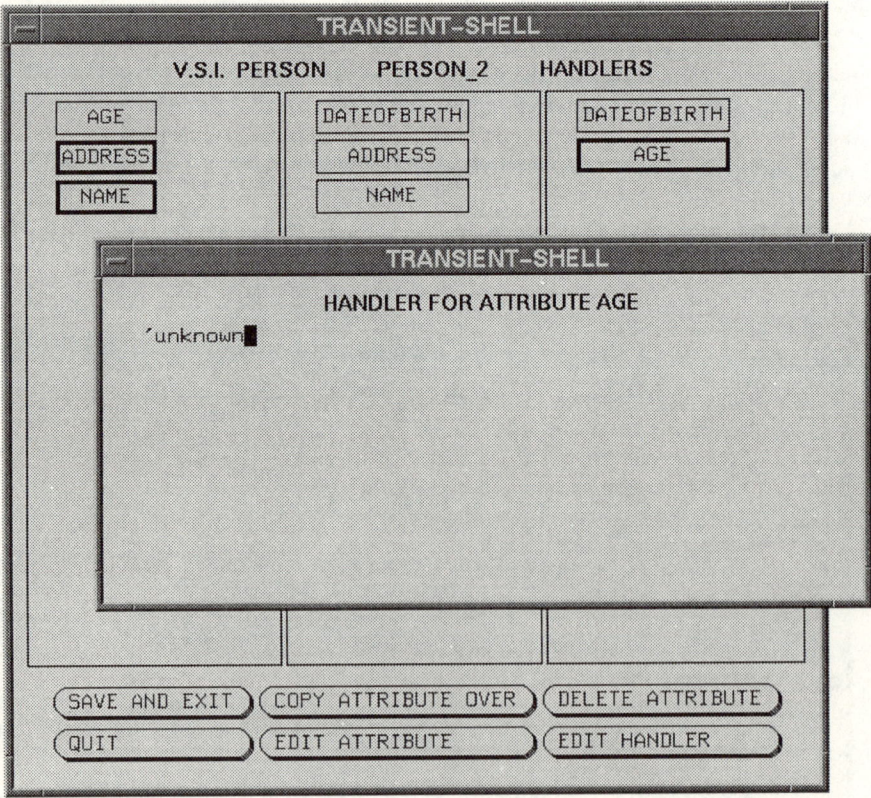

Figure 9. Schema change window for ENCORE.

The important points about this interface are that :-
- The attributes for which some action is required are listed in the left-hand column, prompting the user to copy over those attributes that are to be retained.
- A column of handlers are automatically generated for those attributes which will require them. Simple default handlers are automatically generated.
- The handler can be edited and new attributes for the new version created.

In both class versioning windows (figures 8 and 9) control is held by the window until the class version has been created or the operation cancelled. This prevents the user from carrying out other changes to the schema that could corrupt the meta-data.

# 5 Conclusions

In this paper, the requirements for GUIs for supporting schema evolution are explored. The GUI to the CLOSQL system is used to illustrate some of these requirements for two different types of schema evolution.

The requirements that have been identified are that of ease of use, support for the schema evolution process and accessibility of information. The latter two are a consequence of the unavoidable complexity of managing the process of schema evolution. Support for the schema evolution process strongly implies the need for the GUI to actively support the process by providing the user with information specific to the methodology in use. This means that more information about the schema change process is kept in the system itself and less in the head of the user.

The general schema browsing tool allows navigation of the class and version hierarchies. The class composition hierarchy can only be navigated at the level of instances. The system would be improved if such navigation were possible at the class level.

The GUI described here represents a considerable advantage over using the DIL (database interface language). The complicated syntax is simplified by the GUI which manages the process of speciying the schema change, helping to ensure that all the required actions are taken by the user.

# Acknowledgement

The work described in this paper was funded by the Science and Engineering Research Council (UK) and Zyqad Ltd, Nottingham, UK.

# 6. References

1. Sjøberg, D. Quantifying schema evolution. Information and Software Technology 1993; 35(1):35-44. .
2. Monk, S R and I Sommerville. Schema Evolution in OODBs Using Class Versioning. SIGMOD Record 1993; 22 (3). 16-22.
3. Skarra, A H and S B Zdonik. The Management of Changing Types in an Object-Oriented Database. In: OOPSLA'86. pp 483-495. 1986.

4. Björnerstedt, A and S Britts. AVANCE: An Object Management System. In: OOPSLA'86. pp 206-221. 1988.
5. Kim, H and H F Korth. Schema Versions and Views in Object-Oriented Databases. In: INFO Japan. pp 277-284. 1990.
6. Abiteboul, S and A Bonner. Objects and Views. SIGMOD Record 1991; 20 (2): 238-247. .
7. Scholl, M H, C Laasch, and M Tresch. Updatable Views in Object-Oriented Databases. In Deductive and Object-Oriented Databases, 189-207. 1991.
8. Urban, S D and K Chalmers. An Investigation of the View Update Problem for Object-Oriented Views. In Computers and Communications, Phoenix, 156-163. 1992.
9. Monk, S R. The CLOSQL Query Language. Computing Dept, Lancaster University, Lancaster, LA1 4YR, UK, Internal Report Number SE-91-15. 1991.
10. Monk, S R and I Sommerville. A Model for Versioning of Classes in Object-Oriented Databases. In BNCOD 10, Aberdeen, ed. P M D Gray and R J Lucas, 42-58. Springer-Verlag. 1992.
11. Almarode, J. Issues in the Design and Implementation of a Schema Designer for an OODBMS. In ECOOP'91, Geneva, ed. P America, 200-218. Springer Verlag. 1991.
12. Deux, O et al. The O2 System. *Comm. of the ACM* 34 (10). 34-48. 1991
13. Kim, W. Introduction to Object-Oriented Databases. The MIT Press. 1990.
14. Mariani, J A and R Lougher. Triplespace - An Experiment in a 3D Graphical Interface to a Binary Relational Database. Interacting with Computers 4 (2). 147-162. 1992.
15. Keene, S E. Object-Oriented Programming in Common Lisp - A Programmers Guide to CLOS. Addison-Wesley. 1989.
16. Steele, G L. Common LISP - The Language. Second Edition, DIGITAL Press. 1990.
17. Harlequin. LispWorks User Guide. Harlequin Ltd.,Barrington Hall, Barrington, Cambridge, CB2 5RG, UK, 1991.

# Unifying Interaction with Persistent Data and Program

R.C.H. Connor, Q.I. Cutts, G.N.C. Kirby,
V.S. Moore and R. Morrison

*Division of Computer Science, University of St Andrews,
North Haugh, St Andrews, Fife KY16 9SS, Scotland*

**Abstract**

Visual interaction with object-oriented databases, such as that provided by generic object browsing systems, has proved to be a convenient and natural way for database users to address informal queries over the contents of a database. Our particular field of interest is browsing and editing in persistent and database programming languages where procedures are treated as data values, with the consequence that executable code may exist in the same persistent environment as the other data that it manipulates. Such systems include object-oriented database systems, where the objects' method code is an intrinsic part of the object database itself.

A new style of browsing is introduced which allows a browser/editor to subsume all the activities normally connected with writing queries and other programs against the database. It therefore provides the only interface to the database that programmers and users require to understand. This is achieved partly by unifying the concepts of source and executable code within a system. This unification relies upon the paradigm of hyper-programming, in which programs may contain direct links to database values embedded in their source representations.

## 1 Overview

This paper is about a new style of browser/editor which allows programmers and users to interact directly with the database, by allowing database accesses to be performed by user gesture. Browsing a database in this style is a well-established technique; the contribution here is an extension of this browsing style which allows the programs which operate over the data to be traversed and manipulated in the same manner as other database values.

Our field of interest is in persistent and database programming languages where procedures are treated as data values, with the consequence that executable code may exist in the same persistent environment as the other data that it manipulates. Such systems include object-oriented database systems, where the objects' method code is an intrinsic part of the object database itself.

The major conceptual difference between procedures and methods, that of late binding to object instances, is unimportant in the context of this discussion. The binding issues which will be discussed, notably those of closure formation, are identical in the different paradigmatic contexts of object-oriented databases and other persistent and database programming languages. The examples in the paper will be given in the context of a procedural database programming language (in fact Napier88 [1]), but the concepts extend to any database system in which the code is conceptually resident in the object store.

## 2  Introduction

Visual interaction with object-oriented databases, such as that provided by generic object browsing systems [2-8], has proved to be a convenient and natural way for database users to address informal queries over the contents of a database. The users of such tools can browse freely around the data structures and values of a database, avoiding the necessity to write down algebraic expressions to perform the equivalent accesses. Where appropriate it is also possible to perform updates or invoke more complex methods over the objects depicted on the screen. Such tools are greatly preferred to a traditional query-based approach for simple queries and updates to object-oriented databases.

The advantages of this style of access are comparable to the advantages of a modern iconic operating system interface over a traditional command-line based approach. In addition, however, a more general programming algebra is required so that more complex and longer-running queries may be handled. This rather frustratingly gives rise to two quite separate mechanisms for manipulating the same values within a system, with the choice of mechanism being somewhat arbitrary for tasks in the middle ground between trivial and complex.

Here we describe a new browser/editor that is being developed for the Napier88 system [9]. The significance of this new browser is that it includes three very strong unifying concepts, the combination of which makes the browser the only mechanism which is required for interaction with the database system. The three important unifying concepts are:

1. Data of any type supported by the system may be browsed and edited in a uniform manner. This includes a uniform treatment of procedure closures; a drawback of previous browsers is that they could not adequately handle procedures.

2. Source code is treated not as a fundamental building block within the programming system, but instead as a transient text-based view of any value. The source does not have a conceptual permanent existence within the system, but is apparently generated from any value that may be browsed. Compilation and linking still occur within the system, but are presented to the programmer simply as a reification of the transient source.

3. As a further consequence of the generic treatment of procedure values and source code, the artificial distinction between source and executable values

within a running system is completely removed. If a run-time error occurs, for example, the actual value of the procedure in which it occurred may be displayed by the browser. The source will still be available for necessary purposes such as correction and adaptation; however the source will not exist as a separate entity accessible in isolation from the executable value.

The major difference between this and other browsers is therefore in the uniform treatment of the executable and source code forms of procedures, and hence programs. Furthermore, as will be seen, the manipulation of code made possible by the unification strategy is sufficiently general to subsume the usual process of program editing, compilation and linking which is normally associated with the manipulation of code bodies within a system. This means that the browser/editor is the only interfacing tool required to perform queries of any complexity against the database, or to introduce new data and program to it.

The unification of the source and executable code within a system is not possible with a conventional source representation. Section 3 explains the basic problems, and highlights a new style of source representation, that of hyper-programming, as a way of solving them. Section 4 then introduces the main concepts of the new-look browser/editor.

# 3  Unifying Source and Executable Forms

This section examines the essential problem with the uniform visualisation of persistent source and executable code representations; namely, that many different executable forms may share the same source representation. It is shown how the paradigm of hyper-programming, where direct links to values may exist as part of the source code, may be used to create a one-to-one mapping between source and executable, with the direct consequence that the concepts may be merged in the programmers' view of the system.

## 3.1  Code and Closure Representations

There is normally a clear distinction in persistent systems which support first-class procedures between the concept of procedure code, and the concept of closure; it is this distinction which traditionally makes the unification of source and executable values impossible. The concept of closure represents the executable version of code; it is formed by a pair consisting of the procedure code and the environment in which this code is to be evaluated. Thus the difference between code and closure can be summed up as the meaning of any free variables in the code at the time the procedure value is instantiated.

For a procedure without free variables, the environment is not significant and there is no conceptual difference between code and closure except for the fact that one form is regarded as source and the other as executable. The system's compiler performs a mapping from one form to the other; it is quite possible to construct a reverse mapping from executable to source. This is true in any system, and indeed many systems do keep such reverse mappings for debugging purposes. If all procedures within a system have the property of containing no free variables, then this mapping is one-to-one; that is, no two different executable forms map to the same source form. This is a direct consequence of the executable semantics being wholly captured by the procedure code. If all the code in the system may be defined in terms of such source-executable pairs, then the conceptual unification of source and executable may be achieved with an appropriate user interface design.

However, most procedures in database systems do contain free variables. Thus in general the conceptual division of the code and closures into pairs cannot take place, as many different executable procedures, each with its own different semantics, may derive from the same source description. It is therefore not possible at the interface level to unify the concepts of code and closure. This is illustrated in Figure 1.

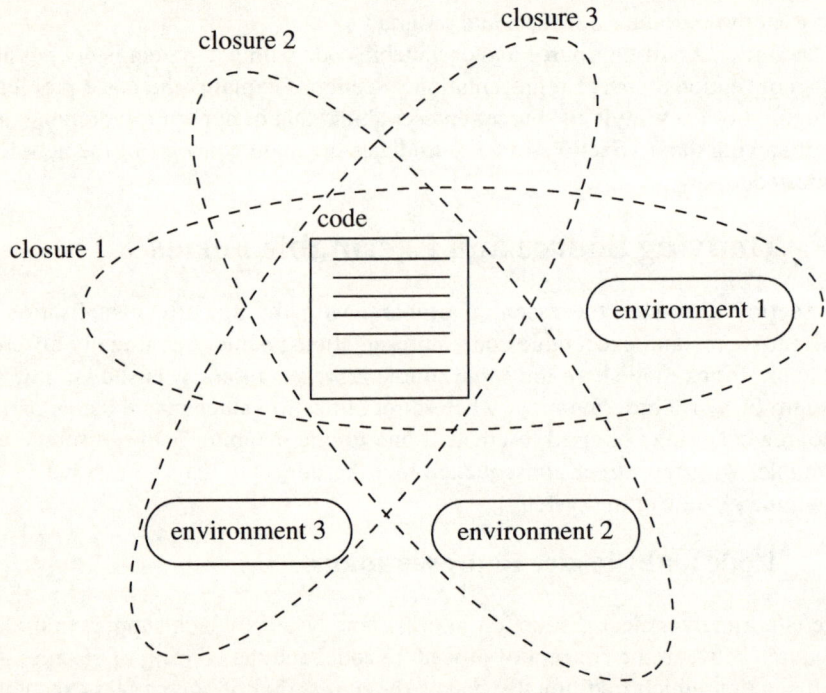

Figure 1: One to many mapping of code to closure

This problem may be overcome, however, by the use of a new paradigm for program source descriptions. This paradigm is known as hyper-programming [10], and is described in the next section. The original motivation for the design of the hyper-programming paradigm was to ease the task of source code construction; we show here how it can be further used to derive a one-to-one mapping between source and executable forms, and thus lay the foundation for their conceptual unification within a persistent programming system.

## 3.2 Persistent Hyper-Programming

Traditionally programs are represented as linear sequences of text. Where a program requires access to an external object during its execution, it must contain a textual description of how that object may be located. At some stage during the software process the description is resolved to establish a link to the object itself. Commonly this occurs during linking for code objects and during execution for data objects, and the environment in which the resolution takes place varies accordingly.

In such systems programs are typically constructed and stored in some long-term storage facility, such as a file system, separate from the run-time environment which disappears at the end of each program execution. By contrast, in persistent systems, programs may be constructed and stored in the same environment as that in which they are executed. This means that objects accessed by a program may already be available at the time the program is composed. In this case it is possible for a link to an object to be directly included in the program, replacing the traditional textual description. A program containing both text and links to objects is called a *hyper-program*.

Figure 2 shows a schematic view of a hyper-program. The links embedded in it are represented by some kind of non-textual token to allow them to be distinguished from the surrounding text. The first link is to a first class procedure value which when called writes a prompt to the user. The program then calls another procedure to read in a name, and then finds an address corresponding to the name. This is done by calling a procedure *lookup* to look up the address in a table package linked into the hyper-program. The address is then written out. Note that code objects (*readString*, *writeString* and *lookup*) are treated in exactly the same way as data objects (the table).

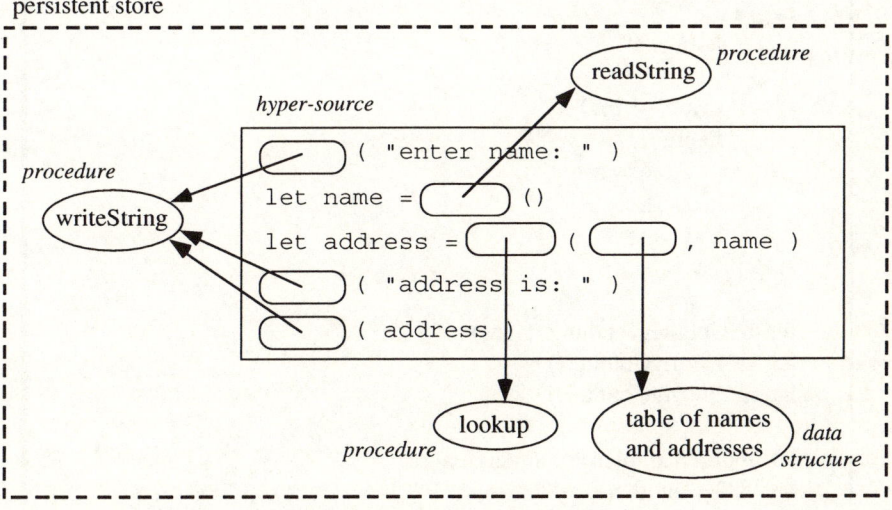

**Figure 2: A hyper-program**

The original motivation behind the hyper-programming paradigm was to allow programmers to incorporate uses of external data and procedures by user gesture, rather than by algebraic expression, when the external data was already present at composition time. The mechanism necessary to achieve this is composition time binding.

Non-textual tokens, referred to as hyper-links, are used within programs to denote composition time bindings. This enhanced source representation gives a way of representing non-local information in the source of a procedure; this non-local information can only be represented in textual source by the use of free variables which are resolved with respect to an evaluation environment. In Figure 2, the code contains no free variables, as all normal variable uses are superseded by hyper-links. This gives rise to the observation that the meaning of this program is independent of an evaluation environment, and is captured directly in the hyper-source.

By a simple extension of the hyper-programming paradigm it is possible to describe a hyper-source representation for any executable procedure. The concept of composition time binding is slightly widened to one of binding all free variables at closure formation time; these variables may be represented by hyper-links in exactly the same way. An example of a procedure with a free variable is shown in Figure 3. Each time the outer procedure *counterGen* is called, it creates a new integer variable *a* and returns a new procedure operating on *a*. The action of the procedure returned is to increment the variable and return its new value. All the procedures generated by *counterGen* share the same code. Their closures differ, however, since the name *a* is bound to a different location in their respective environments.

```
let counterGen = proc( → proc( → int ) )
begin
        let a := 0

        proc( → int )
        begin
                a := a + 1
                a
        end
end

let myCounter = counterGen()
let val1 = myCounter()
let val2 = myCounter()

let anotherCounter = counterGen()
let val3 = anotherCounter()
```

**Figure 3: Free variable binding**

The procedure *myCounter* in Figure 3, whose meaning depends critically upon its evaluation context, may be represented by the hyper-source shown in Figure 4.

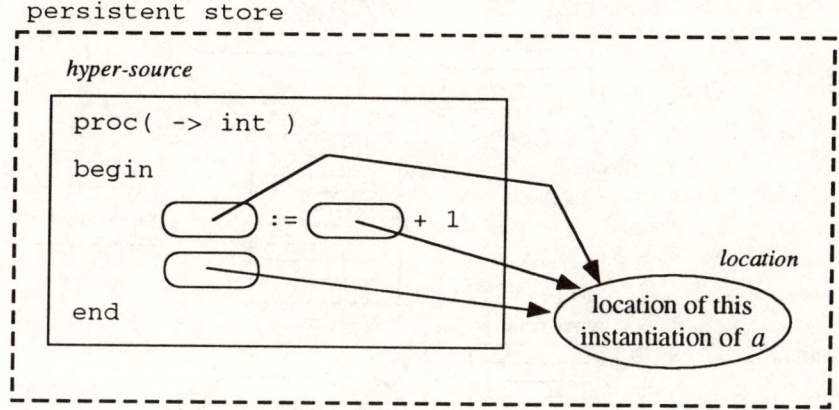

**Figure 4: Corresponding hyper-source**

Thus hyper-source may be used to give a source representation for any arbitrary procedure, with the property that its semantics is independent of its evaluation environment. This is quite simply achieved by representing the necessary parts of the traditional evaluation environment within the source itself, by means of hyper-links. Notice for example that successive evaluations of the procedure *counterGen* will result in different hyper-source representations, as although the textual code is the same the hyper-links are different, reflecting the different semantics. The use of hyper-source is thus able to achieve the desired one-to-one mapping between procedure source and executable forms, as illustrated in Figure 5. This clears the way to the presentation of a unified visualisation of the two representations to the programmer, leaving concepts such as compilation and linking to be matters of system efficiency rather than system building essentials.

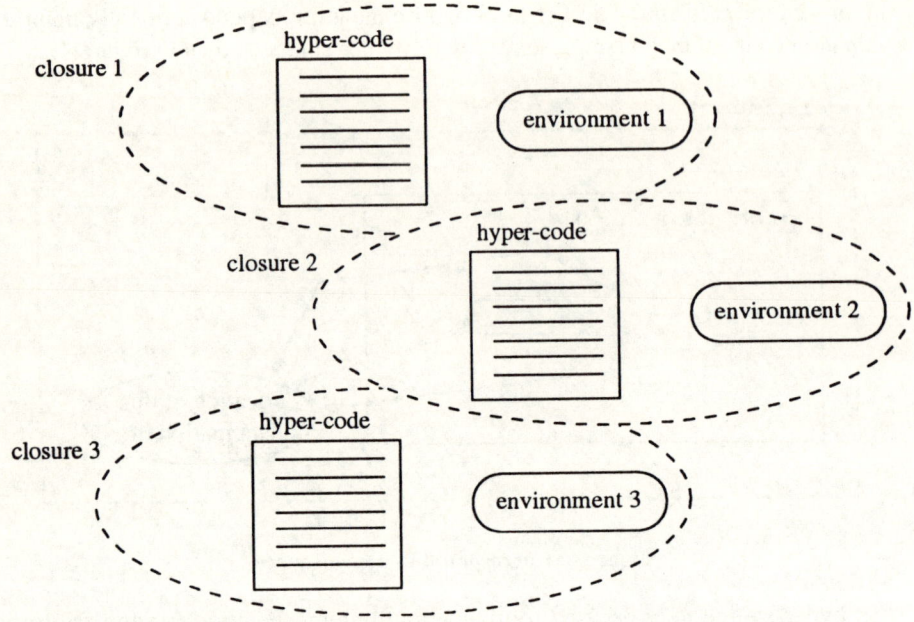

Figure 5: One-to-one mapping of hyper-code to closure

## 4 The Generic Browser

Values are displayed differently by the browser according to their particular type constructor. The following concepts however are upheld across all type constructors:

- Component values and locations are displayed in a uniform manner, with identical operations available. Hyper-links within procedures are deemed to be component values; thus an integer field in a structure (record) appears in a manner identical to an integer hyper-link within a procedure representation.

- Type constructors which represent abstractions over the type system are dealt with uniformly; thus a value typed as a variant which is actually a structure is displayed as a structure, with appropriate annotation to show the type widening. Thus types corresponding to value constructors, such as structure and vector, are distinguished from those representing type system abstraction, such as variants and abstract data types.

- Source code may be generated for any value displayed in the browser. If the value is a procedure, then the source "generated" will correspond to the programmer's original description of the procedure. However source will be generated automatically for any other value also, which may or may not correspond to its original derivation. The source presented is hyper-source.

- Operations on source include textual editing and "reification", which corresponds roughly to compilation and evaluation. If the source is incorrect this results in an error; otherwise the resulting value is displayed as an anonymous value in the browser. Source representations may also be stored in some other environment if required.

## 4.1 General Browser Interface

In general, values are displayed in the browser in one of two formats, called *maxi* and *mini*. The mini representation is roughly equivalent to an iconic view of the value, with the maxi representation showing the full details of its construction. A maxi view will typically contain representations of its component values depicted as minis. A useful parallel may be drawn with the Macintosh operating system, where the windows displayed correspond to a type constructor representing a heterogeneous set, and the icons in these windows correspond to the mini representations of the values contained in the set.

Different styles of windows are also required, one for each data type in the language corresponding to a value constructor; as already mentioned, this includes procedures. These constructors in general contain their component icons in a rather more rigid framework than that of a heterogeneous set, but the basic principles are the same. The browser also supports the kind of user gesture associated with this interface, such as copying and moving values, and the expansion of a mini or icon representation into its own maxi or window level representation.

Another concept which is modelled at this level is that of a location, along with destructive update. Data types which support locations, such as structures, vectors and procedures, display the mini representations within a bounding box which represents the location. Destructive update is modelled by dropping another value within this box; this will only succeed if the new value has an appropriate type.

The last general concept in the browser is that of generating source. This may be done with either a maxi or mini representation; the effect is to produce a new window which contains editable hyper-source. Source may be edited and evaluated; its evaluation (if successful) results in a new anonymous value being depicted within the browser. The source produced from a value has the property that, when evaluated, the resulting value is equal to the original in every respect except for identity. Thus for any scalar value $v$, $evaluate(source(v)) = v$, whereas for objects with store semantics this is not the case where the equality operator is interpreted as identity. The source generated is not a part of the conceptual value space of the browser, but is treated as a transient entity as depicted in Figure 6.

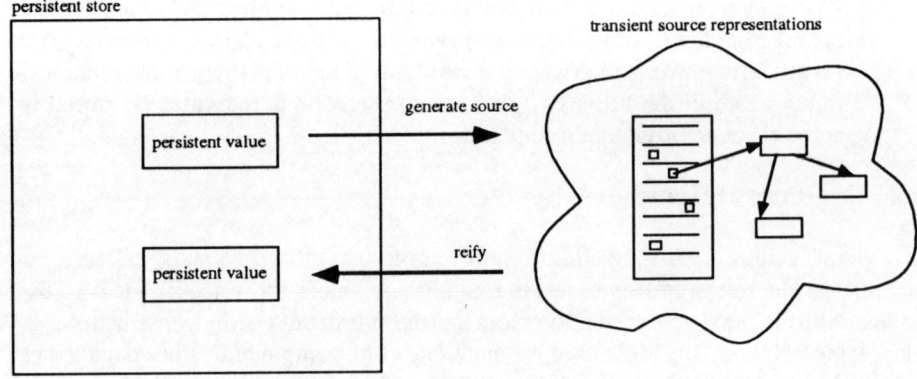

Figure 6: Persistent values and transient source

The source generated for a value is calculated only to the first level; that is, any component values—those displayed as mini representations within a maxi view—are represented as hyper-links within the source. Thus there is a very close correspondence between mini views and hyper-links, and in fact it may be reasonable in the future to merge the concepts. They are kept distinct at present to emphasise the separation between the transient source forms and the concrete maxi views of procedure values.

## 4.2 Browsing Values and Locations

### 4.2.1 Mini Representations

An example of a mini representation for an integer value is shown in Figure 7. There are two parts to the representation: the type and value areas. The type area indicates the base type or constructor; for constructors the user can double-click on the type area to pop up a more detailed representation of the type. In general the type information is displayed by means of an icon; this may be user-defined in the case of user-defined types. Our examples, however, show simple strings rather than icons for the sake of readability. Double-clicking on the value area, known as *inspecting* the value, shows more detail by replacing the mini representation with a maxi representation.

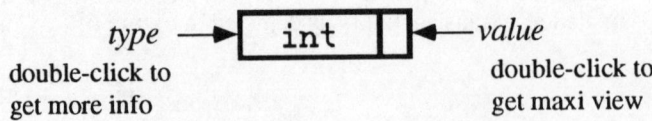

Figure 7: Mini representation

Mutable locations are shown by surrounding the mini representation with a box as shown in Figure 8:

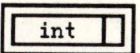

**Figure 8: Mini representation of a mutable location**

A new value may be assigned to the location by dragging the appropriate mini or maxi onto the box. The update succeeds only if the new value has a compatible type.

The user may select either the location or the value which it currently contains by clicking on the appropriate part of the representation. This is necessary for operations such as assigning the value to some other location or including a link to the location or value into source code. These operations will be described shortly.

### 4.2.2  Maxi Representations

Maxi representations of values show more information than minis and may themselves contain mini representations. Figure 9 shows both the mini representation of a structure value, and the corresponding maxi representation obtained by double-clicking on the value area of the mini. The maxi representation may be converted back to the mini by double-clicking on the title bar.

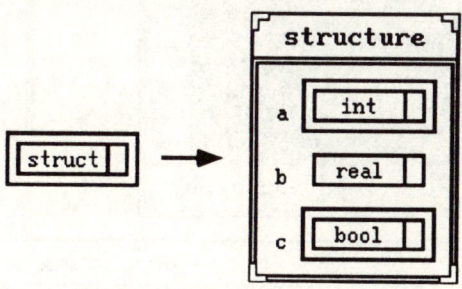

**Figure 9: Mini and maxi representations of a structure**

This shows a structure (record) with mutable fields *a* and *c*, and a constant field *b*. The form of a particular maxi representation depends on the type constructor involved, but the unifying theme is that all components are represented by minis within the maxi representation.

Scalar values have no internal structure; their maxi representations display the value itself in a convenient format, usually textual. An example of an integer value is shown in Figure 10:

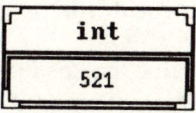

**Figure 10: Maxi representation of an integer**

Figure 11 shows some other examples of maxi representations, for an image, a procedure and a vector. The procedure representation shows a procedure generated by a call of *counterGen* in Figure 3. Each free variable is treated as a component in the same way as a structure field or vector location, and is represented by an embedded mini. Mutable locations can be updated by dragging new values over the box.

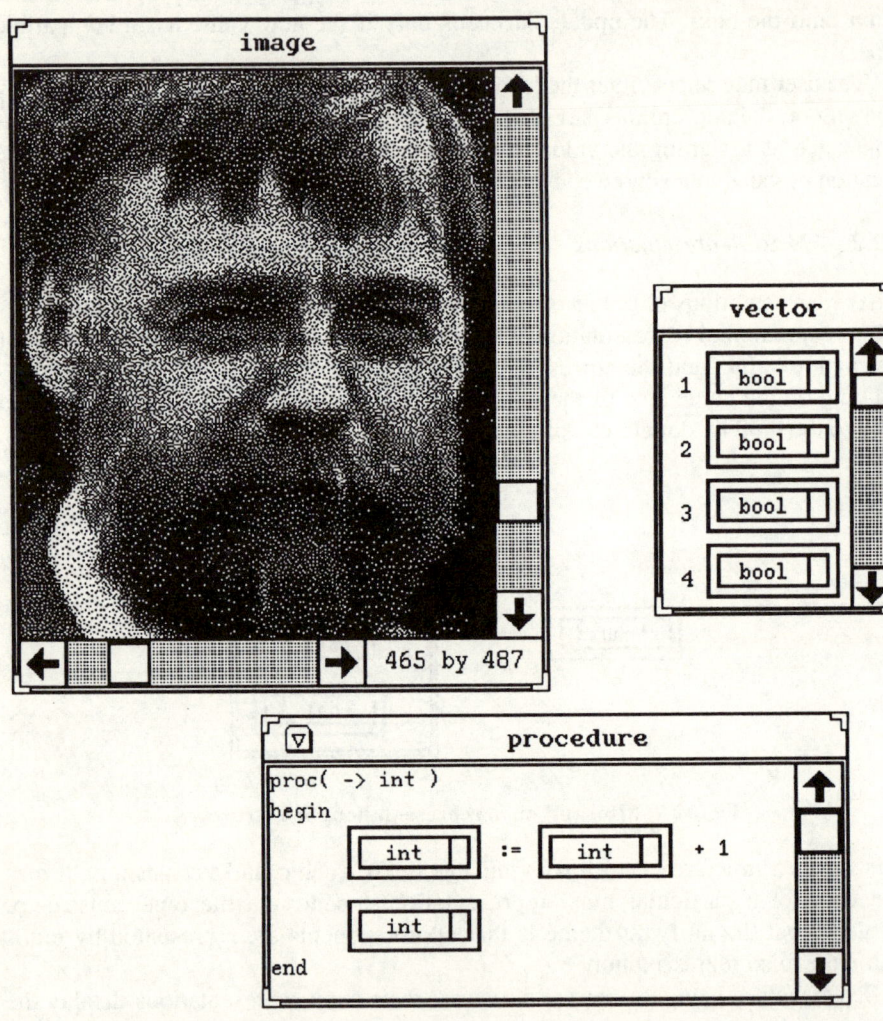

Figure 11: **Maxi representations of an image, procedure and vector**

## 4.3   Inspecting Maxi Components

A component of a maxi representation may be inspected by double-clicking on the corresponding embedded mini representation. If the mini is of a scalar type this results in the mini being expanded into a maxi in place, within the containing maxi.

For other values the maxi is displayed as a separate window and a link is drawn to it from the parent maxi. This approach reflects the treatment of equality in Napier88, in which two scalar values of the same type are equal iff they are bitwise identical, whereas two non-scalars are equal iff they have the same identity.

Figure 12 shows an example of the maxi representation of a structure and the expanded representation of one of its fields.

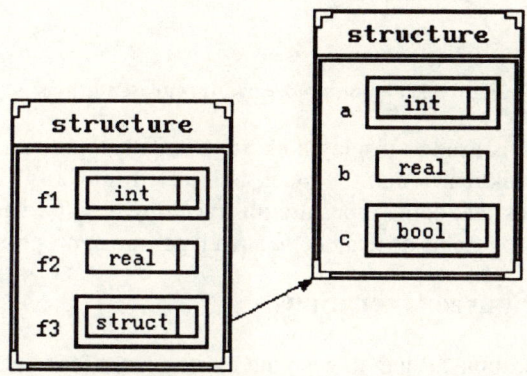

**Figure 12: Inspecting a component of a maxi**

## 4.4 Type Abstraction

Several of the Napier88 types and type constructors involve abstraction over the type of a value. These are **any** (an infinite union), variants (labelled disjoint sums) and abstract data types. The browser displays such values by annotating the mini and maxi representations with extra type information. Figure 13 shows an example of the representations of an instance of the following variant type:

**rec type** list **is variant**( cons : **structure**( hd : **int** ; tl : list ) ; tip : **null** )

The main part of each representation shows the value itself in the normal way. Attached to the edge is an annotation describing the type abstraction through which the value is currently viewed. The example shows an instance of the *cons* branch, indicated in the maxi representation by emboldening that branch name. The user can double-click on the annotation title bar to obtain a detailed description of the type. It is also possible to select the value either as an instance of the variant type, or as an instance of the branch structure type, depending on which part of the representation is clicked on.

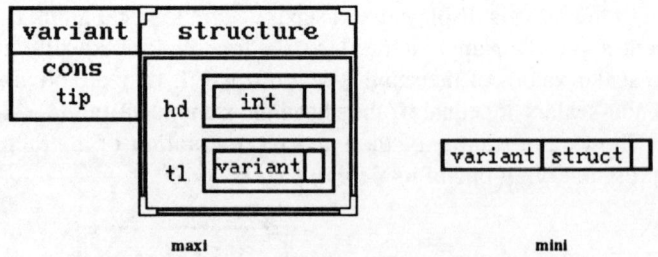

Figure 13: Annotated variant representations

A similar approach is used to display both **any**s and abstypes. In the first case the annotation simply indicates that the value is injected into **any**. For abstypes the annotation indicates that some types are abstracted over—the witness types—and the user operations on fields dependent on such types are appropriately limited.

## 4.5 Hyper-Source Operations

The user may request the system to generate hyper-source for a selected value. This hyper-source may then be edited, involving both normal text editing and insertion of links to values and locations. Insertion of a link is achieved by selecting the appropriate mini or maxi representation and then pressing a *link* button. This inserts a link to the value directly into the source code. Once edited the source code may be reified to give a value which is displayed as a mini or maxi by the browser. Reification involves compilation of the source and execution of the resulting code. These actions, however, are hidden from the user.

Figure 14 shows an example of the hyper-source code generated for a structure value. Components of the structure are shown as embedded links.

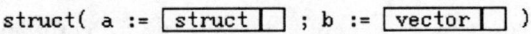

Figure 14: Hyper-source generated for a structure

If source is generated for a value and then reified again without editing, the result is a one-level copy of the original value. Thus the new value has a new identity but any components are shared with the original. It is also possible to selectively copy to any required depth by further generating, in place, source for embedded links. Figure 15 shows how the source in the previous example can be further expanded by selecting only the structure representation and generating source for it. The embedded link is replaced by the corresponding source which may in turn contain further links.

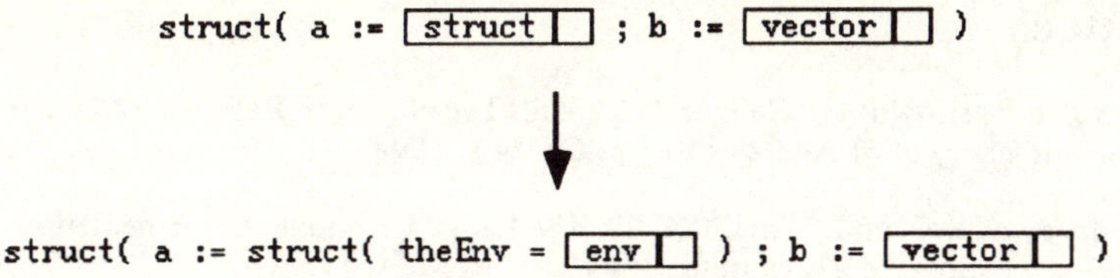

```
struct( a := [ struct  ] ; b := [ vector  ] )
                    ↓
struct( a := struct( theEnv = [ env  ] ) ; b := [ vector  ] )
```

**Figure 15: Selective source generation**

# 5  Conclusions

A generic browsing methodology suitable for use with object-oriented and procedure-oriented database programming languages has been described. The new contribution of this methodology is that the browser traverses data and code in an orthogonal manner, giving a fully general interface to the database which can subsume the normal code construction mechanisms. The interface to the browser is fully generic; the main unifying features are as follows:

- Data of any type are supported in a uniform manner, including procedure closures.
- Source code is treated not as a fundamental building block within the programming system, but instead as a transient text-based view of any value.
- The artificial distinction between source and executable values within a running system is completely removed, as a consequence of using the hyper-source code representation.

The main concepts of the new browser are fully applicable to any database programming language system which treats code as data. Examples have been given in the language Napier88, and are taken from a browser which has been largely implemented. The Napier88 hyper-programming system, complete with window manager, in-store compiler, hyper-program editor and an earlier browser is available from the authors.

# References

1.* Morrison R, Brown AL, Connor RCH et al. The Napier88 Reference Manual (Release 2.0). University of St Andrews Report CS/94/8, 1994

2. Goldberg A, Robson D. Smalltalk-80: The Language and its Implementation. Addison Wesley, Reading, Massachusetts, 1983

3. O'Brien PD, Halbert DC, Kilian MF. The Trellis Programming Environment. In: Proc. International Conference on Object-Oriented Programming Systems, Languages and Applications (OOPSLA'87), Orlando, Florida, 1987, pp 91-102

4.* Dearle A, Brown AL. Safe Browsing in a Strongly Typed Persistent Environment. Comp. J. 1988; 31,6:540-544

5. The LOOKS User's Manual. Altaïr, 1989

6. Bretl B, Otis A, Penney J et al. The GemStone Data Management System. In: W. Kim and F. Lochovsky (ed) Object-Oriented Concepts, Applications, and Databases. Morgan-Kaufman, 1989

7. Cooper RL. On The Utilisation of Persistent Programming Environments. Ph.D. thesis, University of Glasgow, 1990

8.* Kirby GNC, Dearle A. An Adaptive Graphical Browser for Napier88. University of St Andrews Report CS/90/16, 1990

9. Moore VS. A Hyper-Code Browsing System. University of St Andrews, 1994

10.* Kirby GNC, Connor RCH, Cutts QI, Dearle A, Farkas AM, Morrison R. Persistent Hyper-Programs. In: A. Albano and R. Morrison (ed) Persistent Object Systems, Proc. 5th International Workshop on Persistent Object Systems, San Miniato, Italy. Springer-Verlag, 1992, pp 86-106

*Available via *ftp* from
`ftp-fide.dcs.st-andrews.ac.uk/pub/persistence.papers`

or via *WWW* from
`http://www-fide.dcs.st-andrews.ac.uk:8080/Publications.html`

Metaphors

# Bags and Viewers: A Metaphor for Intelligent Database Access

Robert Inder (R.Inder@ed.ac.uk)

Human Communication Research Centre, University of Edinburgh

2, Buccleuch Place, Edinburgh EH8 9LW Scotland

Jussi Stader (J.Stader@ed.ac.uk)

Artificial Intelligence Applications Institute, University of Edinburgh

80, South Bridge, Edinburgh EH1 1HN Scotland

**Abstract**

We present a way of structuring a database query system to form a bridge between current data handling systems and the data requirements of creative work. The interface is based around specifying the contents of "bags" of objects and inspecting them using "viewers", which can then be used to launch further queries.

The operation of such an interface is described and illustrated by an example session using a prototype system. A number of features of such an interface are presented, the metaphor is discussed and a number of areas for future work are indicated.

## 1 Introduction

In many disciplines, a growing number of experts are carrying out creative work using data held, at least in part, on computers. Accessing this data is an increasingly significant part of their work. The data they require at any moment may depend on their interpretation of the data they have already retrieved, making very powerful yet easy-to-use query mechanisms essential.

Formulating queries in conventional database systems requires precise knowledge of the structure of the database and of a query language such as SQL [1]. However, many experts who could benefit from using on-line data neither have, nor wish to acquire, substantial computer skills. Interfaces can be built to allow data to be retrieved without knowledge of database structures—e.g. using on-screen "forms" as described in [2] and [3]—but only to the extent that the user's data needs can be anticipated, which restricts the user to common paths of enquiry (see Figure 1).

Marcus [4] highlights how important it is for any software interface to offer users appropriate *metaphors*, in the sense of "fundamental terms, images and concepts that are easily recognised, understood, and remembered". Work on addressing the database access problem for a particular class of users—geologists working in petroleum exploration [5]—gave rise to a framework for structuring database access activities which embodies *familiar* metaphors. The resulting style of interface is both intuitive and flexible enough to support creative work with unpredictable requirements. In the next section, we outline this framework, presenting the "Bags and Viewers" metaphor as it appears to the

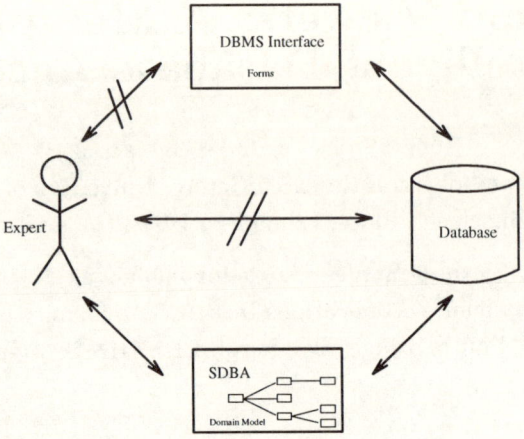

Figure 1: Experts' Routes to Access Data

user. In Section 3 we illustrate the use of such a system using screen dumps from a prototype system that is under development. Section 4 then presents a number of advantages of the approach, Section 5 discusses some specific points in more detail, and Section 6 identifies some areas where further work is required.

## 2 Bags and Viewers: the Metaphor

*Bags and Viewers* describes an approach to structuring the interface to a database query system in such a way that users can incrementally perform complex data retrieval operations without needing to know a query language or the structure of the database being accessed.

Regardless of how the data is actually stored, it is presented to the user as structured in terms of *objects* with *attributes*, and with *relationships* between them. These are specified in an explicit model of the field to which the data applies—the *domain*. This domain model is derived from experts in the field, and is quite independent of any particular database and the pragmatic pressures on its design. This idealised structure is mapped to a particular database by means of a database model, a formal description of the contents of the database in terms of the concepts in the domain model.

Both the domain model and the database are described using a conventional "object-oriented" formalism supporting class hierarchies and inheritance.

An interaction with the system starts with the user selecting an object type and specifying constraints on the values of its attributes by using *constraint editors*—tools customised for handling and constraining the values of a particular attribute.

At any time the user may ask the system to either count the objects that satisfy the currently specified set of constraints, or to "fetch" them. When the system "fetches" objects, it will by default create a new *bag* to contain them, and present the user with a way of referring to it. A bag is a logical container for a collection of objects that satisfy some particular set of constraints. It may be presented to the user in terms of the type and number of objects it contains, using an icon, or an entry in a session-wide menu of bags, or any other reminder of the bag's existence.

Bags are "opaque", and it is not possible to tell much from a bag itself about its contents—typically only the type and number of objects it contains. To see more, it is necessary to attach one or more *viewers* to the bag, each of which will show some attributes of the objects within. Whenever the system creates a bag, it will also attach a default viewer to it, so that the user can see something of the objects the bag contains. This viewer could display a one-line summary of each object; or, depending on the type of object and the user's preferences, it could be a map, a statistical plot, or any form of data presentation that is suitable for groups of such objects. If the default viewer does not give the required information, the user can re-configure it—for instance, by changing the attributes that form the summary or parameterising a cross-plot in terms of attributes to be used for axes, point shape, colour etc.—or select different or *additional* viewers. Thus the user can decide, in the light of what objects have been selected, how they should be displayed.

Whenever objects (or sets of objects) are fetched from the database, the user can choose whether they should be placed into a new bag or an existing one.

Where an existing bag is used, all of the viewers that have been associated with that bag are updated to reflect its new contents. Thus the user can build up an ideal view of a set of objects by associating combinations of viewers with the bag, and then immediately use that view for another set of objects by putting them into the same bag.

Whenever a new bag is used, the system keeps track of how it was created, and can graphically present the complete set of bags created during the session in the form of a *session history* which the user can review easily. As well as containing a set of objects, a bag also retains the constraints that were used to specify that set. These can be used to update the bag, or to re-fill it on subsequent occasions. More importantly the user can return to the constraints at any time and either review them or use them as the basis of another query. This makes it easy to explore alternatives from any point in the session, or refine the query to improve the quality of the results.

Most viewers are interactive, and allow the user to select objects or sets of objects, and thus request more information about them. For example, the one-line object summaries will function as a menu of the entries in the bag. Each selected object is fetched and put into a *box*—a bag for just a single object. Once again, a default viewer will be chosen. This might be a "form"—i.e. a set of attribute names and their values arranged on the screen. However, it could be any display appropriate for the type of object, either pre-stored (such as a photograph) or generated from a collection of data which is retrieved as required. Box viewers, like bag viewers, can be used to seek further details either of the object in the box or of related objects. The user can specify a relationship, and get a bag of the objects to which the one in the box is related in that way. Because viewers are interactive, the interface is very good for generating follow-up queries, and for unconstrained browsing through the data.

A *Bags and Viewers* interface not only hides the structure of the database, but also shields the user from the need to consider the inevitable shortcomings of the data itself, which is often incomplete, sometimes imprecise, and occasionally simply wrong. These factors can be a substantial obstacle for unfamiliar users. However, during the process of mapping the user's query from the domain model to the actual database, the system can ensure that the possibility of missing data is handled appropriately—e.g. by ensuring that missing data cannot cause a match to be rejected. It can also make allowances for uncertainties in the data, and indeed the user's intentions, by allowing constraints to be "fuzzy"—i.e. considering objects which fail to satisfy one or more of the stated constraints, provided that, overall, they are not "too far" away from the stated requirements.

## 3 The Movie

To give an indication of how the system is used we go through a simple session, using SDBA, a prototype *Bags and Viewers* system, to browse a commercially available database about oil wells in the North Sea. This prototype is implemented in Prolog with an external interface to X windows written in C. The oil well data is held in an external relational database system, queried by generating SQL, but SDBA has also been configured to query the Prolog "database" used by the "Chat 80" natural language system [6].

### Query Specification

When the system is started a *Top Window* appears on the screen, from where the user chooses a format to express their initial query. We illustrate a simple form-based approach, and from a menu of types of entities, choose to focus on wells. From the menu of pre-defined forms which pertain to wells, we choose one that contains attributes that relate to its technical, as opposed to, say, financial, aspects.

We are interested in wells that have a result of oil or gas. This will be our first constraint. Clicking on the Result button brings up a constraint editor which is tailored for dealing with the results of wells. As Figure 2 show, it presents us with a list of possible results, from which we select oil and gas, and then OK to dismiss the editor.

Our "oil or gas" constraint appears in the Result button, as shown in Figure 3, as does another constraint, generated in a similar manner, that the Status of the wells of interest must be completed. Figure 3 also shows a numeric constraint editor being used to constrain the value of the Total Depth to a range of values between 9000 and 15000 feet. When this third constraint has been specified, and its editor dismissed, we can collect the set of wells that satisfy them into a *bag* by selecting the fetch into new bag from the Options menu. The form used to generate the query is removed, and replaced (Figure 4) by a viewer onto the new bag, which takes the form of a table showing the eight wells which satisfy the three constraints. In addition, a note of the new bag appears in a list in the query system's Top Window.

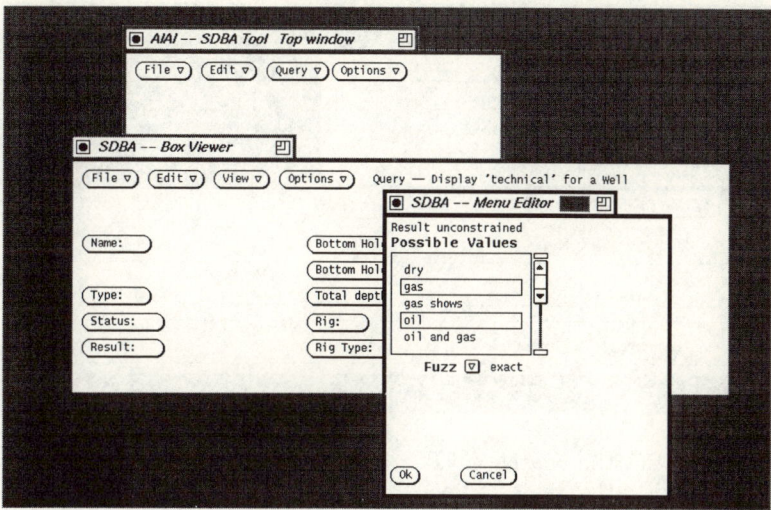

Figure 2: Menu-based Constraint Specification. The front-most window is a constraint editor which allows the user to select acceptable values from a menu of possible attribute values. Behind it is the form being used to compose the query, QBE-style.

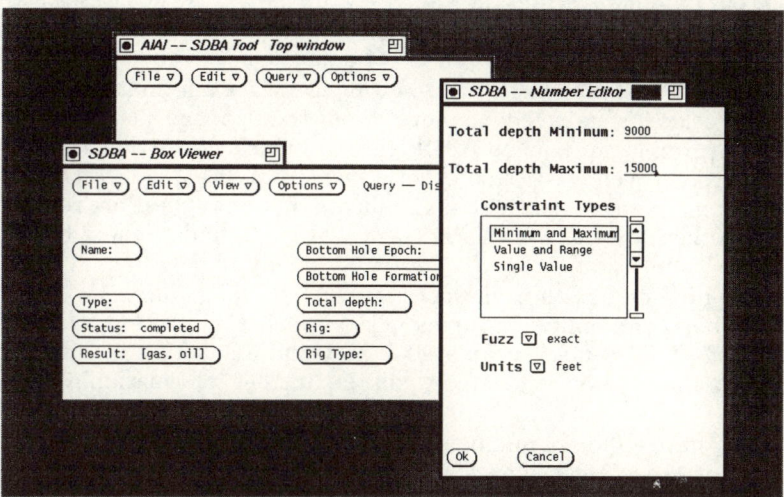

Figure 3: Numeric Constraint Specification. The constraint editor being used to specify a range of depths is tailored to handling numeric values. The form behind now shows constraints already applied to the Status and Result attributes.

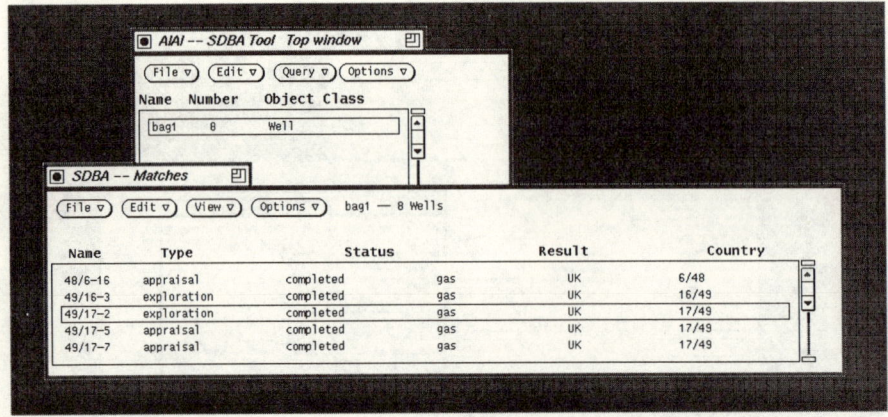

Figure 4: Viewing the Matches. The front-most window is a bag viewer displaying displaying the set of 8 wells in `bag1`. A mouse click on one of the one-line summaries calls up details of the relevant well. The window behind is the system's *"Top Window"*, where `bag1` has appeared on the container menu. The form used to compose the query has been removed.

## Navigation and Viewing

To find out more about a well, we can select it in the bag viewer's table and select `View in detail` from the viewer's `View` menu. This causes the selected well to be placed in a *box*, and its details to be shown using an appropriate form viewer: Figure 5 shows the result of doing this for two wells.

From the details of a single well, we can easily get information about other objects by selecting `related objects` from the `Options` menu for the form viewer. This brings up a menu (see Figure 6), which shows that there are two relationships between a well and other objects: a well has *interests* and a well *is in* one or more areas. The asterisks indicate that both these are relationships to several other objects. We select `is in Area*` to find out which areas well '211/26-7A' is in.

We are presented with a viewer (Figure 7) showing summary information for a new bag containing nine areas, all of which are in the Northern North Sea. As before, we can select an area to view in detail. This is duly placed in a box and a form viewer is created to display further information about it (see Figure 8).

We now have a quite a number of viewers on our screen, and it is beginning to look cluttered. Because each viewer is in a separate window, we can use the facilities of our window manager to open and close, re-size and re-organise them on the screen however we think best. In addition, we can manipulate them from the Top Window. By selecting entries in the bag and box menu and then choosing the `close container` from the Top Window's `Options` menu, we can iconify the viewers that are not immediately relevant. Other entries on the menu let users perform related operations on the viewers, such as re-opening or exposing them, or deleting them altogether.

So far, when we requested details of individual objects from a bag, the

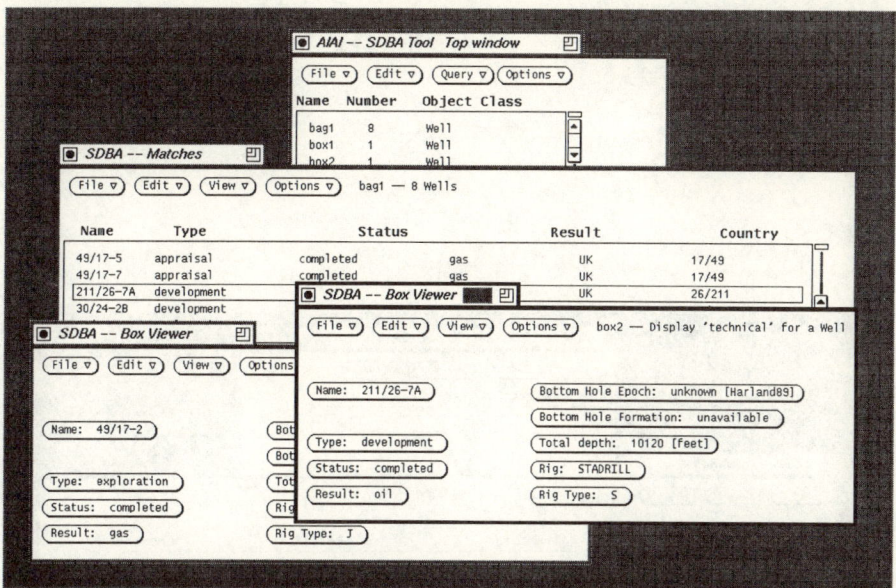

Figure 5: Well Details: the front-most windows contain forms displaying further details of two wells that have been selected from bag1 and placed in boxes for closer examination.

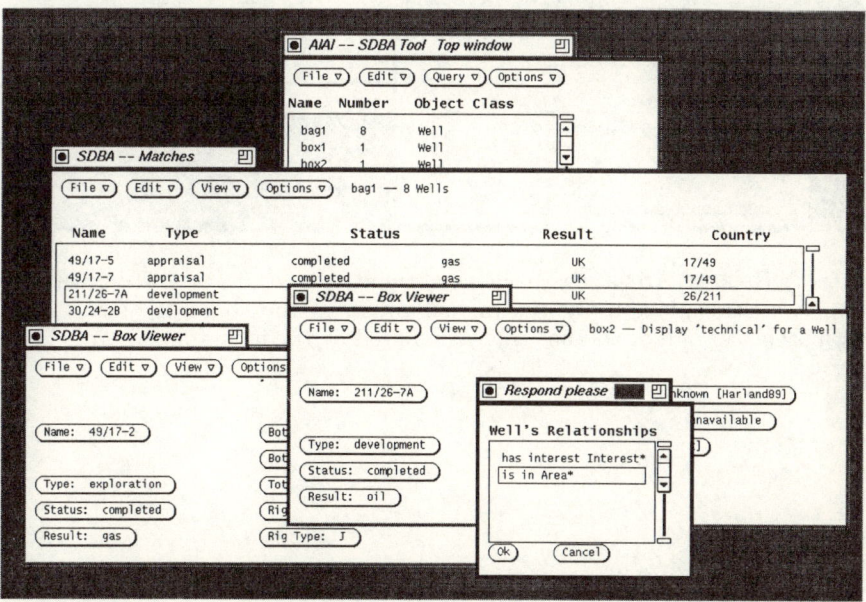

Figure 6: Related Objects: the front-most window contains a menu of the relationships that a well can participate in, and the types of other objects involved. This was called up by selecting related objects on the Options menu of the form behind it.

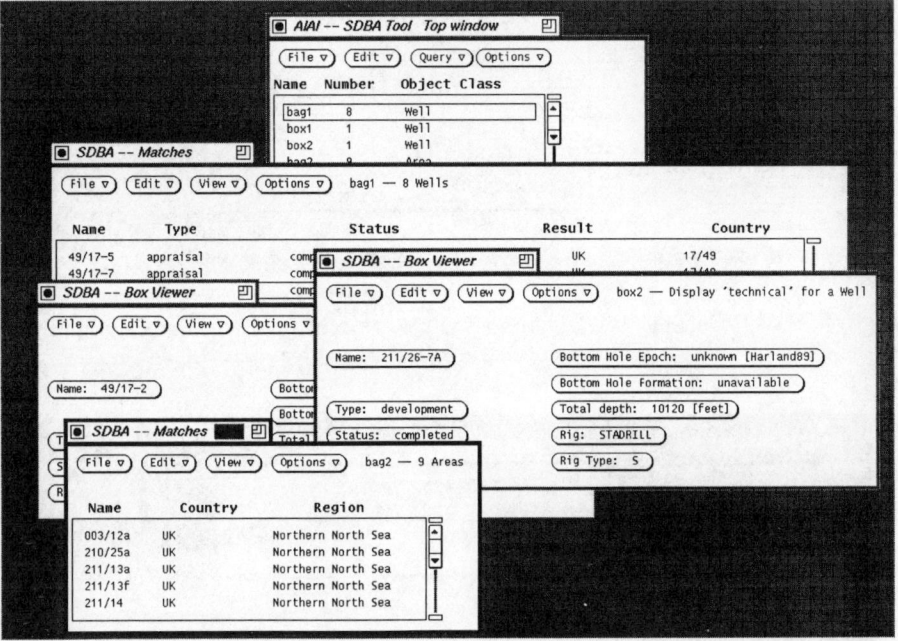

Figure 7: Related Areas: the front-most window contains a newly-created bag viewer which displays a one-per-line summary of the contents of bag2. This contains the set of 9 areas that the well viewed by the form immediately behind it is in.

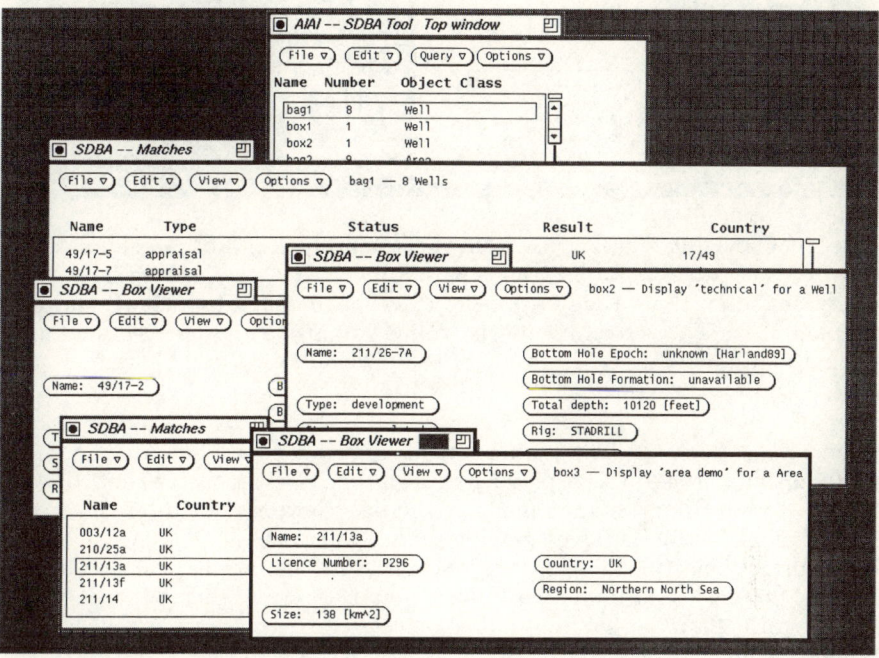

Figure 8: Area Details. The front-most window contains a new form which displays detail of one of an area selected from bag2.

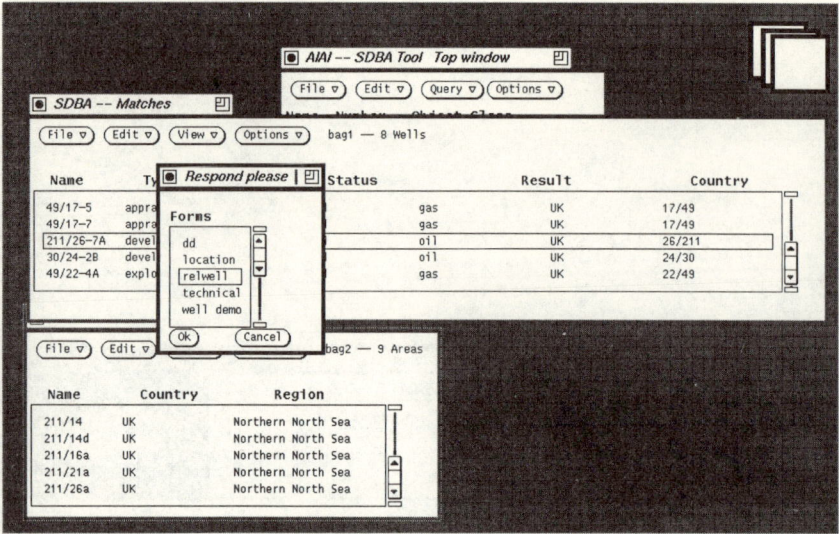

Figure 9: Changing Viewer: the front-most window contains a menu of the types of viewer available for a given type of object. It was called up by selecting the `select details viewer` from the `View` menu of the bag viewer immediately behind it. The screen has been "tidied" by using the menu of containers in the Top Window to iconify some of the previously created viewers.

system chose a default form viewer for us. Figure 9 shows how we can change the details viewer used for displaying information. We use the `select details viewer` option from the `View` menu of the bag viewer, which presents us with a list of available forms for displaying details about wells. We choose the `rel well` form. Selecting a well from the table in the viewer will now display different details (see Figure 10). Note that this viewer has been defined so that the form shows an attribute of some related objects—the areas that Well '49/17-2' is in. The names of these areas, which are the same ones we collected in a bag in Figure 8, are mouse sensitive, and can be used to call up further information on the areas, just as the entries in the bag can.

## Session Summary

We have been browsing for some time now, and have many bags and many windows on the screen which contain our (intermediate) results. It is becoming difficult to remember what information is in which window. However, because the system has retained the connections between the bags we have created, we can ask it, by selecting `view tree` from the `Options` menu in the Top Window, to display a diagrammatic summary of our session so far (See Figure 11). This shows that the session started by generating a bag of eight wells from a query specified from scratch. Viewers onto this bag have been used to create three boxes containing individual wells. One of them was used to obtain a bag of areas, from which we opened a box viewer on an individual area. Another was

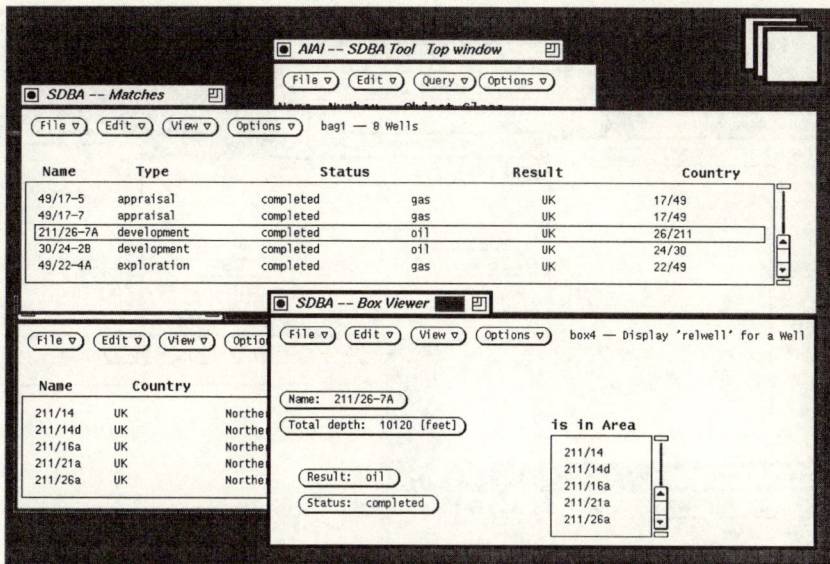

Figure 10: A Well Through Another Viewer. A further form viewer displays a different set of details of one of the areas selected from bag2. Note in particular that the `is in area` attribute is in fact a scrollable list of related objects, identified by some salient attribute. This list is mouse sensitive, and behaves just like the bag viewer in Figure 8.

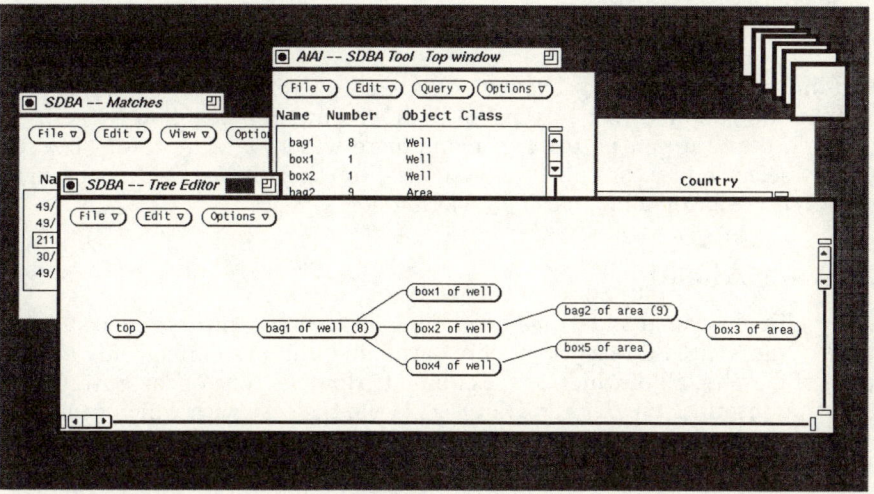

Figure 11: A Session Summary. The front-most window contains a graphical display that shows the relationships between the bags and boxes that have been created during the session. The entries are mouse-sensitive, and can be used to open, close or delete associated viewers.

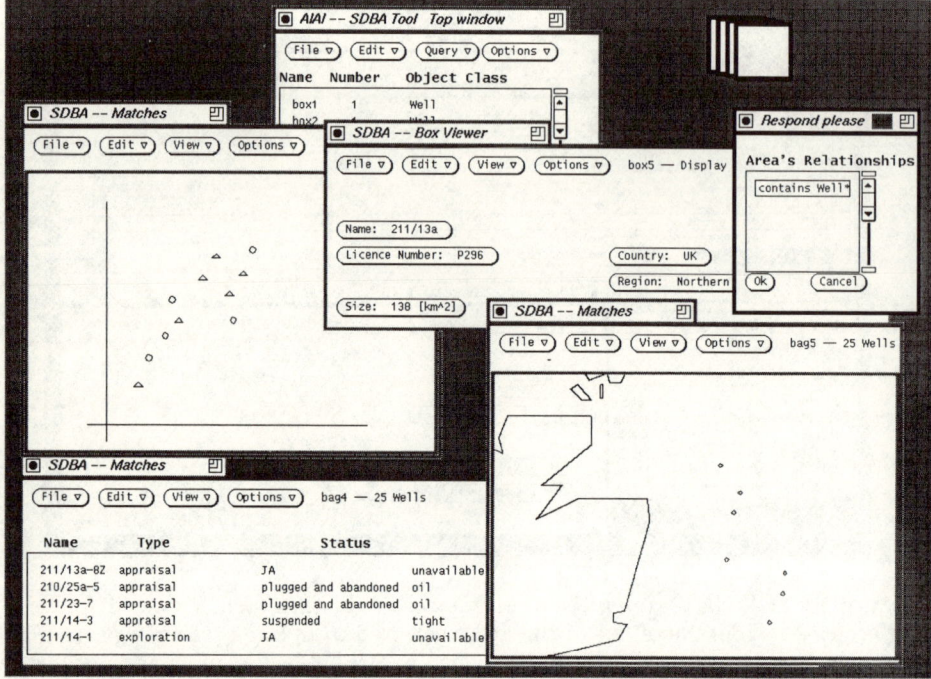

Figure 12: Multi-Media Viewers: an illustration of the way simultaneously active viewers could use different modalities to convey a more complete picture of the contents of a bag.

used directly to open a box viewer on an area.

Like the container list in the top-level window, this summary tree is kept up to date and it can be used to manipulate windows. The tree can also be used to select nodes, or sub-trees of nodes, for the various container-oriented operations—e.g. opening, closing, deleting etc.

## Looking Ahead

Everything described so far has been implemented in a prototype system. Because of the limited development effort available, this system has only a limited range of viewers, all of which are text-based. However, one of the advantages of basing an interface on *Bags and Viewers* is the the ease with which other kinds of data display can be incorporated. It would be straightforward to include other kinds of displays within the overall approach, and Figure 12 illustrates the way that, for instance, map and cross plot viewers could be incorporated within a session.

# 4  Features of the Approach

The *Bags and Viewers* approach has a number of noteworthy features.

- Data can be accessed without knowledge of query languages or database structure. All interaction is mediated by a user-oriented description of the information available, with the query system then mapping this onto the structure of the database being queried. While such an approach is not novel [7, 8, 9, 10], the models used by SDBA are expected to be elicited from domain experts without reference to any particular database, which means it must undertake more radical transformations than other systems [11].

- Because the database structure is hidden from the user, it is possible for multiple databases, possibly with differing structures, to be smoothly integrated (cf [12, 13]). This is especially important in situations involving collaboration or merger between independent database builders or in industries where data is marketed or otherwise distributed.

- Because the domain model is *object-oriented*—that is, it describes the domain in terms of objects positioned within a hierarchical classification scheme—all aspects of the system's behaviour can be tailored to the objects involved. For example, the class of the objects involved in a query is used to determine the appropriate constraint editors and viewers.

- Because the domain model explicitly represents the properties and relationships of the various classes of object that the domain involves, it can be used to help users navigate through the database. Both the properties of a class of object and the relationships in which it can participate can be presented to the user in the form of menus. Because such menus allow the user to navigate through the database on the basis of recognition, rather than recall, using them gives the system the ease of use associated with menu-driven systems in general.

- The constraint editors used in query formulation are chosen and parameterised on the basis of the type of the attribute to be constrained and the object. Some of them can handle very general types of attributes, such as strings, numbers or ranges, and selections from a closed set (menu) of values. Such editors will be tailored to the specific attribute being constrained by giving them information on the possible and normal ranges of values. Other editors can employ notations and embody knowledge specific to that particular attribute: for example, an editor for constraining the age of a rock bed may display a geological time-chart, on which the various periods and sub-periods are mouse sensitive.

    Because the editors embody or have access to the acceptable and normal ranges of values, they can draw the user's attention to unlikely choices as soon as they are made. This use of domain knowledge, rather than query results, to eliminate errors, is also found in [10, 14].

- Viewers were originally conceived as a means of providing a single access mechanism that would work naturally both for textual interformation and for graphics (cf. the *presentation surfaces* of [15]) which could be either prepared in advance for the system ("canned"), or be generated from retrieved data when required. However, individual viewers could perfectly well allow users to interact with any kind of sophisticated data visualisation techniques [16, 17, 18]. Similarly, viewers could present video or audio information, and indeed the overall approach can seamlessly integrate multi-media presentations.

- The system makes it easy to modify both the constraints that define the contents of a bag and the viewers which determine what aspects are presented in what manner, and it can display the effects of these changes immediately. It thus encourages users to build up queries incrementally, refining them in the light of the results being obtained. (cf. [10, 9, 19]).

- Most information displays can be naturally used to launch follow-up queries by either directly indicating the object or set of objects of interest, or by selecting a relationship which will identify them. In effect, the system is using the context, supported by the knowledge in the domain model, to minimise the *gulf of execution* [20] in query formulation. These objects will then be fetched into a bag or box as appropriate. Because any viewer is always associated with precisely one bag, and each bag retains its own record of the constraints that determined its contents, such follow-up queries are entirely self-contained, and the user is free to launch them from any viewer at any time. This makes unrestricted browsing through the database as easy as exploring a hypertext document.

- The various bags that the user generates are self-contained—that is, they each retain the set of constraints that defined the objects it contains. This makes it possible to return to any bag at any time, either to change the constraints (and thus its contents) or the way they are displayed, or to use it as the basis for launching further queries. The user can thus regard the various viewers as "documents" in the sense that [21] calls for. But equally, because viewers are used to request information on other objects, bags can be inter-related. A session with the system has a "discourse structure", with some bags being the "children" of others that provided the context in which they were generated. Because the user is explicitly aware of them, a graphical presentation of the relationships between the bags generated during the session provides a session history that effectively cues recall of their contents and purpose.

- Imprecise queries can be formulated easily using fuzzy matching, with mechanisms which are described in [22]. Any constraint that the user generates can be tagged as requiring either an "exact" match or a "fuzzy" match, which can be one of three degrees of closeness. The domain model can contain definitions of *goodness of fit* functions [22] for each attribute, which indicate how well a given value matches a specified target. The system provides some "common sense" measures of similarity for numeric quantities, but the domain model is expected to contain domain-specific goodness of fit functions. Such a function might indicate the (temporal or geological) closeness between, say, Late Jurassic and Early Devonian, or whether someone asking about Rolls Royces might be interested in Jaguars.

- The underlying fuzzy matching facilities are designed to support a form of true *Query by Example*—that is, queries of the form "find others like this or these". Precisely what constitutes "like" in any particular situation is a matter of domain knowledge, which will in general be applied by an "expert system" embedded in the domain model. The current query system provides a simple mechanism for this expert system to generate fuzzy queries, just by deciding which attributes must be matched precisely, and which "fuzzily".

- The metaphor offers several points in the interaction where limited "intelligence" can easily be built into the software, and thus forms an excellent basis for building an intelligent data access assistant [23]. In addition to the features already mentioned—hiding the database structures by mapping them onto the domain model, supporting fuzzy matching, flagging unusual constraints and queries, ensuring missing data are handled correctly etc.—the system can also employ "intelligence" in a number of other ways. Most obviously, it could select or configure a suitable display for a set of objects, along the lines of [24] and [25], but ideally also taking account of the specific objects (both their number and characteristics), the quality and availability of data, and the user's expressed or inferred preferences and objectives. It can also optimise the query, both in isolation (by generating efficient SQL) and overall, by cacheing or pre-fetching either attributes or object keys. Similarly, the system can offer summaries and comparisons of sets, and provide explanations of failed queries—that is, constraint sets that result in empty bags.

# 5 Discussion

The semantics of the interface is based on treating a bag as a container for a (mathematical) set—i.e. a collections of distinct objects. There is no sense in which the bag contains data, and no distinction between the attributes of the object which are "in" the bag and those which are not: which attributes of the object are visible to the user at any time depends on the set of viewers that are associated with the bag, and of course the data that is present in the database. In addition to the set itself, a bag holds the set of constraints that were used to generate it—in a sense, the "intention" of the set. This can be used to regenerate the contents of the bag, should the database or domain model change, and to form the basis of follow-up queries. Finally, at any moment a bag is associated with a collection of viewers, each displaying some attributes of the objects in the bag in some way.

Despite the familiarity of the concepts involved in the metaphor, their combination within a data-manipulation system in a general manner is novel. It is possible to see other systems as embodying special cases of a *Bags and Viewers* approach. For example, the Macintosh file system allows users to select either a graphical (iconic) or text-based "viewer" to display the set of files in a directory. These can be parameterised to some extent—e.g. by specifying the attribute to be used to determine the order in which files should be listed. Moreover, the elements in the viewers are mouse-sensitive, and can be used to initiate examining specific entities in detail, either by selecting a new viewer on a sub-directory or by invoking the application associated with an ordinary file. Similarly, [26] describes a bibliographic database retrieval system which separates query generation from display, and although it offers only a single "viewer", that viewer can be parameterised to determine which attributes are displayed and how. Finally, the way the system presents the database can be seen as having much in common with the operation of a hypertext system, with viewers offering "pages" of information, many of which contain links to other, related pages. On such a view, every relationship specified in the domain model defines a potential inter-page link, and the pages themselves are constructed, in line with the user's preferences, when they are needed.

Since a set may contain only a single element, the interface could be cleanly specified without making any distinction between bags and boxes. However, there are reasons for making boxes distinct:

- There are only a few ways of presenting data which are equally applicable to both sets and individual objects. Thus, while a map is sensible for any number of locations, a histogram for a single object is absurd, and there is no obvious way of using a form-like display for a set of objects. This could be dealt with by filtering the range of viewers considered by the system, or indeed offered to the user, according to whether the bag contains more than one item. However, if the number of objects in the bag were subsequently changed, many of the viewers associated with it would become silly or even meaningless. This problem is avoided by using boxes, which are known to always contain precisely one object.

- Whether a query is retrieving a set of objects or examining a specific object in more detail is likely to be one of its most salient features. Distinguishing boxes from bags allows this feature to be reflected in the session history, therefore improving its ability to help the user recall the details of the session.

One of the fundamental aspects of any data or domain model is the ontology it imposes upon the world—i.e. what types of objects are deemed to exist. For greatest generality, everything that could possibly be regarded as an object should be. However, this can easily mean that closely related information is distributed across a large number of objects, which can make formulating informative queries a tedious process. Thus, for instance, seeing which company owns a particular oil well might require fetching the object that is linked to the well by means of an "operated by" relationship. A pragmatic solution to this problem can be found by allowing viewers to include attributes of related objects. This is straightforward for one-to-one relationships. It is more complex for relationships where there may be several related objects, which are currently tackled by displaying the attribute's value as a kind of "sub-viewer", from which the related objects can be selected (See Figure 10).

# 6 Further Work

There are a number of aspects of a system based on *Bags and Viewers* which still need to be thought through, and in many cases the alternatives need to be empirically evaluated.

- Many decisions about low-level details of the interface have been made the "obvious" way, and alternatives need to be assessed. For instance, it is not clear whether a single click on an item in a viewer should initiate the display of more details about it, or whether it should simply select the item, with the user obliged to then initiate the query from a separate button or pull-down menu. The answer to this question is likely to depend on the range of operations that can be done with a selected item. If the only option open to the user is to ask for more information, having separate selection and query initiation actions is of dubious merit.

- To date, only a small number of general-purpose viewers and constraint editors have been implemented:

    - configurable forms and one-line-per-object summary displays/menu viewers, and
    - constraint editors for numbers (and ranges), strings, set of options and value hierarchies.

    This range needs to be increased by implementing viewers for, say, maps, charts and histograms, cross-plots, photographs etc. In addition, we think that introducing summary attributes for bags, such as the maximum, minimum and average value for an attribute, will increase the range of queries that can naturally be handled. Finally, we have identified the need for a mechanism for working through a (potentially large) set of objects, considering each in turn in some way (e.g. by putting it into a specific box).

- Constraint editors currently work on a single attribute in isolation, without considering the constraints that have been imposed on others. This is a limitation, since the values of different attributes interact strongly: the Gulf of Mexico ceases to be a possible location for a well which has been constrained to be producing from the Forties field in the North Sea, and vice versa. If constraint editors can be made sensitive to such interactions, feedback about queries that will fail can be given to the user much more quickly. It is also still not clear how some types of complex constraints should be expressed and handled by the system—e.g. to find all the installations being operated by more than two companies, or by companies of two or more nationalities.

- The graphical presentation of the session, which shows how bags and boxes were generated from others, offers a powerful mechanism for helping users to keep track of their interaction with the system. However, we believe that there is considerable scope for improvement by, for instance, using the shape and size of the icons in the display to convey information about, for example, the type and number of objects in the bag. In particular, we believe that the usefulness of the device as a trigger for recall will be greatly improved if the user is allowed to arrange, mark and even label the various nodes in a way that is meaningful to them.

- There are still several areas where the system's "common sense" about data is lacking, and where more knowledge could greatly facilitate building domain and database models, and thus the system's ability to present data effectively. For example, the system has no notion of "time", and thus cannot handle databases that contain many values for a single-valued attribute that apply to different times. The system can be used to access such databases, but only by distorting the domain model. Giving it an understanding of temporal variation should both avoid this and allow a more intelligent handling of such data, such as assuming the most recent value is required unless another time is specified, or presenting the way a value of interest varies over time.

- As the metaphor is developed, the possibility of allowing users to alter the contents of a bag—to add or remove objects—must be given further consideration. Objects could be added by allowing the user to merge two bags or, equivalently, to add the result of a query to an existing bag. In this case, the bag's contents would be described by a disjunction of the constraint sets describing the contributing bags. But there is also considerable appeal to allowing users to simply nominate objects to be added to (or removed from) a bag, perhaps by some kind of "direct manipulation" [27]—"put this, this and this to one side for further investigation", "ignore these two" etc. While this may be very natural, it has the drawback that the system would have no basis for associating a constraint set with the resulting collection of objects, and thus it would be in some sense less than a real bag—a "baguette". It is not clear how baguettes can be handled, and the matter of whether the additional interface complexity of doing so is justified by their usefulness needs to be investigated.

Finally, one of the objectives of the work that led to the formulation of the *Bags and Viewers* approach was to support combining multiple sources of data. This can be supported very naturally within the interface paradigm, since users do not explicitly initiate queries and the underlying database structures are hidden. The encapsulation of database-specific information within the database description makes it straightforward to enable the system to query a new database in isolation. However, there are many problems associated with attempting to combine information from different databases being accessed at the same time. At its simplest, answering a query on the basis of several databases involves querying one database to extract attributes which are missing from another. Doing this effectively obviously depends on cross-referencing between the databases—identifying the same object in two databases which have not been designed or maintained to ensure agreement. However, making the situation only slightly more general involves many more complex issues.

In many cases, there will be overlap between databases available to the system—indeed, this *must* be the case for at least some attributes, to allow entries to be cross-referenced. As a result there will, in general, be more than one source of any piece of information. It is straightforward to use multiple sources of an attribute value within a single database, and to use information about the database to indicate how to obtain the best value. For example, a database may define a field to represent a particular attribute, but may only actually have data present for some objects. In such situations, the system can be given not only the details of how to locate the explicit data, but also a formula for deriving a value from other attributes. The system can then is able to make sensible use of both in answering a question.

Such mechanisms could probably be extended to deal with separate database systems, with the required data being assembled from the results of multiple queries. More awkwardly, if the set of objects of interest may be determined by attributes drawn from multiple databases, then either *join* operations must be carried out outside the databases, or appropriate object-identifying information must be translated and transported between them. In both cases, though, the interface must become involved with determining, rather than just presenting, query results. This will require efficient but general-purpose means of sifting and combining potentially large volumes of partial results to be devised. More subtly, not all databases are created equal: the data they contain can differ not only in range, but also in quality and completeness. Not only must these variations be taken into account when formulating a query, they also mean that the user must be able to see, and indeed constrain, the provenance of the information being displayed. Making this kind of information available to users without overwhelming the data itself will be a significant task.

# 7 Conclusion

*Bags and Viewers* provides a framework for structuring interfaces to systems which involve accessing collections of data. Such systems should be very flexible—they are capable of generating arbitrary queries—yet should also be very simple to use, in that they involve only a few operations and concepts, and these are reasonably familiar. A prototype system has been developed to illustrate these ideas, and has been ported to three different databases in quite distinct domains. Work on the system is continuing, and we are looking for other domains to which it can be ported.

# References

[1] Date CJ. A guide to the SQL standard. Addison-Wesley, Reading Mass., 1989

[2] Oracle. SQL*Forms: operator's guide. Oracle, 1986

[3] Oracle. SQL*Forms: designer's reference. Oracle, 1987

[4] Marcus A. Human communications in advanced UIs. Communications of the ACM 1993; 36:101–109

[5] Inder R, Wells B. PEXES: combining knowledge and data in a tool for the explorationist. In: Proceedings of Conference on AI in petroleum exploration and production (CAIPEP '91)

[6] Warren DHD, Pereira FCN. An efficient easily adaptable system for interpreting natural language queries. American Journal of Computational Linguistics 1982; 8:110–122

[7] Santucci G, Sottile PA. Query by diagram: a visual environment for querying databases. Software: Practice and Experience 1993; 23: 317–340

[8] MacGregor RM. ARIEL—a semantic front-end to relational DBMSs. In: Proceedings of the 12th conference on very large databases, VLDB Endowment, 1985.

[9] Wong HKT, Kuo I. GUIDE: graphical user interface for database exploration. In: Proceedings of the 8th conference on very large databases, VLDB Endowment, 1982, pp22–32

[10] Tou FN, Williams MD, Fikes R, Henderson A, Malone T. RABBIT: an intelligent database assistant. In: Proceedings of the National Conference on Artificial Intelligence. AAAI, 1982, pp 314–318

[11] Stader J, Inder R, Chung PWH. Transforming databases for experts. In: Proceedings of the 7th international conference on the industrial and engineering applications of artificial intelligence and expert systems. Gordon and Breach, New York, 1994

[12] Hurst S. Database Fusion. Project Report AIAI-PR-47, AI Applications Institute, University of Edinburgh, 1990

[13] Piatetsky-Shapiro G, Jakobson G. An intermediate database language and its rule-based transformation into different database languages. Data and Knowledge Engineering 1987; 2:1–29

[14] Jakobson G. An intelligent database assistant. IEEE Expert 1986; 1:65–78

[15] Wilson GA, Domeshek EA, Drascher EL, Dean JS. The multipurpose presentation system. In: Proceedings of the 9th conference on very large databases, VLDB Endowment, 1983, pp56–69

[16] Earnshaw RA, Wiseman N. An introductory guide to scientific visualisation. Springer-Verlag, Berlin, 1992

[17] Robertson G, Card S, Mackinlay J. Information visualization using 3D interactive animation. Communications of the ACM 1993; 36:57–71

[18] Murray BS. Visualizing and representing knowledge for the end user: a review. International Journal of Man-Machine Studies 1993; 38:23–49

[19] Bose P, Rajinikanth M. KARMA: knowledge-based assistant to a database system. In: Proceedings of the 2nd Conference on Artificial Intelligence and Applications. IEEE Computer Society Press, Washington DC, 1985, pp 467–472

[20] Hutchins EL, Hollan JD, Norman DA. Direct manipulation interfaces. In: Norman DA, Draper SW (ed) User centred systems design: new perspectives on human-computer interaction. Lawrence Earlbaum Associates, Hillsdale NJ, 1986, pp 87–124

[21] Nielsen J. Noncommand user interfaces. Communications of the ACM 1993; 36:83–99

[22] Chung PWH, Inder R. Handling uncertainty in accessing petroleum exploration data. Revue de L'Institut Français de Pétrole 1992; 47:305–314

[23] Stader J, Inder R. An intelligent data retrieval asistant. In: Applications and innovations in expert systems: proceedings of Expert Systems '93. Cambridge University Press, 1993, pp 17–32

[24] Mackinlay J. Automating ht edesign of graphical presentations of relational information. ACM Transactions on Graphics 1986; 5:110–1441

[25] Hovy E, Arens Y. When is a picture worth a thousand words? — allocation of modalities in multimedia communication. In: proceedings of the Symposium on HCI. AAAI, 1990

[26] Nowell LT, Hix D. Visualizing search results: user interface development for the Project Envision database of computer science literature. In Salvendy G, Smith MJ (eds) Human computer interaction: software and hardware interfaces (proceedings of HCI International). Elsevier, 1993, pp56–61

[27] Shneiderman B. Designing the user interface: strategies for effective human-computer interaction. Addison-Wesley, Reading Mass., 1986

# Query by Browsing

Alan Dix and Andrew Patrick

School of Computing and Mathematics,
The University of Huddersfield,
Queensgate, Huddersfield, United Kingdom, HD1 3DH.
alan@zeus.hud.ac.uk

**Abstract.**

The paper describes Query-by-Browsing (QBB), which uses machine learning techniques to generate a database query from examples of interesting records supplied by the user. Unlike Query-by-Example, in QBB the user's principal focus is on the actual data rather than on a schema for the database query. The system employs dual representation, displaying both a textual form of the inferred query and highlighting the selected records. This is important so that the user can recognise whether the inferred query is indeed what is required. It also fulfills an important tutorial rôle as the user can learn the form of textual queries.

## 1 Introduction

Most commercial database systems now include some form of Query-by-Example (QBE) [13]. However, this paper argues that QBE is not really 'by example' at all. A new form of querying process is described, Query-by-Browsing (QBB). This works by allowing the user to browse a database and select examples of records. The system then uses machine learning techniques to generate the query from the user's examples.

The basic concept of QBB was described as part of a previous paper [2]. However, the purpose of that paper was to highlight the potential user interface pitfalls of what appears to be straightforward application of existing technology. Also at that time no implementation of QBB existed.

This paper describes the technical details of a prototype version of QBB and some of the problems observed. The paper has a dual thesis. On the one hand, we want to show that QBB is a viable technique. On the other hand, we want to show that the application of artificial intelligence techniques to the user interface is more than the adoption of technical solutions, but requires careful crafting of both the user interaction and the 'intelligent' algorithms.

The rest of this section will describe some related work including traditional Query-by-Example. Section 2 describes the external interface of Query-by-Browsing. This includes a dual representation of queries and Section 3 gives the rationale for this key feature of the design. QBB uses inductive learning to generate a query, the details of which are covered in Section 4. Finally Section 5 discusses some of the problems encountered and some potential solutions. Many of these problems had been anticipated and confirmed the importance of many of the issues raised in [2].

## Related work

There have been several systems which use automatic learning to assist in the browsing of large databases, such as on-line news services. In particular, latent semantic indexing can be used to produce measures of similarity between free text records and hence help guide a reader's browsing [4]. The closest work to QBB is perhaps KNOWBOT [7]. This uses a connectionist approach to generate similarity between records of nuclear accident reports. This is built over a standard relational model of data and is designed to be applied to large incident databases compiled by nuclear regulatory boards. The differences between this and QBB are discussed later.

In a previous paper [2], one of the authors used QBB as an example of the problems of intelligent interfaces. What appears to be a simple technical fix to a problem has, upon deeper reflection, many potential problems at the user interface. These are worst when 'black box' tecnhiques, such as neural networks, are used as the user in this case does not know *why* the system makes its responses. Even where, as in QBB, a more comprehensible learning technique is used, one expects problems managing the dialogue between user and system. The real problem is that AI is not just artificial intelligence, it is non-human – an alien intelligence. Seen in this light, it is not surprising that communication problems arise.

## Query *not* by example

The details of Query-by-Example vary among different database systems, but are essentially as follows.

The process starts with some sort of template giving the headings of the entries in the desired table of results. For example, it might consist of the headings `Department`, `Name` and `Salary`. These headings might correspond to attributes from a single database relation, or might be obtained from several as the result of a join. The specification of this template is itself a non-trivial process, but for the purpose of this paper the user interface for this phase will not be discussed further.

Given such a template, the user must then fill in the slots to produce a sort of archetypal line of the listing.

| Name | Department | Salary |
|------|------------|--------|
|      | = 'Accounts' | > 15000 |

Formulating this query is clearly much simpler for the naïve user than the equivalent textual query:

```
SELECT Department, Name, Salary
WHERE Department = 'Accounts'
      and Salary > 15000
```

However, it still demands that the user thinks in terms of queries. In both textual queries and QBE, the user has to formulate the desired listing in abstract terms and be able to predict from the query what records will be in the final listing. As many database systems are not incremental in displaying the results of queries, the user may have to wait for the whole query to be processed before being able to see whether the resulting listing is as required.

In short, QBE is little more than an alternative format for a standard SQL-like textual query, and is not really 'by example' at all.

## 2 Query by Browsing – the interface

Like QBE, Query-by-Browsing assumes that the user has already defined an appropriate template. However, rather than starting off with a blank form for the user to fill in, QBB generates a complete on screen listing of all records. In a large database, this listing can be generated incrementally as the user browses through the listing, so the cost need not be prohibitive. The user then browses the listing and marks those records which are required and those that are not. In Figure 1, the user has ticked the records of interest and has put a cross against others. Only a representative sample of records have been marked by the user.

| Listing | | | |
|---|---|---|---|
| Name | Department | Salary | |
| William Brown | Accounts | 21,750 | ✓ |
| Margery Chen | Accounts | 27,000 | ✓ |
| Thomas Herbert | Accounts | 14,500 | ✗ |
| Janet Davies | Accounts | 16,000 | ✓ |
| Eugene Warbuck-Smyth | Accounts | 17,500 | |
| Fredrick Blogia | Cleaning | 7,500 | |
| Mary O'Hara | Cleaning | 5,670 | |

**Fig. 1.** Query-by-Browsing — user ticks interesting records

At some point the system infers the pattern underlying the user's selections. It then highlights all those records which correspond to the pattern and displays a textual form of the query it has inferred. At this point, the user has merely to verify that the query the system has generated is correct and if so confirm it by the click of a button. This is shown in Figure 2.

Note that the user has not had to generate an abstract query. Instead, from *examples* of relevant records the system has generated the query. The user only has to recognise that it is correct.

Unlike standard Query-by-Example, Query-by-Browsing really is 'by example'.

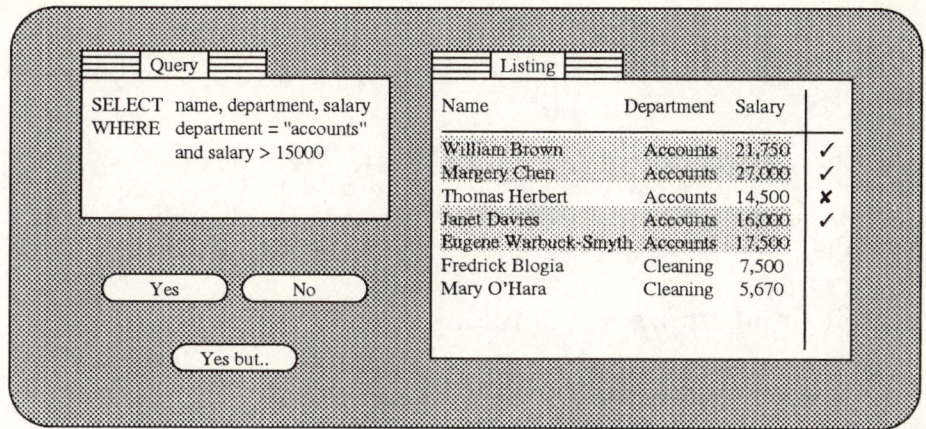

**Fig. 2.** Query-by-Browsing — system highlights inferred selection

## Continuing interaction

When the system has inferred a query, the user has four options:

1. Accept the query by clicking the 'yes' button. This completes the query construction process, the listing is then reduced so that only the selected records are displayed.
2. Ignore the query and continue entering ticks and crosses. The system may at some stage change the presented query when it has been given more examples to work on.
3. Reject the query by clicking the 'no' button, thus telling the system that it has got it completely wrong. The user can then continue to enter ticks and crosses as in the previous option. However, the system has the added clue that the user's intended query is nothing like the one it presented!
4. Refine the query by clicking the 'Yes but ...' button. This then allows the user to give more guidance as to what is right and what is wrong with the query. The simplest such refinements are: 'too many' and 'too few'. Too many tells the system that it has selected all the desired records but some more besides. The user will thereafter only enter negative examples from the selected records and the system will retain the query but try to make it stronger. Too few is similar, but the user enters more positive examples and the system weakens the query.

So long as the query is right, this interaction is quite smooth. However, as predicted in [2], it is much more difficult to design a graceful interaction when the query is wrong.

## 3  Dual representation

In Figure 2, the system's inferred selection is shown in two ways, by highlighting and by the display of the inferred query. Some of the reasons for this dual representation are described in detail below, but in short:

- The highlighting is necessary as we cannot assume that the user is able to predict accurately what records will be generated from a query.
- The displayed query is necessary as the user must be able to verify that the query is *precisely* as required.

Note however, that the form of highlighting and of query display is not critical. For example, we could substitute the textual display of the query with a QBB template that has been filled in by the system, or with a natural language rendering of the query.

### Precise and imprecise domains

In similar domains where intelligent systems have been used to aid in the browsing or searching of databases, the matching has only been required to be useful, not exact. The users of on-line news services cannot possibly read the all the available information. Any facility to prioritise and present more relevant articles will be helpful. Even if an automatic aid sometimes fails to present articles which are wanted or presents those which are not, it is still better than nothing!

Even in the safety critical domain of nuclear accidents, Knowbot can still afford to be imprecise. As with the news service, the user cannot expect to see all accident reports and thus the interface is successful if the user views more relevant reports than before. However, the critical nature of this application favours more inclusive selections and this is reflected in the Knowbot interface. The user originally makes a 'query' by selecting keywords. The system then selects *all* those records which match the keyword, but *in addition* it displays records which are semantically close to the user's original selection.

In both cases the only disadvantage of displaying extra records is that they act as noise for the reader, and in neither case does the user have a fixed idea of what records are 'right', there is a fuzzy idea of more or less interesting records.

Contrast this with generating a standard database query. Now there is a precise set of records that are to be addressed. For example, if we want to select all the employees with certain characteristics in order to give them a pay rise, it is critical that we select exactly those which match the criteria, a fuzzy match is *not* acceptable. In addition, the user needs to be able to verify that the match is as desired.

Hence we see the importance of displaying of the query. Even if the system has correctly inferred the user's desired selection, the user must *know* that it has. Merely browsing the highlighted records would tell the user that the query is correct for the records which have been seen, but unless the user browses the whole database (in which case why use a query!) it is not possible to be sure that the query is exactly as required. Furthermore, if the query is to be reused as the database changes, even an exhaustive search of the database is insufficient to confirm the correctness of the query. For example, in Figure 2 one cannot tell from the highlighted selection whether the selected salary is '> 15000' or '> 15500'.

### Recognition vs. generation

The astute reader may wonder at the apparent contradiction. On the one hand, we say that users find queries complex and hence need some new method (QBB) of generating queries *really* by examples. On the other hand, we also assert that the user needs to be able to verify the correctness of the query.

However, there is a great difference between the effort and knowledge needed to *generate* a query and that needed to *recognise* that a query is indeed what is wanted. This difference is important at various levels.

- At the syntactic level, the user may not be able to remember the keywords and format of a query. This is clearly helped by menu based or other more direct forms of query input and is the level at which Query-by-Example aids the user.
- At the semantic level, the user may know what is wanted but may have difficulty articulating it. This process of externalising knowledge is often very difficult and has been a major problem in expert system design.

Even though it is easier to recognise a query than to generate it, there are still residual problems. The user may be confused as to the meaning of logical connectives, especially where the natural language meaning differs from the mathematical meaning. Also it is well known that people find it hard to understand statements including negation, especially double negatives:

"Select all employees except those where department is 'Accounts' and the manager is not 'Thomas'"

It is here that the dual representation becomes important. If the user is uncertain about the interpretation a glance at a few key records can confirm which interpretation is correct.

## Learning

Last, but not least, dual representation can perform an important tutoring rôle. By seeing the query presented as well as the selection highlighted, the naïve user can begin to learn the appearance of textual or QBE queries, and eventually perhaps move on to become a 'power user'.

## 4 Inductive learning – the internals

The current implementation of QBB uses a variant of Quinlan's ID3 algorithm [10]. The ID3 algorithm takes a number of examples of data values taken from different classes and builds a decision tree which can be used to sort unseen examples into their appropriate classes. That is it *learns* how to recognise the class of a data value. In the case of QBB we only have two classes: wanted (ticked) and not wanted (crossed).

ID3 is used because its data model, being based on frame-and-slot models as used in artificial intelligence, is very similar to the tuples of relational databases. Also, the decision trees generated are relatively easy to represent as database queries.

In the original ID3 each attribute had only a finite number of possible values, for example, a colour attribute might be in the set { red, blue, green } or a rating in the set { 1, 2, 3, 4, 5, 6 }. However, in common with other variants of ID3, QBB uses a richer range of data types. Attributes can in addition have general string values or be integers. These were chosen as they were typical of most other kinds of data type. For example, dates or real numbers behave very similarly to integers in that they can be compared for equality or inequality. Figure 3 shows an example data set suitable for the algorithm.

---

A database for a bank might have the following attributes:

| | |
|---|---|
| **forename** | string |
| **surname** | string |
| **title** | enumerated: { Dr, Mrs, Mr, Ms, Miss } |
| **balance** | integer |
| **overdraft-limit** | integer |

A typical set of records would be

| | forename | surname | title | balance | overdraft-limit |
|---|---|---|---|---|---|
| 1. | Jo | Parkin | Ms | 575 | 0 |
| 2. | John | McCawber | Mr | -101 | -100 |
| 3. | Liz | Windsor | Mrs | 27629 | -9999 |
| 4. | Peter | Coney | Dr | -730 | -1000 |
| 5. | Gladys | Green | Ms | -15 | 0 |
| 6. | Bob | Maxwell | Mr | -7329 | -5000 |

---

**Fig. 3.** Example bank database

In the decision tree built by the algorithm each internal node contains a decision based on the values of attributes of a datum. The branches are labelled by the possible choices of that decision. In the original ID3 the branches were labelled by the possible values of an attribute, for example, a decision might be of the form 'colour = ?' with branches for 'red', 'blue' and 'green'. In QBB all the branches are binary (yes/no) decisions so that all the different forms of decisions can be treated equally. The leaves of the tree are labelled by the classes and in the case of QBB these are simply wanted and not wanted.

Consider the decision tree in Figure 4 which can be used to classify the records from Figure 3. This represents a query for all customers who have exceeded their overdraft limit and are at least 100 pounds overdrawn excluding anyone called 'Maxwell'. (Perhaps Maxwell owns the bank.) Underneath each leaf node is the list of records which are classified at that node.

Notice that the decisions allowed include comparisons of attributes with constants: 'balance > -100' and 'surname = Maxwell', and between attributes: 'balance < overdraft-limit'. Variants of the ID3 algorithm have normally included only the former. However, the use of inter-attribute matching adds considerable power. We have seen this for numeric comparison, but also equality tests between strings can be important. For example, the bank's auditor might want to check records where large overdrafts were authorised by sub-managers with the same surname as the customer!

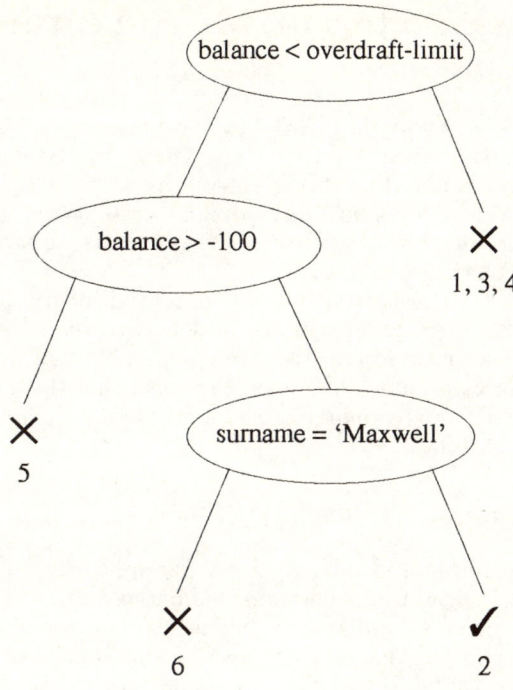

**Fig. 4.** Example decision tree

The ID3 algorithm builds the tree top down. Imagine the user has marked records 2 and 6 as interesting and marked the rest uninteresting. The algorithm first looks at all single decisions. If one of these simple decisions splits the data perfectly into the two classes that one will be chosen. In fact, for the sample data set, the decision 'title = Mr' would do this and would lead to a very simple tree. However, let's assume that the learning algorithm has been forbidden from using gender information. In this case, the algorithms looks at the non-perfect decisions and looks for the best as measured by an entropy based measure. In this case, the decision 'balance < overdraft-limit' splits the data so that the 'no' partition has three uninteresting records and the 'yes' partition has two interesting and one uninteresting records. This is not far from perfect and is thus chosen as the first attribute. The algorithm then considers each branch. Down the 'no' branch all the records are from the same class and therefore it becomes a leaf node classifying as uninteresting. The 'yes' branch is more complex as it has mixed records. The algorithm is then applied recursively to these three records (2, 5 and 6) and looks for another simple decision to split them. The decision 'balance > -100' does this perfectly and is thus chosen leading to two new leaf nodes. The resulting tree is a simplified version of Figure 4 without the last test.

# 5 Problems, alternatives and future developments

As we said in the introduction, there are two reasons for producing a prototype of Query-by-Browsing. First we think Query-by-Browsing is a potentially powerful technique for naïve database users. However, we also want to investigate the potential problems outlined in [2] concerning the interaction between human users and 'intelligent' systems. The problems we have encountered are thus as valuable as the successes!

The discussion of these problems and potential future directions is divided into those principally concerned with the learning algorithms and those concerned with the user interaction. However, the reader will notice that the separation is not perfect and indeed, one would expect that the design of an effective system would involve an intimate connection between the interface and the 'intelligent' engine within.

## Types of decision

We saw in the example above how the naïve application of inductive learning could come up with a spurious decision tree based on the title of the customer. Note that this is not a wrong answer, it does explain the examples. In general, there can be several different decision trees to explain the same example set. In the context of an interactive session this is not critical as the user can always add more examples. However, if the initial decisions are really obscure this can be both confusing for the user and reduce the user's confidence in the system. Even experiments using more knowledge rich learning algorithms have found that automatically generated classification criteria are both different from human criteria and hard for the human reader to comprehend [5]. This is a very difficult problem, but some of the very worst cases can be addressed.

One reason for the production of obscure trees is that the number of examples from browsing is relatively small compared with those generally expected by inductive learning systems. Indeed, one of Quinlan's papers includes the phrase "*large* collections of examples" in its title [9]! The small number of examples means that by the time one gets to the leaves of a complex tree there may be only one or two records in each class on which to base the learning. Obviously these may be distinguished by virtually anything. One solution to this is for the system to refrain from presenting a query until it has a certain level of confidence in its solution.

A more interactive solution is for the system to assign confidence to each leaf of a tree. A possible measure to use for this is the 'gain ratio' as described in [12]. The system can then specifically mark those records (say with a question mark) indicating to the user which records it would be useful for the user to classify. Alternatively, it could specifically ask the user 'do you want this record'. Hopefully a small number of records classified in the uncertain areas of the tree will serve to build a confidence and generate a robust query. This sounds in fact very close to the interaction of a user consulting a database expert who was constructing the query. The expert would explicitly probe the boundaries of the query in order to check that it was as required.

In order to make the query more 'human', the inductive learning algorithm can be biased towards certain types of query. For example, some of Quinlan's work on ID3 has investigated the biasing of the algorithm towards degenerate trees – that is effectively conjunctive queries and other forms of more comprehensible query [11]. ID3 is derived originally from the Concept Learning System and there have been other algorithms developed in this area which learn different sorts of rules, often including more complex domains. This includes purely conjunctive and disjunctive formulas and formulas based on 'internal disjunctive concepts' [6] — that is, rules which are conjunctions of terms of the type:

'department = Accounts or Computing'.

Whereas ID3 will return *any* tree which separates the classes, some algorithms will give the most specific rule to specify the positive examples. That is a rule which includes everything which is true about all of the examples. The query shown in Figure 2 is of this form. The examples shown can be classified by the criterion 'salary > 1500', but the most specific rule also includes the fact that all the positive examples are also in the accounts department:

'department = Accounts and salary > 1500'

In order to make ID3 give this query negative examples had to be given in other departments (not shown on the screen shot). In principle, a system using most specific criteria can learn mainly from positive examples, which would probably lead to a more natural interaction style for the user.

In addition, we may want to add some knowledge to the learning process. For example, in a banking system we may bias the system to favour queries dependent on monetary fields over those using personal attributes such as title or address. In [2] it was argued that inadvertent discrimination was a danger of the use of example based approaches. QBB clearly portrays what decisions are being made which reduces (but does not eliminate) this problem. Despite these dangers, it is likely that knowledge should be in the form of a bias rather than a prohibition. For example, a bank's market research may have shown that its male middle-earning customers are likely to purchase redundancy insurance and so it may want to send insurance brochures to that group.[1] There has been little work on such hybrid learning systems which employ a combination of rich knowledge with relatively 'blind' techniques such as inductive learning [8]. However, fairly simple techniques should be sufficient to improve the performance of QBB. In fact, the current implementation does employ some minimal general knowledge in that when making integer comparisons it chooses nice numbers. For example, in Figure 2, the examples have a ticked record with salary £ 1600 and a crossed one of £ 1450. Rather than choosing the midpoint of these £ 1525 the algorithm instead chooses the round number £ 1500.

Finally, in this area it is worth emphasising the unsuitability of neural networks as the primary mechanism for QBB. Although they can be highly effective as classifiers, the nature of their decision making is such that they must be regarded as 'black box' methods. It would be virtually impossible to generate a readable query from standard networks, thus ruling out a dual representation. That is, they are possibly acceptable in imprecise domains, but not where the user needs confidence that the classification performed by the system is exactly as required.

---

[1] Whether such direct mailing is socially acceptable is, of course, questionable in itself.

## Complex interaction

The difficulties with interaction come when the system gets the wrong query. The 'no' button is particularly problematical as it gives no indication of what is wrong. Such an answer would be rather rude if delivered to a human expert, but perhaps one of the advantages of a computer assistant is that one can be as rude as one likes! At present the 'no' answer means that the system never displays that precise query again. However, this might involve a long period of inactivity as the additional examples that the user enters may all agree with the incorrect query. As the inductive learning algorithm is deterministic the system will keep on coming up with the same tree until an example is given which disagrees with it. There are two ways out of this impasse. The user can be encouraged to select helpful records by continuing to show the highlighting of the incorrect query. This will suggest marking which of the highlighted records aren't wanted and which of the unhighlighted ones are wanted. The other option is to alter the algorithm so that it finds a different tree to explain the examples. One way to achieve this is to make the algorithm slightly random, so that repeated invocations are likely to give different trees. Although deliberately making the interface non-deterministic sounds rather extreme, there are situations when it can be extremely effective [1].

QBB is an example of a system where autonomous intelligent agents interact with the user. General interface guidelines for such systems are given in [3]. In particular, it is important that it is clear which interface objects (windows, buttons, etc.) are under the control of the user, which belong to the agents, and which are under shared control. We can apply this analysis to the present QBB system.

The listing window is a shared object where the user controls the marking and the agent (inductive learning component) controls the highlighting. The labelled buttons are a communication medium from the user to the agent and the query window is a form of communication from the agent to the user (not to forget that the shared listing window is also a medium of communication).

However, if we want to allow continuity between the novice, example based interface and an expert, query based interface, it suggests that the query window should also be shared and that the user ought to be able to make contributions there as well as to the listing.

For example, imagine the query generated in Figure 2 was correct except that the criterion the user was really after was those with salary over £1550. Rather than trying to find examples to force the system to the correct value, the user might find it easier to simply edit the query. However, in such cases the system would have to remember which bits of the query had been generated by the user and which by the system so that subsequent work by the inductive learning agent does not overwrite the user's work. This could be achieved by marking some of the tree's nodes as fixed.

# 6 Summary

We have described Query-by-Browsing a novel database query mechanism where the system generates the query. As opposed to traditional Query-by-Example, QBB really does work by example. The dual representation of the system's query by highlighting the selected records and by textual representation ensures that the user understands both the specific and general implications of the query. In addition, dual representation may serve an important tutoring rôle for the naïve user.

The current prototype exposes various shortcomings, several of which had been predicted in previous work. It serves as an exemplar of the general design problems where interfaces include autonomous intelligent agents. The prototype demonstrates the care and attention to detail which is needed in the design of such systems. In particular, it emphasises the close connection between the nature of the underlying algorithms and the details of user interaction.

We believe that Query-by-Browsing is a promising method which we hope will one day be included in many database systems alongside QBE and SQL queries.

# Acknowledgements

Alan Dix is funded by SERC Advanced Fellowship B/89/ITA/220. The work was carried out while both authors were at the University of York.

# References

1. Alan Dix. *Formal Methods for Interactive Systems*, chapter 6. Academic Press, 1991.
2. Alan Dix. Human issues in the use of pattern recognition techniques. In *Neural Networks and Pattern Recognition in Human-Computer Interaction*, pages 429–451. Ellis-Horwood, 1992.
3. Alan Dix, Janet Finlay, and Jonathan Hassell. Environments for cooperating agents: Designing the interface as medium. In *CSCW and Artificial Intelligence*. Springer Verlag (in press), 1994.
4. P. W. Foltz. Using latent semantic indexing for information filters. In *Proceedings of the Conference on Office Information Systems*, pages 40–47, April 25–27 1990.
5. Stephen José Hanson. Conceptual clustering and categorisation: Bridging the gap between induction and causal models. In *Machine Learning: An Artificial Intelligence Approach, Volume III*, chapter 9, pages 235–268. Morgan Kaufmann, 1990.
6. David Haussler. Applying Valient's learning framework to AI concept-learning problems. In *Machine Learning: An Artificial Intelligence Approach, Volume III*, chapter 22, pages 641–669. Morgan Kaufmann, 1990.
7. A. Sharif Heger and Billy V. Koen. Knowbot: An adaptive database interface. *Nuclear Science and Engineering*, 107:142–157, 1991.
8. Ryszard S. Michalski and Yves Kodratoff. Research in machine learning: recent progress, classification of methods, and future directions. In *Machine Learning: An Artificial Intelligence Approach, Volume III*, chapter 1, pages 3–30. Morgan Kaufmann, 1990.
9. J. R. Quinlan. Discovering rules by induction from large collections of examples. In *Expert Systems in the Micro Electronic Age*, pages 168–201. Edinburgh University Press, 1979.
10. J. R. Quinlan. Induction of decision trees. *Machine Learning*, 1(1), 1986.

11. J. R. Quinlan. Simplifying decision trees. *International Journal of Man-Machine Studies*, 27(4):221–234, 1986.
12. J. R. Quinlan. Decision trees and multi-valued attributes. In *Machine Intelligence 11*, pages 305–318. Oxford University Press, 1988.
13. M. M. Zloof. Query by example. In *Proc. AFIPS National Computer Conf. 44*, pages 431–438. AFIPS Press, New Jersey, 1975.

This article was processed using the LaTeX macro package with LLNCS style

# A Dynamic Form-Based Data Visualiser for Semantic Query Languages

Giuseppe Santucci and Francesco Palmisano

Dipartimento di Informatica e Sistemistica
Università di Roma "La Sapienza"
Via Salaria 113 - 00198 Roma, Italy
e-mail: santucci@infokit.dis.uniroma1.it

### Abstract

Most Data Base Management Systems lack in offering adequate tools for handling in a sophisticate way the query result. Generally, the output to a query is a table of tuples, offering a flat, boring (and sometime confusing) presentation of data. In this paper we present a dynamic form based data Visualiser whose main goal is to manage the query output in such a way to overcome the above problems. The Visualiser strategies are based on the hypothesis that, when performing a (SQL) query against a set of relational tables, a high level description of the database, through the Entity Relationship model is available. The cardinality of the relationships involved in the query is exploited in order to cluster the tuple attributes in homogeneous subsets and to suitably handle meaningless repetitions of values. In this way the data are presented to the user in a more compact and understandable way.

## 1 Introduction

A wide variety of computer applications have the main goal of allowing several people to access and manipulate data stored in a database. Much work has been done, and a lot is still in progress, for devising user-friendly interfaces able to significantly reduce the user effort in interacting with such systems. Most Data Base Management Systems, however, still lack in offering adequate tools for handling the query result. Generally, the output to a query is a table of tuples, offering a flat, boring (and sometime confusing) presentation of data. In few cases, the user is provided with formatting facilities, allowing her/him to rearrange the query output structure, i.e., to alter the order in which the tuples are presented and/or to reduce the tuple components. Moreover, rearranging the result of a query is just one of the possible user needs: user requests are often related to further navigation in order to achieve more information "on the run" (instance grouping and sorting, visual density feedback). Moreover, the join of two or more relational tables may result, in general, in a table that is not in second normal form, i.e., exhibiting a tedious repetition of values.
The above considerations are still true also in the context of the new generation of Visual Query Languages (a comprehensive survey is in [2]) that provide the user

with a high level presentation of data through the usage of semantic data models. Systems based on such kind of query language include both a language to express the queries in a visual form and a variety of functionalities to facilitate human-computer interaction. As such, they are oriented to a wide spectrum of users, having limited technical skills and generally ignoring the inner structure of the accessed database. They are often implemented on relational DBMSs, so while the query formulation is performed in a friendly way, the output is still a flat set of tuples, in which the additional knowledge stored in the semantic representation of data is totally ignored.

Recently, the research focused on the way in which to present the result of a query mainly adapting the interface to the special nature of the involved data (sounds, pictures, graphs, quantitative information, etc.) (see, for instance, [7, 15, 19, 21] where the data characteristics strongly influence the way in which the result of the query is presented to the user. In a number of cases, however, the underlying database is a relational one, and the types of the data are no so suggestive (text, integer, etc.) as the case of multimedia databases. So the output of the query is a "simple relational table."

We strongly believe that the above situation still deserves more attention that the one it gained till now. "Pure relational database" are widely diffused, and the research shows us that luckily in the future the end user interfaces for those databases will be mainly based on the visual query paradigm instead of the SQL paradigm. The additional knowledge embedded in the semantic model used as means by the user to query the database can be fruitfully used also to nicely arrange the output of the query process.

A variety of form-oriented systems have been developed and are available now; notable among them are Star Rp [14], Obe[20, 25] and Qbe [25, 26], Fads [16], Opas [12] and Formal [18, 24], Formdoq [10, 11], and Formanager[23, 24], ranging from flat tables to network structures. However, most of them are mainly devoted to system design (Formal, Formanager, and Fads) and to query expression (Obe, Qbe). Among the ones more oriented to data manipulation and showing a nonflat table structure, Star Rp uses a file system rather than a DBMS, while Formdoq and Opas are based on extensions of the relational model. A novel contribution of our proposal is to adopt a semantic model "on the top" of the logical (relational) one as a source of information for arranging the query result in a nonflat table. In this way our system is able to interact, in principle, with any "pure" relational DBMS.

In this paper we present a dynamic form based data Visualiser whose main goal is to manage the query output in such a way to overcome the above problems. The Visualiser strategies are based on the hypothesis that, when performing a (SQL) query against a set of relational tables, a high level description of the database, through a semantic data model is available. In particular, we have chosen the Entity Relationship model (ER in what follows) proposed by Chen [5] and actually at the base of the definition of the Information Resource Dictionary System (IRDS) [22]. However, our approach can be fruitfully adopted with any semantic data model supporting cardinality information. The cardinality of the relationships involved in the query is exploited in order to cluster the tuple attributes in homogeneous subsets and to suitable handle meaningless repetitions of values. In this way the data are presented to the user in a more compact and understandable way. It is worth noting that the ER relationship cardinality is only one of the possible way of representing the required knowledge: it is possible to devise a suitable formalism directly in terms of the relational model, making possible, in principle, the usage of the prototype also in a simple relational environment.

The paper is organised as follows. In Section 2 we briefly recall the main features of the so called semantic visual query languages, i.e., visual languages defined on semantic models. In Section 3 we discuss the structure of the tabular output of actual systems, In Section 4 we describe the main ideas underlying our Visualiser and the adopted algorithm. In Section 5 the functionalities of the Visualiser are shown. Finally, in Section 6 we briefly discuss the implementation of the a prototype of the Visualiser, drawing some conclusions and open problems.

## 2 Semantic visual query languages

The growth of the class of database users, including more and more non-expert and casual users, has motivated the development of easy-to-use query languages that are part of friendly interfaces for databases. A number of proposals are concerned with the usage of a semantic or object structured model as a means for representing the information content of the database (comparative analyses of semantic data models can be found in [9, 13]). The availability of graphic representations of such models results in the natural building of systems in which the user interacts visually with a diagram, representing the underlying semantic schema. We call that class of query language *semantic visual query language*.

In most of the above cases, the graphic representation of the semantic model is a graph, and the user is provided with a set of graphic operations whose semantics is expressed in terms of a formal internal query language (a very general analysis on that approach is in [4]). The user is usually provided with simple mechanisms for expressing selection and projection condition on a single class and for relating two or more classes by following the relationships linking them. In this way the query language reaches the expressive power of the conjunctive queries. More sophisticate strategies allow the user to relate classes independently of the relationships existing on the schema and to compose two intermediate results through set-oriented operator; the underlying language has gained the relational completeness.

The way in which the user formulates the query is based on one of two main paradigms of interaction, each of them more suitable for certain class of queries: navigational (see for instance, [1, 6, 8]) or view based (see for instance, [3, 4]).

In the navigational approach, the user specifies a path among the classes and the relationships of the schema. Roughly speaking, it corresponds to an ordered sequence of "join" between the pairs <entity, relationships> constituting the path, followed by a final selection and projection. The explicit presence of the relationships prevents the user from looking for concepts like "foreign keys" and the system can perform in the right way the join operations.

In the view based approach, the user simply specifies a view on the graph representing the database and the query corresponds to an unordered sequence of "natural joins". It is possible to show that the view based approach is equivalent to the navigational one [17], i.e., given a view v on a schema S there always exists a path p on S whose meaning is the same as the view v and vice versa. In the following, for the sake of simplicity, we will drive our discussion under the light of the path based approach.

We will not dwell on problems like expressive power or interaction strategies: what we want to point out is that the semantic model the user is interacting with is very often more expressive of the underlying relational model and that the representation structures and constraints of the semantic model can be usefully adopted for devising more friendly and expressive query outputs arranging them in a nonflat tabular structure. In fact, whatever is the chosen approach (view based or navigational) and the expressive power associated with the query language, it is always possible to deduce from the analysis of the cardinalities of the relationships involved in the query the pieces of information useful to give a structure to the flat set of tuples constituting the DBMS query output.

## 3 Viewing a Table

A query to a Data Base Management System often results in a "simple relational table" containing text in various formats (strings, numbers, alpha-numeric, dates, character, etc.). Every application dealing with such tables usually provides its own way of showing a single tuple in the most readable way, but very often it fails to offer an adequate tool for handling the entire table presentation. It is not an easy task to give a particular and structured overview of a large amount of data, especially when the data semantic is unknown. Moreover, tables are considered to be the end point of some kind of analysis of data (a query) and therefore they are not supposed to be further manipulated, except for sorting or attribute inversion. This is not always the case. We know by experience that those "simple relational tables" are often subjected to further 'manual' division or restructuring, to obtain better readability on several hidden data properties. This is primarily due to the semantics of data and it is hardly predictable during table formatting. As a matter of fact a query result can be further navigated to extract more specific information.

### 3.1 Tables Format

A relational table is a set of tuples made up of fields that are filled with attribute domain values. In the representation of a table there is usually nothing more than that: rows of values, equally spaced and possibly sorted. Most of the time a table is not even in second normal form, i.e., it exhibits a tedious repetition of values in its rows -- think of a telephone book. This offers a flat, boring and sometimes confusing presentation, which is almost inevitable, considering that the attributes with the repeated instances are usually 'key' to other attributes. In few cases is the user provided with formatting facilities, allowing her/him to rearrange the query output structure, i.e., to alter the order in which the tuples are presented and/or to reduce the tuple component and/or to "group" the instances of single attributes -- think of the SQL statement "Group By". These tools however, never get rid of one of the things that decreases readability in a table: the contiguity of unrelated data. Many tables can be the natural join of two or more tables, thus gathering attributes whose coupling may be meaningless, though each one has its precise meaning within the original table. Moreover, joining two tables in third normal form results, in general, in a table that is not in third normal form anymore, i.e., showing tedious value repetitions. Although many tricks can be thought of to avoid this problem, some undesired proximity will always exist.

### 3.2 Tables Use

In spite of all the formatting handicaps, a table is a potential source of further analysis. Beside the obvious fact that the table itself, as a "relational table", could be involved in subsequent queries, we should focus on the operations performed "manually" on it. This kind of analysis is again relational or statistic. New simple queries, usually projections or selections, can be made on this relational table, even equijoins. Those operations are definitely too simple to involve a DBMS, and should not alter the original table either. Let us examine the example shown in fig. 2.1.

A table is given, presenting the winners of state lotteries in all the states of US, formed by the attributes: State-Name, City-Name, Person-Surname, Person-Name, Person-Tel# and Win-Date. The first column is alphabetically sorted; for each unique entry in the first column the relative section of the second column is alphabetically sorted, and so on. Suppose that this table is the result of a query on a bigger one (it could contain all the people who have won a state lottery in the past five years).

| State-Name | City-Name | Person-Surname | Person-Name | Person-Tel# | Win-Date |
|---|---|---|---|---|---|
| NY | Albany | Smith | John | 555-1234 | 01/01/94 |
| NY | New York | Jones | Tom | 555-4321 | 01/01/94 |
| NY | New York | Smith | Susan | 555-3421 | 02/02/94 |
| ... | ... | ... | ... | ... | ... |
| WY | Casper | Chang | Lawrence | 555-4312 | 03/03/94 |
| ... | ... | ... | ... | ... | ... |
| WY | Casper | Zangler | Bela | 555-1423 | 12/12/94 |

**Fig. 2.1.** A State lottery winners table

Typical interactions with these data could be:

- Finding values of one attribute relative to the values of another one. Notice that this simple operation could be very easy (all the Surnames of the winner in Casper) or a little more tedious (all Win-Dates of the winners whose Surname is Smith), according to the proximity of the attributes involved;
- Finding instances of one attribute relative to the instances of many others. This could be very tedious, as in the search for all Tel# of all the "Smiths" living in the state of New York. Those people in fact do not appear next to each other in the list, but are spread through all the cities of New York.

Many other even more complex interactions can be derived from the ones described above. The main task of a table analysis is the highlighting of a sub-table formed by pieces of the original table that could possibly not be related in its raw form. This is the kind of work a DBMS does; but, as we stated above, it is too simple a job to involve such a powerful tool. At the same time we need an easy, highly interactive tool to let the user obtain a variety of views, without getting trapped in a complicated, abstract query language. The tool must be accurate in finding the exact sub-table of interest, but it is even more important that it be immediate in sketching the result. Should it lack this quality, it would not be very different from other spreadsheet-like applications, which require a large number of manipulations to obtain that result.

# 4 The Visualiser Guidelines

The main goal of our Visualiser is to obtain a highly readable table and a multi-stage browser. To achieve this objective, additional information is needed. This information can be retrieved in the ER schema representing the (relational) database on which the query is performed. This does not add a strong constraint to the Visualiser, which has been designed to be a part of a semantic visual query system based on an ER diagrammatic representation of the database.

The first step is to devise an algorithm for automatic attribute sorting. Such an algorithm is necessary, as it is not acceptable to rely on a canonical structure as supplied by the DBMS for the generic table that will be shown by the Visualiser. The main idea is to find a connecting property, derived from both the ER schema and the path corresponding to the query (see Section 2), linking attributes in such a way to suggest their proximity and order in the presentation.

The simple but powerful approach we have chosen, consists in ordering the attributes according to their mutual numerical relationship, which can be found in the ER model; if such a numerical information cannot help us in ordering the attributes, as shown in the following, we refer to the query path in order to suitably devise an attribute presentation sequence.

As a preliminary position, we have chosen to cluster attributes coming from different relational tables and belonging to the same entity. An Entity represents a class of real world objects sharing common properties, giving to the common attributes a strong cohesion. That is why it would be potentially useless to separate the Names from the Surnames in a table. So when a table is composed, the natural choice will be to group together the attributes relative to the same entity. Such groups of attributes -- at least under the hypothesis that the ER schema satisfies the first normal form requirements -- share another important property: they are all in a one-to-one relationship with one another.

Thus, in the Visualiser, attributes coming from the same entity are represented together and considered in one-to-one relationship. The problem we are dealing with now is to devise the arities of a relationship between two clusters of attributes coming from two different ER concepts. Two cases are given:

1. the attributes under consideration are part of two concepts of the query path directly linked;
2. they are still on the same path, but "far" from each other.

In the first case the numerical proportion can be derived directly from the cardinality of the ER schema, the maximum one being an indication of the greatest number of instances of one for each instance of the other. The second case is more complex. Evidence must be found navigating through the schema from one attribute to the other; cardinalities found through a path must be composed to determine a "super-arity" between two objects belonging to the path not directly linked. In the following examples, we assume the path has been specified from left to right.

Let us start with the simple case of two near entities in the path shown in Fig. 4.1, in which we denote with a pair of numbers the minimum and maximum cardinalities of a relationship. Note that we consider the cardinalities from the point of view of the relationship itself: the pair (1,1) between Person and Lives_in means that each instance of the entity Person is involved in the relationship Lives_in at least and at most once; each instance of the entity City is involved in the same relationship at least once and at most n times[1]. Moreover, when comparing two entities each other we often talk only about the maximum cardinalities and we say, for instance, that Person and City when related through the relationship Lives_in are in many-to-one relationship (when no ambiguity occurs we omit the relationship name).

**Fig. 4.1.** Two near entities

The trivial case of a one-to-one relationship between two entities has been omitted. There is no doubt that, in the schema shown in fig. 4.1, the attributes of Person are in a many-to-one relationship with the attributes of City. Adding another piece of path to the above example results in the ER schema shown in Fig. 4.2.

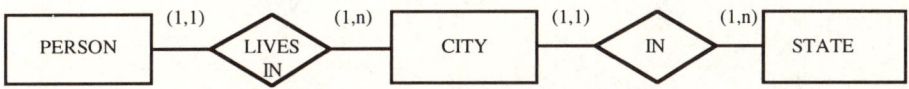

**Fig. 4.2.** A three-step path

Composing the cardinalities, Person is found to be in a many-to-one relationship with State -- more specifically a (many-to-one)$^2$ relationship. Person is in many-to-one relationship with City and City is in many-to-one relationship with State. In this case, the natural presentation of attributes is in contrast to the specified path flow. It is more effective, in fact, to present first the attributes coming from state, showing for each state the set of its cities and for each city the set of its inhabitants[2]. If we show the attributes in the order corresponding to the path, there is no way of avoiding the tedious repetition of the attributes of city for all the person living in the same city and the repetition of the attributes of state for each city in that state (we are assuming that the natural way of reading a table is from left to right; for different culture people, like Arabian people that read from right to left, the considerations presented in this paper on the matter must be reversed).

The algorithm for arity composition is based on the following approach. Given a path on an ER schema:

$$E_A - R_{AB} - E_B - R_{BC} - \cdots \cdots - R_{YZ} - E_Z$$

the problem of finding a "super-arity" between $E_A$ and $E_Z$, (or between any pairs of non adjacent entities in the path) could be divided in two steps: (a) finding the "arity" between $E_A$ and $E_B$, and then (b) between $E_B$ and $E_Z$. Iterating this procedure will yield the result. So, we can limit our analysis on two-step paths, in which different cases of arity composition could occur. The way they are considered depends on the

---

[1] We have chosen this notation because of it allows for describing cardinalities of more of two way relationships in a homogeneous way
[2] This happens through the Visualiser mechanisms of expansion and contraction, as shown in Section 5.

orientation of the path under examination. This means that, according to the direction, a one-to-many relationship is different from a many-to-one relationship -- i.e., the same relationship is considered in different ways depending on the direction of the path.

For the sake of simplicity, a reduced notation will be used instead of the ER model notation. Entities will be represented by labelled nodes, linked by edges that represent relationships; labels on edges represent maximum cardinalities.

Three base cases are shown in fig. 4.3.

The 4.3a case is easily seen to yield a one-to-one cardinality between A and C; 4.3b and 4.3c result in a one-to-many relationship between A and C. In these cases the numerical information and the path furnish non contrasting results, so the order of presentation of the attributes in the table is A, B, and C. Note that, from the point of view of numerical relationships, the order of presentation of A, B, and C can be

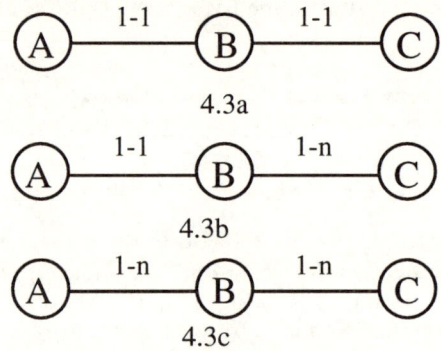

Fig. 4.3. Three base cases

arbitrarily permuted in the 4.3a case; the same happens for A and B in the 4.3b case. In the 4.3c case any permutation will result in repetition of values. However, being the user path A,B, and C it makes no sense to alter it.

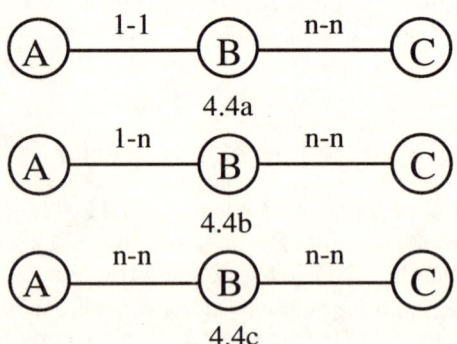

Fig. 4.4. Paths resulting in one-to-many relationship

The slightly more complex situations shown in Fig. 4.4 result in an overall many-to-many relationship between A and C. However, under the light of the presentation of the attributes, a many-to-many relationship can be considered as a "two-way" one-to-many relationship, always concordant with the orientation of the path. It results that the order of presentation of the attributes is still A,B, and C. Moreover, while in the 4.4c case it is possible alter the presentation in any way, in the 4.4b case the permutations in which A follows B are meaningless, so the unique alternative is C, A, and B. Finally, in the 4.4a case it makes no sense split A and B, so the admissible alternatives are C,B, and A and C, A, and B. Again, being the topological choice of the user not in contrast to numerical information the Visualiser choice will be A, B, and C.

Standing the position of considering a many-to-many relationship as a pair of one-to-many relationship, all remaining different cases can be restricted to the pair of patterns shown in fig. 4.5.

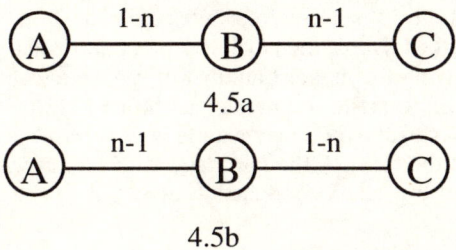

**Fig. 4.5.** Remaining path possibilities

It can be shown that there is not a general solution for the 4.5a case and the arity between A and C depends on the semantics of the involved data. A safe approach would be that of considering the arity between A and C as a many-to-many one. Different positions would need additional information to be supported. It is possible, in principle, to enrich the ER model with additional constraints, like more-than-one-step cardinality or inclusion dependencies, but we have chosen to use the common adopted constraints for the ER model instead of devising new ones. Moreover, using this approach, the order of attributes derived from the path is preferred where there is not another outstanding property. It is likely in fact, that the order in which the path has been formed is more important for the user than the order suggested by the semantics. It is interesting to remark that this method is purely a topologic one rather than a semantic one. All deductions obtained give a trend or a worst case analysis of the potential numerical fig. of attributes on a table. No semantics is involved in deduction, though all efforts were pointed to finding what of topology is derived from semantics. Considering 4.5b case, we find a many-to-many relationship as well.

This pure topologic approach is found to be very useful because it allows us to obtain a "super-arity" between entities semantically unrelated. This is the case when branches are present in the path. Complex queries can be formed by means of operators such as 'union' or 'intersection'. In terms of path on an ER schema those queries can form branches parting from the same root. Entities at the end of the branches are in general unrelated one to another, and could hardly be checked for mutual numerical relationship. Anyway some order must be chosen in the case attributes from those entities are shown in the table. The topologic approach allows for deriving that order.

Under the circumstances described above, solution obtained by means of that algorithm are at least a sub-optimum. The preference accorded to the path mutual position however, always turns into the right choice from the user's point of view -- which in the end is the most important.

The results described in this Section will be used as the means for arranging the table attributes in the Visualiser, as described in the next Section.

## 5 The Visualiser Functionalities

The algorithm described in Section 4 creates, on the basis of the arity of the relationships of the ER schema, a partial order relation on the table attributes. Such a partial order is matched against the total order defined by the user path that, when necessary, is altered in order to present attributes according to the considerations driven in Section 4. In the Visualiser, attributes are placed on the screen according to that precedence; in other words, the attributes in a one-to-many relationship with all the others -- i.e., showing the greatest number of repeated instances -- appear first on the left. The more we go right, the greater is the number of distinct instances that form a column. This is exactly the way a table is expected to be: more general to the left, more specific to the right. Although many cases are given in arity composition, it has been shown that they can be reduced to two:

1. a one-to-one arity, which suggests grouping;
2. a one-to-many arity, which suggests hierarchy.

In this section we introduce the functionalities of the Viewer through an incremental example. With no loss of generality, we have chosen an example formed by a plain cascade of one-to-many relationships, with no inversion. This would make the following description easier. Equally, the number of attributes has been limited to one for entity, typically the 'name', keeping in mind that, in a real situation, attributes coming from the same entity can form homogeneous groups.

Once the numerical relationships are defined following the strategies shown in Section 4, the next step is to provide a proper layout that takes advantage of them. The idea is to represent the fewest tuples we can, without loss of information. Let us consider the schema shown in Fig. 5.1.

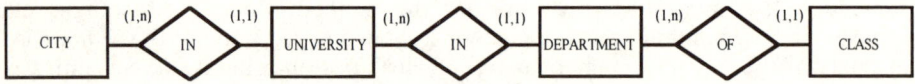

**Fig. 5.1.** A simple university database

That schema can yield a plane table like the one shown in fig. 5.2.

Many tedious repetitions appear in the table. The first column especially, presents only two distinct instances, namely New York and Cambridge. This means that the entire table can be split in two by choosing one of them. So, it makes sense to show the first column composed of a single instance in place of the repetitions, as shown in fig. 5.3.

| CITY | UNIVERSITY | DEPARTMENT | CLASS |
|---|---|---|---|
| NEW YORK | COLUMBIA | SCIENCE | ARITHMETIC |
| NEW YORK | COLUMBIA | SCIENCE | PHYSICS |
| NEW YORK | COLUMBIA | ART | MUSIC |
| NEW YORK | NYU | MEDICINE | PATHOLOGY |
| NEW YORK | NYU | MEDICINE | ANATOMY |
| NEW YORK | CUNY | HISTORY | HYSTORY |
| CAMBRIDGE | MIT | SCIENCE | PHYSICS |
| CAMBRIDGE | MIT | SCIENCE | ARITHMETIC |
| CAMBRIDGE | MIT | SCIENCE | MATHEMATICS |
| CAMBRIDGE | MIT | SCIENCE | BIOLOGY |

Fig. 5.2: The table corresponding to the university database

| CITY |
|---|
| NEW YORK |
| CAMBRIDGE |

**Fig. 5.3.** The distinct values of the first column

Regarding the subsequent columns, consistency must be maintained. Moreover, the user should feel completely free to browse through the table; every layout that may be confusing or constraining has to be avoided. Thus the remaining columns must complete one of the tuples -- typically the first -- relative to each instance of the nearest expanded attribute to its left. The resulting table is the one shown in fig. 5.4.

| CITY | UNIVERSITY | DEPARTMENT | CLASS |
|---|---|---|---|
| NEW YORK | COLUMBIA | SCIENCE | ARITHMETIC |
| CAMBRIDGE | MIT | SCIENCE | PHYSICS |

**Fig. 5.4.** The compact representation of the table of fig. 5.2

At this point, a method must be introduced to allow the selectively presentation of parts of the table, through easy, visual primitives. To expand sub-parts of the table, at least one instance of one attribute must be selected -- by selecting its cell -- in order to decide which instances to pick. It can be thought of as the argument to the relational operator of 'selection'. Now a column on the right can be 'expanded' to uncover all the instances of that attribute (or group of attributes) relative to the one selected to the left. In fig. 5.5 the selection of "NEW YORK" and its further expansion is shown.

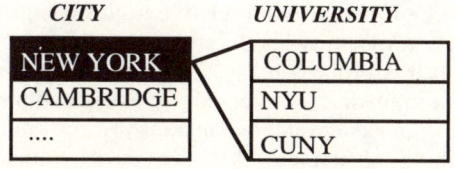

**Fig. 5.5.** Expansion of the value "NEW YORK"

Expansions are possible only to the right of a selection, since everything that is on

the left acts as a 'key' to the sub-table; thus there are no further distinct instances that can be found to the left, on the basis of the selection. The columns to the right of the expanded one -- for which the expansion is not directly requested -- must fit the new layout, as shown in fig. 5.6, while columns in the between of the selection and the expanded one (if any) remain unchanged (see fig. 5.7).

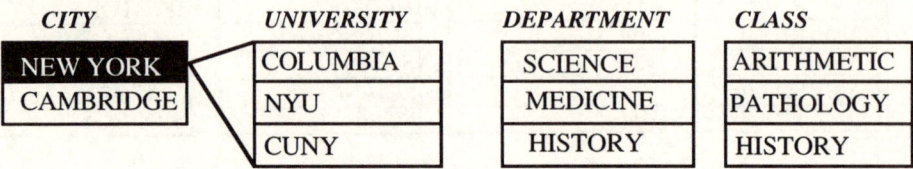

**Fig. 5.6.** Automatic rearrangement of the table after an expansion

Notice that those columns are not expanded, but only adapt themselves to maintain consistency. Any other possibility -- columns remaining unchanged or being expanded individually -- is neither requested by the user, nor consistent, nor clear.

From the expanded attribute proceeding to the right a sub-table is obtained, which follows the same rules of the initial one: a single tuple for each distinct instance of the leftmost attribute. Thus applying again the expansion procedure to an instance in the sub-table, a similar result is reached.

Selection and expansion can involve almost every pair of columns, the only constraint being the expansion performed on the right of the selection. When the involved attributes are not adjacent, the columns lying between them need are not expanded, for two reasons:

1. no operation was required on them;
2. repetitions would be introduced, worsening readability.

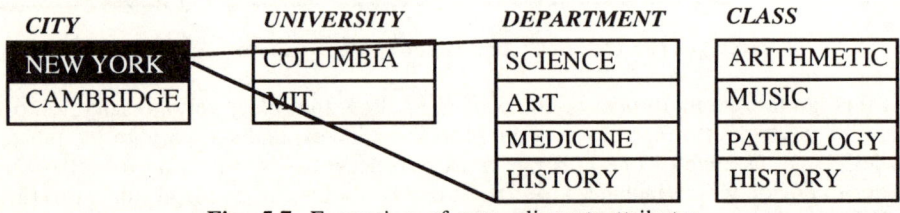

**Fig. 5.7.** Expansion of non adjacent attributes

This solution also helps multiple expansions based on a single selection. There is in fact nothing that prevents the user from asking details about two or more different columns independently. In this case, each column should act separately, presenting each and every instance of that attribute relative to the selection. As an example, in fig. 5.8 the expansion of University and Class with respect to New York is shown.

The only constraint to this process regards the selection to be used as a point of reference. The need for immediacy prevented supplying complex binding procedure, causing the adoption of an easier one: expansions always refer to the first selection met going to the left. Such a method, however, restrains the order in which expansions can be performed. For example, the only way to reach a situation like the one shown in Fig. 5.9, is to select the first column and expand the third prior to selecting the second and expanding the fourth.

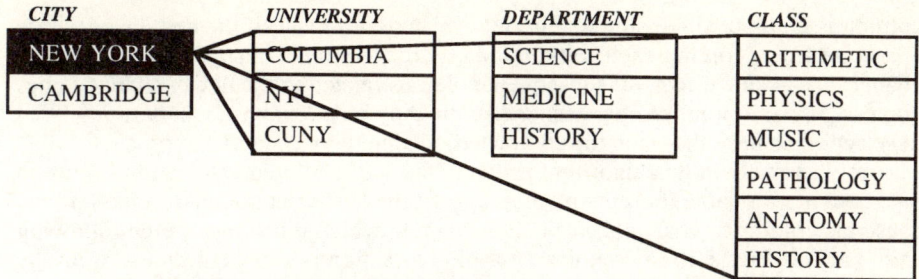

**Fig. 5.8.** Multiple expansion based on a single selection

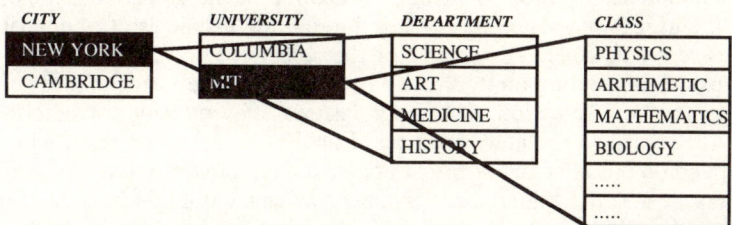

**Fig. 5.9.** Multiple expansion based on two different selections

Figure 5.9 also shows that expansions can be unrelated, or overlapping, or crossed, allowing the maximum freedom of browsing.

Till now, only one operator was described, but at least other two interaction procedures might be introduced to complete the instrument: contraction and selection changing.

Not only can a column be expanded, it must also be possible to undo or backtrack the browsing. The user should be able to bring things back to a situation equal -- or at least compatible if something else has changed -- to the one present before the expansion. A contraction can have three main causes:

1. the user request it;
2. the reference selection has been removed;
3. the contraction has been caused from the contraction of previous columns.

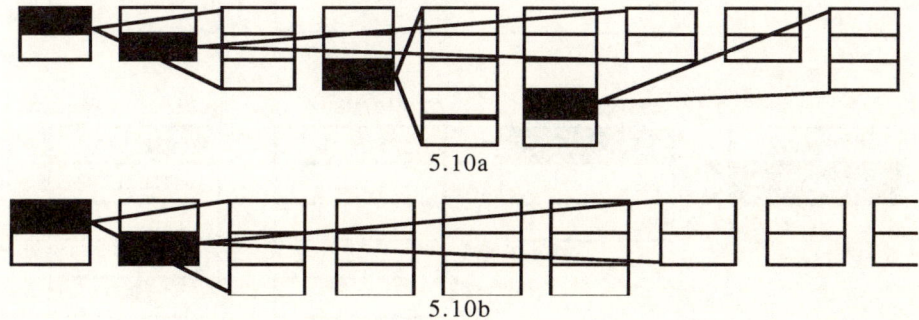

**Fig. 5.10.** An example of contraction

The main difficulty is to supply a rule for propagation. It is clear in fact that once a column is contracted, all subsequent ones related to it must fit the new layout. This is accomplished forcing each column directly related to the changed one to join the changes. As a side effect, all subsequent columns related to the newly changed ones are also forced to join the changes, and so on. Any other expansion pattern involved in selection chains other than the contracted, remain untouched by the process.

The only anomaly in this algorithm is due to the way a reference selection is chosen backtracking the table. Forcing a column to fit the first selection met to the left can cause the column to change the selection chain to which it belongs. In the following example (see Fig. 5.10) a complex case of contraction is shown, deriving from the removal of the selection of the fourth column in Fig. 5.10a.

Finally, a method is supplied to manage a change in the selected instance. It is likely that the user is interested in moving through the instances of one attribute to browse different sub-table. To the left of the selection, however, there might be many expansions depending on it, directly or indirectly. The former simply changes according to the new selection. The latter instead, may or may not be consistent anymore with regard to the new instances. Equally the selection from which they directly depend on has changed or might not exist anymore even as a physical cell -- there may not be a 'fifth' cell anymore. As a consequence it might be correct to keep the pattern or to release it. Both possibilities are allowed, letting the user to choose -- through a system option -- whether restart browsing when changing selection or not. In Fig. 5.11b, both situations are shown; starting from the case depicted in the first table (Fig. 5.11a).

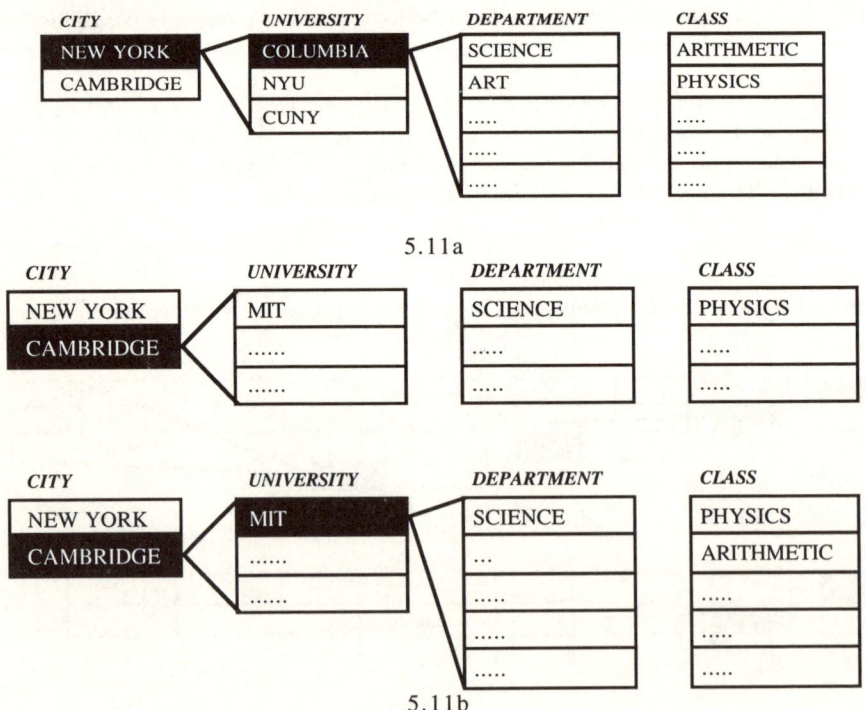

**Fig. 5.11.** Browsing the table by changing the selected value

In any case, all dependent columns following the changed one, are modified in order to show the new part of the table.

## 6 Conclusion and further research

In this paper we have presented a form based Visualiser able to nicely arrange the output to a query against a relational database under the hypothesis that a semantic description of the database is available. In particular, on the basis of the cardinality constraints the proposed Visualiser is able to cluster the result attributes with the same arity and to avoid tedious value repetitions.

A prototype of the Visualiser has been implemented under the Unix operative system, using C++ language and the XVT graphical toolkit. This toolkit is a set of libraries designed for multi-platform programming and ensures portability over several environments (hardware and software). The prototype takes as input an ER schema, an ER query, the corresponding SQL query, and the table corresponding to the SQL query. It produces a dynamic table, whose attributes are arranged according to the strategies described in the previous sections. The format of input is row ASCII files, to allow the use of the Visualiser as a stand-alone application. In fact, given a table as ASCII, file with fixed length attributes, it is possible to construct the additional information needed, and to put it in a text file, without relying on other application.

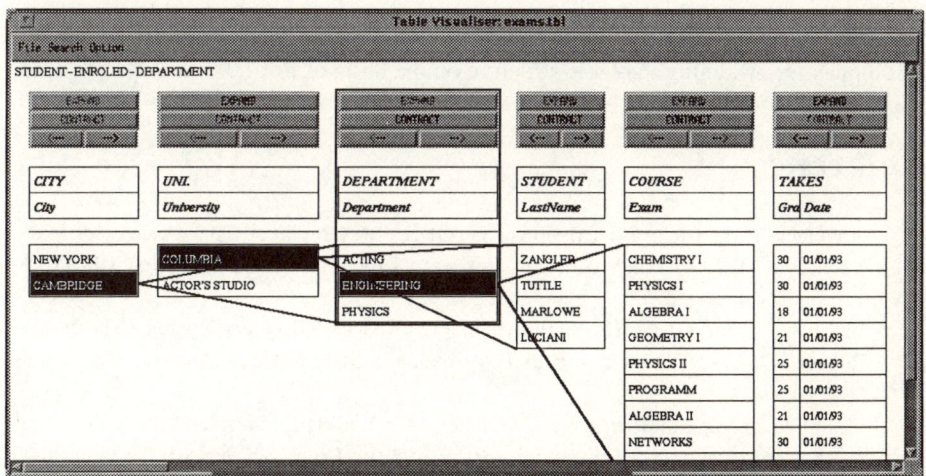

**Fig. 6.1.** A screen grabbed from the Visualiser prototype

The initial layout of the table is formed by a subset of the initial tuples having distinct values in the leftmost group of attributes. Main goal is to shrink information at the highest level without compromising browsing capability. The single tuple of the new table represents one tuple (typically the first) of the sub-table derived from the initial one, through a selection on the first group of attributes.

All features described in Section 5 are fully supported. Selecting ('clicking' with a pointing device) a cell on the screen -- cell containing one instance of a group of attributes -- tells the system that future operation will refer to that instance. Expansions button on following columns (to the right) are enabled, so that depressing one of them will force the involved column to show all the distinct values related to the nearest selection. Such an operation can be iterated on several groups to browse through different levels of detail. Expansion can also be disjoined to allow unrelated analysis. To easily keep track of the relationship between selection and expansion, guiding lines has been added to the graphical presentation, as well as a frame around the currently selected column. Each column changes reflecting the changes in the selection to which it refers, maintaining consistency. User can backtrack expansions at every level, possibly forcing related columns to the right to join the operation.

Some options have been added to the prototype. Sorting facilities allow to alphabetically sort each group or the first one only, still maintaining consistency. A tool for string search, acting on each group, helps instance retrieval in big tables. It is possible to scroll a selected column and all related ones independently from the others. Finally, an option -- namely 'keep expansions' -- allows the user to choose between two behaviours while changing a selection: 1) all subsequent expansion, related to the changed selections, are contracted, forcing them to fit the expansion level of the column containing the selection; 2) expansion pattern is maintained in order to allow the user to jump to the different instances while browsing the same details.

From a practical point of view we are planning to integrate the Visualiser prototype within the QBD* system [1], a visual query system able to manage recursive queries and more than relational set oriented operators.

From a theoretical point of view we are studying how to better exploit the high level description of data coming from the ER model. In particular, we are analysing techniques for arranging the table structure on the basis of ISA relationships.

# References

1. Angelaccio M., Catarci T., Santucci G. QBD*: A Graphical Query Language with Recursion. IEEE Transactions on Software Engineering, Vol.16, No. 10, 1150-1163 (1991)
2. Batini C., Catarci T., F.Costabile M., Levialdi S. Visual Query Systems. Technical Report N.04.91, Dipartimento di Informatica e Sistemistica, Università di Roma "La Sapienza".
3. Campbell D.M., Embley D.W., Czejdo B. A relationally complete query language for an entity-relationship model. pp. 90-97 in Proc. of the 4th International Conference on Entity-Relationship Approach, Chicago, Illinois, October 1985.
4. Catarci T., Santucci G., Angelaccio M. Fundamental Graphical Primitives for Visual Query Languages. Information Systems, Vol. 18 No.2 (1993)
5. Chen P.P. The Entity-Relationship Model toward a Unified View of Data. *ACM Transactions on Data Base Systems,1*, 1 (1976)
6. Consens M., Mendelzon A.O. Graphlog: A Visual Formalism for Real Life Recursion. Proc. of the ACM Symp. on Principles of Database Systems, 404-416 (1990)
7. Consens M., Mendelzon A.O. Hy+ : A Hygraph-based Query and Visualization System. Proc. of the ACM SIGMOD 93, Washington, DC USA (1993)
8. Cruz I.F., Mendelzon A.O., Wood P.T. G+: Recursive Queries Without Recursion. Proc. of the 2nd International Conference on Expert Database Systems, April, 355-

368 (1988)
9. Hull R., King R. Semantic Database Modeling: Survey, Applications and Research Issues,. *ACM Computing Surveys*, vol. 19, n. 3, pp. 201 - 260 (1987)
10. Kitagawa H., Kunii T.L., et al. For ngraphics: A Form-Based Graphics Architecture Providing a Database Workbench. *IEEE CGA, Vol.4,* No.6, June pp.38-56 (1984)
11. Kitagawa H. *Structured Forms Handling By Nested Table Data Model,* D.Sc. Thesis, Department of Information Science, Faculty of Science, the University of Tokyo, Japan (1987)
12. Lum V.Y., Choy D.M., Shu N.C. OPAS: An office procedure automation system. *IBM Syst. J.*, Vol.21, No.3, pp.327-350 (1982)
13. Peckham J., Maryanski F. Semantic Data Models. *ACM Computing Surveys*, vol. 20, n. 3, pp. 153 - 189 (1988)
14. Purvy R., Farrell J., Klose P. The design of STAR's records processing: Data processing for the noncomputer professional. ACM *Trans. on Office Inf. Syst.,* Vol.1, No.1, pp.3-24 (1983)
15. Rhiner M. Object Description and Representation for Visual and Multimedia Databases. IFIP Transactions on Visual Database Systems, II, North-Holland (1992)
16. Rowe L.A., Shoens K.A. A Form Application Development System. Proc of ACM Sigmod '82, pp.28-38 (1982)
17. Santucci G. A Multilevel Query Language for the Entity Relationship Model. Technical Report, Dipartimento di Informatica e Sistemistica, Università di Roma "La Sapienza", in printing. (1994)
18. Shi N.C. FORMAL: A Forms-Oriented, Visual-Directed Application Development System. Kunii, T.L.(ed), Application Development Systems, Springer, Tokyo and Berlin, 1986, pp.2-26.
19. Tufte E.R. The visual Display of Quantitative Information. Graphics Press, Cheshire, Connecticut, (1983)
20. Whang K.Y.et al. Office-by-Example: An Integrated Office System and Database Manager. *ACM Trans. on Office Inf. Syst.,* Vol.5, No.4 pp.393-427. (1987)
21. Wilson G.A. Semantics vs. graphics -- to show or not to show. Proc. of the 6th Very Large Data Base (1980)
22. Winkler J. The Entity Relationship approach and the Information Resource Dictionary system standard. Seventh International Conference on the Entity Relationship Approach, North Holland (1989)
23. Yao S.B., Hevner A.R., Z.Shi, Luo D.: FORMANAGER: An office forms management system. *ACM Trans. on Office Inf. Syst.,* Vol.2, No.3, pp.235-262 (1984)
24. Yao S.B., and Kitagawa H. Structured Application Generation Using XDB. *Proc. AFIPS National Computer Conference,* Chicago (1985)
25. Zloof M.M. Query-by-example: A data base language. *IBM Syst. J.,* Vol.16, No.4, pp.324-343 (1982)
26. Zloof M.M. Office-by-example: A business language that unifies data and word processing and electronic mail. *IBM Syst. J.,* Vol.21, No.3, pp.272-304 (1982)

# Domain Restrictive User Interfaces Using Databases

**Peter Messer and Nitin Patel**

School of Computing Sciences
De Montfort University
The Gateway
Leicester LE1 9BH

pm@dmu.ac.uk
patel@dmu.ac.uk

**Abstract.**

Many important computer applications require that users be able to use them effectively with little or no formal training [1]. DRAGEN (Domain Restrictive Application GENerator) is a suite of tools which allows the designer of an application to automatically create interfaces to restricted application domains. It does this by providing a small set of stylised interface structures which help the designer to create the interface. The information with respect to the interface is stored in the database, as well as application data and the map of possible interactions. This paper provides an overview of DRAGEN and the underlying methodologies used in the development of DRAGEN.

# 1 Introduction

The interface requirements of database systems are particularly stringent. In the search for powerful paradigms to release information to users, many disparate techniques are being brought to help users. One class of user who it is easy to ignore is the naive user with static requirements. Such users often require access to database information infrequently and will never become skilled users. The present work covers the case where:

1. the user is database naive;
2. the user requires database access infrequently;
3. the user's requirements can be satisfied by database queries;
4. the required database queries are of a static nature.

The user is considered to be a novice with regard to the interface (in particular mouse expertise is assumed), but naive with regard to the underlying database. The four conditions imply that the interface should be of a walk up and use type [1, 2].

The queries made by the user must appear simple, but there is no restriction on the complexity of the underlying database query that a user may require.

The approach taken to the problem is the development of DRAGEN (Domain Restrictive Application GENerator), a tool to generate a stylised walk up and use interface. The tool is intended to act as an experimental testbed for this type of interface rather than as a commercial product. DRAGEN has the following characteristics:

1. it generates the interface;
2. it generates an analytic model of the interface;
3. it stores the interface entirely within the database;
4. it embeds generation routines in its runpack.

The interface has the following characteristics:

1. it represents data from the database;
2. it follows a hierarchical menu structure;
3. only five types of data display are allowed;
4. the database query language is totally hidden from the user.

Modern relational and object oriented databases have very powerful tools for querying and updating the information content. These tools are very general in nature and tend to require knowledge of the structure of the database and be relatively difficult to learn and use (e.g. SQL). Many different approaches are being taken to address these issues [3]. Thus specialised domain specific interfacesexist [4, 5] along with tools which make learning and use of general interfaces much easier.

DRAGEN is a fully working prototype tool and has been evaluated using fifty subjects. The results of these evaluations are still being analysed. Early observations from the analysis show that the two groups of users (naive and novice) take similar times to carry out the same type of task. This leads us to believe that the interfaces that are generated by DRAGEN are of the 'walk up and use' variety.

Modern user interface tools allow the designer to specify how the interface will look, though these tools tend to have a large learning curve. The tools are very powerful and allow the user to develop the look of the interface within a short period of time. The designer of the interface has the added responsibility of handling any events that may occur when interaction with the interface takes place. In many cases the language used to write the interaction code is specific to the application generator (for example TeleUSE uses a language called D). The designer is also responsible for the handling of data transfer between application and interface. DRAGEN differs from this approach in a number of different ways. A major difference is that DRAGEN automatically generates the interface as well as generating all interactions that can occur within the interface. Hence, there is no necessity for the designer to write code to achieve interaction. All retrieval, storage and manipulation of application and interface information is handled automatically by DRAGEN.

DRAGEN currently generates interfaces for a specified number of applications, i.e. those that require some form of scheduling, hence there are a limited number of stylised interface structures. There is the potential to increase the number of applications that can be generated by DRAGEN; this would entail the study of different application domains, to investigate the different types of interface styles that are present in those applications. These can then be implemented by adding the new styles to the ones that already exist. The designer of the application can have available a number of different styles, similar to the approach adopted by X-Windows and Motif. This has the added side effect that the types of interface that are developed tend to be more complex, without walk up and use characteristics.

## 2 The Interface and the Analytical Model

Since DRAGEN is designed to generate simple interfaces, the underlying model used is analytic [6], based on the GOMS model [7, 8] and Cognitive Complexity Theory (CCT) model [9, 10, 11]. The designer uses the tool to produce an automatic interface and a set of production rules based on GOMS analysis. This is achieved by using strictly stylised interfaces which allow macro expansions to give the GOMS model.

The work in cognitive psychology in developing analytical models (GOMS, CCT) for constructing and analysing computer interfaces enables designers to predict the performance of their interface. A user's method selections can be predicted with 90% accuracy with a root mean square error of 35% [7]. For interfaces with strictly stylised designs a large part of the model can be generated automatically.

To justify the class of interfaces generated by DRAGEN it is required to show that the analytic model predicts successful use of the interfaces. Since the interfaces have a walk up and use characteristics, GOMS/CCT analysis should predict the error free performance characteristics of the generated interfaces with a high degree of accuracy [7].

In the present work it is assumed that the queries required by novice users should hide the structure of the database. Instead a hierarchical menu system is presented which allows the user to answer a set of restricted questions. The designer of such an interface should have expertise in human computer interaction sciences, but DRAGEN is constructed to help minimise the expertise needed. Thus the designer should exhibit the following characteristics:

1. A knowledge of the method level of the analytic model.
2. A knowledge of the database query language (typically SQL) and how to partition queries into separate sub queries.
3. A knowledge of the interface generation tool and how sub-queries are implemented.

The analytic model method level is used to generate an appropriate menu structure for a given set of queries. The queries are broken down into a partial ordering of sub-queries, one for each level of the menu hierarchy.

The generation tool is now used to construct the interface. At any stage of the construction the designer may generate the partial interface for testing purposes. The tool generates:

1. The interface;
2. A GOMS/CCT set of production rules for the interface;
3. A set of timing predictions for moving from one level of the interface to another by a novice user.

From these generated results predictions can be made of the performance of users for any specific query. So by using a carefully chosen sample set of queries, predictions can be made about the performance of users. It is proposed that the tool provides a testbed for the testing of different ways of implementing the same set of queries and predicting which will prove superior.

A series of experiments have been carried out to demonstrate that generated interfaces perform well and have the characteristics predicted by the analytic model. The results of the experiments conform with previously published figures [7, 12, 13, 14, 15] for GOMS/CCT models.

DRAGEN provides a number of different stylised interface structures which allow the user to put application-specific data into the structures provided. The types of information structures are presented here:

1. Designer-Defined and System-Defined Menu Structures;
2. Name Structure;
3. Grid Structure;
4. Information Retrieval Structure;
5. Label Structure.

## 2.1 Designer-Defined and System-Defined Menu Structures

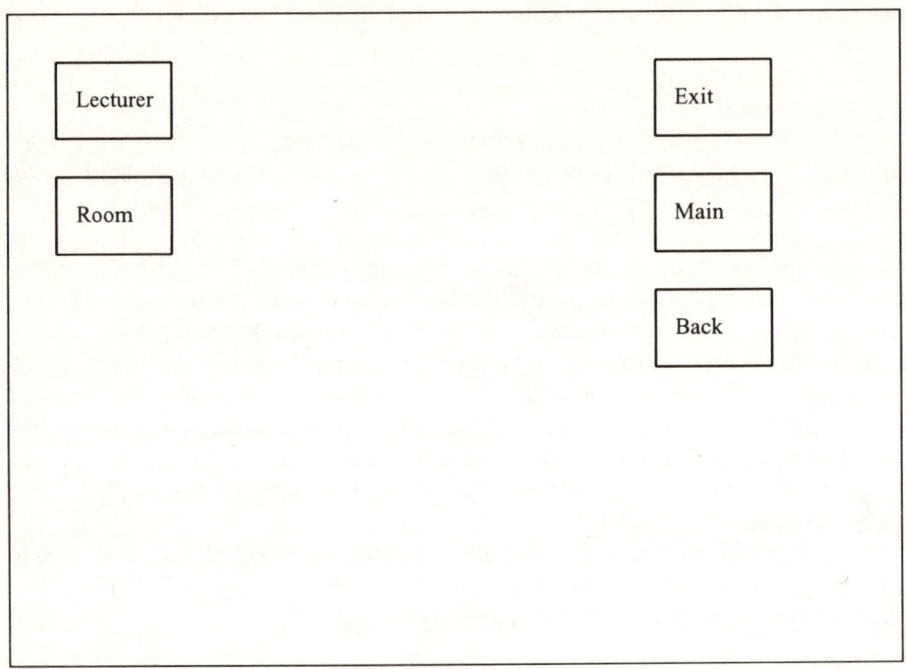

**Figure 1**
Designer defined and system defined menu structures

A typical generated screen is shown in figure 1. The menu buttons on the right hand side are standard (at least for a given application) and involve traversal of the paths through the structure. A user is given the option to Exit, Start again with a new query, and to backtrack one step. Once defined for an application these buttons appear on every screen. These allow simple navigation paths within the menu structure and provide consistency. The left hand side of the interface presents material that has been generated from the database. Further information can be derived by clicking with a mouse on the appropriate box.

Menu structures are similar to buttons found in most windowing systems, where a single click causes some action to be taken by the name indicated on an icon. The icons should have meaningful names; this assists the naive user and the experienced user to traverse to the correct screen required to achieve the given task. System menu buttons/icons, take the user to previous screens by back-tracking along the path hierarchy. This is indicated by a system button labelled 'Back'. Other system buttons take the user back to the top level in the hierarchy, indicated by the button 'Main', and another button labelled 'Exit' allows the user to exit the system. At the top level of the hierarchy only one system menu button is automatically provided; this is the 'Exit' button. From the top level hierarchy the user is only able to advance forward or exit as further traversal backwards is not possible. The diagram represents two designer-defined menu buttons, 'Lecturer' and 'Room', as well as three system buttons 'Exit', 'Main' and 'Back'.

The designer of the system is responsible for ensuring designer-defined menu buttons are named so that they are meaningful for the end-user of the system. If they are labelled so that the user of the end-system does not understand or has to guess which button to press this is likely to cause traversal to the wrong screen, hence causing user errors which could have been avoided. This makes the system intuitive for the user to use as it provides the user with meaningful text labels on each button to allow them to make the correct decision [16]. This concept of meaningful text labels on each icon reduces the cognitive overload of the size of the system. At any one time the user is concerned with the task at hand. During the initial stages the user is learning by exploration [17]. As the user becomes more familiar with the layout of the hierarchy then tasks of the same complexity will be carried out at a faster rate [12]. This is because there is a cognitive overlap as the user becomes familiar with the layout of the system and knows the appearance of each screen. It is at this stage that the user can carry out tasks in parallel. The user can begin to move the mouse as the next screen is appearing and at the same time know what will be required to achieve the sub goal for that screen. The user when learning creates a mental model of the device [18, 19, 9] which assists the user in learning and operating the device. In this case the device is the hierarchical structure of the application.

The general structure for designer-defined menu structures is based on the system structure. The designer has the ability to create any number of menu options that will fit on the screen. When selecting a menu structure the designer is prompted for the number of menu options required. The designer is then prompted for the text that should appear for that specified menu icon. It is possible to create any number of menu options, but the designer should be familiar with interface design guidelines for the maximum number of menus that should be present on any one screen [20, 21] and the system gives warnings when these standard guidelines are flouted.

## 2.2 Name Retrieval Structure

| Comp Sci | Maths Sci | Info Sys |
|---|---|---|
| Brown | Davidson | Farmer |
| Dowson | Gregson | Fidler |
| Jackson | Palmer | McBride |
| Sexton | Smith | Oldroyd |
| Skipper | | Thornton |
| Williams | | |

Exit

Main

Back

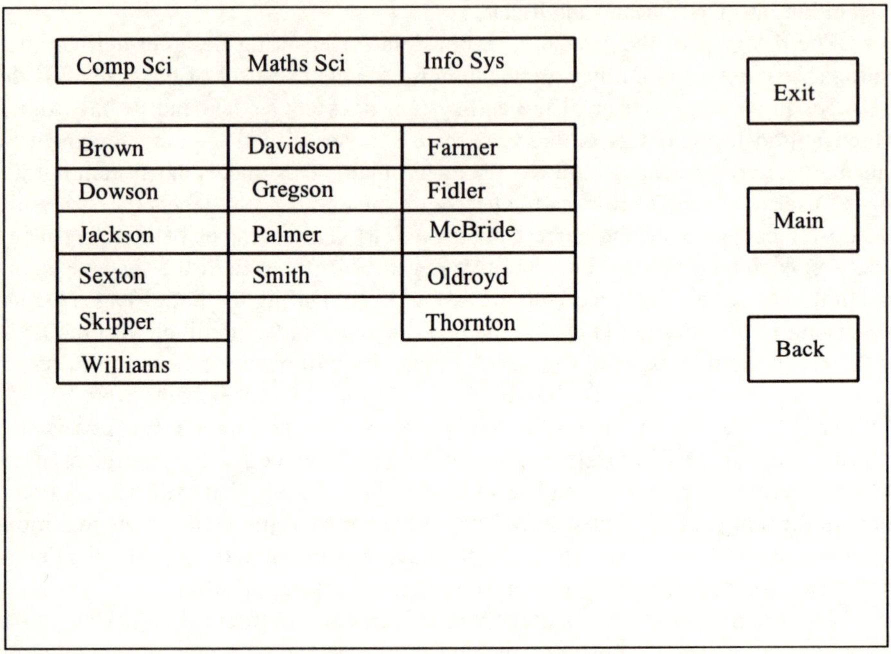

**Figure 2**
Name retrieval structure

Figure 2 shows a name retrieval structure, this can be thought of as a series of buttons with the difference being the shape, positioning and physical appearance of the structure. The designer specifies the number of name columns that are desired. For each name column the designer specifies an SQL query which retrieves from a designer-defined database table (or tables) a list of names that should appear in the name structure. The number of rows that appear in a name column structure is dependent on the number of names that are retrieved by the query. Unlike the grid structure (discussed in section 2.3), the appearance is not uniform. For example, if the columns were a representation of the lecturers in three different departments, there would be three name columns, and for each name column there would be a certain number of lecturer names, i.e. the number of lecturers present in each of their respective departments. A mouse click on any name retrieval structure box produces more information. Each box provides similarly structured information, but it need not be uniform.

## 2.3 Grid Structure

Figure 3 shows a grid structure which is analogous to a spreadsheet, representing information as if they were cells. However, it is not the aim of the grid structure to provide facilities that are provided by spreadsheets, as this would go against the principles of a naive user interface. The grid structure, although different in appearance, is composed of many buttons organised in grid formation, i.e. a specified number of rows by a specified number of columns. The designer can specify the number of columns that the grid contains and then carry out an SQL query for each of the columns. The number of rows retrieved by each of the queries makes up the number of rows. Typically a retrieval of a row will be the text label that will appear in each of the grids. The grid structure is usually a structure of uniform appearance; each column will have an equal number of rows. The second way in which to create a grid is to specify a single column. The designer will be asked if the grid is to contain a certain number of rows. For example, for the single column, if the numbers of rows contained has been specified as four, and the number of rows retrieved by the SQL query is twenty.

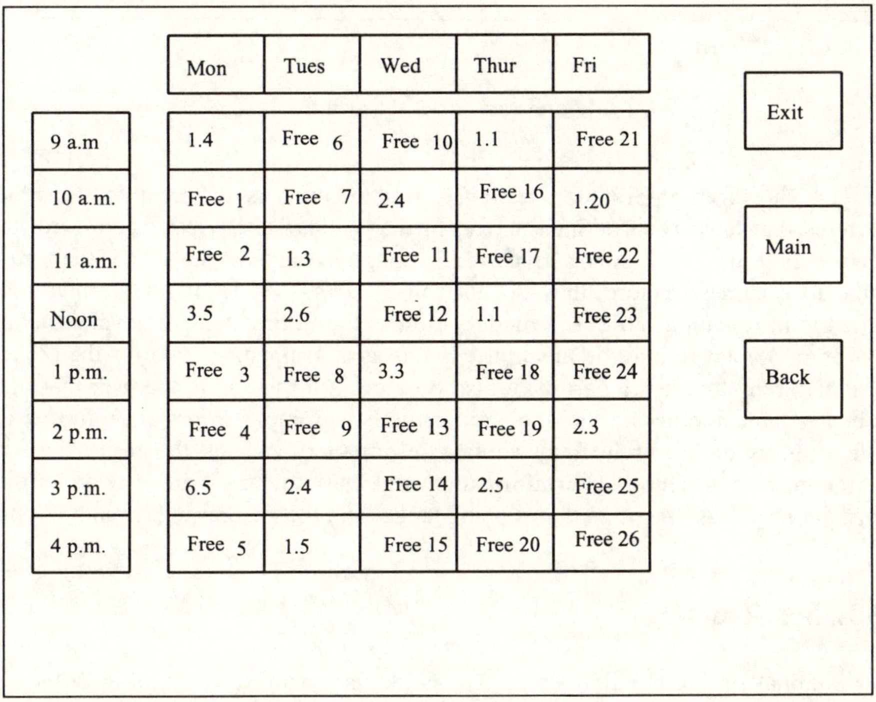

|         | Mon    | Tues   | Wed     | Thur    | Fri     |
|---------|--------|--------|---------|---------|---------|
| 9 a.m   | 1.4    | Free 6 | Free 10 | 1.1     | Free 21 |
| 10 a.m. | Free 1 | Free 7 | 2.4     | Free 16 | 1.20    |
| 11 a.m. | Free 2 | 1.3    | Free 11 | Free 17 | Free 22 |
| Noon    | 3.5    | 2.6    | Free 12 | 1.1     | Free 23 |
| 1 p.m.  | Free 3 | Free 8 | 3.3     | Free 18 | Free 24 |
| 2 p.m.  | Free 4 | Free 9 | Free 13 | Free 19 | 2.3     |
| 3 p.m.  | 6.5    | 2.4    | Free 14 | 2.5     | Free 25 |
| 4 p.m.  | Free 5 | 1.5    | Free 15 | Free 20 | Free 26 |

Exit | Main | Back

**Figure 3**
Grid Structure

## 2. 4 Information Retrieval Structure

| Name  | Farmer          |
|-------|-----------------|
| Dept  | Information Sys |
| Time  | 9.00            |
| Day   | Monday          |
| Room  | 1.4             |
| Group | BSc Comp Sci 1  |

Exit

Main

Back

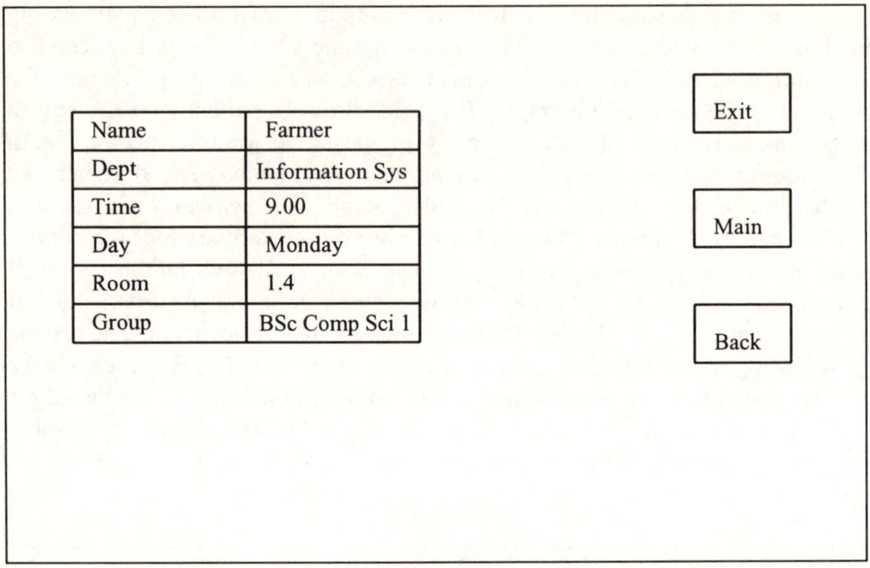

**Figure 4**
Information retrieval structure

Figure 4 shows an information retrieval structure, this is different to the other structures that have been defined above, in that no interaction can occur with the structure. It is strictly a viewing structure. Although the appearance of the structure is similar to a name structure, they do not cause traversal to levels in the hierarchy below the information retrieval structure. Hence, the information retrieval structure plays an important role in the hierarchy. It acts as a termination state for the branch in the hierarchy that it is a part of. It also provides information to the user that may not be available at other levels in the hierarchy. For example, information further up in the application hierarchy may contain information such as the room that the lecturer may be teaching. The information retrieval structure will provide further information such as the group that is being taught and the number of students.

## 2.5 Label Structure

An additional structure which also provides the user with information is called the label structure. It is in some respects similar to an information retrieval structure in that no interaction occurs with this structure. Instead its aim is to provide the user with information about the structures. For example, a grid structure without a label structure is simply a collection of squares across and squares down with no apparent meaning, except for text labels which appear within each grid. The label structure puts further meaningful information above each grid structure and beside each row if it is required, to inform the user the meaning of the grid arrangement. For example, in the scheduling of rooms in a University, a five column grid with eight rows would represent days for each of the columns and each of the rows would be a representation of times within that day from 9.00 a.m. to 4.00 p.m. This is shown in figure 3. Both information retrieval structures and label structures are indicated in different colours to denote that no interaction is possible. This saves user interaction time if they know that interacting with those structures will have no effect.

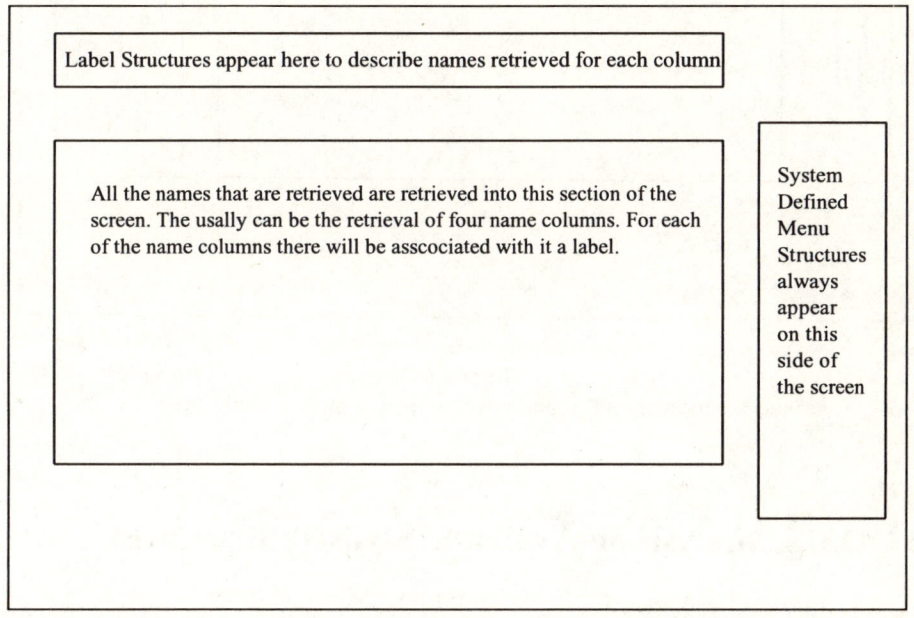

**Figure 5**
General appearance of a label structure with respect to a name retrieval structure

Figure 5 and figure 6 show a generalised view of the location of a label structure with respect to grid structures and name structures, which are the only two structures which accommodate label structures. Figure 5 show the general view of a name structure. Labels only appear above each of the columns in a name structure (one label for each of the name columns). Figure 6 shows the location of label structures where a grid is being used. The normal layout for labels with respect to a grid structure is above each column grid and along each row grid, as is the case with spreadsheets, where the column cells are labelled with letters and the rows are labelled with numbers.

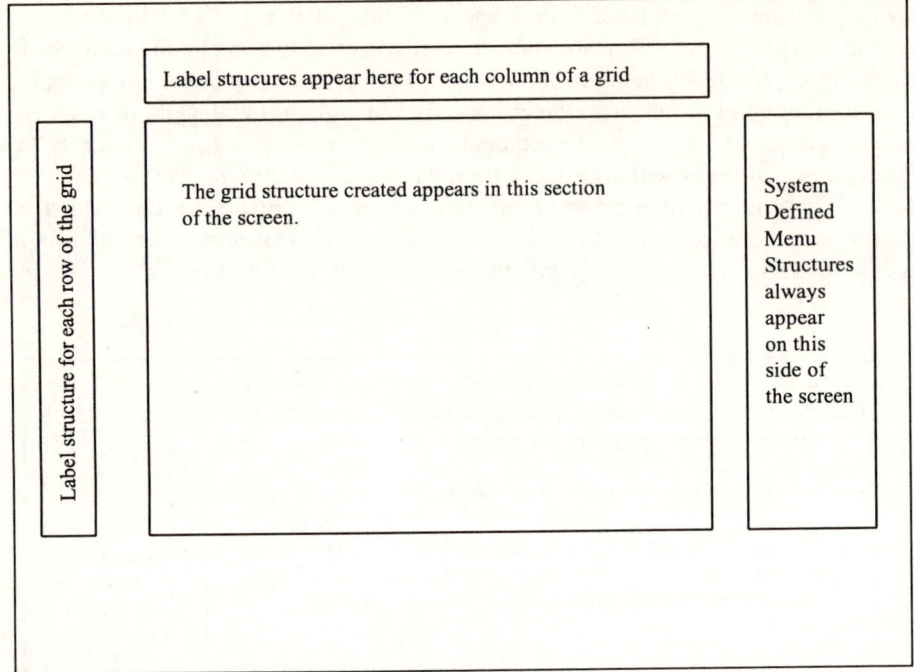

**Figure 6**
General appearance of a label structure with respect to a grid structure

## 3 GOMS Analysis on Available Stylised Structures

This section shows the GOMS analysis of the structures that are available in DRAGEN. The example shows the GOMS analysis for one of the structures, and shows all the possible structures that can be created from that structure. The GOMS/CCT analysis is also carried out on the structure to show the created production rule set for the structure on a particular screen.

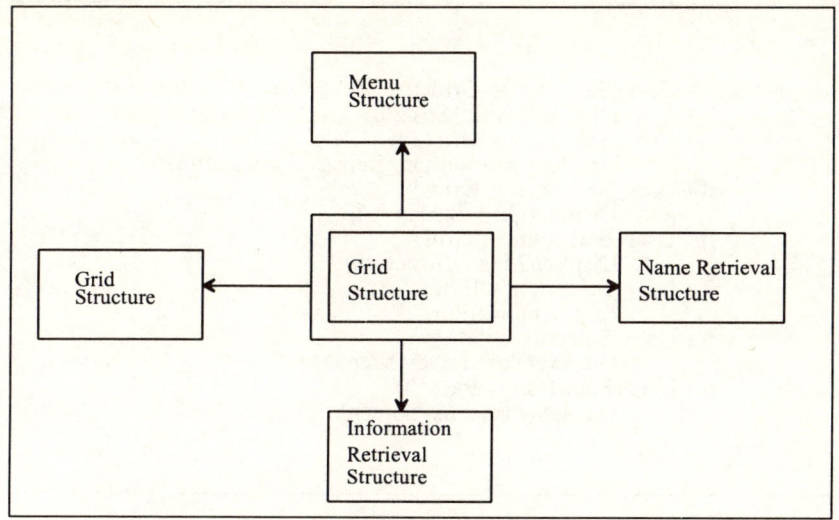

**Figure 7**
Available structures that can be created from a grid structure

Figure 7 shows that if interaction was to occur with a grid structure then the structures that can be created are a menu structure, another grid structure, a name retrieval structure or an information retrieval structure. Figure 8 demonstrates this by showing a two by two grid to illustrate the different structures that can be generated from a grid structure.

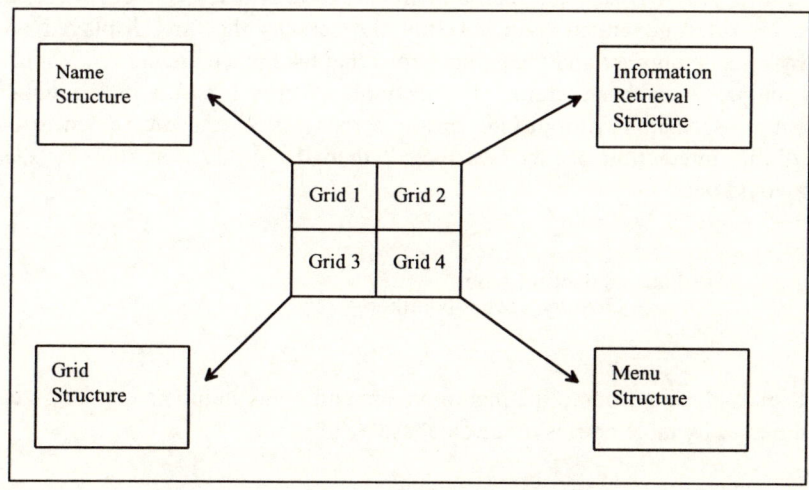

**Figure 8**
Example showing structures that could be generated from a grid structure

```
if ( User_Selection = 'Grid 1')
        Display(Name_Structure);
if ( User_Selection = 'Grid 2')
        Display(Information_Retrieval_Structure);
if ( User_Selection = 'Grid 3')
        Display(Grid_Structure);
if ( User_Selection = 'Grid 4')
        Display(Menu_Structure);
if ( User_Selection = 'Exit')
        Exit_Application;
if ( User_Selection = 'Main')
        Display(Top_Level_Menu);
if ( User_Selection = 'Back' )
        Display(Previous_Screen);
```

**Figure 9**
Generated GOMS/CCT production rules

In figure 9 when the user selects the appropriate grid structure icon, traversal occurs to a screen which displays the appropriate structure. If the user selects grid 1 then traversal to a name structure occurs; if grid 2 is selected then traversal to a information retrieval structure occurs; if grid 3 is selected a grid structure is displayed; and if grid 4 is selected then a menu structure is displayed. However, in the production rules generated by DRAGEN the screens that are displayed are identified by a scene number and the comparisons that take place are numeric values which are unique to each structure. For example if grid 1 had a pick number (number that is associated with an icon on the screen) of 35 and the screen to be displayed if this interaction occurs is screen 7 then the production rule for that interaction would be:

```
if ( User_Selection = 35)
        Display(Scene_Number = 7 );
```

If required for analysis purposes the pick numbers and scene numbers can be given meaningful names by table entries in the database

# 4 Design Process

## 4.1 Analytic Design

The stylised menus allow the standard design process [22, 23] to be simplified. The four stages of the iterated process can be described as follows:

- Stage 1 is effectively carried out with the aid of DRAGEN. The designer breaks down the allowed information into a hierarchical set of database queries. These queries are implemented using the available structures within DRAGEN.

- Stage 2 is carried out by the designer specifying goals and DRAGEN generating the GOMS/CCT detailed analysis.

- Stage 3 and 4 are handled by the interactive part of DRAGEN following the standard production rule model [Kieras & Bovair, 1986]. From the generated GOMS/CCT of stage 2 performance and predicted times can be generated for novice users. This means that the interface generated can only predict behaviour in an aggregate sense.

The four steps are iterated until a satisfactory model is obtained.

## 4.2 Use of DRAGEN in the Design Process

The design process is considered to be carried out by a domain expert with regard to the database. Considerable knowledge of SQL is required. In terms of the interface the designer must have knowledge of the types of menu available. Since the interface is highly stylised there is very little to learn in this respect.

For a given task there exist queries and sub queries which allow the user to select the correct icons from the generated interface for the types of interface generated. The example below demonstrates how the designer generated the queries and sub- queries which allow the user to make the correct choices to reach the desired goal.

A typical example could be to browse the interface to locate room 1.1 on floor 1 on Monday at 9.00 a.m. to see whether the room was occupied. The user would first select room from the menu illustrated in figure 1. This would cause traversal to another menu which contains a list of all possible floors ranging from floor 1 to floor 5. The example states that the room is on floor 1, hence the user selects the appropriate menu box, this causes a grid structure, as shown in figure 10 to be displayed.

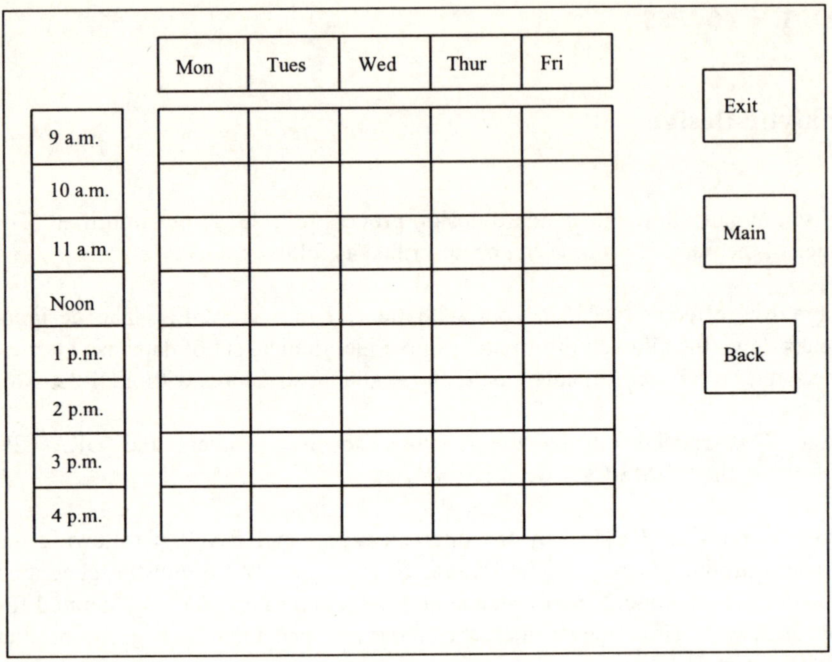

|        | Mon | Tues | Wed | Thur | Fri |
|--------|-----|------|-----|------|-----|
| 9 a.m. |     |      |     |      |     |
| 10 a.m.|     |      |     |      |     |
| 11 a.m.|     |      |     |      |     |
| Noon   |     |      |     |      |     |
| 1 p.m. |     |      |     |      |     |
| 2 p.m. |     |      |     |      |     |
| 3 p.m. |     |      |     |      |     |
| 4 p.m. |     |      |     |      |     |

[Exit]  [Main]  [Back]

**Figure 10**
Grid structure prompting the user to select a cell for a specified day/hour.

An SQL query would be required to retrieve information into the grid structure specified. The designer is constrained by the required task to break down the queries so that the required information is displayed in a suitable position corresponding to the user's expectations. The labels at the top of each of the columns and along the side of each row assist the user to realise what the contents of each of the grid boxes represent, and also assist the user to find the correct row/column combination (in the example Monday at 9.00 am). The designer is able to either carry out an SQL query for each row, or carry out a single query to retrieve the entire grid structure in one query and display the information in a suitable format. In this example the later option is chosen.

The associated SQL query is:

*Select TextForGrid*
*From DefaultGrid;*

DefaultGrid has been set up to contain the information relating to the grid shown in figure 10. From the designers point of view this speeds up the creation process when the same grid is to be displayed many times. In this instance no text is required and the grid structure is equivalent to having two menus one for each of the days of the week and the other for each of the times of the day. Instead, the user selects a day/hour combination for the specified floor to retrieve further information. The resultant screen is shown in figure 11.

When a single query is used, the designer is asked whether row and column labels are required. If the designer replies with yes then the designer is prompted for the number of rows. The designer in this case replies with eight (one for each hour from 9.00 to 4.00) which causes the output to appear with eight rows in each column. The total amount of information retrieved in this case is forty rows hence we have an eight by five grid. The designer is prompted for the 8 row labels and DRAGEN calculates the number of column labels that will be required.

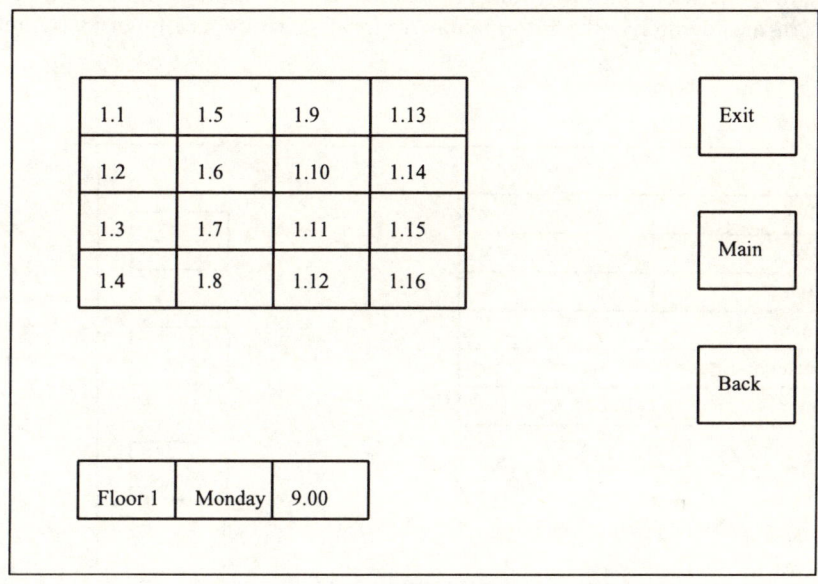

**Figure 11**
A grid structure caused by selecting grid box 9.00/Monday

The associated query for the retrieval of the above screen would be:

*Select RoomNumber*
*From RoomInfo*
*Where Day = 'Monday' and Floor = 1 and Time = '9.00'*
*Order by RoomNumber;*

Figure 11 shows another grid structure which is displayed when the user selected the grid with the labels 9.00 and Monday from figure 10. This shows all the rooms that are available for floor one at 9.00 on Monday. There would be 40 other similar screens to show information for different day/time slots for floor 1. Having a grid structure call another grid structure causes many rows to be put into the database to represent the information. In this example of a grid structure there are no labels along the top or along the sides. Instead labels at the bottom show the information that has been traversed to reach this screen; this reassures the user that they are at the correct location in which to retrieve the desired results. The query used for the retrieval of information for figure 11 is a single query which retrieves a four by four grid. The designer this time did not require row and column labels and instead opted for another form of label which is illustrated in the bottom left hand corner. The designer also specifies that each column will contain four rows, hence because sixteen rows are retrieved by the query the appearance is a four by four grid. The original question asked whether room 1.1 was occupied on Monday at 9.00 on floor 1. This requires the user to select room 1.1 from figure 11 causing traversal to the last screen in the hierarchy (the information retrieval structure as shown in figure 12).

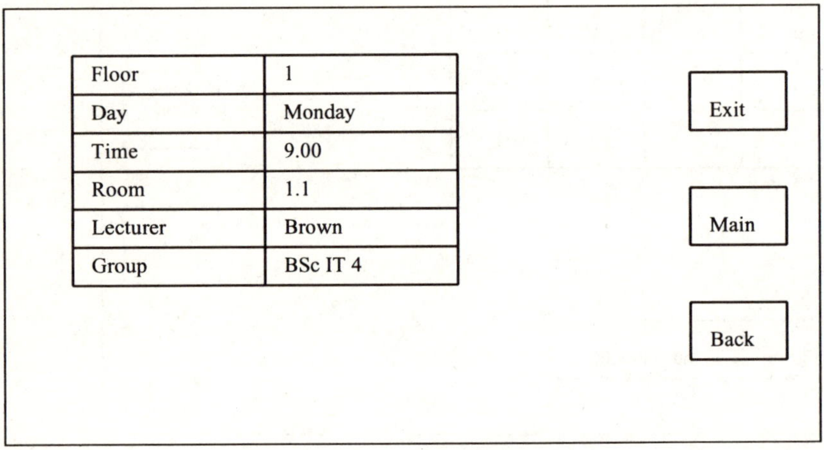

| Floor | 1 |
|---|---|
| Day | Monday |
| Time | 9.00 |
| Room | 1.1 |
| Lecturer | Brown |
| Group | BSc IT 4 |

Exit

Main

Back

**Figure 12**
An information retrieval structure caused by selecting room 1.1 from figure 11

Figure 12 shows an information retrieval structure. This is the last structure on that branch, hence no further interaction can occur. The user is only able to go back to previous levels in the hierarchy. The user has reached the desired goal to see who is in room 1.1 on Monday at 9.00 a.m. on floor 1, this was achieved by following the meaningful labels provided by the system.

The SQL statement to retrieve the information is:

*Select Floor, Day, Time, Room, Lecturer, Group*
*From RoomInfo*
*Where Floor = 1 and Day = 'Monday' and Time = '9.00' and Room = ?;*

The significance of the '?' is that this is a repeated query. In this case information retrieval structures were generated for all rooms on floor 1 at 9.00 a.m. on Monday (Figure 11). The above query retrieves all the information about room 1.1, and creates the appropriate information retrieval structure, then does the same for all the other rooms. This saves the designer valuable time by not having to enter the same query over and over again when only one variable changes, in this case room number. The question is replaced by the appropriate room number as the query is executed repeatedly.

## 5 The Database

An important characteristic of DRAGEN is its integration with the target database. The design technique applies to different styles of database. DRAGEN generates interfaces for a sample relational database (Ingres) and a sample object oriented database (ONTOS). In principle DRAGEN can be adapted for any database with a robust query language.

DRAGEN constructs the interface by creating tables and storing information within the database. This information is used by the runtime libraries to generate the interface. Thus all information to construct the interface is held in the database itself. This is the normal process in commercial interfaces such as Oracle Forms and Windows 4GL.

Changes to the interface are easily accommodated by updating the database, with the analytic model being updated simultaneously. This provides a flexible and responsive system for studying differing interfaces to obtain the same objectives within the restrictions of DRAGEN.

## 6 Summary

A prototype interface generation tool DRAGEN (Domain Restrictive Application GENerator) has been developed to generate naive/novice interfaces for point and click query systems. This allows quick and effective development of interfaces to database systems. Generated interfaces have been experimentally compared with the predictions of the corresponding analytic model and the results compared with the published literature. DRAGEN is now being used to test various hypotheses about variations in interfaces. In particular these studies are being used to give more detailed quantitative results related to the work on the relationship of design to user performance. Cognitive issues explicitly assume that the better design is the one that minimises the amount of complexity of the new knowledge necessary to use an application effectively [25, 26, 27, 28, 22].

DRAGEN has been evaluated by fifty subjects. Early statistical analysis of the results show that the two groups (Naive and Novice) have very similar response times to carry out the same task. This leads us to believe that the generated interface is of a 'walk up and use' variety.

Studies are also being carried out to relate the complexity of the queries required by the designer to the complexity of the resultant interface for the user.

# References

[1]  Polson, P.G. & Lewis, C.H., (1990). Theory-based design for easily learned interfaces, in Human Computer interaction, Vol. 5, pp. 191-220, Lawrence Erlbaum Associates.

[2]  Lewis, C., Polson, P.G., Wharton, C. & Rieman, J. (1990). Testing a walkthrough methodology for theory-based design of walk-up-and-use interfaces, in Empowering People Proceedings of the CHI '90 Conference on Human Factors in Computing Systems, pp. 235-242.

[3]  Trimble, J.H. & Chappell, D., (1990). A Visual Introduction to SQL, New York: John Willey & Sons.

[4]  Zloof, M.M., (1977). Query-by-Example: A database language, IBM Systems Journal, Vol. 16, pp. 324-343.

[5]  Huang, K.T., (1990). Visual interface design systems, in S.K. Chang (Ed.), Principles of Visual Programming Systems, Englewood Cliffs, NJ: Prentice Hall.

[6]  Gugerty, L., (1993). The use of analytical models in human computer interface design, in International Journal of Man Machine Studies, Vol. 38, pp. 625-660.

[7]  Card, S.K., Moran, T.P., & Newell, A., (1983), The Psychology of Human-Computer Interaction, Hillsdale, NJ: Lawrence Erlbaum Associates, Inc.

[8]  Kieras, D.E., (1988). Towards a practical GOMS model methodology for user interface design, in M. Helander, (ed.), Handbook of human computer interaction, pp. 135-158, Amsterdam: Elsevier.

[9]  Kieras, D.E. & Polson, P.G., (1985). An approach to the formal analysis of user complexity, in International Journal of Man Machine Studies, Vol. 22, pp. 365-394.

[10]  Bovair, S., Kieras, D.E., Polson, P.G., (1990). The acquisition and performance of text editing skill: a production system analysis, in Human computer interaction, vol. 5, pp. 1-48.

[11]  Vossen, P.H., Sitter, S. & Ziegler, J.E., (1987). An empirical validation of cognitive complexity theory, in H. Bullinger & B. Shackel (eds.), Human computer interaction INTERACT '87, pp. 75-82, Amsterdam: Elsevier, North Holland.

[12]   Olson, J.R. & Olson G.M., (1990). The growth of cognitive modelling in human computer interaction since GOMS, in Human Computer interaction, vol. 5, pp. 221-266, Lawrence Erlbaum Associates.

[13]   John, B.E. & Newell, A., (1987). Predicting the time to recall computer command abbreviations, in Proceedings of the CHI '87 Conference on Human Factors in Computing Systems, pp. 33-40, New York: Association for Computer Machinery.

[14]   John, B.E. & Newell, A., (1989). Cumulating the science of HCI: from S-R compatibility to transcription typing, in Proceedings of the CHI '89 Conference on Human Factors in Computing Systems, pp. 109-114, New York: Association for Computer Machinery

[15]   Olson, J.R. & Nilsen, E., (1988). Analysis of the cognition involved in spreadsheet software interaction, in Human Computer interaction, Vol. 3, pp. 309-350, Lawrence Erlbaum Associates.

[16]   Polson, P.G., Muncher, E. & Engelbeck, G., (1986). A test of a common elements theory of transfer, in Proceedings of the CHI '86 Conference on Human Factors in Computing Systems, pp. 78-83, New York: Digital Press.

[17]   Howes, A. & Payne, S.J., (1990). Semantic analysis during exploratory learning, in Empowering People Proceedings of the CHI '90 Conference on Human Factors in Computing Systems, pp. 399-405, Association for Computing Machinery.

[18]   Gentner, D. & Stevens, A.L. (Eds.), (1983). Mental Models, Hillsdale, New Jersey: Lawrence Erlbaum Associates.

[19]   Kieras, D.E. & Bovair, S., (1984). The role of a mental model in learning to operate a device, Cognitive Science, vol. 8, pp. 255-273.

[20]   Sutcliffe, A., (1988). Human Computer Interface Design, Macmillan Education Ltd.

[21]   Shneiderman, B., (1992). Designing the User Interface: Strategies for Effective Human Computer Interaction, Second Edition, Addison Wesley.

[22]   Polson, P.G., (1987). A quantitative theory of human computer interaction, in J.M. Carroll, (ed.), Interfacing Thought: cognitive aspects of human computer interaction, pp. 184-235, Cambridge, MA: MIT Press.

[23]   Gould, J.D. & Lewis, C.H., (1985). Designing for usability and what designers think, Communications of the ACM, vol. 28, pp. 300-311.

[24]　　Kieras, D.E. & Bovair, S., (1986). A production system analysis of transfer of training, in Journal of Memory and Language, vol. 25, pp. 507-524.

[25]　　Bennett, J.L., Lorch, D.J., Kieras, D.E. & Polson, P.G., (1987). Developing a user interface technology for use in industry, in H. Bullinger & B. Shackel (Eds.), Human Computer Interaction INTERACT '87, pp. 75-82, Amsterdam, Elsevier, North Holland.

[26]　　Card, S.K. & Newell, A., (1985). The prospects of psychological science in human computer interaction, in Human Computer Interaction, vol. 1, pp. 209-242, Lawrence Erlbaum Associates, Hillsdale, NJ.

[27]　　Hutchins, E.L., Hollan, J.D. & Norman, D.A., (1985). Direct manipulation interfaces, Human Computer Interaction, vol. 1, pp. 311-338, Lawrence Erlbaum Associates, Hillsdale, NJ.

[28]　　Norman, D.A., (1986). Cognitive Engineering, in D.A. Norman & S.W. Draper (Eds.), User Centred System Design, pp. 87-104, Hillsdale, NJ: Lawrence Erlbaum.

# Data Model Issues II

# A Graphical User Interface for a Cooperative Design Database

Marek Machura[*]

Department of Applied Computing and Electronics, Bournemouth University
Poole, United Kingdom

**Abstract**

A summary of a model of sharing objects in cooperative applications is presented first, followed by a brief description of a cooperative design environment. Information management tools (node browsers, node editors, event/status monitors) and their user interfaces are then presented. The design of cooperative user interfaces based on the adopted model of object sharing is discussed in more detail, with emphasis on monitoring changes to objects, physical and logical object locking, refreshing the application cache, supporting change propagation and maintaining data consistency.

## 1 Introduction

The graphical user interface presented in this paper was developed as part of a research project aimed at (i) investigating software techniques and tools for cooperative design environments and (ii) building a cooperative software framework for a specific design environment. Although the discussion revolves around a particular application domain, namely that of control system design, the examined issues are common to a broad class of cooperative applications [1]. Cooperative applications dealt with in this paper can be described as systems that support:
- common, distributed information space,
- highly interactive, cooperative work,
- long-lived transactions,
- various data representations (complex objects, rules, as well spatial, temporal and uncertain data),
- construction/composition and reuse of objects,
- version management,
- project control,
- location of objects by navigation (in addition to location by query), and
- access control.

---

[*] The work reported in this paper was funded by the Science and Engineering Research Council and carried out by the author at the Engineering Design Research Centre, Glasgow.

It is assumed that the above class of cooperative applications is based on an object-oriented data model in which objects are treated as units of consistency, concurrency and distribution. The primary goal of these applications is to support 'controlled simultaneous multi-user access to objects' [2], and thereby increase the degree of user cooperation. An important feature of such applications is the interplay of technical support for cooperation and human decision making.

Object-oriented database technology [3] offers a particularly suitable framework for the development of cooperative applications. The cooperative design environment described in this paper was implemented by means of the object database management system ONTOS DB [4]. The current generation of object management systems [5] does not provide adequate support for the development of cooperative applications. Not surprisingly, support for the construction of cooperative user interfaces is practically non-existent. A survey of main issues related to graphical user interfaces for object-oriented databases can be found in [6].

It is well known that the design and expressive power of a graphical user interface depends on the underlying data model [7]. Similarly, a model of sharing objects among users has a considerable influence on the design of a cooperative user interface and, as will be shown in the paper, adds significantly to its complexity. The characteristic feature of the proposed model of object sharing is that centrally scheduled transactions typical of traditional database applications are replaced by centrally provided change notification services and user-scheduled (local) actions [8].

The paper can be broadly divided into two parts. The first gives a summary of a model of sharing objects in cooperative applications, focussing on such issues as object locking, concurrency control and object change notification. A sample cooperative database application is then briefly overviewed, with emphasis on the structure of the database and a suite of information management tools that form the foundation of the application.

The first part of the paper serves the purpose of setting the scene for the presentation of a cooperative user interface. Although a specific user interface is used as an illustration, the paper aims to describe a general solution to the problem of building cooperative user interfaces. Three basic types of information management tools that constitute a cooperative user interface are identified, i.e. node browsers, node editors, and event/status monitors. The design of cooperative user interfaces based on the proposed model of object sharing is examined in more detail. The following design issues are discussed: retrieving objects and registering them for change notification, physical and logical object locking, refreshing the application cache, supporting change propagation, maintaining data consistency and closing windows. The paper concludes with some general remarks on further work in this area.

## 2  Model of Object Sharing

The proposed approach to object sharing encourages a shift from the centralized, server-based transaction processing to a more decentralized, client-based approach, thereby allowing the client application to play a more active role in concurrency control. Application-independent transaction processing is replaced by application-dependent processing of user actions. In particular, the detection of update conflicts is handled by the client application. Access to the database objects is controlled by users who decide by whom and in what order the necessary actions are carried out.

This section gives a summary of the model of object sharing. The proposed model attempts to create a decentralized framework for sharing persistent objects and, at the same time, provide central services for change notification. The main goal of client applications is to ensure that every user action preserves the intended semantics of objects shared by several simultaneous processes.

## 2.1 Object Locking

It is useful to make a distinction between physical and logical access control. Physical access is user-controlled and results in physical locks being allocated to selected database objects. Logical access, on the other hand, is controlled by the client application itself and is based on the properties of objects (no physical locks are allocated). This distinction is important, as by identifying objects that need not be locked physically, we can expect to reduce unnecessary network traffic.

*Physical access control* requires that shared objects be locked at the database level. Physical locks are allocated to objects in order to preserve data consistency for the duration of a user action. A physically locked object may be viewed, but it cannot be modified or deleted by other simultaneous processes.

A selected object is usually locked together with all its private objects, i.e. objects owned by the selected object. However, instead of locking the whole group of objects, the user can allocate a physical lock to the owning object only. When another process receives lock notification, it determines access rights to all private objects of the locked object using the logical access control mechanism.

*Logical access control* is based on user types, the properties of objects, such as object type or lock status of the owning object, and relationships between objects. In general, the following rules apply:

- Objects that may not be viewed by a given user will never be shared by this user with others.
- Objects that may not be modified or deleted by a given user can always be shared with others without having to allocate locks to them.
- Physically locked objects carry information indicating which of their private objects should be locked as well.

The logical locking rules, once established, are valid for a long period of time (usually for the lifetime of the database). They can be used by the user interface to disable certain operations and make certain data entry fields insensitive.

## 2.2 Concurrency Control

Cooperative database transactions are characterised by long duration and may very well span entire interactive sessions. This has obvious implications for the way in which transactions have to be managed: (i) a transaction should never abort as it might lead to an unacceptable loss of results, (ii) intermediate results should be made visible to concurrent transactions, and (iii) as much work as possible should be recovered in a crash. Maintaining data consistency in cooperative transactions is more complex than maintaining data consistency in conventional on-line transactions, since application-level correctness must be ensured.

Continuous update and sharing of data in a highly interactive multi-user setting cannot be implemented satisfactorily using the traditional database concurrency strategies which are based on the idea of serializing short transactions against a single copy of data. Current research in the field of transaction management concentrates on improving the degree of concurrency in database systems by allowing weaker notions of correctness than serializability and atomicity [9]. It seems, however, that extending the traditional transaction concepts to support cooperative work is not straightforward and leads to increasingly complex transaction management. Alternative approaches still need to be researched in order to improve concurrent access to shared information and simplify the development of cooperative database applications.

In general, a cooperative session can be treated as one long transaction with checkpointing being done at suitable points, e.g. at the time of closing windows, after operations which changed the arrangement of objects or the values of object attributes, or on user request. A cooperative session can thus be viewed as a series of actions of a length dictated by the interactive process. The governing principle is to break up the cooperative session into small logical actions and make the results of those actions immediately visible to all interested parties.

Physical locks are used as the means of concurrency control. As no locks are allocated automatically, it is the user's responsibility to lock temporarily those objects that should not be modified by other users. The user can unlock the locked objects, or the locks are released automatically when the user quits a given tool.

The proposed model of object sharing aims to minimize the number of locked objects by giving individual users a possibility to decide which objects and when to lock. However, if users are negligent about locking shared objects, conflicting updates may invalidate some parts of cooperative work. Although such situations will be rare[1], appropriate protection mechanisms must of course be built into the client applications. Prior to committing an action, the notification procedure (see the next section) is queried to find out whether any of the objects to be affected by this action have recently been updated by another process. If this is the case, the intended action is discontinued. In general, an action is not allowed to modify/delete an unlocked object that was modified by another user after it had been acquired by the given action.

The above model is basically a 'no-conflict' concurrency control model. If the user requests a lock for an object that is already locked by another user, then a warning is issued and the intended action cannot be carried out. Once all requested locks are allocated, the action cannot conflict with others.

## 2.3 Change Notification

The major element of the proposed model of object sharing is a mechanism for monitoring changes to shared objects and making these changes visible to all client applications. The obvious solution is to have a centralized server-based process (a publisher) that keeps track of changes made to database objects and sends appropriate messages to client processes (subscribers). Each client application tells the server which objects are to be monitored. When a requested object is changed, the publisher sends change notification to all interested subscribers.

The subscriber is expected to refresh its cache upon receiving notification. However, the cache is not refreshed each time new notification arrives. Instead, the publisher gathers all notifications addressed to a given subscriber in a special table,

---

[1] This remark is based on the observation that collaborators usually have a good idea of who is doing what, and that contention in high-granularity cooperative work is relatively infrequent.

called *notification table*. The refreshing of the cache takes place at a suitable point at the request of the subscriber.

Two operations are performed by the subscriber at refresh time:
- all changes recorded in the notification table are physically carried out in the cache, i.e. the contents of all modified objects are updated and all deleted objects are removed from memory, and
- references to all changed objects together with indications of how they changed (i.e. whether they were modified or deleted) are added to a special list called *changed object list*.

What operations are performed afterwards, depends on a particular process context and on the content of the changed object list.

## 3 Cooperative Design Environment

EDICS (Environment for the Design and Implementation of Control Systems) is a multi-tool software system operating on symbolic, textual and graphical representations at various levels of detail, and providing mechanisms for hierarchical system decomposition, version management and project control.

The crucial task in the EDICS design process is the construction of a system model upon which various design operations are performed. The structure of a system and the behaviour of its components are specified by means of so-called base system representations. The hierarchical modelling tools use those representations to generate a behaviour representation for the whole system.

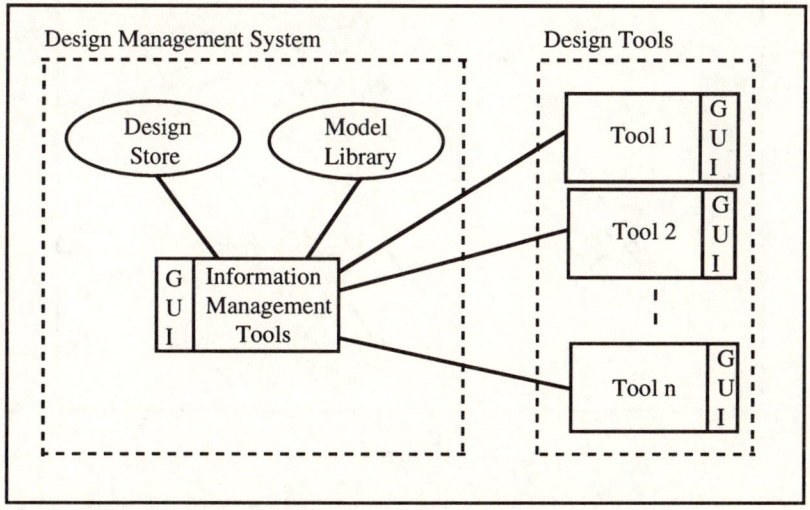

**Fig. 1.** Design support environment

EDICS consists of the Design Management System and a suite of design tools (Figure 1). The Design Management System is composed of three parts: the Design Store, the Model Library, and a collection of information management tools. The Design Store is a repository of all design objects created in EDICS, such as descriptions of design projects, component models, system models, system versions and other data associated with them. The Model Library stores re-usable models of components and subsystems which can be used as building blocks in the construction of models of other systems.

The information management tools are viewed as basic utilities of the environment. They organize the structure of design data and communicate directly with the Design Store and the Model Library. They provide a framework within which all other design tools are used, enabling designers to create, access and manipulate all objects in a uniform and consistent way. The information management tools (and some design tools) effectively implement the model of object sharing described in the previous section.

The design tools constitute the application-domain part of the environment and include behaviour representation editors, model transformation tools, simulation tools, model validation tools, fault diagnosis tools, etc.

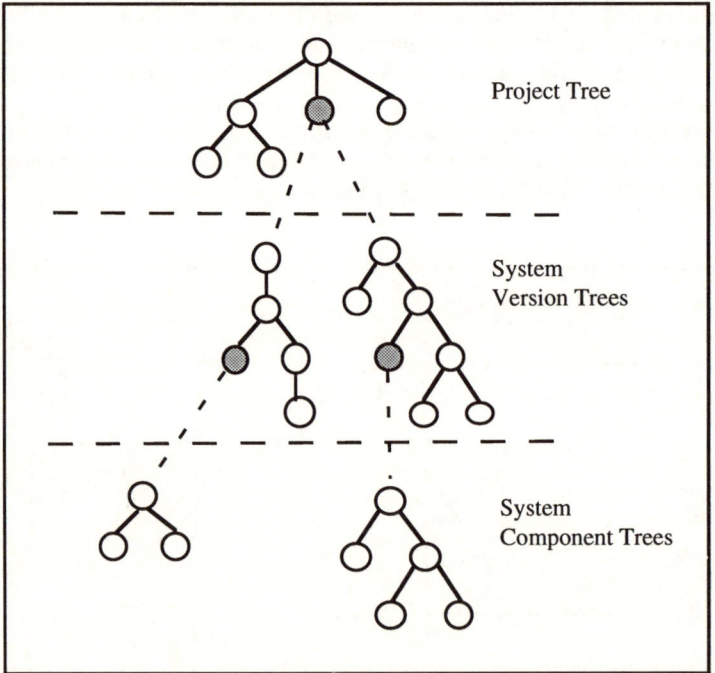

**Fig. 2.** Design Store tree

From the user's point of view, all design objects created and manipulated within EDICS are classified into three groups: (i) system components and system configurations, (ii) versions of system configurations, and (iii) projects. The Design Store can be viewed as a three-layered structure (Figure 2). Components stored in the lowest System Component layer are used to build system configurations. The System Version layer contains descriptions of system versions, each of which refers to a system configuration stored in the System Component layer. The Project layer contains descriptions of all projects defined in EDICS. Each project refers to a number of systems whose descriptions are stored in the System Version layer. Hierarchical organisation of the Design Store enables the user to access all objects by navigating along the branches of the Design Store tree. Direct access to all design objects is used consistently by designers and design tools.

The following operations can be performed on the nodes of the Design Store tree: adding a child node, adding a parent node, deleting a node (either terminal or non-terminal), deleting subtrees of nodes, defining/viewing node forms (structures containing node attributes), and opening nodes, i.e. accessing nodes in the Design Store layer below the current one (the shaded nodes in Figure 2 are open).

The following graphical tools support information management in EDICS [10]:
- Design Store Browsers (Project Browser, System Version Browser, System Structure Editor),
- Project Form Editor, Version Form Editor and Component Form Editor,
- Consistency Checkers,
- Library Model Browser,
- Model Class Editor,
- Document Editor,
- User Definition Browser.

Note that the System Structure Editor is treated as an information management tool ('system structure browser') that directly manipulates system components stored in the Design Store. In reality, it is a design tool whose purpose is to describe the architecture of a system and the interconnections between its components.

The use of tools in EDICS follows the browse/select/modify pattern typical of interactive database applications. Each user action is preceded by a browsing phase during which a large number of objects are displayed. Once an action has been carried out on the selected objects, the user returns to the browsing mode and the whole process is repeated. Other users who share the affected objects expect the modifications to be displayed immediately on their screens.

## 4 Cooperative User Interface

The diagram in Figure 3 shows the activation of the information management tools as seen by the user. The Main Menu Handler activates the Project Browser, the Library Model Browser, and the User Definition Browser which provides access to the descriptions of all registered users. The Main Menu Handler performs a number of other functions, such as:
- logging in the user,
- initializing the environment (opening the database), and
- exiting the environment (closing the database).

Four graphical tools are provided to manipulate design objects in the database. Three of them, the Project Browser, System Version Browser and System Structure Editor, serve to retrieve objects from the Design Store; the Library Model Browser retrieves objects from the Model Library. The Design Store browsers enable the designer to access objects in the respective layers of the Design Store. In order to do so, the System Version Browser can be activated for a selected project from within the Project Browser. Similarly, the System Structure Editor can be activated for a selected system version from within the System Version Browser.

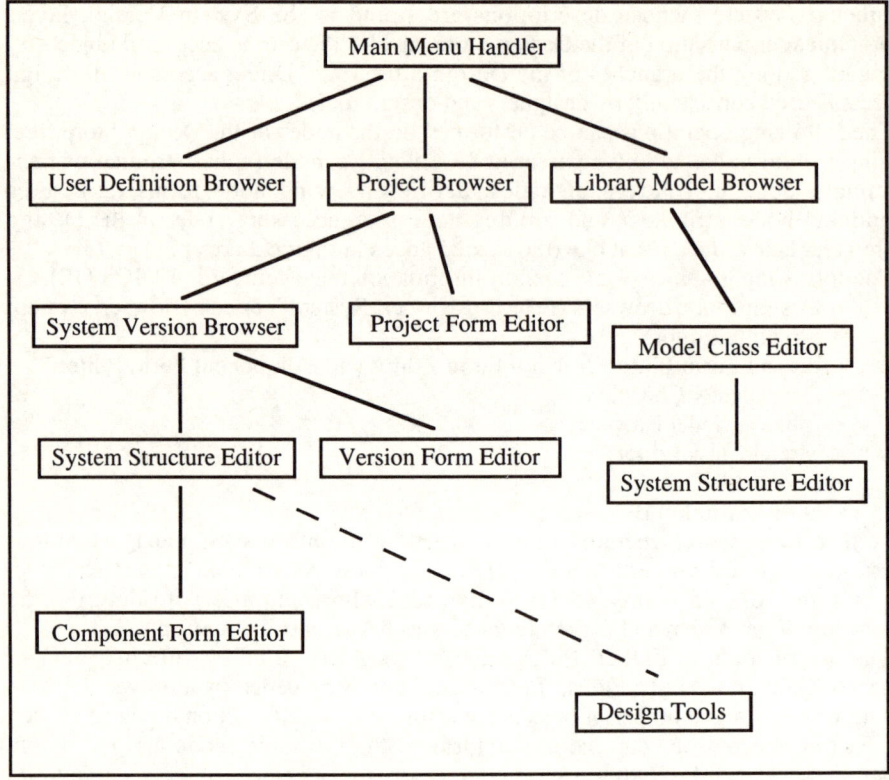

**Fig. 3.** Tool activation diagram

Node forms associated with tree nodes are handled by form editors. A separate form editor is provided for each type of node: project, system version, system component and model class. Note that the System Structure Editor can also be activated by the Model Class Editor to view the definition of a system model.

The activation of some information management tools is not shown in Figure 3. The Consistency Checkers are automatically invoked whenever object attributes are updated and prior to the activation of certain design tools. The Document Editor is invoked from within the node form editors. All design tools, including the behaviour representation editors, are activated for a selected component node from within the System Structure Editor.

In general, three types of information management tools can be identified in cooperative design environments: node browsers, node editors and event/status monitors.

## 4.1 Node Browsers

Node browsers enable users to retrieve, view, add and delete database objects. Due to their similarities, all four node browsers used in the environment are implemented as one tool.

The user interface of the System Version Browser is shown in Figure 4. Two systems *ModSys* and *CORS* are part of project *DEV*. They are the root nodes of the corresponding version derivation trees (only the derivation tree of system *ModSys* is expanded). When the user presses the View button for a selected system version node, the Version Form Editor is activated and the corresponding node form is displayed. The user can add a new system to project *DEV* or derive a new system version from an existing one by pressing the Add/Derive button. The Add Parent button is permanently disabled. Similarly, the Delete button is always disabled for non-terminal versions since all non-terminal versions are by definition immutable. The project manager can make a terminal version immutable using the Freeze button. The Who button serves to identify all users who are currently working on a selected system version.

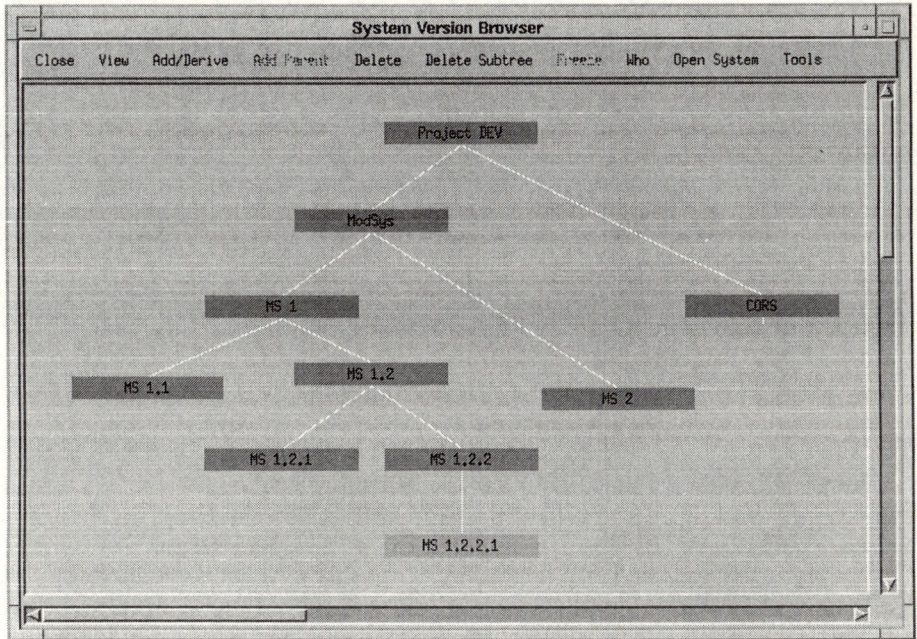

**Fig. 4.** System Version Browser

When the user selects version node *MS 1.2.2.1* and presses the Open System button, the System Structure Editor for the chosen system version is activated (see Figure 5). System version *MS 1.2.2.1* consists of component *A* and subsystem *B*, which in turn consists of components *Bx* and *By*. The Copy and Paste buttons enable the user to copy a selected component, or a whole subsystem consisting of several components, either within the same System Structure Editor or between the System Structure Editors activated for different system versions. The Behaviour Editor is a design tool that is used to specify behaviour representations for terminal component nodes.

The node browsers enable users to follow navigation paths determined by the existing node hierarchies (or node networks in general), as well as backtrack from the previously made selections. Since large collections of objects are typically involved, appropriate measures must be taken to accelerate the search processes. One of them is support for so-called 'set-at-a-time' navigation which allows the user to pursue many navigation paths in parallel by activating as many node browsers as required.

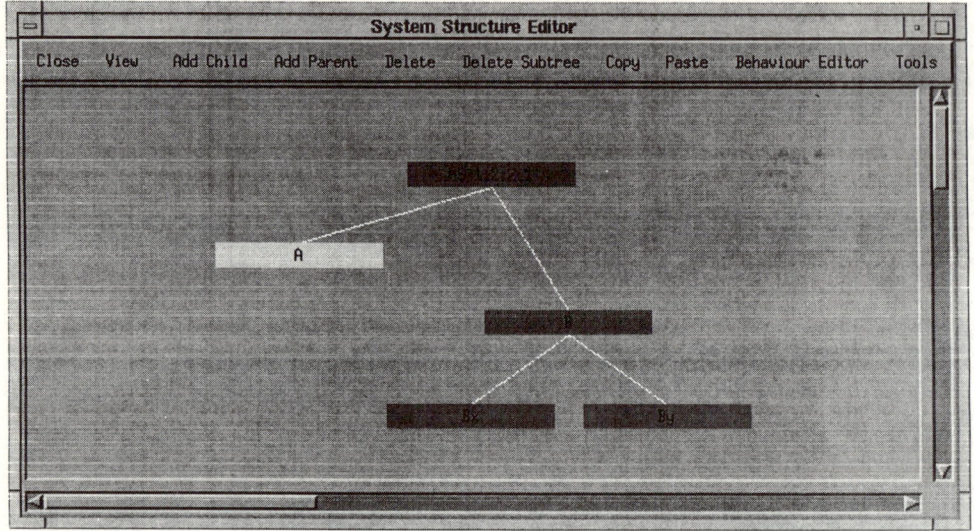

**Fig. 5.** System Structure Editor

Another important measure is to keep a record of selected nodes and their screen layouts. Nodes can be expanded/collapsed by making their immediate child nodes visible/invisible. The layout of nodes on the screen is determined automatically by the browsers, but the user may choose to change it by moving some nodes to new locations. In order to be able to re-create the screen layouts in subsequent interactive sessions, an indication of which nodes have been expanded or moved must be recorded in the database. Obviously, it is not necessary (if not impractical) to store this information for all node browsers activated by a given user, so only the screen layouts for the highest-level node browsers are kept in the database, i.e. the layouts for the Project Browser and several most recently activated System Version Browsers and System Structure Editors.

### 4.2 Node Editors

Node editors serve the purpose of manipulating node-related information. This includes node descriptions (forms) and other node-associated data, such as behaviour representations, derived behaviour representations, documents, drawings, user-provided test data, etc. In general, node editors can be divided into *node form editors*, *node representation editors* and *node document editors*. Node form editors and node document editors are regarded as general-purpose information management tools.

For example, when component *MS 1.2.2.1* is selected and the View button is pressed (see the System Structure Editor in Figure 5), then the Component Form Editor is activated and the respective component form is displayed. Figure 6 shows the description of component *MS 1.2.2.1* which includes, among other things, the definitions of its ports, and the connections between its ports and the ports of subcomponents *A* and *B*. A new connection definition is about to be added to the component.

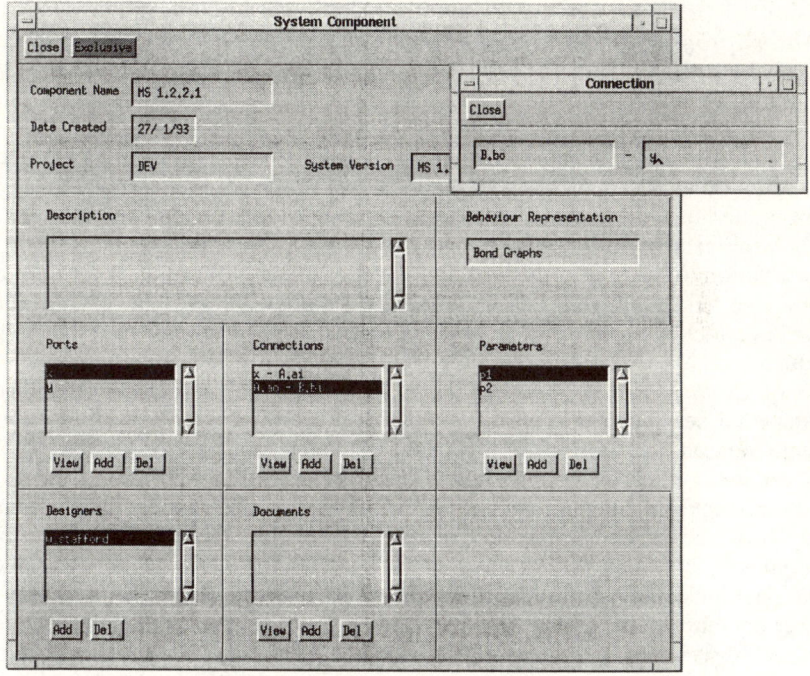

**Fig. 6.** Component Form Editor

Figure 6 also shows the way in which physical locks are applied to selected objects. When the Component Form Editor is activated for an unlocked component, the editor is started with the Lock button. When the user chooses to lock the selected component, the depressed Lock button changes to the green Exclusive button. When later on the user presses the Exclusive button, the lock allocated to the component is released, and the Exclusive button assumes its original appearance. Obviously, the lock can also be released by closing the Component Form Editor. When, on the other hand, the Component Form Editor is activated for a component that is already locked by some other user, the editor is started with the red Locked button instead of the usual Lock button.

When a node editor is activated for an object that is already locked, the logical locking mechanism is used to determine which related objects should be locked as well. When, for example, a form of some node is locked, all objects that represent the elements of this form are locked automatically. However, other representations associated with that node remain unlocked. This means that, in general, all node editors must provide their own Lock buttons to enable users to lock the associated representations individually.

## 4.3 Event/Status Monitors

Event/status monitors enable users to watch changes in and to make enquiries about the state of the environment. Examples of event monitors are work progress monitors and lock release monitors. An example of a status monitor is a lock owner monitor.

A *work progress monitor* sends the interested user a message each time a decision is made by a chosen collaborator. Here, by making a decision we understand writing (committing) new data to the database. In this way, the user is immediately notified of the completion of each successive action of his collaborator.

The purpose of *lock release monitors* is to check the status of objects that are locked by other users. As soon as the locks are removed, the interested user is sent appropriate notification which subsequently enables him to acquire exclusive access to those objects.

In addition to being informed that an object is already locked, the user may want to know who has actually locked it. *Lock owner monitors* track the identity of users who have locked selected objects. Based on this information, users can negotiate exclusive access to the contested objects. Note that the Who button of the System Version Browser (Figure 4) is not implemented as a lock owner monitor. Instead, it is a special service that keeps a record of all users working currently on a given system version, i.e. those users who have activated the System Structure Editor for this version.

The current implementation of EDICS does not include any event/status monitors. They could have been implemented by means of the ONTOS change notification mechanism, but then each EDICS object would have had to be equipped with additional lock status attributes. Since physical locks are dealt with internally by the object database management system, it is unreasonable to expect that cooperative applications should duplicate the lock mechanism for their particular purposes. Future object database management systems will undoubtedly, among other things, provide support for tracking the identity of users who are holding locks on selected objects, and for monitoring the progress of cooperative work by means of checkpoint and lock release notifications.

# 5 Design of a Cooperative User Interface

The following design and implementation issues are relevant to all information management and problem-domain tools which are to be equipped with cooperative user interfaces based on the proposed model of object sharing.

## 5.1 Retrieving and Registering Objects

The primary mode of locating objects in the design database is by link traversal. Browsing through a network of persistent objects is intimately connected with data retrieval. Consequently, the user interface is responsible for initiating database read operations (and database write operations for that matter as well).

As already mentioned, EDICS stores layouts of nodes for certain node browsers in order to accelerate browsing. These layouts are used to automatically retrieve objects from the database. Each tree node has a corresponding shadow node, called *graph node*. A screen layout is stored in the database as a collection of relevant graph nodes. A graph node describes the position of a node on the screen. It also contains a reference to the corresponding node object in the database. Graph nodes owned by different users may point to the same node object in the database, so if a particular node is deleted some graph nodes may be left with 'dangling' references. A cleanup service must be provided to remove graph nodes containing references to non-existent node objects.

Objects retrieved from a cooperative database are subject to change, so some (if not most) objects selected by a given user should be registered with the centrally provided change notification service. This is typically done at the time of making a retrieval request. From this moment on, all relevant change notifications are gathered in the change notification table associated with the given client application. The user interface must decide which objects need not be registered (e.g. some shared objects are immutable). Decisions of this kind are based on object types and user types.

## 5.2 Physical Locking

The cooperative interface must enable the user to physically lock objects for the duration of an intended action. It must also notify the user whether the retrieved objects are already locked by other users. As already explained, the Lock button is used to meet those two requirements.

The user interface sends a lock request to the database server when the Lock button is pressed. A lock request can be accepted or rejected. Object database management systems usually provide appropriate services for allocating physical locks to objects.

## 5.3 Logical Locking

Another responsibility of the cooperative user interface is to ensure that logical locks are applied to all objects designated by objects that are locked physically by other users. The current generation of object database management systems offers no support for logical locking, so this mechanism must be implemented by the developers of cooperative applications.

The logical locking rules can be implemented as user interface functions or, preferably, as methods associated with the relevant objects. The user interface calls these functions to find out whether it should disable certain operations or make some data entry fields insensitive.

## 5.4 Refreshing the Cache

There are two types of strategic point at which the application cache should be refreshed: (i) prior to opening a new window (browsers, forms, etc.), and (ii) before an action on selected objects is executed, i.e. before the objects are written to the database (data is usually saved at the time of closing a window). In both cases, the aim is to make objects in the application cache and their locks match exactly the current state of the database.

When opening a new window, the contents of all 'refreshed' objects are displayed and references to those objects (if any) are removed from the changed object list (see Section 2.3).

Different operations are required prior to executing an intended action. As already explained, the adopted model of object sharing ensures that no update conflicts occur even if a user fails to lock shared objects properly. To this end, the following *conflict detection procedure* must be adhered to:

- find out whether the selected objects, or any of their private objects that participate in the action, are on the changed object list, i.e. whether they have been changed by other users.

If this is the case, then

- discontinue the action and issue an appropriate warning,
- remove all references to the changed objects from the changed object list.

If no objects participating in the action have been changed by other users, then

- carry out the intended action.

The above procedure must be implemented by all cooperative user interfaces. Once appropriate environment-wide services are provided, this becomes a relatively straightforward task.

## 5.5 Supporting Change Propagation

The process of refreshing the cache is followed by a process called change propagation. The purpose of the latter is to ensure that the graphical representations of objects on the screen and the objects stored in the database match as closely as possible. Basically, two types of graphical objects must be considered: (i) spatial objects that consist of spatially arranged graphical elements, and (ii) text fields. If the user interface is notified that a spatial object (e.g. a node tree) has changed, the whole object must be re-displayed in accordance with its modified layout. If an attribute value has changed, the corresponding text field must be re-displayed.

The user interface must maintain two lists with references to graphical representations of objects: one storing references to spatial objects, the other storing references to text fields. In the case of node trees, only references to the root nodes are stored. There is no need to store references to graphical representations of objects that are immutable. Change notifications are used to identify references to graphical representations that need to be re-displayed.

## 5.6 Maintaining Data Consistency

The rules for maintaining semantic consistency of data stored in the database are provided by a particular problem domain [11]. Once established, the data consistency rules are usually valid for the lifetime of the database. They are typically implemented as services of the problem-domain classes.

Although many errors can be detected at the time of creating and updating objects (data correctness), the consistency of an evolving design can only be checked completely after the structure of the system and the behaviour of its components have been fully defined. In EDICS, the completeness checks are performed on model definitions (Component Nodes) only. These checks are automatically carried out prior to activating any of the hierarchical modelling tool. An example of a completeness rule is "The name of each component port must be used at least once in the connections of the parent component or the component itself."

Updating object attributes may make some of the existing model definitions inconsistent. Therefore the data consistency procedures are also responsible for maintaining consistency of all related objects. The contents of updated objects (if displayed) must be updated on the screen as well. For example, any change made to a Component Node definition causes automatic modification in all its related definitions. In particular, if a port is deleted from some component definition, all affected connections are removed from this component and its parent component.

The user interface usually 'knows' which graphical objects should be re-displayed when a local update takes place. If it does not, it can always fall back on the general change propagation mechanism described above.

## 5.7 Closing Windows

The user interface of a design environment must support simultaneous access to different parts of the project/version/component tree. On the screen, the nested node browsers are represented graphically as hierarchies of open windows (links between the browsers are traversed by opening new windows). The drawback of this approach to browsing is that the screen inevitably becomes cluttered with many overlapping windows.[2] Closing a large number of windows can be a cumbersome task as well, so some rules must be established to simplify it.

A number of related windows can be opened for a given browser window: a lower-level node browser, a node editor or simply a dialogue box. Instead of closing all open windows one at a time, the user may choose to close the owning window, and thereby close all its related windows automatically. A whole hierarchy of node browser windows with all its related windows can be closed in this way.

This seemingly simple process is, however, complicated by the fact that closing a window means also writing data to the database and performing some additional housekeeping tasks. These tasks are carried out by destroy callback functions associated with the windows. In particular, each window maintains a dynamically allocated data structure which stores references to all its open windows. If no subordinate windows are open, this data structure can be deallocated by the destroy callback function of the owning window. Otherwise, the deallocation must be deferred until the activation of a destroy callback function associated with the subordinate window which is closed last.

The destroy callback functions are also responsible for some additional housekeeping operations. In particular, object references stored in various lists must be removed and the lists themselves modified or deleted. For example, the lists maintaining references to graphical objects used in the change propagation procedure must be updated. Similarly, design objects that are no longer displayed need not be monitored by the change notification mechanism, i.e. the user interface should automatically withdraw the relevant change notification requests.

## 5.8 Summary of User Interface Tasks

1   Prior to opening a window for a cooperative tool, refresh the cache and propagate the changes reported by the change notification procedure. In case of a node browser, activate the cleanup service to delete graph nodes containing references to node objects removed from the database by other users.

2   Open the window.

---

[2]  The user interface should at least ensure that the same window is never opened twice.

3   If the window was opened for an object that is already locked by some other user, change the Lock button to the red Locked button and apply all logical locks (the window is open for viewing only).

4   Otherwise:
    4.1   On user request, lock the object and change the Lock button to the green Exclusive button.
    4.2   Carry out user actions.
    4.3   Prior to closing the window, check data for consistency.
    4.4   If any errors are discovered, issue a warning and return to 4.2.
    4.5   If the user did not request locks for the changed object, activate the conflict detection procedure:
          4.5.1   Refresh the cache.
          4.5.2   If the object in question was changed in the meantime by another user, issue a warning, propagate the changes, and go to 3.
    4.6   Write data to the database.

5   Close the window.

# 6  Conclusion

The purpose of the paper was to present a user interface developed for a particular cooperative application and, at the same time, to propose a general solution to the problem of building cooperative user interfaces. To this end, a model of sharing objects in cooperative applications was built. The characteristic feature of this model is that centrally scheduled transactions typical of traditional database applications are replaced by centrally provided change notification services and user-scheduled (local) actions. Based on the proposed model, the following issues were addressed: retrieving objects and registering them for change notification, physical and logical object locking, refreshing the application cache, supporting change propagation and maintaining data consistency.

In general, three models must be defined when developing graphical user interfaces for cooperative applications. First, a data model suitable for a particular problem domain must be chosen. Second, a model of human collaboration to be supported by the intended application must be constructed. Third, a detailed model of sharing objects within the cooperative application must be developed. Only then the work on the design and implementation of the cooperative user interface can begin. In our case, the model of object sharing was built in parallel with the application itself. Inevitably, several errors were made in the process. Probably, the most serious mistake was to develop a single-user prototype of the design environment first, instead of building a multi-user prototype right from the beginning. As a result, even though the problem domain requirements remained unchanged, the cooperative user interface had to undergo a significant re-design.

The cooperative user interface presented in this paper supports navigational access to database objects. It would be a worthwhile exercise to extend it with querying facilities and investigate its usefulness in other cooperative information systems. Another interesting task would be to examine a possibility of building a cooperative user interface framework, so that the connection between the cooperative user interface and the application is made easier. Needless to say that such a framework would have to be developed with some model of human collaboration and object sharing built into it.

**Acknowledgements**

Thanks to Arshad Mahmood for making available his Tree widget and implementing the node browser user interface.

# References

1.  Rodden T. *et al.* Supporting cooperative applications. Computer Supported Cooperative Work 1992; 1(1-2): 41-67

2.  Daniels J., Cook S. Strategies for sharing objects in distributed systems. Journal of Object-Oriented Programming 1993; 6(1): 27-36

3.  Bertino E., Martino L. Object-oriented database management systems: concepts and issues. IEEE Computer 1991; 24(4): 33-47

4.  ONTOS DB, Release 2.2, ONTOS, Inc.,1992

5.  Ahmed S. *et al.* Object-oriented database management systems for engineering: a comparison. Journal of Object-Oriented Programming 1992; 5(3): 27-44

6.  Kapel G., Min Tjoa A. State of art and open issues in graphical user interfaces for object-oriented database systems. Information and Software Technology 1992; 34(11): 721-730

7.  Schrefl M. Interfaces for advanced database systems: on the impact of data models. In: E.Batini (ed) A Bridge to the User, Proceedings of the 7th International Conference on ER Approach. North-Holland 1989, pp.41-46

8.  Machura M. Sharing objects in a design database system. In: Proceedings of the International Conference on Information Systems and Management of Data. New Delhi, 6-8 October 1993, pp. 218-228

9.  A.K. Elmagarmid *et al.* Introduction to advanced transaction models. In: Database Transaction Models for Advanced Applications. Morgan Kaufmann Publishers, 1992, pp. 33-52

10. Machura M. Design management tools and design processes in EDICS. Research Report, Engineering Design Research Centre, Glasgow, 1992

11. Machura M. Object manipulation and consistency maintenance in EDICS. Research Report, Engineering Design Research Centre, Glasgow, 1992

# Interfaces to Data Models: Taking a Step Backwards

Peter Barclay
Alison Crerar
Department of Computer Studies

Kirsteen Davidson
Department of Mathematics

Napier University, 219 Colinton Road
Edinburgh, EH14 1DJ
e-mail: {pete, mac}@dcs.napier.ac.uk

**Abstract**

This paper is concerned with data modelling and the question of how to improve the quality of software tools to provide more effective support for the modeller. With the increasing interest in building intelligent interfaces to databases and associated support tools, we thought it instructive to embrace human-computer interaction (HCI) concepts, particularly ideas of user needs analysis and methods of interface evaluation. In the pilot study reported here, we step back from implementation issues to learn more about what goes on during the modelling process. Three competent student modellers were filmed giving a spoken commentary as they tackled an on-line modelling task. Two subjects, ST1 and ST2 used a software tool developed in-house, while subject FC modelled the same scenario using a flip-chart. Analysis of the resulting video film yielded a number of interesting insights into how the three subjects approached the task, and in particular, about how their medium helped or hindered. In this report we concentrate mostly on subjects ST1 and FC who proved to be well matched in ability, neither evidencing any conceptual difficulties. The observations made from this preliminary experiment confirm the untapped potential of this technique among the database community. Moreover, on the basis of the findings, it seems that we have much to learn from going back to pen and paper, about the features a successful data modelling tool should provide.

# 1 Background

The need for better interfaces to database systems has been identified as a key area for research [Ston93]. We have been interested in object-oriented data models [BaKe91], exploring novel application areas [BaKe92], creating interfaces to these applications [BaFK92] and to the data model itself [Mull92]. However, it has become apparent that providing a 'good' interface to a data model is not as easy as it seems — attractive features can be implemented, but it is not clear what the user *needs*. For this reason, we have decided to take a step back from construction and evaluation of data model interfaces in order to gain a better understanding of what tasks the modelling process entails, and how these might be supported.

The work reported here is a pilot study to explore the potential of using video techniques, coupled with a speaking-aloud protocol (verbal commentary given by a subject while modelling), to elucidate the requirements for a successful data modelling tool. We deliberately avoid speaking just of the interface to a data modelling tool, as if it were a matter simply of bolting on the 'right' one. Though the functionality of such a tool may at first seem obvious (*e.g.* entities can be created, deleted, moved, named, associated and so forth), we find from studying modellers in action, that a full specification of requirements can only be completed after analysing the target users performing typical tasks. The related activities of profiling the user (user modelling) and decomposing the activities to be performed (task analysis) are often referred to under the heading of 'user needs analysis' [Lind94].

Speaking-aloud protocols are not a new idea, they have been profitably employed by cognitive scientists for 30 years or more, to study human problem solving in progress [Feig63], [NeSi72]. This early work on the automation of reasoning processes such as the construction of mathematical proofs, lead eventually to the development of knowledge based systems which captured expertise in the form of production rules. Speaking-aloud protocols have been extensively used in the AI community to elicit expertise for incorporating into knowledge bases. Lewis [Lewi82] is credited with having introduced the technique into user interface research, where it has been widely applied both for design and evaluation [Jorg90], [WrMo91]. Speaking protocols are generally recorded on audio or video tape for off-line analysis.

Like speaking protocols, videotaping is a technique that has been used by cognitive scientists both to study human performance and as documentary evidence of the behaviour observed, for future reference. With the proliferation of point and click software and the associated growth in concern for software 'usability', HCI researchers have used video extensively for capturing human-computer interactions; large software companies such as Microsoft now have usability laboratories where subjects are studied performing predefined tasks by means of video cameras and one-way mirrors [Whee92]. Split-screen video filming, used in the present study, is especially useful, providing a sound track (giving voice, mouse clicks, keyboard depressions, *etc.*), together with twin video windows, one showing the computer screen (from which operations and mouse movements can be followed) and the other showing the user's upper body (from which behavioural data including eye movements and facial expressions can be observed). Videotaping is the most effective way of capturing interaction data, it provides the opportunity to analyse and re-analyse the session and to time sequences of actions carefully off-line. Analysing video film is notoriously time consuming, but fortunately there is evidence to show that most usability problems detected will be found by a small set of testers. Nielsen and Landauer [NeLa93] reported that detection rates can be modelled by a Poisson distribution where the most favourable cost-benefit ratio is achieved with about four to six subjects; enlarging the sample size beyond this number yields very little additional information. Our previous work in the context of usability analysis has tended to confirm that finding [CrDa94], [Davi93].

In the database community there has been surprisingly little transference of methods such as these from cognitive science and HCI, despite overlapping interests in areas such as data modelling and an awareness in the literature of the relevance of HCI issues [Coop92], [Drap92]. The work described here is the first stage of an interdisciplinary project involving the database and HCI groups in an academic computing environment. The long term aims of this collaboration are concerned with finding out more about the nature of difficulties encountered during the process of data modelling, utilising these findings in the construction of supportive software environments and evaluating the effectiveness of the resulting tools. From teaching experience and industrial contacts we know that data modelling is widely found to be a difficult task. We are interested to explore the reasons why this is so, particularly in the case of object-orientation, which is claimed, on cognitive psychological evidence, to be compatible with human internal knowledge representation [Sull93]. There may be fundamental inadequacies with the models proposed, with the ways they are taught, with the computer-based tools that are used to design and manipulate the models, or with a combination of such factors. The systematic teasing apart of these possibilities is a major undertaking, but the potential impact of new findings makes it worthwhile to try.

Though the problems we have outlined have been acknowledged in the database community for some time, recent developments in programming environments have in some ways exacerbated the situation. In particular, the emergence of powerful graphical user interface (GUI) development tools [HaHi89] has made the implementation of sophisticated data modelling prototypes feasible even within the short time frame of an undergraduate project. In the Computer Studies Department at Napier University, and no doubt others are the same, we are spawning apparently high quality software tools for different modelling paradigms. Other research is focusing on increasing the generality of these tools so that they may support a variety of models [Coop90]. Using GUI development environments these products are relatively easy to modify and enhance, especially in terms of altering the interface. Thus, there is an ever widening gulf between the ability to construct complex software and knowledge about how to evaluate it and how to maximise its effectiveness from a user's point of view. In the database field, the ability to give a full and reasoned specification of requirements for modelling support tools lags well behind the pace of change in the software development arena: the means to build sophisticated interfaces relatively easily has arrived before we really know what to do with them. There is a need somehow to regain intellectual control and to be in a position to lead the advancement from the current generation of tools that *permit* models to be constructed, to tools that actively *support* the process; true 'tools for thought' [Wadd77].

## 2    Objectives

As a first step, and as a means of demonstrating the application of HCI techniques to the data modelling domain, we conducted an experiment using just three subjects. The purpose of this was twofold, firstly to establish some rough benchmarks on issues such as how complicated a scenario to present and how much a modeller can be expected to achieve in 30 minutes on camera, and secondly, to obtain some preliminary insights into how modellers go about the task using paper (flip-chart), compared with using a typical windows-based tool. We therefore decided to use competent student modellers as subjects. In this experiment we were not studying data modelling problems *per se*, but getting a feel for standards against which novices might later be measured, and for differences of approach that might be attributable to the media used. The reason for looking at flip-chart versus software environment was to compare the arguably 'natural' pre-computing paper and pen method with working at a VDU with mouse and keyboard. At this stage the details of the software tool are not crucial; this is not a usability study as such (*i.e.*, it is not an in-depth analysis of the usability of a particular product). We are taking a step back from interface details to ask, before arguing about the fine detail of automated tool design, is there anything more fundamental we are missing? Are there, perhaps, important aspects of traditional paper and pen working, that software tools in general have so far neglected?

## 3 Procedure

Three mature computing students who were known to be competent modellers, volunteered to take part in the study. Two of these subjects, ST1 and ST2 were asked to use a Windows-based software tool developed in-house, to produce their models, while the third, FC, was asked to work at a flip-chart. ST1 and ST2 were given copies of the software prior to the experiment so that they could familiarise themselves with it; they were also given written instructions containing the minimum operation set that would allow them to complete the experimental task, *viz.* creating an entity (object), labelling an entity, creating a relationship (association), labelling a relationship, indicating the degree of a relationship, creating attribute (property) lists for entities and editing the diagram (moving, deleting, re-sizing). The implementation of these operations in the tool used is similar to that of commercial modelling tools such as **team***work*/IM [Cadr90]. Although our main interest is in object-oriented data models, in this study our subjects were invited to use an extended entity-relationship approach (EER) adding optional use of subtyping/inheritance to the basic approach of Chen [Chen76]. A textual scenario was created (see Appendix I) using a familiar domain, that of the library, from which the subjects were required to construct an EER diagram.

The subjects were filmed consecutively, the same afternoon, with no opportunity for collaboration. ST1 and ST2 were filmed split-screen, as described above, so that there were twin windows on the resulting video, one showing the computer screen and the other showing the modeller. FC, who stood at the flip-chart, was filmed full screen, which captured both him and his model very adequately. At no time did the researchers discuss supplementary use of paper and pen with ST1 and ST2 who were assigned to the software tool; we were interested to see what would happen. ST1 arrived with pad and paper which he placed purposefully beside the computer; he obviously felt the need for it and did not consider asking permission to use it. The researchers made no comment about this. ST2 was more tentative in asking if he would need paper and pen; we neither encouraged nor discouraged him. All three subjects were required to give a speaking-aloud protocol, or verbal commentary as they worked. The purpose of the study was explained to the subjects, in particular, the two subjects using software were aware that we did not want an appraisal of the product they were using, but a commentary on the thought processes they were going through in formulating an EER model.

Each subject was filmed for 30 minutes. The subjects did not see the scenario until filming began. During filming the third author sat beside each modeller. Her rôle was to give them somebody to explain their thinking to, and to intervene occasionally when she felt she could elicit a little more information than the subject had verbalised spontaneously. These interjections were few, and consisted of prompts such as "Describe what you mean by that a bit more" and echoing a phrase by the modeller to encourage elaboration. The second author was present to ensure standardisation of procedures and to observe the sessions from the control room. Both experimenters made notes during the interactions, which allowed the most interesting parts of the films to be located quickly during later viewing sessions[1]. While on-line observations guided subsequent analysis, the entire videos and portions of them were re-run several times to collect detailed timings for sequences that turned out to be important, to glean deeper insights into thought processes from the commentary and to seek quantitative information (such as number of primitive operations required to achieve a high level objective, *e.g.* creating an entity).

## 4 Observations

This section outlines the main observations about the subjects' interactions with their supplied modelling media. Prior expectations were that the computer-based tool would provide a more convenient medium for the construction of the diagram, since it allows easy re-arrangement of layout and obviates the need to re-draw. We suspected, though, that the software environment might prove to be a constraining medium by comparison with the flip-chart, the latter allowing freer expression, and thus perhaps valuable insights into the process of modelling. This prediction was borne out; however, we emerged from the study chastened by the realisation that there is a great deal more to be learned from paper and pen that we imagined, not just as a means to studying the process of modelling, but as a means to eliciting software interface requirements.

### 4.1  Observations of Flip-Chart Use

The entire output of subject FC, who used three pages of an A2-size flip-chart, appears photo-reduced as Appendix II. FC gave a very fluent monologue; he treated the third author as an audience and modelled in the style of a tutorial presentation. FC put pen to paper almost as soon as he had finished reading the scenario. He started out by drawing the entities Book (Bk) and Paper (Pr), which he felt were central to the whole system. He then worked on the attribute lists beneath, starting with the attributes of Book and Paper and later adding those for Copy and Book key/Subject key (BkSk).

To give an example of the information FC was able to give as he modelled we include a short transcript. Here FC is explaining why he is keeping the

---

[1] We highly recommend having two researchers present during filming. The interchange of ideas between observers who have viewed the sessions live can be very enlightening; moreover, agreement about the key observations greatly assists in directing subsequent analysis.

entities Bk and Pr separate and how the need for the attribute Book-number (Bk-no) arises.

> "There's not a lot in common between books and papers, so I'm going to keep them as separate entities. For each book, if I tabulated books as being a copy of a book there would be a lot of duplicate information, so instead I could give a book a number ..."

After completing the first page of Appendix II, FC removed the sheet from the flip-chart, laid it face-up on the floor and proceeded with sheet two. On the second sheet he began by transcribing his two entity boxes, scaled down in size to accommodate the forthcoming elaboration. It was interesting to watch the way he worked through the notion of Location. This was first modelled as an entity, FC jotting himself a freehand note as a reminder that this related to *who* had the item. After adding the relationship between Person (Pers) and Room, FC realised that Location was redundant. He therefore crossed it out and connected Copy (Cp) direct to Person. The deliberate actions of crossing out and drawing the relationship line vertically through the Location entity together with the real time verbalisation were mutually reinforcing. Later, as he worked on sheet three, FC referred back to this second sheet (which was now beside the first, on the floor) as he went through the final refinement to subsume Room as an attribute of Person. It was clear to the observers, that having the history of his interaction visible at all times was very helpful in maintaining FC's stream of thought.

The transition from sheet two to sheet three (16 minutes after the start) was particularly interesting. At first glance there seems to have been a considerable re-arrangement. This all happened very spontaneously, FC had the shape of the final version in his head before he started drawing and we were struck by the graphical commentary that accompanied it:

> "Copy is going to be central. We're going to have the Subject, then two sister entities Book and Paper, which only differ in their attributes, but otherwise can be treated in the same way."

Video analysis allowed us to discover that the centrality of Copy (Cp) was something that FC had identified (and verbalised) just after deleting Location on sheet two. In the re-drawing of the diagram on sheet three, two interesting things were observed. The first was the rotation of the leftmost three entity boxes clockwise through 90°, a transformation that FC had performed mentally, but which one would probably not think to support in a software tool. The second concerned the oblong box FC used to embrace both Book (Bk) and Paper (Pr) as instances of an entity Publication (Pub) (he suggested that they might share the same record structure, perhaps using JVol as a switch). Of course, such an oblong, with annotation, is not a part of the formal EER notation, but it was a useful *ad hoc* representation of his proposed operation. Although he was digressing into implementation details[2] here, his approach

---
[2] His idea of utilising a single record for Book and Paper, as shown in the attribute list on his third sheet of working (Appendix II) is neither a modelling issue, nor a technique we have advocated. On retrospective protocol it emerged that he had recently been reading a paper where two record types had been merged in this way for compression reasons.

alerted us to the need for a high level representation for operations such as the merging of two entity types.

To summarise, refinements were made by two means. The first was the use of additions and scorings-out on the page of the flip-chart currently in use. The second was by copying (with rearrangement) the model from the current page onto a new one. Each page of the chart thus documented one version in the history of the model, with a complete record of the history of changes by which that version was derived from the previous one. Such an approach might be called 'multi-page working', indicating that at each successive stage the modeller has a current and some previous version(s). The extent of this is indicated by the video analysis of head movements, which shows that FC made 17 consultations of the first page while working on the second, and 18 consultations of the previous two pages while working on the third. Pages one and two were arranged on the floor so that all previous workings were visible to the modeller.

In his working, we were particularly impressed by the ease with which FC could interrupt a task such as completing an attribute list to annotate the diagram, returning afterwards to the place he had left off.

## 4.2 Observations of Software Tool Use

It is interesting to note that both subjects filmed using the software tool, ST1 and ST2, made initial notes on paper, spending nearly 10 minutes each on this; the preliminary jottings of ST1 are shown in Appendix III. Recall that the researchers were careful neither to encourage nor discourage the use of paper. This suggests that these two users did not feel that the tool was either appropriate or convenient for formulating their initial ideas. Though ST1 and ST2 spent a significant proportion of their allotted time using paper, they both switched to the modelling tool without prompting. Clearly it would be senseless to use a software tool if all working were done on paper and the tool used merely to document the results! Fortunately, our observations do not indicate this to be the case; however, Appendix III shows that ST1 had done a great deal of his analysis by the time he felt ready to transfer this information to the tool. The observers were struck by the duplication of effort involved in entering the data (rather akin to using a word processor as a device to input a finished hand-written document, instead of as an aid to its creation).

ST1 is an avid computer-user working daily in a Windows environment, so we asked him retrospectively about his use of paper. He was clearly surprised it was noteworthy. He replied that working on paper one does not have to think about operating another device and that the act of moving the mouse away from the place you want to work, to a menu, for example, destroys the thought process. *ST1, a highly competent computer user was aware of the extra cognitive load software tools impose over pen and paper.* A throw away remark was "Paper, same interface every time!"

Having sketched out the major components of his model on paper, ST1 on moving to the software tool, straight away created a stack of five blank entity boxes, by rapid clicking, then dragged them out into place following his sketched model, and began to label them. In stark contrast with FC's performance, the authors were impressed with the amount of work ST1 had to do to effect his entity labelling, attribute lists and relationship connections. These operations often involved him being three windows deep — far removed both physically and we suspected cognitively, from the diagram that lay (invisible) beneath.

A related observation regarding the transition from paper to screen concerns subject ST2, who created several entity boxes, arranged these and linked them with their relevant relationships — all while the boxes remained unlabelled! The reason was that he was employing multi-page working, his previous version being on paper, and his current version on screen. Thus he knew which entity type each box represented because it corresponded spatially to his paper diagram which was fully annotated. This shows a reliance on the paper similar to ST1's.

However, ST1, having transferred his model from paper to screen, deftly performed several refinements that showed the tool to advantage, including rearranging and scaling the model. His interaction did, though, point up some potential short-comings of the medium. At one point he realised that the two entity types Book and Article in his diagram should have a common supertype Item; the corresponding rearrangement of the diagram was not simple since it had to be effected by a sequence of simple operations such as add entity, add generalisation arc, add attribute, add relationship, remove attribute and remove relationship. Interestingly, the original paper-based version already contained this inheritance (see Appendix III), but ST1 on transferring to the software tool simplified out his first analysis, feeling that somehow this would make the entities clearer to see. He said on film:

> "It's maybe not really necessary to have book and paper as separate entities. I've done it this way because I can see what I've got in my model. I thought it would be better to get an overview then go back and fill in the detail."

## 4.3 A Comparison of Flip-Chart and Computer-Based Working

Use of the flip-chart supported two methods of refinement: amending the current page, and copying with rearrangement onto a new one; the software tool supported only the former method. Thus, the flip-chart maintained the history of working on each page, whereas this information was lost using the modelling tool. Here, the main disadvantage of the paper-based approach is the overhead of copying unaltered portions of the model from the previous to the current page. In the present study, this alleviation of the need to copy unaltered information across versions (or, equivalently, the ability to rearrange the diagram incrementally on-screen) seemed to be the major advantage of the software tool over the flip-chart.

Another potential advantage of the tool was the ability to hide unnecessary information (such as details of attributes) on the main diagram where not required. A reasonable tool might support various levels of abridgement [HGPN92], such as allowing all attributes to be hidden, all attributes to be displayed, or attributes of specified entities only to be displayed (the tool used in this study supported only the first and second alternatives). However, at least for this small model, subject FC using the flip-chart achieved nearly the same functionality by writing the attributes at the foot of the page, where they did not clutter the diagram, but were available for inspection. Further, the tool would need to provide operations such as 'indicate all entities with an attribute of this name', and 'globally change the name of this attribute wherever it appears' to ensure that hiding attribute information does not make it harder to manage.

One additional observation is that since the tool used does not maintain a history of working, it possesses no mechanism to annotate that working. For example, one can specify details of an attribute recorded for a certain entity type, but cannot record why one chose to drop a certain attribute from an entity. We believe this restriction to be widespread since modelling tools typically are oriented towards the model developed rather then the process of developing it.

# 5 Preliminary Conclusions

We have presented some results from the use of a speaking-aloud protocol to gain insight into the process of data modelling. The observations reported are in no way presented as a definitive set of user-needs for this task, but rather as evidence that even a very modest investment of time in this technique can provide useful insights; for example, after only 30 minutes of filming a subject using a flip-chart, we have already obtained some useful ideas for features to provide in our modelling tools which might otherwise not have been considered. Such observations allow specific hypotheses to be framed which may then be investigated by further experimentation using the speaking-aloud protocol. The insights gained from this pilot study are presented under the subheadings of 'support for method of working', including provision of history, and 'provision of appropriate operations on the model'.

## 5.1 Support for Method of Working

It has been noted that both ST1 and ST2 made rough notes before making use of the modelling tool. What advantages did this provide to them? We believe that the following factors may be significant. First, pen and paper is a highly flexible and fast-to-use medium, that permits diagram realisation at a speed and in a manner that keeps pace with mental processes. Specifically, this study has highlighted the remarkable characteristics of spatial, temporal, notational and orientational freedom which contribute towards making paper-based working a seamless extension of mental life. Thus, initial notes can be in any desired form such as lists, sketches and annotations; they do not need to conform to any particular means of representation, they can be captured as and when they occur. Another point is that paper, unlike the software tool, provides a clear history of the modellers' working. It may be that during these initial stages, perhaps the most difficult in arriving at a model, this history is felt to be indispensable. Finally, as ST1 commented, paper presents a familiar and standard interface, leaving its user free to concentrate on modelling tasks.

From this preliminary study, it seems that a scratchpad might be useful for data modelling: an area for working which has no understanding of the model's semantics. The scratchpad should provide the ability to work spontaneously, and support multi-page working. ST1 and ST2 both invested time in copying their initial workings from paper into the tool; an integrated software scratchpad should provide the ability to copy information to the main workspace in a convenient manner. For example, when in 'create entity' mode, the user could drag a piece of text from the scratchpad into the workspace, the required entity box appearing around it as it crossed the boundary. This would address the problem highlighted by both subjects: creating boxes and labelling them are activities sufficiently different from one another that they may mutually interfere. ST1 created boxes as a batch, and then labelled them in a batch; ST2 became involved in connecting up his boxes, and neglected to label them. The need at times to free the developer from the semantics of the model is also shown by the facility in some commercial data modelling tools to check the consistency and correctness of the model; this is typically provided as a push-button operation, because it is too distracting and constricting for it to be performed as the model is elaborated.

The subjects using the tool had available to them only the current state of their model; unlike FC, no information was presented to them which indicated how they had arrived at this model. Even a versioning mechanism is not sufficient to provide this functionality; this allows various designated versions of the evolution of the model to be recovered, but does not document how one was transformed into the next. We can envisage being able to add (possibly audio) comments to each transformation, and later step through all the operations performed on one particular version of the model, recovering the comments at each stage. This would document the transformation of each version of the model into the succeeding one. Clearly, the ability to do this in a useful manner depends on identifying semantic and graphical operations at the correct level of abstraction so that each atomic transformation of the diagram can represent a meaningful refinement of the model.

Such a facility would be similar to the ability to undo edits, though it serves a different function; rather than providing the ability to recover from errors, it provides the ability to recover the evolution-history of the model. An undo function [Thim90, chapter 12] is often implemented by maintaining an undo stack; saving this stack between sessions would immediately provide a basis for the incorporation of a history mechanism into our tools.

Observation of ST1 and ST2 showed that the tool did not provide support for the multi-page working which FC favoured; both subjects at times remedied this by their additional use of paper. Although it remains for further research to determine whether multi-page working is generally a preferred approach to the task of modelling, we see the opportunity for an analogous approach which might be called multi-window working in modelling tools. This is intended to mean something other than the customary use of multiple windows where a user may perform (associated or totally unrelated) tasks in separate windows, or may use subwindows for specific subtasks. Currently, it is not usual to have available simultaneous presentations of different parts of the same model[3], or of the same part at different levels of development, or at different degrees of abridgement.

---

[3] One notable counter-example is the document preparation environment provided by the Oberon system [Reis92].

## 5.2 Provision of Appropriate Operations on the Model

One major factor to emerge from analysis of the video footage was the need to identify appropriate graphical and semantic operations which will assist the data modeller. Such operations allow manipulation and presentation at an appropriate level of graphical and semantic abstraction [Rade93]. Clearly, the flip-chart had no 'understanding' of the intended semantics of the model drawn upon it — unfortunately, the tool did not always do that much better! While some tools are undoubtedly better than others in this respect, (and we are not concerned here with comparisons of software), the experiment has indicated a number of semantic operations which we suspect receive too little attention from tool-builders in general.

Consider first the need for graphical operations at the correct level of representational abstraction. Here we mean graphical operations such as moving a box which do not affect the semantics of a model, only its representation. For example, when a box is moved, the lines representing any relationships in which it participates should follow it; here a reasonable software tool is superior to a flip-chart, since moving a box between pages (or on paper erasing and redrawing it on one page) require that all attached lines be individually adjusted. In this case the automated tool supports the semantics of the graphical operation better than paper. Similarly, other tools with which we have experimented provide useful graphical operations such as calculating routes for association arcs which incur minimal line crossing [Watt93]. However, FC's amendment where part of the diagram was rotated and re-integrated with the remainder of the diagram would be little easier to perform on screen than on paper. It is not hard to speculate on other such graphical operations which should be better supported by our modelling tools: *e.g.*, find a convenient location for this box towards the left of the diagram, swap the locations of these two boxes and readjust the connecting arcs, create some free space in this area *etc*. Some further experimentation with a larger number of subjects should enable us to identify which operations of this sort would be of most benefit.

Secondly we can consider what we might call semantic operations, meaning operations which alter the semantics of the model when performed. Analysis of both flip-chart and automated tool use revealed subjects performing these operations, although no support for them was given by either modelling medium. One example of such an operation was merging two entity types, the need for which was highlighted by FC's working. This requires that one of the two names (or a new one) be chosen to represent the resulting type, and one of the existing boxes be removed. Further, the box representing the entity type after merging should have associated with it the set union of the attributes of the two former types, and should participate in the set union of the relationships participated in by the two former types. This ensures that all the relevant information about this type is retained; if at the current stage of working, the entity type were incompletely modelled under each of its guises, all the relevant information is drawn together after merging. Of course, problems may arise from incomplete and inconsistent modelling; for example, if the same attribute has been recorded twice under different names in the two former types, this attribute will now be duplicated in the new type, requiring user-intervention to correct the merged attribute list. To represent the performance of this semantic operation on screen requires an appropriate graphical operation to transform the diagram, which will be an appropriate combination of the basic graphical operations mentioned above.

The need for another such semantic operation emerged during analysis of the video of ST1's interaction with the data modelling tool: he recognised that two existing entity types on the diagram were in fact specialisations of a common supertype. Creation of a supertype requires that if both the subtypes have any common attributes or participate in any common relationships, these should be ascribed to the supertype and removed from the direct definitions of the subtypes since they will now be inherited. Any such feature possessed by only one of the subtypes may be assumed to be a specialisation and should remain ascribed to *that* subtype; of course, there is always the possibility that it is really held in common and has been omitted by error from the specification of the other entity. As before, resolution of such issues will require further user-intervention.

Again, an appropriate graphical representation of this operation would considerably simplify the amendment of the model. Since an EER diagram specifies both the aggregation and the generalisation structure of the enterprise model [SmSm77], alterations will be required to various different types of graphical object to represent the addition of a supertype of existing entity types. In the absence of such a high-level graphical operation, a considerable amount of mouse-clicking and typing was required to introduce the new supertype, set the attributes and relationships common to the subtypes, connect these by a generalisation arc, and remove the common attributes and relationships from the entity types newly defined as subtypes.

Of course, it is possible to generalise from the semantic operations actually observed and infer the existence of others which should also be supported; however, analysis of the video is useful as it provides the seeds of such generalisations and raises awareness of the need for classes of operation which might otherwise be wholly overlooked. Furthermore, analysis of larger quantities of video footage could reveal which such operations are most commonly performed and therefore most useful to support.

# 6 Indications for Further Research

We have stressed that this was an exploratory study designed to assess the potential of techniques imported from HCI and to identify research issues worthy of further investigation. Although only three subjects were studied, the results have provided some insight into the process of data modelling, and into limitations of an automated tool compared with a flip-chart; this certainly merits follow-up studies.

We would like to investigate the preference for initial paper-based working by ST1 and ST2, to ensure that it is not an artefact either of studying these particular subjects, or of the software used. If the finding persists in larger, controlled studies using other software tools, we will proceed to identifying features which would more adequately support initial drafting of a data model by studying more closely the way that initial sketches are produced.

Likewise, multi-page working has emerged as a concept worthy of further investigation. Is it an artefact of the use of paper as the modelling medium (or the way modelling is taught), or is it a natural way in which people like to work? If further experimentation suggests the latter, there is much work to be done in devising and evaluating ways of implementing multi-page working and history maintenance.

Further, we intend to identify appropriate graphical and semantic abstractions for model building. Some initial ideas have already been mentioned, but further thought and user-needs analysis is necessary to draw up full requirements specifications for these operations.

One area which the initial study has not addressed is issues of scale. We expect that an automatic tool will gain further advantages over the flip-chart when enterprise models become larger, since they may provide operations such as scrolling, rescaling, and centring the viewer on a specified entity, as well as some support for consistency across large models. However, while not denying the importance of these factors, we believe that issues concerning support for small-scale working must be addressed before considering scaling-up.

The next stage will be to test the insights gained here by constructing prototype modelling tools which reflect them, and evaluating these more formally in comparison to existing in-house and commercial products. Some features may be evaluated fairly soon; the ability to provide others is more remote. Our initial findings certainly suggest that a multi-disciplinary approach to interface analysis and design taking in the theory and techniques of human factors research is a profitable way to proceed. In the longer term we anticipate that multi-modal systems will be required to support the emerging requirements for an adequate automated data modelling environment, in which case continuing HCI and database collaboration will be crucial.

Our long term goal is to create a supportive environment that helps the data modeller as a human expert sitting beside him might. Clearly, this requires a great deal of further research, especially into the nature of modelling problems themselves as well as HCI issues. To understand how such a tool might interact with its users, we anticipate extending our video experiments to embrace co-discovery learning, where user-pairs co-operate on a modelling task; previous work has indicated that speaking-aloud dialogues are an even richer source of insight than speaking-aloud monologues [Kenn89].

# 7  Summary

In order to build better data modelling tools it is necessary to have a better understanding of what the modelling process entails. The use of split-screen filming coupled with speaking-aloud protocols has been presented as a suitable technique to perform the required user-needs analysis, and to generate hypotheses which can then be tested by developing prototypes and evaluating them using standard statistical techniques [SiCa88]. The effectiveness of this approach has been demonstrated by reporting a number of interesting insights which were gained during the course of a very small pilot study.

# 8  Acknowledgements

We are grateful to Craig Cockburn, Bryn Marshall and Paul Holmes, who acted as subjects in this study, and Ritchie McMahon, the author of the software tool used. Ken Barclay, Jessie Kennedy, and Ken Chisholm, colleagues in the Department of Computer Studies at Napier University, contributed many valuable suggestions for this research. We also wish to thank Andy Methven and his team at Napier University TV studio for all their help.

# References

[Cadr90]     Cadre Technologies Inc. 1990. **team**work documentation. Providence, RI.

[Chen76]     Chen, Peter Pin-Shan. 1976. The Entity-Relationship Model — Towards a Unified View of Data. ACM TODS, 1(1), 9 – 36.

[BaKe91]     Barclay, Peter J., & Kennedy, Jessie B. 1991. Regaining the Conceptual Level in Object Oriented Data Modelling. In *Proceedings of BNCOD-9*. Butterworths.

[BaKe92]     Barclay, Peter J., & Kennedy, Jessie B. 1992. Modelling Ecological Data. In *Proceedings of the 6th International Working Conference on Scientific and Statistical Database Management*, 77 – 93. Eidgenössische Technische Hochschule, Zürich, Switzerland.

[BaFK92]     Barclay, Peter J., & Fraser, Colin M., & Kennedy, Jessie B. 1992. Using a Persistent System to Construct a Customised Interface to an Ecological Database. In *Proceedings of the 1st International Workshop on Interfaces to Database Systems*, 225 – 243. Springer Verlag (workshops in computer science series).

[Coop90]     Cooper, Richard L. 1990. Configurable Data Modelling Systems. In *Proceedings of the 9th International Conference on the Entity-Relationship Approach*, 35 – 52. Lausanne, Switzerland.

[Coop92]     Cooper, Richard L. 1992. The Interaction between DBMS and User-Interface Research. In *Proceedings of the 1st International Workshop on Interfaces to Database Systems*, 1 – 5. Springer Verlag (workshops in computer science series).

[CrDa94]     Crerar, A., & Davidson, K. April 1994. *Teaching and Learning through CAL Development: an HCI Perspective.* Paper to be presented at XXIX Annual International Conference of the Association for Educational and Training Technology. Napier University, Edinburgh.

[Davi93]     Davidson, K. 1993. *GLIP, an Interactive Graphical Linear Programming Tool.* MSc dissertation, Dept. of Computer Studies, Napier University, Edinburgh.

[Drap92]     Draper, S.W. 1992. HCI and Database Work: Reciprocal Relevance and Challenges. In *Proceedings of the 1st International Workshop on Interfaces to Database Systems*, 455 – 465. Springer Verlag (workshops in computer science series).

[Feig63]     Feigenbaum, E. A. 1963. The Simulation of Verbal Learning Behaviour. In Feigenbaum, E. A., & and Feldman, J. (Eds), *Computers and Thought*. New York: McGraw-Hill.

[HGPN92]   Halper, Michael, & Geller, James, & Perl, Yehoshua, & Neuhold, Erich J. 1992. A Graphical Schema Representation for Object Oriented Databases. In *Proceedings of the 1st International Workshop on Interfaces to Database Systems*, 282 – 310. Springer Verlag (workshops in computer science series).

[HaHi89]    Harton, H.R., & Hix, D. 1989. Human-Computer Interface Development: Concepts and Systems. *ACM Computing Surveys*, 21(1), 5 – 92.

[Jorg90]     Jorgensen, A. H. 1990. Thinking-Aloud in User Interface Design: a Method Promoting Cognitive Ergonomics. *Ergonomics*, 33 (4), 501 – 507.

[Kenn89]    Kennedy, S. 1989. Using Video in the BNR Usability Lab. *SIGCHI Bulletin*, 21(2), 68 – 71

[Lewi82]    Lewis, C. 1982. *Using the 'Thinking Aloud' Method in Cognitive Interface Design*. IBM Research Report RC 9265 2/17/82, IBM, T.J. Watson Research Center, Yorktown Heights, NY.

[Lind94]    Lindgaard, G. 1994. *Usability Testing and System Evaluation*. London: Chapman & Hall.

[Mull92]    Mullen, Anthony. 1992. *An Object Oriented Modelling Tool*. Honours dissertation, Napier University, Edinburgh.

[NeLa93]    Neilsen, J., & Landauer, T. K. 1993. A Mathematical Model of the Finding of Usability Problems. In *Proceedings of the Conference on Human Factors in Computing Systems, INTERCHI '93*, 206 – 213.

[NeSi72]    Newell, A., & Simon, H. 1972. *Human Problem Solving*. Engelwood Cliffs: NJ: Prentice Hall.

[Rade93]    Radermacher, Klaus. 1993. Abstraction Techniques in Semantic Modelling. In *Information Modelling and Knowledge Bases IV*. Amsterdam: IOS Press.

[Reis92]    Reiser, M. 1992. *The Oberon System: User Guide and Programmer's Manual*. ACM Press.

[SiCa88]    Siegel, S, & Castellan, N. R. Jnr. 1988 (second edition). Non-Parametric Statisistics for the Behavioural Sciences. McGraw-Hill.

[SmSm77]   Smith, J.M., & Smith, Diane C.P. 1977. Data Abstractions — Aggregation and Generalisation. *ACM TODS*, 2(2), 105 – 133.

[Ston93]    Stonebraker, Michael. 1993. Database Research at a Crossroads: the Vienna Update. In *Proceedings of the 19th International Conference on Very Large Data Bases*, Dublin. Morgan Kaufmann.

[Sull93]  Sully, P. 1993. *Modelling the World with Objects.* Prentice Hall.

[Thim90]  Thimbleby, Harold. 1990. *User Interface Design.* Addison Wesley.

[Wadd77]  Waddington, C. H. 1977. *Tools for Thought.* London: Cape.

[Watt93]  Watt, R. 1993. *Conceptual Modelling for Logical Design.* Honours dissertation, Department of Computer Studies, Napier University, Edinburgh.

[Whee92]  Wheelwright, G. 1992. Friendly Persuasion. Microsoft Usability Lab. *Personal Computer World*, April Issue, 250 – 254.

[WrMo91]  Wright, P. C., & Monk, A. F. 1991. The Use of Think-Aloud Evaluation Methods in Design. *SIGCHI Bulletin*, 23 (1), 55 – 57.

# Appendix I

## Reproduction of Task Sheet Given to Subjects

**Produce an Entity-Relationship model to capture the following scenario.**

Members of the Computer Studies Department would like a bibliographic catalogue system to hold details of books and journal articles available in the Department. Staff have specialist research areas and would like to be able to locate relevant literature efficiently.

The information needed for each book is author(s), title, edition (optional), place of publication and publisher, whereas journal articles are referred to by author(s), date of publication, title, journal name, volume number, issue number, and start and end pages of the paper.

Both books and papers may be relevant to more than one research area. On storing a new item in the catalogue, members of staff will supply appropriate keywords selected from a previously compiled list. There may be multiple copies of books and journal articles in the Department, but individual academics will not own duplicate books.

Typical queries might be:

List all papers on a given subject.

List all publications by a given author.

For a given item, which member of staff has a copy and what is his/her office number?


Sample book reference

Berkeley, P. 1994. *Colourful booting routines.* Edinburgh: The Alternative Computing Press.

Sample journal reference

Pecan, P. W., & Banoffee, J. R. 1991. Data visualisation and tasty pie charts. *International Journal of Digestive Computing,* vol 8, no. 2, pp123-314.

# Appendix II

The Three Successive Sheets of Subject FC who Used the Flip-Chart

FC's Workings — Sheet 1

[ Bk ]

[ Pr ]

Copy Bk-no, copy {location?}

Bk $\underset{\sim}{Bk\text{-}no}$ Auth Title [Ed]
   Place Pub

Pr $\overset{Pr\text{-}no}{Auth}$ Title JName
   JVol JIss StP End

~~Sk~~
Bk Sk   Bk-no, Pr-no   Subject

## FC's Workings — Sheet 2

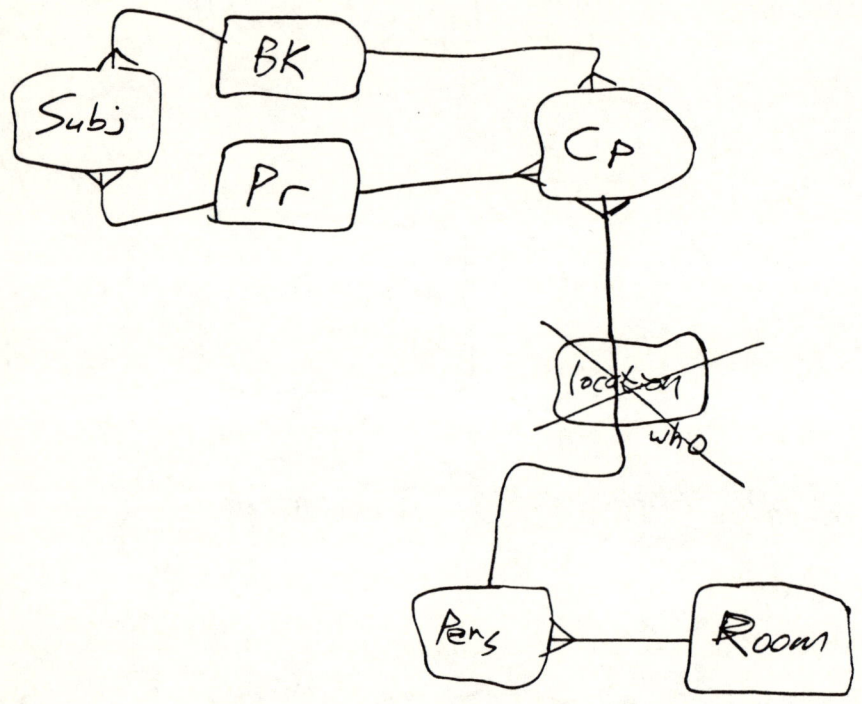

# FC's Workings — Sheet 3

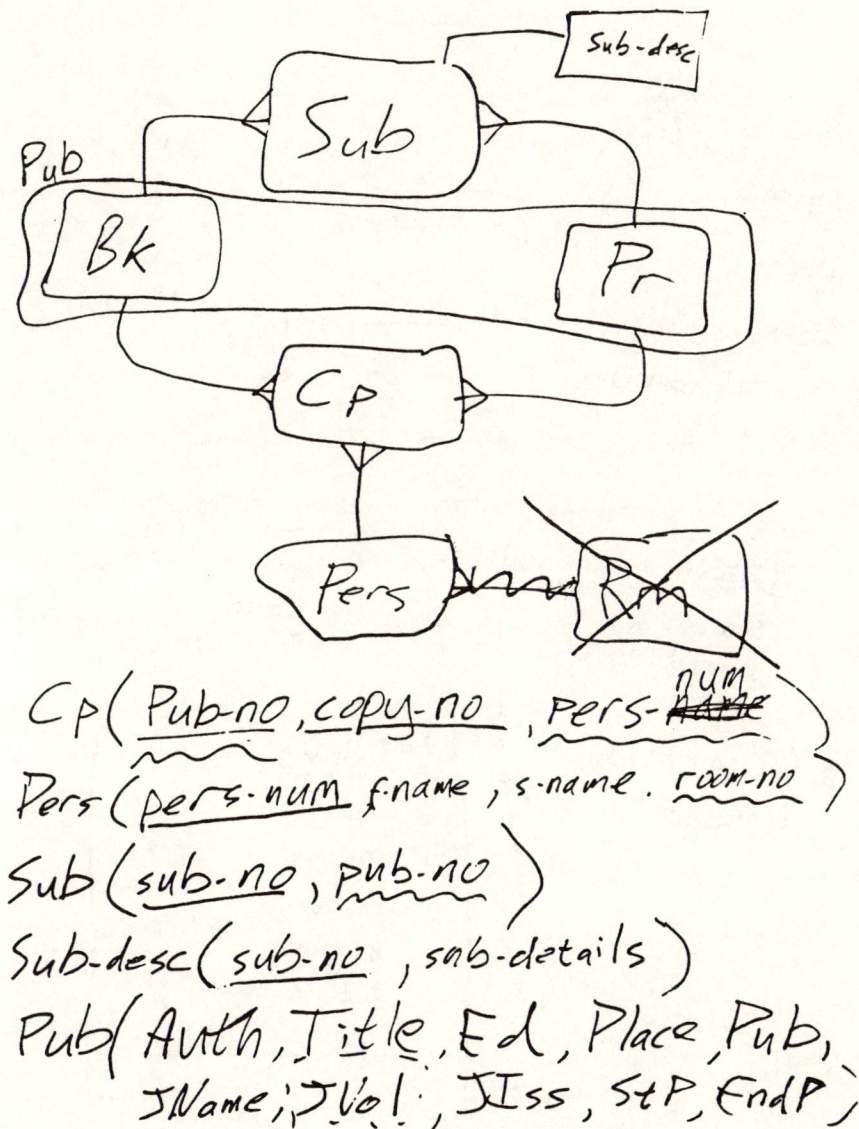

Cp( <u>Pub-no</u>, <u>copy-no</u>, Pers-num )

Pers( <u>pers-num</u>, f-name, s-name, room-no )

Sub( <u>sub-no</u>, pub-no )

Sub-desc( <u>sub-no</u>, sub-details )

Pub( Auth, Title, Ed, Place, Pub,
    JName, JVol, JIss, StP, EndP )

# Appendix III

## Preliminary Jottings of Subject ST1 Prior to Using the Software Tool

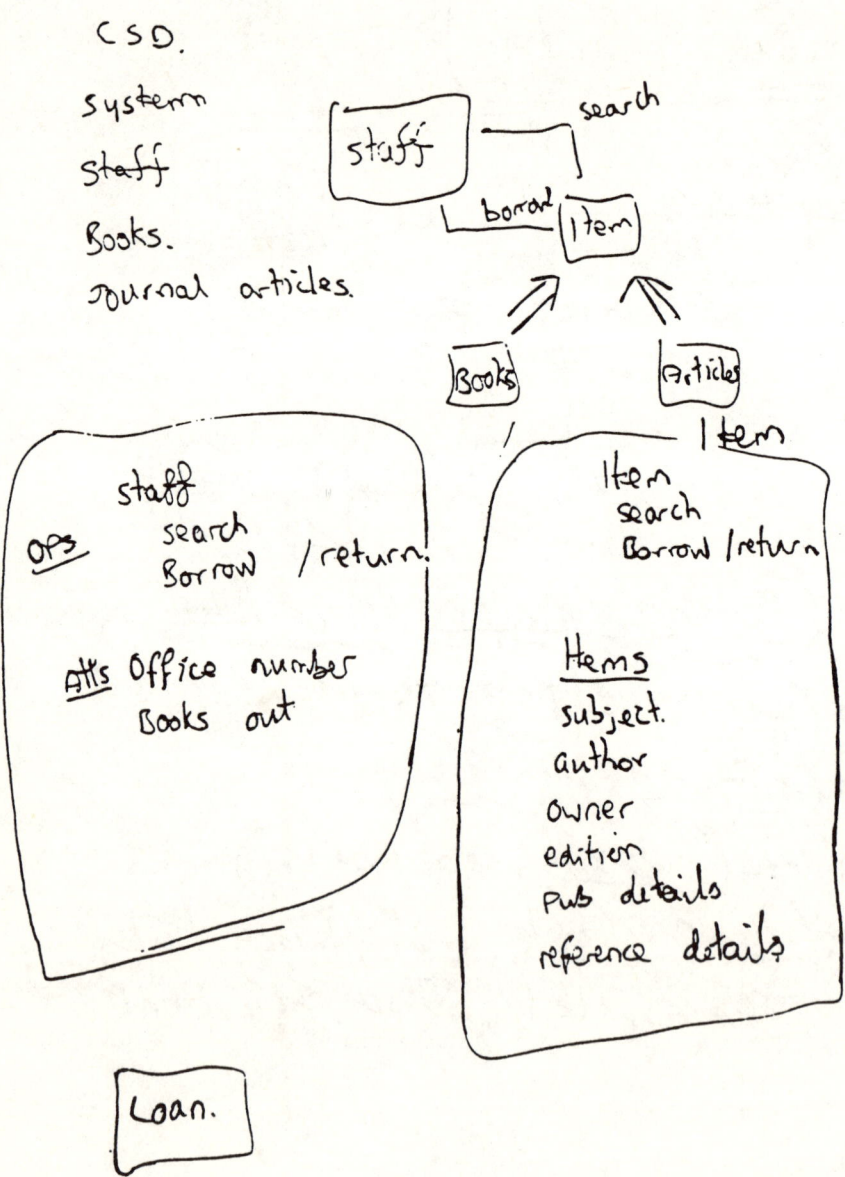

# Evaluation and Experimentation

# Intuitive Human Interfaces for an Audio-database

Barry Eaglestone
Department of Computing, University of Bradford
Bradford, UK

Roel Vertegaal
Department of Ergonomics, University of Twente
7500 AE Enschede, The Netherlands

**Abstract**

Database technology can now host multimedia applications through the representation of sounds and images, but such new applications also require extensions to HCI technology. This paper examines the problems of querying and manipulating audio information. We argue that no single "style" of user interface can provide a complete solution, and propose two novel types of interface to complement conventional database languages. The first is gestural, and allows users literally to reach into spaces of sounds and to "grab" the required objects. The second involves retrieval by mimicry. The main part of this paper describes our research into the viability of the gestural interface. We have experimented using the ISEE (Intuitive Sound Editing Environment) interface, a four-dimensional perceptually-based space of sounds. Our experiments have involved a user population and a range of multidimensional input devices, and have provided strong evidence that the approach is viable, but that the choice of input devices has a significant impact on the usability of the system. The second proposed interface, which we are currently researching, involves the use of neural networks within the data model to derive perceptually-based attributes. The neural networks can be trained on expertly created sound spaces, together with vocal imitations of the sounds, and subsequently used to retrieve on the basis of vocal imitations of the required sounds.

## 1 Introduction

Audio information is now an important dimension in multimedia systems. In particular, there are a number of specialist applications in the arts and in the sound industries concerned with music, television, cine and video, where there is a requirement for large databases of sounds [9, 16]. However, current database solutions to this problem are inadequate. Though physical storage of sounds is well researched (e.g. through the ESPRIT multimedia projects), this is less true of sound retrieval and manipulation interfaces. This weakness is particularly acute for artistic design applications in which design objects must be retrieved, manipulated and evaluated on the basis of their perceptual features [11, 12].

This paper proposes two novel "styles" of intuitive audio-database interface which complement conventional database languages. The first is a gestural interface [31], which allows users to select sounds from a database by literally reaching into spaces of sounds and "grabbing" the required objects. The second involves querying the database by vocally mimicking the required sound - query-by-imitation (QBI) [7]. Both techniques are being researched as part of the work of the Sound Information Technology (SIT) project [9]. SIT is researching a technology to support audio-related design projects, and involves specialists in music, digital signal processing, and computer science. The research is focused and coordinated within the framework of an extended IPSE architecture [10], and has concentrated mainly upon the repository/database component [10, 11, 12]. Ideas are being implemented and tested through the construction of a music composition demonstrator.

The structure of the paper is as follows. Section 2 analyses the problems of providing intuitive interfaces to audio-information, and includes the review of related research. The proposed gestural interface (that of the ISEE system) is described and discussed in section 3. Section 4 describes our experimentation with the ISEE interface and various input devices. Experimental results and conclusions are in section 5. Query-by-imitation is briefly discussed in section 6, and finally, sections 7 and 8 gives details of conclusions and acknowledgements.

## 2 Intuitive Querying of Audio-Information

Though artistic designers may be constrained by functional requirements, their main criteria for the acceptability of designs are usually non-functional, since they are to do with subjective aesthetic judgement [11]. Where the product includes an audio component (as in multimedia authoring, musical composition and instrument design, soundtrack creation, etc.), it is therefore necessary that the design support system should support the representation of audio signals and the manipulation of them on the basis of their perceptual properties. Standards already exist for representation of audio signals. These are typically stored as sample values (perhaps using some destructive compression techniques) (e.g. AES 3-1985, MADI, 8-bit A-law, 16-bit linear, 24-bit linear, ISO/MPEG-Audio-standard), but can also be represented in an analysed form (e.g. group additive synthesis representation [8]), or as parameters for some sound synthesis algorithm. However, we know of no general database languages for perceptually-based definition and manipulation of audio information. There are two gaps in our knowledge which hinder the creation of this type of facility:

- lack of sophisticated and widely accepted perceptual models of sound;
- lack of knowledge about the mapping between audio signals and their perceptual properties.

These respectively deny us a standard vocabulary for characterising perceptual sound, and a basis for automatic derivation of perceptual properties from audio signals.

These two problems have been researched, mainly in the field of computer music and psycho-acoustics, but we believe the results provide a basis for more general applications, for example in multimedia design systems. In particular, progress has been made through the study of timbre space representations -

a timbre space is a multidimensional space of sound, where each dimension models the variability of sounds with respect to some perceived characteristic. The viability of timbre spaces as perceptual interfaces to objects in an audio-database depends on achieving adequate characterisations of sounds within a manageable number of dimensions. However there are a number of results which indicate that these objectives are achievable. [32, 15, 25], for example, have established that it is possible to explain differences in timbre with far fewer degrees of freedom than are needed by most sound synthesis algorithms. Wessel [33] suggested using multidimensional scaling techniques [26] to map sounds into a timbre space. He derived a timbre space from a matrix of timbre dissimilarity judgements made by humans comparing all pairs of a set of timbres. In such a space timbres that are close sound similar, and timbres that are far apart sound different. However, this work highlights two problematic areas. Firstly, the manual construction of dissimilarity matrices is clearly not viable for indexing large audio-databases. Secondly, multidimensional scaling can lead to a proliferation of dimensions. [25] established that when using this technique, the number of timbre space dimensions increases with the variance in the assessed timbres.

The problem of implementing a mapping between sounds and their perceptual features is an example "soft confusion" problem [34], since the nature of such a mapping is sensitive to many contextual criteria, including the identity and health of the listener, the acoustics, and juxtaposition with other sounds, and the evaluation of the correctness of solutions is subjective. Candidate technologies for this type of problem include connectionist theory, fuzzy logic and fuzzy set theory. Advancements have been made towards automatic creation of timbre spaces using connectionist technology. For example, Feiten and Ungvary [13] are making progress in training neural networks to automate the organization of sounds in a timbre space based upon the timbre characteristics identified in [5]. There is also evidence that for sound retrieval purposes (rather than manipulation) from classes of "similar" sounds, a few parameters may suffice. Grey [15] for example experimented with similarity comparisons of 16 closely related re-synthesized instrument stimuli with similar envelope behaviour (varying from wind instruments to strings). He concluded that one dimension could express instrument family partitioning, another could relate to spectral energy distribution, and a third could relate to the temporal pattern of (inharmonic) transient phenomena.

A query language can use a timbre space interface to an audio-database by allowing users to specify coordinates in the space. The sounds at or neighbouring specified locations may then be retrieved, or alternatively sound synthesis parameters may be generated (by interpolation between neighbouring timbres). The latter is necessary if the language also allows modifications to stored sounds e.g. for sound synthesis control in music applications, as in the ISEE system [31]. A crude approach to implementing a perceptual timbre space interface is as an aggregation or set (a relational view for example) comprising for each sound in the space, its object identifier and timbre space coordinate values. Conventional retrieval techniques can then be used to access and re-synthesise the specified sound or neighbouring sounds from their physical representations. However, this approach imposes problems if automated interpolation is also required, for example to synthesize the sound associated with an unoccupied location in timbre space. An alternative or complementary approach is to represent the timbre space in terms of the functional mappings from perceptual coordinate to sound synthesis algorithm parameter values. In this latter approach the timbre space is characterised by its behaviour, rather than by describing each of its inhabitants, and can therefore be implemented in an object-oriented database through encapsulation of the mapping functions within the timbre space object. The work of Lee and Wessel [20, 21] provides a basis for this second implementation. They have successfully trained a neural network to generate parameters for several synthesis models with timbre space coordinates as input, thus providing timbral interpolation automatically. The neural network code therefore provides the mapping function (method) encapsulated with the timbre space object. This approach however involves substantial computational power in order to train the neural network.

Though specific to music, the above research addresses some general problems of providing perceptually-based facilities for querying design objects. The timbre space solution described is an example of a perceptually-based object space in which each dimension models some variable perceived property of the objects. There are a number of advantages to using such a model as an interface. Objects can be retrieved by describing some of their perceptual properties, and then projecting along the axes corresponding to the other uninstantiated perceptual properties. The fuzzy nature of this type of querying means it can be viewed as an extension of the class 2 search in [1, 28]. It is therefore appropriate to return objects which are in some sense "closest" to the query key. In fact the object space metaphor provides an implementation of a notion of "distance" between objects. A further advantage is the ability to "browse" or "explore" object spaces. This can be provided if the interface supports some "pointing" input device, such as a mouse or joystick, with which the user may "point to" locations within the space. If, in addition, the system provides instant retrieval (playback) of the objects as they are pointed to, we believe users can learn to navigate their way around the spaces, and locate objects with some required property without first having to formulate a query.

The approach does have limitations, in that it does not provide direct definition or manipulation of all design object attributes, or completeness with respect to the underlying data or object model. A consequence is that users are restricted to a pre-specified subset of objects, taken from a possibly infinite domain. In this respect it must be considered as a presentation model which is complementary to other more conventional querying facilities.

The following three sections describe the ISEE timbre space interface, and our experimental research, using ISEE, into the viability and effectiveness of the above type of "point and play" interface to an audio-database.

## 3  The ISEE Timbre Space Interface

The practicality of using timbre space as a basis for a sound design system is demonstrated by the ISEE (Intuitive Sound Editing Environment) system [31]. ISEE is a synthesizer and synthesis model independent user interface designed for musical sound design applications in both composition and performance. However, we also view ISEE as a demonstrator system with which the general concept of a perceptually-based multidimensional object space interface can be evaluated. Accordingly, the following description of ISEE omits technical details concerning signal processing and musical applications - those interested should refer to [30, 31].

The ISEE interface is a four-dimensional timbre space. The dimensions were identified through qualitative observation of the working methods employed by expert designers of synthesized sounds. Because of their high level of abstraction, these parameters have important orthogonal properties which make them suitable as a basis for the high level ISEE sound synthesis model. The actual implementation of the abstract parameters depends on the required refinement of synthesis control. ISEE refers to a scaled implementation of the four parameters as an instrument space because as well as allowing control of the timbre, it also defines the range and type of pitch and loudness behaviour of the instrument(s) it encloses. The four parameters are presented to the user as a pair of two-dimensional spaces called the Control Monitor (see figure 1). The first two of the abstract timbre parameters relate to the spectral envelope and the last two to the temporal envelope: the Overtones parameter controls the basic harmonic content; the Brightness parameter controls the spectral energy distribution; the Articulation parameter controls the spectral transient behaviour as well as the persistent noise behaviour; and the Envelope parameter controls temporal envelope speed. The first three parameters are similar to those identified by [15]. The Violin instrument space (see figure 2) is a good example of a refined application of ISEE timbre parameters. In this space, the Overtones parameter describes the relation of the bow to the bridge, from flautando to sul ponticello. The Brightness parameter relates to the bow pressure on the string, the Articulation parameter controls the harshness of the inharmonic transient components (the force with which the bow is "dropped" on the strings) and the Envelope parameter controls the duration of the attack. The problem of defining the functions which map from timbre space dimensions to synthesis parameters is simplified by decomposition of the timbre space into a hierarchy of instrument spaces, each of which defines sub-classes of "similar" sounds. Separate mapping functions are then defined for each sub-class. Generally, each component instrument space is organised using the following heuristics: from low to high, from harmonic to inharmonic, from mellow to harsh, and from fast to slow. The instrument space hierarchy (see figure 2) is based upon a categorisation scheme derived from expert analysis of existing instruments using think-aloud protocols, card sorting and interview techniques. Using the hierarchy, the user can structure a search by "zooming in" on specific instruments spaces from grosser higher level spaces. Alternatively, when interested in a broader perspective of instruments, the user can jump to a broader instrument space by "zooming out". More expert users can also make use of a traditional hierarchy browser, for example, when constructing new instrument spaces. ISEE embodies the essential features of a perceptually-based multidimensional object space interface: each dimension models variability of a particular perceptual feature, dimensions are orthogonal, and the interface behaviour is characterised by mapping functions which relate locations in the space to specific objects. Two factors which determine the usability of this type of interface are the visual representation of the space, and the means by which users specify locations within it. The following section describes our experimental research toward establishing the significance of the second of these factors.

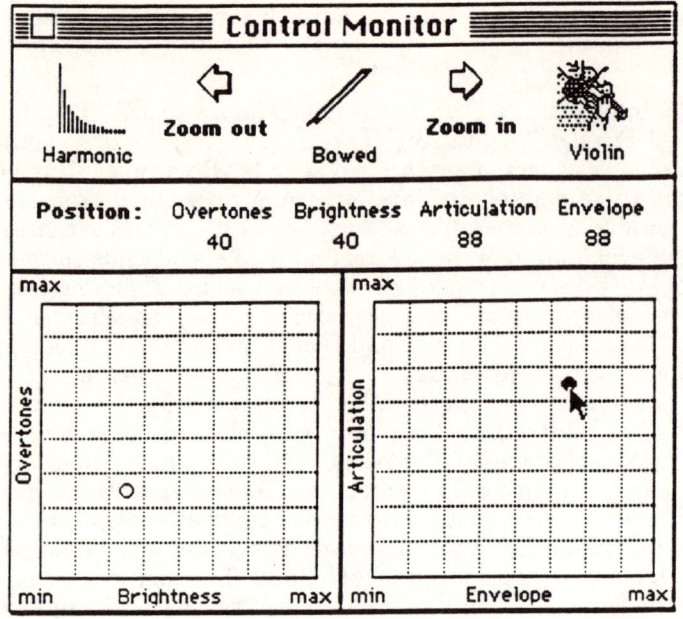

Figure 1: The Control Monitor application is used to control and monitor the position in the hierarchy (depicted by the middle icon) and the position in the current instrument space (indicated by the two dots). Two buttons are used to zoom out to the parent space (Harmonic) or zoom in to the child space (Violin) closest to the 4D position indicated by the dots.

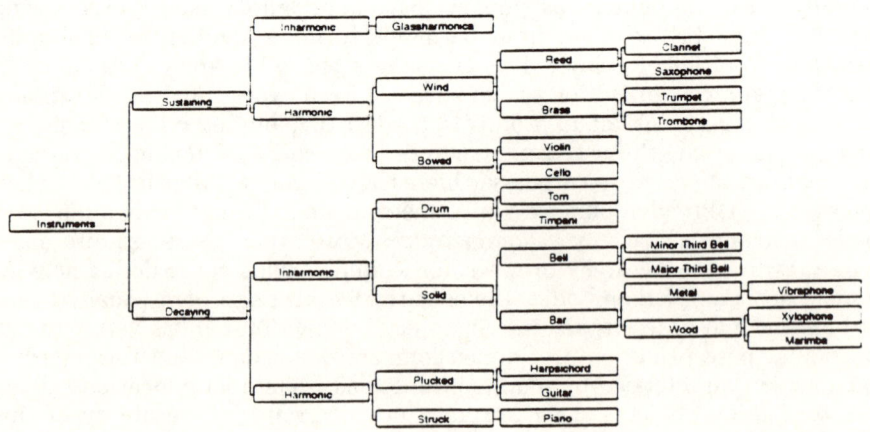

Figure 2: An example partial taxonomy of instrument spaces.

# 4 Experiments with a hardware audio database interface

We believe that the choice of appropriate hardware input devices can increase the efficiency of an audio-database query by increasing the sense of direct manipulation of the audio-objects [14, 27]. This is particularly true in music applications where many users will have a strong bond with direct manipulation of sound using musical instruments of some sort. We tested this assertion through experimentation using three low-cost hardware input devices (two general, low-dimensional devices and one specialized multidimensional device) to assess their usability in this relatively new application of information technology. The ISEE general sound specification model (described in the previous section) was used to provide the generalised low to high- dimensional mapping needed for gestural control of the search process.

## 4.1 Input Devices

Many studies have tested and compared usability of input devices for manipulation of on-screen graphic objects. We have therefore used this literature to assess which input devices were most suitable to test as timbre-parameter controllers for querying an audio-database.

According to [4] a multidimensional input device does not necessarily perform better in a multidimensional task than a low-dimensional input device. [17] states that performance in a multidimensional task with simultaneous control of all dimensions depends on the perceptual composition of the task's dimensions. We therefore selected both multi- and low-dimensional devices to control the ISEE interface. ISEE control consists of four medium resolution timbre parameters and one discrete scale parameter. The experiments focused on the usability of the input devices controlling the four medium resolution parameters, of which the control integration is unknown.

Another issue is whether absolute or relative devices are easier to use for audio-database query tasks. With an absolute device, the position of the device directly corresponds to the position of the controlled parameter. A relative device controls the direction in which the parameter changes. The nulling problem (i.e. the inconsistency between the state of the device and the state of the parameter that occurs when changing the parameter an input device operates on) that will occur when switching between the two 2-dimensional coordinate systems (see figure 1) using an absolute low-dimensional device might, according to [2], easily be solved by using a relative device instead. However, when using an absolute device, the position within an instrument space matches that of the controlling limb, which, according to [18, 19, 27], reduces cognitive processing load and corresponds more closely to control of most musical instruments. We therefore experimented with both direct and relative interfaces.

An excellent taxonomy of current input devices is given by [22]. It indicates that multidimensional devices are mainly absolute devices. Of the relative devices, the mouse is the most commonly used. Joysticks can be changed from absolute to relative, which makes them ideal for comparing the usability of an absolute vs. a relative device. [24] has studied the use of two multidimensional input devices, the Nintendo Power Glove and the Polhemus 3Space Isotrak, as virtual reality controllers. However, since the magnetic field sensors of the Polhemus cannot be mass-produced, the Polhemus is too expensive to consider for regular database query applications. The low-cost Nintendo Power Glove, however, uses ultrasonics to sense three spatial coordinates and variable resistor material for sensing finger bend. Finger bend can be used to provide information about the status of the glove and to control the scale parameter. The three spatial coordinates can be used to control the first three ISEE parameters. The low resolution of the roll information of the Power Glove (only 12 positions) however, would make specification of the fourth ISEE parameter rather crude. The roll information would only be useful for our purpose when used as a relative controller. This makes it impossible, however, to assess the control integration of all four ISEE parameters with a Power Glove.

## 4.2 Methods

We selected the following input devices: Apple Standard Mouse (a relative input device); Gravis Advanced MouseStick II - an optical high-resolution joystick (absolute or relative); Nintendo Power Glove (absolute and relative). Our sample population consisted of music students from the Department of Music of the University of Huddersfield, England, with experience in the use of electronic instruments and synthesized sounds, but with little experience in sound synthesis. A repeated measures design [6] was used with a group of 15 paid subjects who were asked to search an audio-database for objects matching target sounds using the different input devices. The experiments were conducted using an audio-database containing a broad selection of musical instrument sounds. These were generated by simple FM synthesis [3] (technical details of the parameters of the instrument space can be found in the appendix). An Apple Macintosh SE was used to filter the erratic Power Glove information and record the experiments. An Apple Macintosh LC was used as the database query platform running the ISEE system. A YAMAHA SY99 synthesizer was used to generate sounds according to the synthesis specification generated by the database objects. All systems were interconnected by MIDI, a general synthesizer LAN.

Four interfaces were constructed. In the first, the mouse was used to change the coordinate indicators in the Control Monitor (see figure 1) by clicking and dragging the indicator dots. The joystick was used in the second and third interfaces. In the second the joystick provided absolute control - the position of the stick corresponded directly to the position of the indicators in the Control Monitor. In the third, the joystick provided relative control - the position of the stick controlled the speed and direction of the Control Monitor indicators. In both, the two buttons on the top of the stick were used to select the coordinate system to be controlled with the stick. The fourth interface used the Power Glove for four- dimensional positioning in the Control Monitor. Motion on the Y-axis controlled Overtones, the X-axis controlled Brightness, the Z-axis controlled Articulation, and roll information was used to control the Envelope parameter in a relative fashion. Holding the wrist level would produce no change, rolling the wrist anti-clockwise would decrease the Envelope parameter and rolling clockwise would increase the Envelope parameter. The glove was engaged by clutching and inactive when not clutching. The interfaces each provided feedback in the form of tones corresponding to the current position in the ISEE search space.

The subjects were given five minutes to get used to each device, except for the Power Glove, with which they were allowed to practice for 15 minutes because of the special technique involved. Each subject was given 10 test blocks of four experiments, one for each of the four device types. To prevent an order effect due to training, the order of the 4 types of input devices in each test block as well as the order of the test blocks was randomised. A questionnaire was answered by each subject after the experiments.

In each experiment the subject was required to listen to a sound, and then locate it in the audio-database, using one of the four interfaces. The location of the target sound could be seen in the Control Monitor while the target sound was being played (five times), and in a separate window throughout the rest of the experiment. After the initial sounding of the target sound, the indicators in Control Monitor centred, with the sound changing accordingly, giving the subjects an audio- visual cue to start manipulating the indicators with the input device. The tones were repeated throughout the experiment to give the subjects sufficient auditive feedback on their position. When the match was considered good enough, the subjects released the input device and recording was stopped.

Recording the experiments in this way enabled us to simulate retroactively an experiment where the subject would have been required to reach a certain accuracy criterion, which would then automatically terminate the trial.

## 5 Experimental Results and Conclusions

The efficacy of each device was established by measuring the time needed to reach the appropriate 4-dimensional position within a certain accuracy (where accuracy is overall Euclidian distance to target in 4-dimensional space). This combines speed and accuracy into a single measure and removes the effect of individual subjects' subjective accuracy criteria for terminating trials. Since a subject might briefly, inadvertently pass through a point that lies within the required accuracy, retroactive analysis allows us to correct this by measuring the time until the subject passed the criterion for the last time during the trial. The data was recorded at millisecond accuracy using a MIDI sequencer. The accuracy criterion was set to 1.13 cm in 4-D Euclidean distance to target, which was the 75th percentile of the final accuracies achieved over all trials in this experiment by the least accurate device, the Power Glove. The choice of the 75th percentile is not critical; analysis with other criteria gave similar results.

Analysis of variance showed that the choice of input device had a highly significant effect on performance ($F(3, 483) = 68.99$, $p < 0.001$). This indicated that differences in performance were related to the choice of input device and not just due to differences between subjects. Figure 3 shows the mean time for each device. All differences were highly significant. The mouse was 1.5 times faster than the absolute joystick (paired two-tailed t-test; $p < 0.0001$), 2.1 times faster than the relative joystick ($p < 0.0001$) and 5.1 times faster than the Power Glove ($p < 0.0001$). The absolute joystick was 1.4 times faster than the relative joystick ($p < 0.0001$) and 3.5 times faster than the Power Glove ($p < 0.0001$). The relative joystick was 2.4 times faster than the Power Glove ($p < 0.0001$).

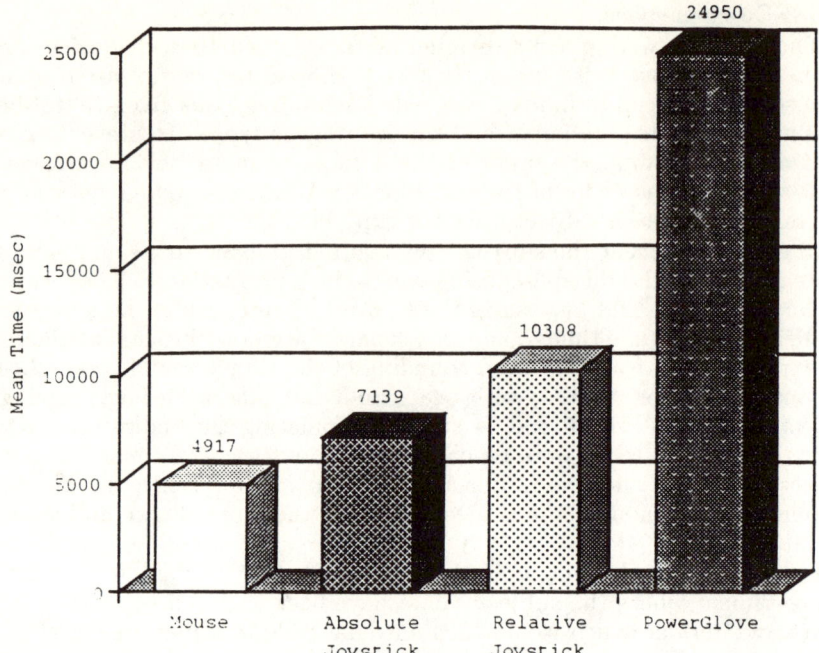

Figure 3: The mean time (in msec) for each input device used in the experiments.

It is clear from these findings that the Power Glove was not very effective in this 4-dimensional task. The subjects found it physically tiring, and very hard to control. However, the bad performance of the glove can also be partly attributed to the lag that occurred because of the filtering, the insufficient resolution of the device beyond 3 degrees of freedom and the fact that this device had not been used before by any of the subjects. During regular audio-database queries a mouse will suffice. When a keyboard is used for additional pitch and loudness specification, the absolute joystick is the most likely option, since it can easily be placed on top of the control panel of the keyboard. Also, in dark studio circumstances, absolute control can be very useful. The relative joystick only seems useful in a musical context where subtle changes in timbre need to be made, and no sudden jumps may occur. The ISEE user interface was judged by most subjects as being "pleasant to work with" and "intuitive".

# 6 Future work towards a "Query-by-imitation" interface

This penultimate section briefly describes our current research towards automating the creation of timbre space, and extending the intuitive search facilities.

ISEE timbre spaces used in HCI experiments (see sections 4 and 5) were manually created by a sound design expert. The functions which map from timbre space dimensions to synthesis parameters were "hand coded". The problems of perceptual object space definition is analogous to the more general problem of indexing within information retrieval systems. Both are skilled labour-intensive tasks which involve induction of object semantics so as to facilitate object retrieval with high precision and recall. However, the work of [13, 21] indicates that automatic creation of timbre spaces may be possible using neural networks. Neural networks can be trained, using expertly created spaces as training sets, and can then be used to re-apply the induced design expertise in order to create other object spaces.

A "query-by-imitation" (QBI) search facility is a potential by-product of the above strategy. The idea for this type of interface was researched by Vertegaal, De Koning and Oates [7]. They researched an interface where-by users query an audio- database by vocally or textually imitating the required sound. The idea is based upon observed use of this vague form of query specification by film soundtrack engineers [9]. However, it was also observed that the lack of an onomatopoeia indexing system could then necessitate a lengthy search for the required audio material, even when there was a common understanding between the requester and the searcher of what the required object sounded like. The search mechanism of the system proposed in [7] is based upon the conversion of the sound imitations into phonetic keys, which are then matched with stored sounds using conventional search techniques. The phonemes in fact provide a canonical form for both queries and stored sounds. Their approach builds upon techniques developed for speech recognition.

We believe our proposed neural network solution for automatic creation of timbre spaces can be extended to include vocal imitations of the characteristic component sounds, and thus provide a mechanism for associating sound imitations with locations in perceptual space. The advantage over the phoneme-based searching is its greater generality. The system does not rely upon a notional phoneme-based granularity of sounds, and can be adapted to the individual user, since users can generate their own training set of vocal imitations. We also believe that the QBI approach has some generality. There is an obvious analogy with image-databases whereby the user queries the database by sketching the require object. We are currently developing and experimenting with a prototype implementation of the above QBI system.

# 7 Conclusions

The gestural and QBI interfaces to audio-databases described are complementary to conventional database languages. For example, we envisage a situation in which QBI provides a mechanism by which a user specifies an approximate location within an object space. The user then refines the query, perhaps through a gestural search. Finally, the required multimedia information is retrieved through the use of some database model-complete language.

We believe that the techniques have some generality within artists design systems, since they provide a general strategy for perceptually-based manipulation of physically represented non-textual design objects.

The main contribution of this paper is the experimental evidence concerning the choice of input device for a gestural interface. The experimental results strongly indicate that the mouse, already used in most applications, is the best input device for audio-database queries with a timbre space approach. The absolute joystick is best used when a keyboard is applied to specify pitch and loudness. Multi-dimensional input devices need not necessarily perform better in a multidimensional query task.

# 8 Acknowledgements

We would like to thank Apple Computer Inc., and in particular, S. Joy Mountford of the Apple Human Interface Group, for supporting the above research, and Dr Michael Clarke of the University of Huddersfield Music Department for facilitating the experimental work. We would also like to thank the other members of SITRG, Geoff Davies, Tamas Ungvary, Bernhard Feiten and Iain Millns, for their contributions to our research.

# References

[1] W.A. Burkhard, Some Approaches to Best-Match File Searching, **Comms ACM**, 1973, 16(4), pp. 230-236.

[2] W. Buxton, There's More to Interaction than Meets the Eye: Some Issues in Manual Input, in D.A. Norman and S.W. Draper (ed), **User Centered System Design: New Perspectives on HCI**, , 1986, Lawrence Erlbaum Associates: Hillsdale, N.J. pp. 319-337.

[3] J. Chowning, The synthesis of complex audio spectra by means of frequency modulation, **Journal of the Audio Engineering Society**, 1973, 21(7), pp. 526-534.

[4] M. Chen, S.J. Mountford, and A. Sellen, A Study in Interactive 3-D Rotation Using 2-D Control Devices, **Computer Graphics**, 1988, 22(4), pp. 121-129.

[5] R. Cogan, **New images of Musical Sound**, Havard U P, 1984.

[6] H. Coolican, **Research Methods and Statistics in Psychology**, London: Hodder and Stoughton, 1990.

[7] K De Koning and S. Oates, Sound Base: Phonetic Searching in Sound Archives, **Proceedings of the International Conference on Computer Music, Montreal**, 1991, pp. 433-436.

[8] B.Eaglestone and S. Oates, Analytical tools for Group Additive Synthesis, **Proceedings of the International Conference on Computer Music, Glasgow**, 1990.

[9] B. Eaglestone and A. Verschoor, Dichtslaande deuren en mens-machine interfaces, **Kennissystemen**, jrg 5 nr 5 mei, 1991, pp. 17-21.

[10] B. Eaglestone and A. Verschoor, An Intelligent Music Repository, **Proceedings of the International Computer Music Conference, Montreal**, 1991, pp. 437-440.

[11] B. Eaglestone, G.L. Davies and T. Ungvary, An Extended Version Model for Artistic Design, **5th International Conference on Computing and Information**, IEEE, Sudbury, Canada, 1993, pp. 502-506.

[12] B. Eaglestone, G.L. Davies, M. Ridley and Hulley N, Implementation of an Artists Version Model using Extended Relational Database Technology. Advances in Databases, BNCOD-11, Keele, UK, July 1993, **Lecture Notes in Computer Science**, 696, Springer Verlag, 1993, pp. 258-276.

[13] B. Feiten and T. Ungvary, Organisation of Sounds with Neural Nets, **Proceedings of the International Computer Music Conference, Montreal**, International Computer Music Association, 1991.

[14] P. Fitts and M. Posner, **Human Performance**, London, Prentice-Hall Inc., 1967.

[15] J. Grey, An Exploration of Musical Timbre, Ph.D. Dissertation, Dept. of Psychology, Stanford University. **CCRMA Report STAN-M-2**, 1975.

[16] M. Jaslowitz, T. D'Silva and E. Zwaneveld, Sound Genie - An Automated Digital Sound Effects Library System, **SMTE Journal**, May 1990, pp. 386-391.

[17] R.J.K. Jacob and L.E. Sibert, The Perceptual Structure of Multidimensional Input Device Selection, **Proceedings of ACM CHI'92 Conference on Human Factors in Computing Systems**, 1992, pp. 211-218.

[18] S. Keele, Movement Control in Skilled Motor Performance, **Psychological Bulletin**, 70, 1968, pp. 387-402.

[19] S. Keele, **Attention and Human Performance**, Pacific Pallisades, Goodyear Publishing Company, 1973.

[20] M. Lee, A. Freed, D. Wessel, Real-Time Neural Network Processing of Gestural and Acoustical Signals, **Proceedings of the International Computer Music Conference, Montreal**, 1991, pp. 277-280.

[21] M. Lee and D. Wessel, Connectionist Models for Real-Time Control of Synthesis and Compositional Algorithms, **Proceedings of the International Computer Music Conference, San Jose**, International Computer Music Association, 1992.

[22] J.D. Mackinlay, S.K. Card, and G.G. Robertson, A Semantic Analysis of the Design Space of Input Devices, **Human-Computer Interaction**, 1990, 5, pp. 145-190.

[23] A. Monk, Statistical Evaluation of Behavioural Data, in A. Monk (ed), **Fundamentals of Human-Computer Interaction**. 1985, Academic Press, London, pp. 81-87.

[24] R. Pausch, Virtual Reality on Five Dollars a Day, **Proceedings of ACM CHI'91 Conference on Human Factors in Computing Systems**, 1991, pp. 265-270.

[25] R. Plomp, **Aspects of Tone Sensation**, London, Academic Press, 1976.

[26] R. Shepard, Representations of Structure in Similar Data: Problems and Prospects, **Psychometrica**, 1974, 39, pp. 373-421.

[27] B. Shneiderman, **Designing the User-Interface: Strategies for Effective Human-Computer Interaction**, Reading, MA, Addison Wesley, 1987.

[28] D.Shasha and T.-L. Wang, New Techniques for Best-Match Retrieval, **ACM TOIS**, 1990, 8(2), pp. 140-158.

[29] B. Truax, Organizational Techniques for c:m Ratios in Frequency Modulation, **Computer Music Journal**, 1977, 1(4), pp. 39-45.

[30] R. Vertegaal, ISEE: ontwerp en implementatie, **Music Technology Dissertation**, Utrecht School of the Arts, The Netherlands, 1992.

[31] R. Vertegaal and E. Bonis, ISEE: An Intuitive Sound Editing Environment, **Computer Music Journal**, 1994, 8(2), pp. 21-29.

[32] D. Wessel, **Report to C.M.E. University of California**, San Diego, 1974.

[33] D. Wessel. Timbre Space as a Musical Control Structure. In C. Roads and J. Strawn (ed), **Foundations of Computer Music**, Cambridge, MA, MIT Press, 1985.

[34] L.A. Zadeh, Soft Confusion and Fuzzy Logic, **5th International Conference on Computing and Information**, IEEE, Sudbury, Canada, 1993.

# A   Experimental Instrument Space Definition

The four parameters of the instrument space were defined as follows. The Overtones parameter was used to control the harmonicity of the spectrum using FM frequency ratios (c:m = 1:1, 2:1, 3:1, 4:1, 5:1, 1:2, 1:4, 1:3, 1:5, 4:5, 6:5, 1:9, 1:11, 1:14, 2:3, 3:4, 2:5, 2:7, 2:9 (see [29] for a more detailed explanation)). The Brightness parameter was used to control the cutoff frequency of the low-pass filter. The Articulation parameter controlled the ratio of the higher partials' attack rate to the lower partials' attack rate. The Envelope parameter controlled the duration of the attack. These mappings were designed by an expert to approach as consistent a perceptual mapping as possible with simple FM.

# Techniques for the Effective Evaluation of Database Interfaces

Norman W. Paton, Ghassan al-Qaimari,
Khoa Doan and Alistair C. Kilgour

Department of Computing and Electrical Engineering,
Heriot-Watt University, Riccarton
Edinburgh, Scotland.
e-mail: < norm,ghassan,vibama,ack >@cee.hw.ac.uk

### Abstract

Many proposals have been made for database interfaces which support a wide range of tasks in a variety of different ways using a wide selection of visual or textual languages. In this context of widespread experimentation, it is important that the proposals be effectively evaluated. If they are not, then flawed approaches could become widely accepted, good ideas could be let down by inappropriate implementations, or novel techniques overlooked in the absence of suitable supporting evidence. This paper summarises our experience using several different evaluation techniques in the context of a multi-paradigm query interface and a browser which supports visualisations of advanced data modelling constructs. It is shown how different evaluation techniques are suitable for evaluating different aspects of database interface functionality, and that different techniques yield different kinds of information on the usability of an interface.

## 1 Introduction

A database management system is likely to be among the most complex pieces of software used by an organisation, with a wide range of associated tasks (schema design, performance tuning, applications programming, schema modification, data entry, querying) carried out by many different user groups. Are the tools which are presently being used for such tasks effective? Could they be improved upon? What sort of changes would be most effective? In the absence of carefully conducted evaluations, these questions are likely to be met by responses such as 'They seem to get the job done', 'I'm sure they're not perfect', and 'They could have more facilities'. In many cases, it is known that certain tools are cumbersome to use, lack essential features, have steep learning curves, or are avoided at all cost. This is not surprising, given the range of tasks and users associated with database systems, but it behoves those who are developing new interfaces, or who aim to produce tools, visualisations and languages for use in future database systems, to donate some time to evaluating new ideas, lest they merely replicate the usability problems of existing interfaces.

What, then, can evaluation do for developers of database interfaces? What are the most effective techniques? How long do they take to use? What sort of thing is learned from different approaches? This paper does not endeavour to answer these questions in general terms, but does present pertinent observations on a range of techniques applied to the evaluation of two novel interfaces to an object-oriented database (OODB) developed at Heriot-Watt.

The paper is structured as follows. Section 2 presents the framework within which the evaluation techniques will be compared. Section 3 outlines two approaches to the evaluation of visualisations for advanced data modelling constructs. Section 4 indicates how qualitative and quantitative evaluation results were obtained for a multi-paradigm query interface. Section 5 summarises our experience to date, and draws some conclusions.

## 2  Evaluation Framework

This section itemises issues relevant to the interface evaluation process, which are subsequently revisited in sections 3 and 4 where specific approaches are described in more detail.

- **Aim:** It is important to be specific about the aim of each evaluation exercise. Different evaluation techniques yield insights on different aspects of an interface, and it is difficult to test multiple hypotheses at the same time. It is best if the designer can express a putative property of the interface as a simple hypothesis, e.g. 'inexperienced users make fewer errors with a form-based than with a command language interface'. Experiments can then be designed to test such hypotheses.

- **Technique:** A range of techniques have been proposed, which can be applied to evaluating database interfaces (e.g. expert evaluation, observational evaluation, experimental evaluation, survey evaluation [16, 5]), from which different kinds of information can be gathered using a range of techniques (e.g. think-aloud protocols, questionnaires, observation, timing). A technique can be selected after the aim of the evaluation has been identified, taking into account the cost of the technique.

- **Nature:** Techniques may yield qualitative or quantitative results, or a mixture of the two. What is required depends very much upon the aim of the evaluation – an existing interface can often be improved without quantitatively measuring the improvement, whereas an effective comparison of alternative approaches to the same problem is likely to require statistically significant quantifiable results.

- **Cost:** Some evaluation strategies are relatively inexpensive to perform, involving the evaluator and a small number of users, whereas other approaches are highly resource intensive. Certain kinds of information (in particular quantitative results) are intrinsically expensive to obtain, but a straightforward evaluation may yield valuable qualitative insights at minimal cost.

In the field of human-computer interaction, techniques for evaluating aspects of the usability of a system or interface are well developed and widely described, although they have yet to become part of the standard armoury of the conventionally-trained software engineer. The techniques mostly derive, with suitable modifications, from the domain of experimental psychology. Recent descriptions aimed at the practical system developer include the guide by Monk *et al.* to their *Co-operative Evaluation* technique [11], the comprehensive and authoritative review by Nielsen of the philosophy and range of techniques usually referred to as *Usability Engineering* [13], and a training video on *User Interface Performance Measurement* produced by Jordan, Oatley and Draper at Glasgow [9].

For completeness, the major approaches to usability evaluation are reviewed in the following sections; later our specific experience in applying a selection of these methods to a range of novel database interfaces is described. Our aim is threefold: to draw the attention of the database community to the need for a systematic approach to interface evaluation in order to reap the full benefits of the new database technologies, and avoid the mistakes of the past; to encourage more practitioners in the HCI community to address themselves to the rich, demanding and stimulating domain of database interface design, where their skills are greatly needed, and are likely to be of immediate and substantial benefit; and to provide pointers from our own experience as to the most challenging problems and the most promising techniques.

The following subsections summarise a number of evaluation strategies which could be applied to database interfaces, with reference to the above characteristics. The role of evaluation in system design is discussed in [13].

## 2.1 Expert Evaluation

This approach belongs to the category referred to as *heuristic evaluation* by Nielsen [13]. Unlike most other approaches, it does not involve the co-operation of sample users representing the target user population. Rather, the usability of the system under test is assessed by usability specialists, possibly guided by reference to an agreed set of usability heuristics. Experiments have shown that a single usability specialist is likely to uncover on average only around 35% of usability problems, whereas assessment by 5 specialists acting independently can be expected to uncover 75% of problems [13]. Nielsen has also shown that *double specialists*, i.e. those who have knowledge of the application domain as well as specialist knowledge of HCI, are likely to perform better than HCI specialists unfamiliar with the application domain.

As well as identifying potential usability problems, possibly related to violations of one or more usability heuristics, the specialists may also be asked to rate the relative severity of the problems identified, so that the work of fixing the problems may be prioritised. The specialists asked to assess the severity may optionally be different from those identifying the problems in the first place. Expert evaluation is useful both at the very early stages of design (possibly even before a computer interface has been built, e.g. using a *pencil and paper* prototype), and also in critiquing extant systems which are known or believed to have problems. Reference to one or more experts at an early stage of design can avoid the more obvious problems which might be difficult or tedious to fix later, and in addition the feedback from experts is a valuable learning experience for the interface builder, providing an apprenticeship situation through which the expertise of the specialists may be progressively passed on.

There are however important limitations to expert evaluation which mean that it is never safe to rely on it on its own (although, as Nielsen emphasises, any evaluation is better than none). Expert evaluation cannot yield figures for error rates, performance times or learnability by different categories of users, let alone levels of subjective user satisfaction. Most important of all, no specialist however skilled can anticipate all the assumptions, expectations, and generalisations that *normal* users are likely to bring to their use of the system. It is these factors which lead to most of the surprises in interface design: users behaving in perfectly rational, sensible and intelligent ways which nevertheless lead to breakdowns in their ability to express their requirements via the given interface. Because it is unlikely that in the near future there will be a rich enough cognitive model of a typical human user to allow all such situations to be anticipated a priori, presently there is no substitute for empirical testing with real users. This point has been succinctly and cogently argued by Landauer [10].

## 2.2 Controlled Experimentation

Central to most evaluation methods which involve *real* users is the experimental performance by sample users (the *subjects*, also sometimes referred to rather confusingly as *evaluators*) of one or more tasks which are representative of what the final system is intended to be used for. There are a range of objections to this kind of experimental procedure, for example the laboratory situation which removes the user from the normal work situation, the presence of at least one observer and possibly a tape recorder and video camera as well, the distortion due to the unavoidable pressure felt by the participants in being the focus of close scrutiny and measurement, and the arbitrary and perhaps artificial nature of the selected tasks. In spite of these and other factors, however, there is now a large body of evidence attesting to the effectiveness of the approach in practice, even when used by practitioners who are relatively unskilled (in experimental psychology). Major usability problems and effects are generally detectable even with relatively ill-focussed or poorly directed instruments.

A major choice in experiments which ask subjects to perform specified tasks is between measuring performance (in terms of completion time, error rate, etc.) and gathering subjective or informal usability information, through so-called *think aloud* methods, in which subjects are asked to verbalise their thoughts, deductions and uncertainties during the performance of the task. It is well known that verbalising one's actions interferes with smooth performance of a familiar task, and indeed may render it impossible to complete. However, the effect is much less when performing an unfamiliar task, which is the case in most usability experiments, and through careful design it may be possible to garner both objective performance measurements and some informal feedback through the same experiment, though the experimenter must have a clear plan as to the primary purpose of the experiment. In section 4, we describe a novel approach in which qualitative feedback is garnered during the initial training session, prior to quantitative measurement of a subjects' performance on specified specimen tasks.

Experiments where collection of qualitative information is the primary goal normally use fewer subjects (typically between three and six), whereas those aimed at producing a statistically significant quantitative result usually require at least ten subjects, and need to be carefully designed so that meaningful conclusions can be drawn.

## 2.3 Questionnaires and Interviews

Eliciting information prior to an experiment about the subjects' previous experience, knowledge and expectations is a necessary part of the experimental process, and may be done either through questionnaires or interviews. In terms of minimising the overhead on the time of the experimenter, questionnaires are much more efficient. Interviews have the advantage that misunderstandings and uncertainties as to the meaning of questions, or the kind of answers expected, can be dealt with by the experimenter at the time.

The same techniques may be used to gather feedback after an experiment as to the subjects' impressions of the system, their views on its good and bad points, whether they would wish to use it again, and their suggestions for improvement. Some of these results can form part of a quantitative study (e.g. a rating of the ease of use on a scale of 1 to 5), while others provide a spectrum of indicators which the designer must analyse individually looking for common themes or patterns.

## 2.4 Formative and Summative Evaluation

Evaluation may take place either during the interface design process, or at the end (or long after delivery of the system), for example to gain quantitative usability measures for a system, or a range of systems being compared. The former is referred to as formative, the latter as summative evaluation. Formative evaluation is usually part of an iterative design process, and an important issue is how the system should be modified subsequent to an evaluation in order to improve usability, so that the iterative process actually converges.

One approach to formative evaluation which gets round this problem to some extent is for the designer, when faced with a major design decision, to implement two or more versions of the interface, each instantiating one possible answer to the design question. Then experimental evaluation can focus on a quantitative comparison of the alternatives, aimed at deciding which is best in some predetermined sense. Although this approach is expensive in terms of the time required to construct the alternatives, and is subject to the plausible objection that low-level details of each implementation may affect the usability in ways which swamp the high-level differences which the experiment is designed to measure, it nevertheless has many attractions, not least in that it can lead to creative new syntheses which combine the best features of the different alternatives, and can also give insight into cognitive processes affecting users' comprehension and learning. Our experience, in particular in comparing database query interfaces based on alternative paradigms, reported later, points to the conclusion that no one interface is best: giving the user a choice, and in particular allowing simultaneous access to two or more alternatives, may provide usability benefits in excess of anything achievable with any of the alternatives on its own.

## 3 Evaluating Modelling Constructs

The evaluations described in this section relate to the development of an interface to the extensible OODB described in [8, 14]. The database system includes extensibility features which have allowed a range of new modelling constructs (relationships, versions, composite objects) to be added to the underlying data model. Where the data model can be readily extended, it is also necessary for the interface to be extended [15] with new visualisations [2], so that the interface continues to reflect the nature of the database.

The visualisations designed for depicting the modelling constructs in a browser/schema design tool were evaluated using two prototypes – one based upon paper mock-ups of displays, and the other running on a workstation, using the interface described in [15]. As well as assessing general reactions to the visualisations presented, an additional aim of the evaluation was to ascertain whether or not the meaning of the underlying construct was effectively conveyed to the user.

### 3.1 Evaluating Paper Prototypes

Paper prototypes are normally used to provide rapid, low-cost feedback on the usability of interface constructs/systems [12]. Identification of inappropriate designs at an early stage saves wasted effort developing systems which incorporate fundamental design faults. In fact, for the evaluation of the modelling constructs, we chose to implement all visualisations for which paper prototypes were developed, in order to allow an assessment of the extent to which the results with the paper prototypes were repeated with an implementation. The results of this comparison are presented in section 3.3.

- **Aim:** To assess the relative merits of different styles of visual representation for presenting assorted modelling constructs, and to identify weaknesses in the specific proposals made.

- **Technique:** Paper mock-ups were devised of a range of constructs which were shown to expert users who were then asked to respond to a range of questions on a checklist relating to features of specific interfaces, and then to give an overall score to each of the visualisations. As an example, figure 1 presents a mock-up of a visualisation of a *vehicle* composite object. The expert users were also invited to give off-the-cuff comments on the specific evaluations.

- **Nature:** This approach principally yielded qualitative feedback on the specific approaches, partly through the questions on the checklist, and partly through the informal feedback. As many of the checklist questions were visualisation-specific, quantitative feedback could not always be used to compare different proposals. Only the final rating, through which the 20 users were asked to rate the alternatives on a 5 point scale, yielded quantifiable relative results. The main disadvantage of the approach is that it is difficult to simulate the *dynamics* of the interface, or system output.

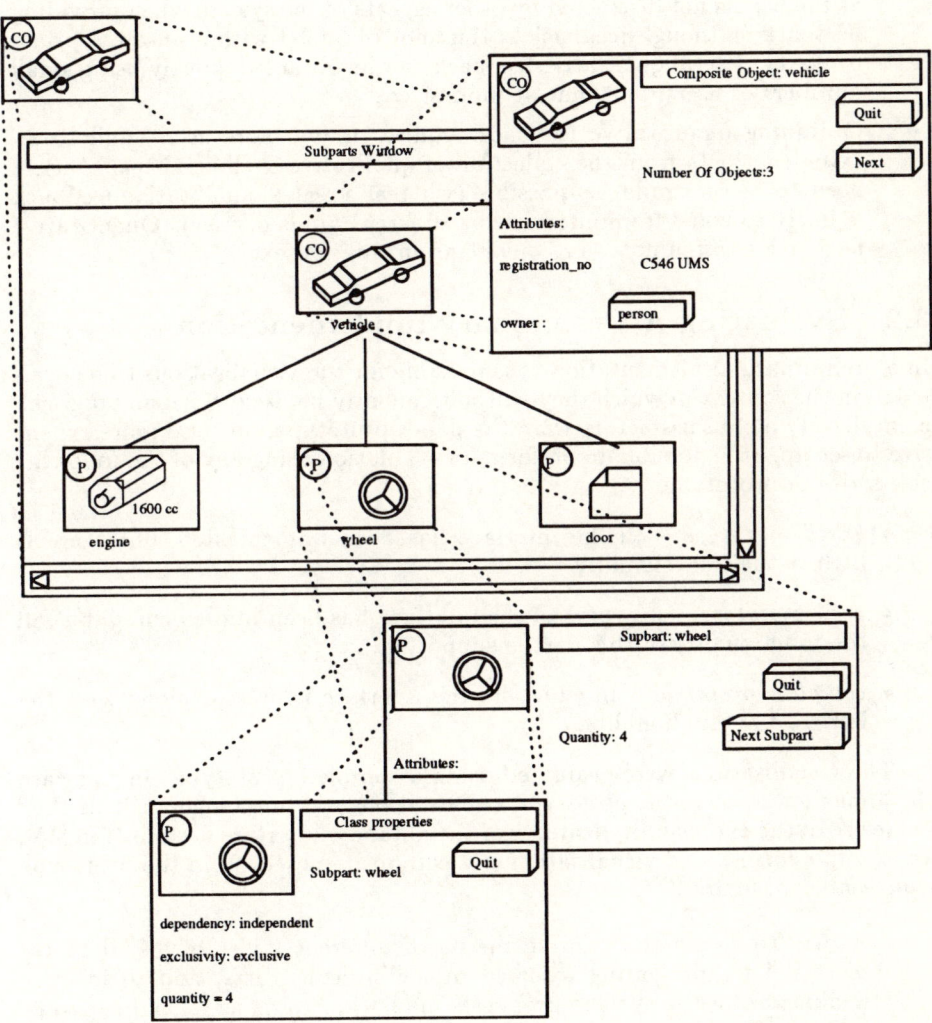

Figure 1: A mock up of a graph-based visual representation of a *vehicle* composite object.

- **Cost:** Paper mock-ups can be produced using computer-based drawing packages in a modest period of time compared with implementations, even when the implementation is built using a rapid prototyping system. Such paper prototypes are particularly suitable when evaluating visualisations, as the user is not distracted by other aspects of the system when providing feedback (although feedback is thus not obtained within an appropriate context). Useful qualitative feedback can be obtained quickly using small numbers of users, and thus at modest cost.

Obtaining quantitative feedback requires many more users, and to an extent detracts from the collection of qualitative feedback because users need to be as similar as possible (whereas greatest qualitative feedback is likely to come from interviewing different kinds of user). Quantitative feedback is often not very convincing in this context.

## 3.2 Evaluating A Preliminary Implementation

In a preliminary implementation, it is possible for the visualisations to be evaluated in the context in which they will subsequently be used. Such an approach is intuitively more satisfactory than the paper prototype, but also more expensive to set up. It is possible to perform an evaluation using any of the following categories of prototype:

- *broad prototype* – all the interface has been implemented, but there is little actual functionality.

- *deep prototype* – only part of the interface has been implemented, but all the functionality of this part is supported.

- *complete prototype* – in which all the interface is present along with the bulk of the functionality.

The visualisations were evaluated using a complete prototype. In this case the implementation of the prototype visualisations was not a huge task, as they made use of the extensibility features of the database interface described in [15]; an example form-based visualisation of a composite object from the prototype is presented in figure 2.

- **Aim:** To assess the relative merits of different styles of visual representation for presenting assorted modelling constructs, and to identify weaknesses in the specific proposals made (i.e. same as for paper prototype); to ascertain the extent to which the characteristics of a modelling construct were revealed to users of its visualisation.

- **Technique:** A number of tasks were identified which users carried out using the system. Feedback was obtained by observing users (both expert and semi-naive) performing the tasks, encouraging users to think aloud when using the system ('Why do you think that?'...), and by using checklists to elicit opinions on specific aspects of the system. Questions were included which endeavoured to find out if the visualisations successfully put across the meaning of the various constructs ('Are relationships represented as normal database objects?', 'Why do you think that?').

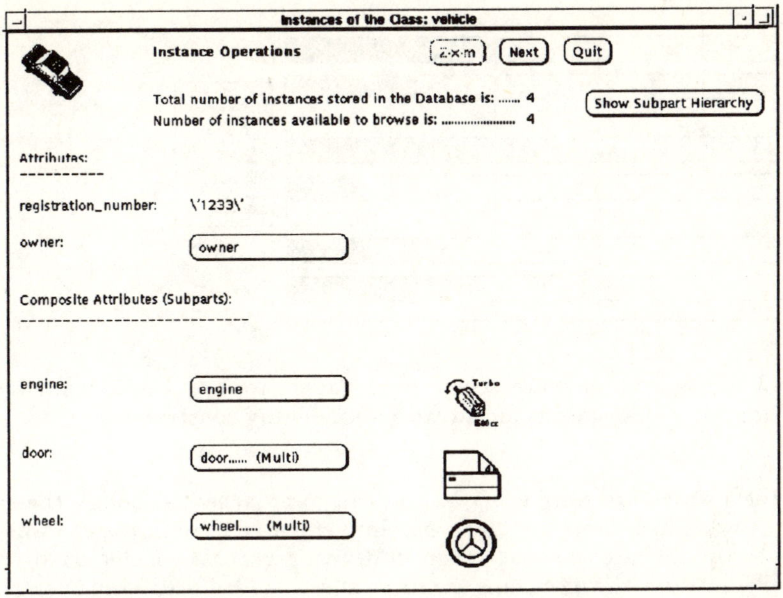

Figure 2: A prototype implementation up of a form-based visual representation of a *vehicle* composite object.

- **Nature:** The bulk of the feedback obtained was qualitative – many of the questions were visualisation-specific, and only summary questions on overall visualisation quality were amenable to tabulation and comparison.
- **Cost:** The cost of carrying out this evaluation, which involved 20 users, was similar to the cost of evaluating the paper prototypes once the implementations had been constructed. The desire to obtain some quantitative results meant that more users were involved in the evaluation than was necessary to obtain effective qualitative feedback – a law of diminishing returns quickly takes hold when recording qualitative feedback.

## 3.3 Comparing Paper/Practical Evaluations

The feedback obtained during both evaluations enabled a range of minor design errors to be detected (confusing labels, unclear button behaviour (e.g. knowing what 'quit' actually shuts down), ...), and enabled general opinions to be drawn as to which visual paradigms were most suitable for different constructs. The evaluation with the actual system provided additional feedback on how certain visual constructs could be integrated with the existing interface in an unobtrusive way. Thus the paper prototype was effective at screening out initial faults, but tended to gloss over uniformity and integration issues which only came to the fore in the practical implementation.

Figure 3 presents the relative scores assigned to three different visualisations of composite objects in the paper and practical evaluations. In two of the three

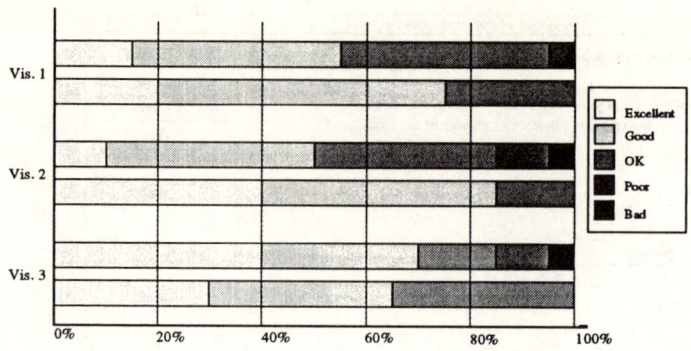

Figure 3: Relative preference scores from paper (top) and practical (bottom) evaluations of visualisations for advanced modelling constructs

cases, the ratings are similar across the two approaches, although the second approach was much more popular when implemented than in paper form. This shows that some care must be taken in drawing general conclusions from the paper evaluation – the mock-ups are more effective for identifying finer grained usability problems.

## 4 Evaluating Query Interfaces

The evaluations described in this section relate to the multi-paradigm query interface described in [7]. A screen dump of the evaluated version of the graph-based query interface is presented in figure 4. In this system, queries over an OODB can be written using textual, form-based or graph-based notations, and the system supports automatic mapping between these styles. Earlier work on the evaluation of query interfaces [1, 3, 4] has, like that described here, endeavoured to obtain quantifiable feedback on the effectiveness of different paradigms. However, we had the additional desire to obtain qualitative feedback on the usability of the specific interfaces. To obtain both from the same experiment, qualitative feedback was elicited during the training process which subjects underwent in preparation for the quantitative analysis, which was based upon timing measurements and quantified user opinions.

### 4.1 Qualitative Evaluation

- **Aim:** To identify weaknesses in the design and implementation of specific direct manipulation and textual query interfaces.

- **Technique:** A number of sample query tasks were identified, and a detailed description of how to perform them for a specific interface was given to the users. All tasks made use of a straightforward database relating to a domain which was familiar to the users. The users then stepped through the construction of the example queries, and while doing so they were encouraged to comment on the facilities supported and their realisation in the system. This enabled qualitative results to be obtained during

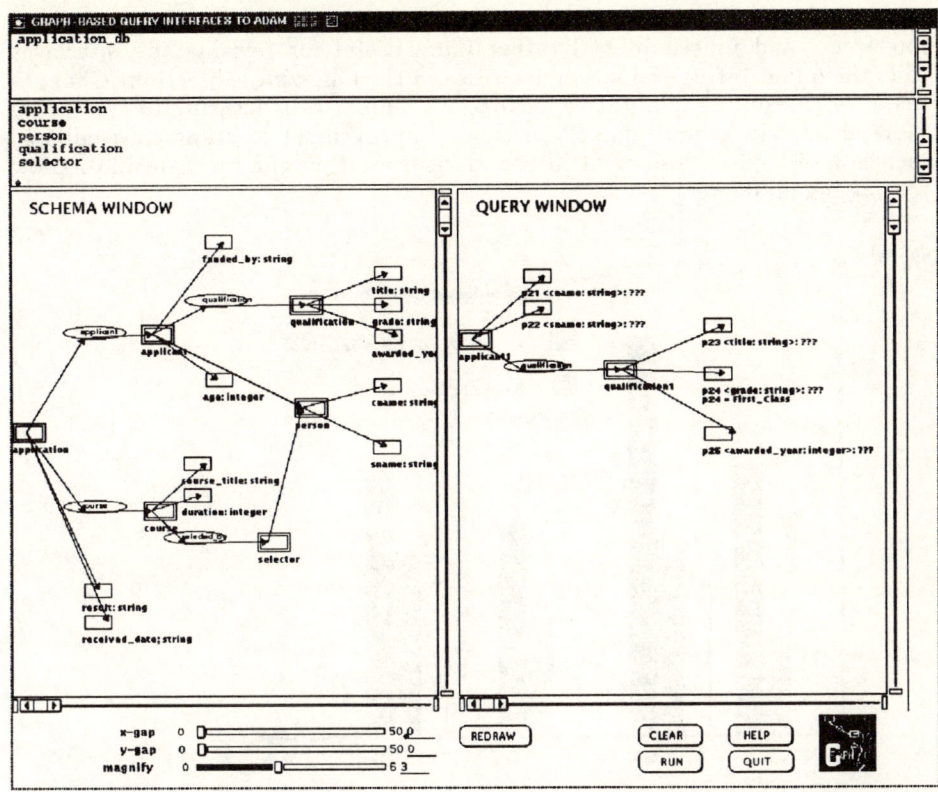

Figure 4: Example display from the graph-based query interface. Queries are constructed in the *query window* as a result of interaction with the *schema window* and the current state of the query.

the training session for the quantitative analysis in a way which was not intrusive to the user when timings were being recorded – indeed, encouraging the user to 'think aloud' during the training session is wholly in step with the user asking questions about the system during the training process.

- **Nature:** Qualitative comments on general approach and nature of specific system. It is straightforward to obtain feedback on specific aspects of an interface by soliciting comments on features as they are used.

- **Cost:** Once a query system has been built, it is straightforward to identify a number of appropriate tasks and to lead representative users through them. Worthwhile results can be obtained with small numbers of users (in our case the users were all of similar background, as they were subsequently to participate in the quantitative evaluation, although this restriction is not normally necessary or even desirable for qualitative evaluation).

This process provided a significant amount of feedback on the different interfaces, and indeed proved rather more useful for revising the interfaces than the quantitative evaluation described in the following subsection. Changes made as a result of qualitative feedback include a restructuring of screens to more effectively group related functions, improvement of graphical feedback, inclusion of a query history facility, and incorporation of a mechanism to allow formatting of answers.

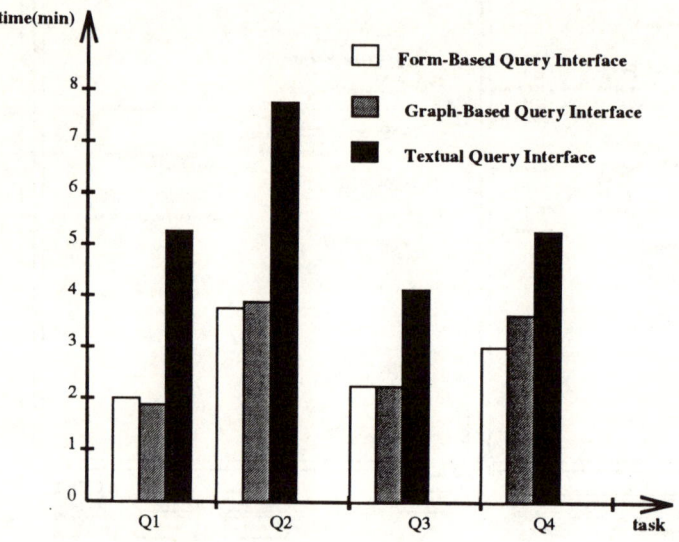

Figure 5: Task completion times using different query interfaces

## 4.2 Quantitative Evaluation

During the qualitative evaluation, the users were encouraged to interact with the evaluator, asking questions about the interface and explaining what they were thinking as they progressed. During the quantitative evaluation such interaction was discouraged, as the aim was to assess the effectiveness of each of the systems after a short, standard training session. The example queries constructed during the quantitative evaluation used facilities introduced during the training session, and were of progressively increasing complexity.

- **Aim:** To compare a range of alternative query interfaces for performing a number of representative tasks.

- **Technique:** A number of users were given (as near as possible) identical training sessions on one of the three query interfaces begin evaluated, and then asked to perform four representative queries using that interface. The time taken to perform each query was recorded along with the number of errors encountered, and users were asked to rank the system they used on a scale of 0-5 for intuitiveness, suitability (by asking if they thought the approach was appropriate for retrieving information from a database) and desirability (by asking the users to give an indication of how happy they would be to use such a system on a regular basis).

- **Nature:** Quantitative – times and preference scores for each interface.
- **Cost:** Expensive to perform – large numbers of users are required (in our case there were 30 users in total – 10 per interface), each of which must spend up to an hour with the system.

The outcome of this evaluation was a collection of tables which indicated how the users performed with and felt about the different interfaces. For example, figure 5 shows the average time taken for a range of sample queries using each of the query interfaces, which suggests that the two direct manipulation interfaces are more easily picked up than their textual counterpart. User preference scores often related very directly to the time taken to perform the different tasks (see figure 6 for a quantified rating of the intuitiveness of each interface).

Further details of the evaluation carried out with the query interfaces is given in [6].

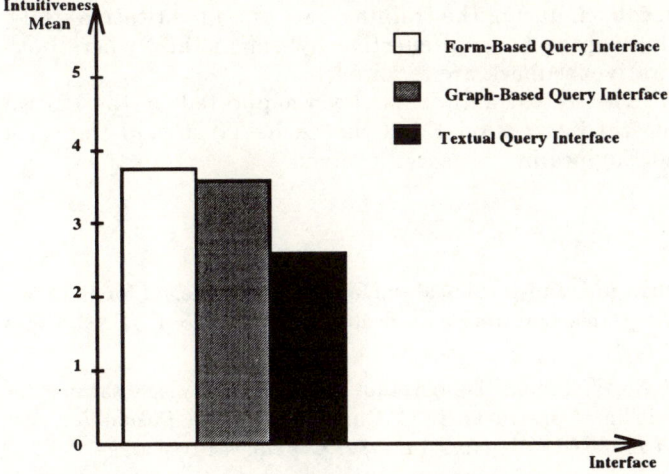

Figure 6: Intuitiveness ratings for different query interfaces

## 5 Conclusions

This paper has summarised our experience during two independent evaluation execises concerned with database interfaces, one involving the visualisation of semantic modelling constructs in a database browser, and the other dealing with the construction and execution of database queries using alternative visual paradigms.

In the evaluation of the modelling constructs, user preferences did not always coincide with the expectations of the designers, and thus prior expectations had to be set aside in the light of the evaluation. Also, lack of attention to detail in the prototype visualisations led to users misunderstanding the construct being presented, indicating a need to revise the layout and textual content of some displays. The paper prototype was better at identifying small changes required to clarify visualisations than at giving an overall perspective – this is a pity, as just the opposite would have been the preferred result in view of the relative costs of the two methods.

In the evaluation of the query interface, it was interesting to see the direct manipulation interfaces clearly out-performing the textual query language in both user preference and query completion times. This result suggests that vendors of OODBs should be seriously considering support for direct manipulation query interfaces alongside the more generally available object-oriented extensions of SQL.

While quantitative results such as those supported above are important when faced with key design decisions, they do not indicate how each of the interfaces being compared might be improved. Furthermore, they are expensive to obtain, which will inevitably lead to more developers performing qualitative evaluations. This will not necessarily be a great loss to the community – effective qualitative feedback can be obtained with minimal effort, and directly reveals weaknesses in the target interface. In practice, we have found it possible to obtain qualitative feedback during the training part of a quantitative study, and we recommend this approach as an effective hybrid method where both qualitative and quantitative feedback are required.

*Acknowledgements:* The second author has been supported by the British Council, Arab Student Aid International and the Leche Trust, and the third by the UK Science and Engineering Research Council.

# References

[1] C. Ahlberg, C. Williamson, and B. Shneiderman. Dynamic Queries for Information Exploration: An Implementation and Evaluation. In *Proc. CHI '92*, pages 619–625. ACM, 1992.

[2] G. Al-Qaimari and N. W. Paton. Design and Evaluation of Visualisations for Advanced Data Modelling Constructs. In C. Chrisment, editor, *Basque International Workshop on IT (BIWIT)*, pages 169–182. Cepadues Press, 1994.

[3] J. E. Bell. The Experience of New Users of a Natural Language Interface to a Relational Database in a Controlled Setting. In *The 1st International Workshop On Interfaces to Database Systems (IDS92), Glasgow*, pages 433–454. Springer-Verlag, 1992. R. Cooper (Ed).

[4] J. E. Bell and L. A. Rowe. An Exploratory Study of Ad Hoc Query Language to Databases. In *Proc. Data Engineering Conf.*, pages 606–613. IEEE, 1992.

[5] J. Crellin, T. Horn, and J. Preece. Evaluating Evaluation: A Case Study Of The Use Of Novel And Conventional Evaluation Techniques In A Small Company. In *Human-Computer Interaction - INTERACT'90*, pages 329–335, (North-Holland), 1990. Elsevier Science Publishers. D. Diaper et al (Eds).

[6] D. K. Doan, N. W. Paton, and A. C. Kilgour. Evaluation of Database Query Interface Paradigms for Object-Oriented Databases. 1994. Submitted for publication.

[7] D. K. Doan, N. W. Paton, A. C. Kilgour, and G. Al-Qaimari. A Multi-Paradigm Query Interface To An Object-Oriented Database. 1994. To be published in Interacting With Computers.

[8] P.M.D. Gray, K.G. Kulkarni, and N.W. Paton. *Object-Oriented Databases: A Semantic Data Model Approach*. Prentice-Hall International(UK), Hertfordshire, 1992. ISBN 0-13-620203-3.

[9] P. W. Jordan. *User Performance Measurement*. Media Services, University of Glasgow, 1992.

[10] T.K. Landauer. Let's get real: a position paper on the role of cognitive psychology in the design of humanly useful and usable systems. In J.M. Carroll, editor, *Designing Interaction: Psychology at the Human-Computer Interface*, pages 60–73. Cambridge University Press, 1991.

[11] A. Monk, P. Wright, J. Haber, and L. Davenport. *Improving Your Human-Computer Interface: A Practical Technique*. Prentice Hall, 1993.

[12] J. Nielsen. Paper Versus Computer Implementations as Mockup Scenarios For Heuristic Evaluation. In *Human-Computer Interaction - INTERACT'90*, pages 315–320, (North-Holland), 1990. Elsevier Science Publishers. D. Diaper et. al. (Eds).

[13] J. Nielsen. *Usability Engineering*. Academic Press, San Diego, 1993.

[14] N. Paton, O. Diaz, and M.L. Barja. Combining active rules and metaclasses for enhanced extensibility in object-oriented systems. *Data and Knowledge Engineering*, 10:45–63, 1993.

[15] N. W. Paton, G. al Qaimari, and A. C. Kilgour. An Extensible Interface To An Extensible Object-Oriented Database System. In *The 1st International Workshop On Interfaces to Database Systems (IDS92), Glasgow*, pages 265–281. Springer-Verlag, 1992. R. Cooper (Ed).

[16] J. Preece, editor. *A Guide to Usability*. Addison-Wesley, 1993.

# Future Directions

# The Ambleside Survey:
# Important Topics in DB/HCI Research

Eben M. Haber
Department of Computer Sciences
University of Wisconsin - Madison
Madison, Wisconsin, U.S.A.
haber@cs.wisc.edu

### Abstract

In 1989, and again in 1993, panels of database researchers were surveyed about which research areas they considered promising. In both cases, the area of user interfaces was chosen more than any other. This paper describes a follow up survey conducted in 1994 at the 2nd International Workshop on User Interfaces to Databases. The aim of this survey was to refine the results of the earlier panels, giving a better picture of work in the Database/Human-Computer Interaction field.

## 1 Introduction

In 1989, and again in 1993, Michael Stonebraker surveyed panels of database researchers about which research areas they considered promising, and also which areas they considered the least likely to produce significant results [1]. The panels' conclusions were somewhat controversial because of their dismissal of several active research areas as unimportant. On the positive side, however, both panels chose user interfaces as the most promising area. This outcome indicates an awareness of the importance of Database/Human-Computer Interaction (DB/HCI) research. It also suggests that more work in the area needs to be done, and that the work that is done needs more exposure in the database community (user interfaces was the only topic from the first survey that maintained its importance in the second survey; all of the other important areas listed in 1989 saw many papers published and reduced importance by 1993).

In order to refine the results of these panels with respect to user interfaces, a survey was conducted of the participants at the 2nd International Workshop on User Interfaces to Databases (IDS '94) in Ambleside, U.K. The survey's goal was to obtain a snapshot of work in the area, and highlight important subareas and problems. Unlike the surveys by Stonebraker, the results are intended to *describe* rather than *direct*; the sample size is too small and geographical distribution too narrow to mark any topics as the most important, or as unsuitable for further work.

## 2 The Survey

This survey was initially performed during IDS '94 to provide data for a panel discussion. The survey results and the discussion that followed were sufficiently interesting to warrant a follow-up survey by e-mail, providing more comprehensive results. Participants were asked to list the areas of their own research, and outside those areas to vote for three topics within DB/HCI that they consider important. In order to maximize the breadth of responses, the survey did not list specific topics (though general categories were listed to suggest the breadth of the field). The survey also asked respondents to optionally specify if they believe that a formal or empirical approach is needed for each of their chosen topics. Twenty people responded, representing about half of the workshop participants.

# 3 The Results

Survey respondents voted for about 30 distinct topics within DB/HCI. To organize this large number of topics, I have created a framework of categories, subcategories, and topics. These topics, subcategories, and categories are listed in the following outline; each is followed by the number of votes it received. Some answers covered two topics, and thus are listed as half votes for each. Votes varied in generality; some votes were for a specific topic, some were for a subcategory, and some were for a category as a whole. In the case of the User Issues category, two votes were cast for that category as a whole, so the total for that category is greater than the sum of the votes of its subcategories.

- Issues of better interfaces for traditional DB tasks (20)
    - Data Visualization (Traditionally Read-only) (8)
        * Data visualization in general (6)
        * Interfaces to manage visualization (1)
        * Formal approaches to visualization (.5)
        * New techniques for visualization (3-D, VR, etc.) (.5)
    - Querying (6.5)
        * Query interfaces in general (3)
        * Querying based on user's view of the data (1)
        * Metaphors for data access/querying (1)
        * Query visualization (1)
        * Formal approaches to query interfaces (.5)
    - Schema Design/Viewing (3.5)
        * Interfaces for schema design (2.5)
        * Schema visualization (.5)
        * New Techniques for visualization (3-D, VR, etc.) (.5)
    - Other DB Tasks (2)
        * DB administration (1.5)
        * DB distribution (.5)

- Issues of better interfaces for new types of DB or new DB functions (15)
    - CSCW and DBs (4)
        * Interfaces for cooperative DBs in general (4)
    - Interactive Data Visualization (3)
        * Interactive visualization in general (1)
        * Direct manipulation of data (1)
        * Interactive 3-D and multimedia views (1)
    - Handling Multimedia (3)
        * Multimedia in general (2)
        * Integrating multimedia into the DB and the interface (1)
    - Other Issues (6)
        * New types/applications of DB in general (2)
        * Visualization of hypertext information (1)
        * Interfaces for heterogeneous multi-DBs (1)
        * Interfaces for fuzzy pattern matching in queries (1)
        * Extending the human-computer interaction paradigm for multi-modal systems (1)
- User Issues (13.5)
    - Evaluating Usability (5.5)
        * Evaluating usability in general (3)
        * Empirical usability evaluation (1)
        * Defining evaluation criteria for DB interfaces (1)
        * Formal usability evaluation (.5)
    - Different Types of User (3)
        * Walk up and use DB interfaces (1)
        * Formal basis for defining suitable visualizations for different types of users (1)
        * Maintaining functionality for different types of users though different interfaces created using user-centered design (1)
    - User Behavior (3)
        * Models of User Behavior (2)
        * User Studies (1)
- Assorted Interface Design Issues (5.5)
    * Architecture of distributed interfaces (1)
    * Facilitating the production and integration of multiple interfaces (1)
    * Standardizing interface behavior (1)
    * Formalize properties of user interfaces in the context of DBMSs (1)
    * Intergration of DB interfaces with those of other software (1)
    * Formal basis to keep different interfaces mutually consistent (.5)

In addition, two votes were cast for formal approaches to all aspects of DB/HCI work.

When describing the areas of their own research, the survey respondents listed topics found in all of the above categories, and all of the subcategories except evaluating usability and user behavior.

The most popular topics are data visualization (6), cooperative databases (4), evaluating usability (3), and query interfaces (3). Six votes specified that a formal approach is needed, and only one vote (for usability evaluation) mentioned an empirical approach.

## 4 Conclusions

This survey has a sample size too small to state with any certainty the opinions of the DB/HCI community. Nevertheless, it does give a good picture of the area and its popular topics. DB/HCI is a broad area, stretching from mainly HCI topics, such as user studies, to mainly DB topics, such as query interfaces. Research into improving traditional DB tasks is popular, but novel DB types and tasks are also receiving attention. In addition, the database user is being studied to understand how these interfaces should be oriented. Finally, there is interest in formal approaches to several topics.

Personally, I believe that some of the less popular topics will prove to be of greater importance in the future. Schema design and visualization has received much less attention than other traditional database tasks, and I see important problems remaining to be solved within that topic. Similarly, I think there is much work to be done in studying database users and forming models of their behavior. In my experience, interfaces are often designed without a clear understanding of the end-user.

## 5 Acknowledgements

Special thanks to all of the IDS '94 participants who provided their input, making this survey possible.

## References

[1] Stonebraker, M., et. al., DBMS Research at a Crossroads: The Vienna Update, Proceedings of the 19th VLDB Conference, Dublin, Ireland, 1993, pp. 688-692.

# Author Index

| | |
|---|---|
| al-Qaimari, G. | 343 |
| Barclay, P. | 306 |
| Benford, S. | 168 |
| Boyle, J. | 127 |
| Catarci, T. | 65, 84 |
| Connor, R.C.H. | 197 |
| Cooper, R. | 3 |
| Crerar, A. | 306 |
| Cutts, Q.I. | 197 |
| Davidson, K. | 306 |
| Dix, A. | 236 |
| Doan, K. | 343 |
| Eaglestone, B. | 329 |
| Ellis, G.P. | 49 |
| Finlay, J.E. | 49 |
| Fothergill, J.E. | 127 |
| Goble, C. | 25 |
| Gray, P.M.D. | 127 |
| Haber, E.M. | 361 |
| Haw, D. | 25 |
| Inder, R. | 215 |
| Kennedy, J.B. | 143 |
| Kilgour, A.C. | 343 |
| Kirby, G.N.C. | 197 |
| Machura, M. | 289 |
| Mariani, J. | 168 |
| McGregor, D.R. | 104 |
| MdSap, M.N. | 104 |
| Messer, P. | 266 |
| Monk, S. | 185 |
| Moore, V.S. | 197 |
| Morrison, R. | 197 |
| Palmisano, F. | 249 |
| Patel, N. | 266 |
| Paton, N.W. | 343 |
| Patrick, A. | 236 |
| Pollitt, A.S. | 49 |

Rapley, M.H. .................................................................................. 143
Rector, A. ....................................................................................... 25
Santucci, G. ........................................................................... 65, 249
Stader, J. ...................................................................................... 215
Tarantino, L. ................................................................................. 84
Vertegaal, R. ............................................................................... 329

# *Published in 1990–92*

**AI and Cognitive Science '89,** Dublin City University, Eire, 14–15 September 1989
Alan F. Smeaton and Gabriel McDermott (Eds.)

**Specification and Verification of Concurrent Systems,** University of Stirling, Scotland, 6–8 July 1988
C. Rattray (Ed.)

**Semantics for Concurrency,** Proceedings of the International BCS-FACS Workshop, Sponsored by Logic for IT (S.E.R.C.), University of Leicester, UK, 23–25 July 1990
M. Z. Kwiatkowska, M. W. Shields and R. M. Thomas (Eds.)

**Functional Programming, Glasgow 1989**
Proceedings of the 1989 Glasgow Workshop, Fraserburgh, Scotland, 21–23 August 1989
Kei Davis and John Hughes (Eds.)

**Persistent Object Systems,** Proceedings of the Third International Workshop, Newcastle, Australia, 10–13 January 1989
John Rosenberg and David Koch (Eds.)

**Z User Workshop, Oxford 1989,** Proceedings of the Fourth Annual Z User Meeting, Oxford, 15 December 1989
J. E. Nicholls (Ed.)

**Formal Methods for Trustworthy Computer Systems (FM89),** Halifax, Canada, 23–27 July 1989
Dan Craigen (Editor) and Karen Summerskill (Assistant Editor)

**Security and Persistence,** Proceedings of the International Workshop on Computer Architectures to Support Security and Persistence of Information, Bremen, West Germany, 8–11 May 1990
John Rosenberg and J. Leslie Keedy (Eds.)

**Women into Computing: Selected Papers 1988–1990**
Gillian Lovegrove and Barbara Segal (Eds.)

**3rd Refinement Workshop** (organised by BCS-FACS, and sponsored by IBM UK Laboratories, Hursley Park and the Programming Research Group, University of Oxford), Hursley Park, 9–11 January 1990
Carroll Morgan and J. C. P. Woodcock (Eds.)

**Designing Correct Circuits,** Workshop jointly organised by the Universities of Oxford and Glasgow, Oxford, 26–28 September 1990
Geraint Jones and Mary Sheeran (Eds.)

**Functional Programming, Glasgow 1990**
Proceedings of the 1990 Glasgow Workshop on Functional Programming, Ullapool, Scotland, 13–15 August 1990
Simon L. Peyton Jones, Graham Hutton and Carsten Kehler Holst (Eds.)

**4th Refinement Workshop,** Proceedings of the 4th Refinement Workshop, organised by BCS-FACS, Cambridge, 9–11 January 1991
Joseph M. Morris and Roger C. Shaw (Eds.)

**AI and Cognitive Science '90,** University of Ulster at Jordanstown, 20–21 September 1990
Michael F. McTear and Norman Creaney (Eds.)

**Software Re-use, Utrecht 1989,** Proceedings of the Software Re-use Workshop, Utrecht, The Netherlands, 23–24 November 1989
Liesbeth Dusink and Patrick Hall (Eds.)

**Z User Workshop, 1990,** Proceedings of the Fifth Annual Z User Meeting, Oxford, 17–18 December 1990
J.E. Nicholls (Ed.)

**IV Higher Order Workshop, Banff 1990**
Proceedings of the IV Higher Order Workshop, Banff, Alberta, Canada, 10–14 September 1990
Graham Birtwistle (Ed.)

**ALPUK91,** Proceedings of the 3rd UK Annual Conference on Logic Programming, Edinburgh, 10–12 April 1991
Geraint A.Wiggins, Chris Mellish and Tim Duncan (Eds.)

**Specifications of Database Systems**
International Workshop on Specifications of Database Systems, Glasgow, 3–5 July 1991
David J. Harper and Moira C. Norrie (Eds.)

**7th UK Computer and Telecommunications Performance Engineering Workshop**
Edinburgh, 22–23 July 1991
J. Hillston, P.J.B. King and R.J. Pooley (Eds.)

**Logic Program Synthesis and Transformation**
Proceedings of LOPSTR 91, International Workshop on Logic Program Synthesis and Transformation, University of Manchester, 4–5 July 1991
T.P. Clement and K.-K. Lau (Eds.)

**Declarative Programming, Sasbachwalden 1991**
PHOENIX Seminar and Workshop on Declarative Programming, Sasbachwalden, Black Forest, Germany, 18–22 November 1991
John Darlington and Roland Dietrich (Eds.)

**Building Interactive Systems: Architectures and Tools**
Philip Gray and Roger Took (Eds.)

**Functional Programming, Glasgow 1991**
Proceedings of the 1991 Glasgow Workshop on Functional Programming, Portree, Isle of Skye, 12–14 August 1991
Rogardt Heldal, Carsten Kehler Holst and Philip Wadler (Eds.)

**Object Orientation in Z**
Susan Stepney, Rosalind Barden and David Cooper (Eds.)

**Code Generation – Concepts, Tools, Techniques**
Proceedings of the International Workshop on Code Generation, Dagstuhl, Germany, 20–24 May 1991
Robert Giegerich and Susan L. Graham (Eds.)

**Z User Workshop, York 1991,** Proceedings of the Sixth Annual Z User Meeting, York, 16–17 December 1991
J.E. Nicholls (Ed.)

**Formal Aspects of Measurement**
Proceedings of the BCS-FACS Workshop on Formal Aspects of Measurement, South Bank University, London, 5 May 1991
Tim Denvir, Ros Herman and R.W. Whitty (Eds.)

**AI and Cognitive Science '91**
University College, Cork, 19–20 September 1991
Humphrey Sorensen (Ed.)

**5th Refinement Workshop,** Proceedings of the 5th Refinement Workshop, organised by BCS-FACS, London, 8–10 January 1992
Cliff B. Jones, Roger C. Shaw and Tim Denvir (Eds.)

**Algebraic Methodology and Software Technology (AMAST'91)**
Proceedings of the Second International Conference on Algebraic Methodology and Software Technology, Iowa City, USA, 22–25 May 1991
M. Nivat, C. Rattray, T. Rus and G. Scollo (Eds.)

**ALPUK92,** Proceedings of the 4th UK Conference on Logic Programming, London, 30 March–1 April 1992
Krysia Broda (Ed.)

**Logic Program Synthesis and Transformation**
Proceedings of LOPSTR 92, International Workshop on Logic Program Synthesis and Transformation, University of Manchester, 2–3 July 1992
Kung-Kiu Lau and Tim Clement (Eds.)

**NAPAW 92,** Proceedings of the First North American Process Algebra Workshop, Stony Brook, New York, USA, 28 August 1992
S. Purushothaman and Amy Zwarico (Eds.)

**First International Workshop on Larch**
Proceedings of the First International Workshop on Larch, Dedham, Massachusetts, USA, 13–15 July 1992
Ursula Martin and Jeannette M. Wing (Eds.)

**Persistent Object Systems**
Proceedings of the Fifth International Workshop on Persistent Object Systems, San Miniato (Pisa), Italy, 1–4 September 1992
Antonio Albano and Ron Morrison (Eds.)

**Formal Methods in Databases and Software Engineering,** Proceedings of the Workshop on Formal Methods in Databases and Software Engineering, Montreal, Canada, 15–16 May 1992
V.S. Alagar, Laks V.S. Lakshmanan and F. Sadri (Eds.)

**Modelling Database Dynamics**
Selected Papers from the Fourth International Workshop on Foundations of Models and Languages for Data and Objects, Volkse, Germany, 19–22 October 1992
Udo W. Lipeck and Bernhard Thalheim (Eds.)

**14th Information Retrieval Colloquium**
Proceedings of the BCS 14th Information Retrieval Colloquium, University of Lancaster, 13–14 April 1992
Tony McEnery and Chris Paice (Eds.)

**Functional Programming, Glasgow 1992**
Proceedings of the 1992 Glasgow Workshop on Functional Programming, Ayr, Scotland, 6–8 July 1992
John Launchbury and Patrick Sansom (Eds.)

**Z User Workshop, London 1992**
Proceedings of the Seventh Annual Z User Meeting, London, 14–15 December 1992
J.P. Bowen and J.E. Nicholls (Eds.)